QUANTUM AND WOODY

MUST DIE!

JAMES ASMUS | TIM SIEDELL | STEVE LIEBER | PERE PÉREZ | DAVE MCCAIG

CONTENTS

Quantum & Woody created by MD Bright & Priest

Collection Cover Art: Mike Hawthorne
with Jordie Bellaire

Editor: Alejandro Arbona
Editor-in-Chief: Warren Simons

VALIANT®

Peter Cuneo
Chairman

Dinesh Shamdasani
CEO & Chief Creative Officer

Gavin Cuneo
Chief Operating Officer & CFO

Fred Pierce
Publisher

Warren Simons
VP Editor-in-Chief

Walter Black
VP Operations

Hunter Gorinson
Director of Marketing,
Communications & Digital Media

Atom! Freeman
Matthew Klein
Andy Liegl
Sales Managers

Josh Johns
Digital Sales & Special Projects Manager

Travis Escarfullery
Jeff Walker
Production & Design Managers

Alejandro Arbona
Editor

Kyle Andrukiewicz
Tom Brennan
Associate Editors

Peter Stern
Publishing & Operations Manager

Chris Daniels
Marketing Coordinator

Ivan Cohen
Collection Editor

Steve Blackwell
Collection Designer

Rian Hughes/Device
Trade Dress & Book Design

Russell Brown
President, Consumer Products,
Promotions and Ad Sales

Jason Kothari
Vice Chairman

TIM SIEDELL
PERE PÉREZ

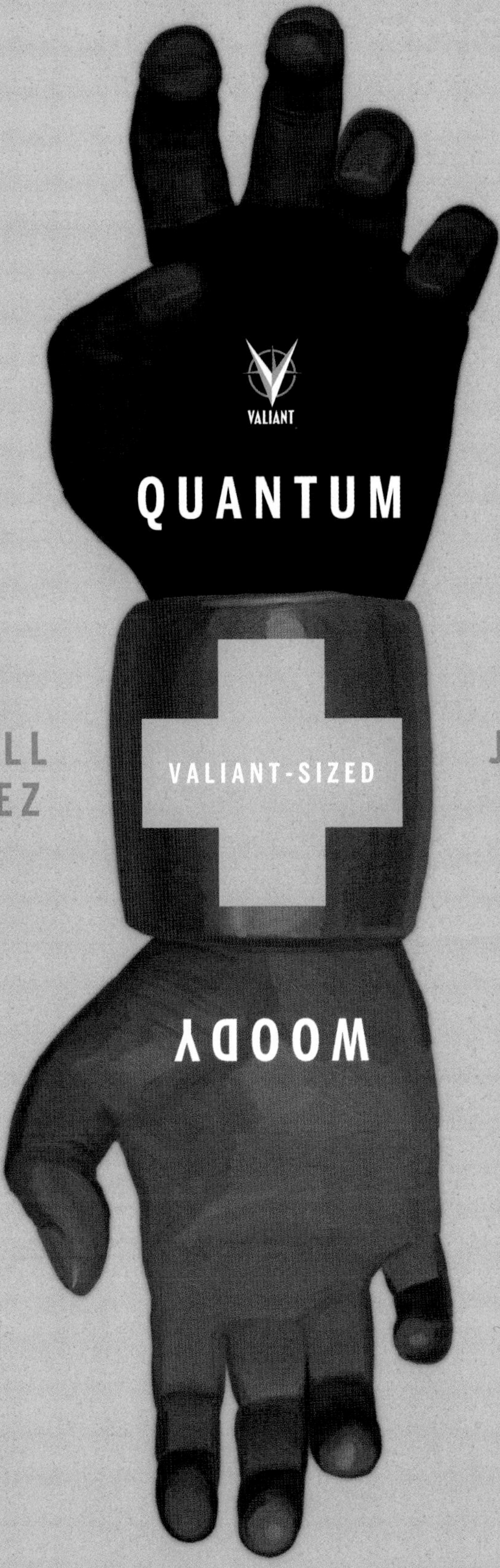
VALIANT
QUANTUM
VALIANT-SIZED
WOODY

JAMES ASMUS
BRIAN LEVEL

QUANTUM AND WOODY!

OUR STORY SO FAR...

Eric and Woody are foster brothers and total opposites, reunited after years of estrangement when their father died mysteriously. An accident at their father's lab imbued the brothers with fantastic power — now Woody shoots blasts and Eric generates shields of pure energy...but they're bound by metal wristbands they have to KLANG together every 24 hours or they dissolve into atoms. The brothers became Quantum!...and Woody...ersatz superheroes.

Investigating their father's death led Quantum and Woody to Edison's Radical Acquisitions, a mad-science cabal that's been strangulating the progress of scientific and technological development for decades...led by the one-man Monster Mash that is (what remains of) Thomas Edison himself.

The brothers exposed and brought down the E.R.A., but Edison and most of his senior agents escaped...

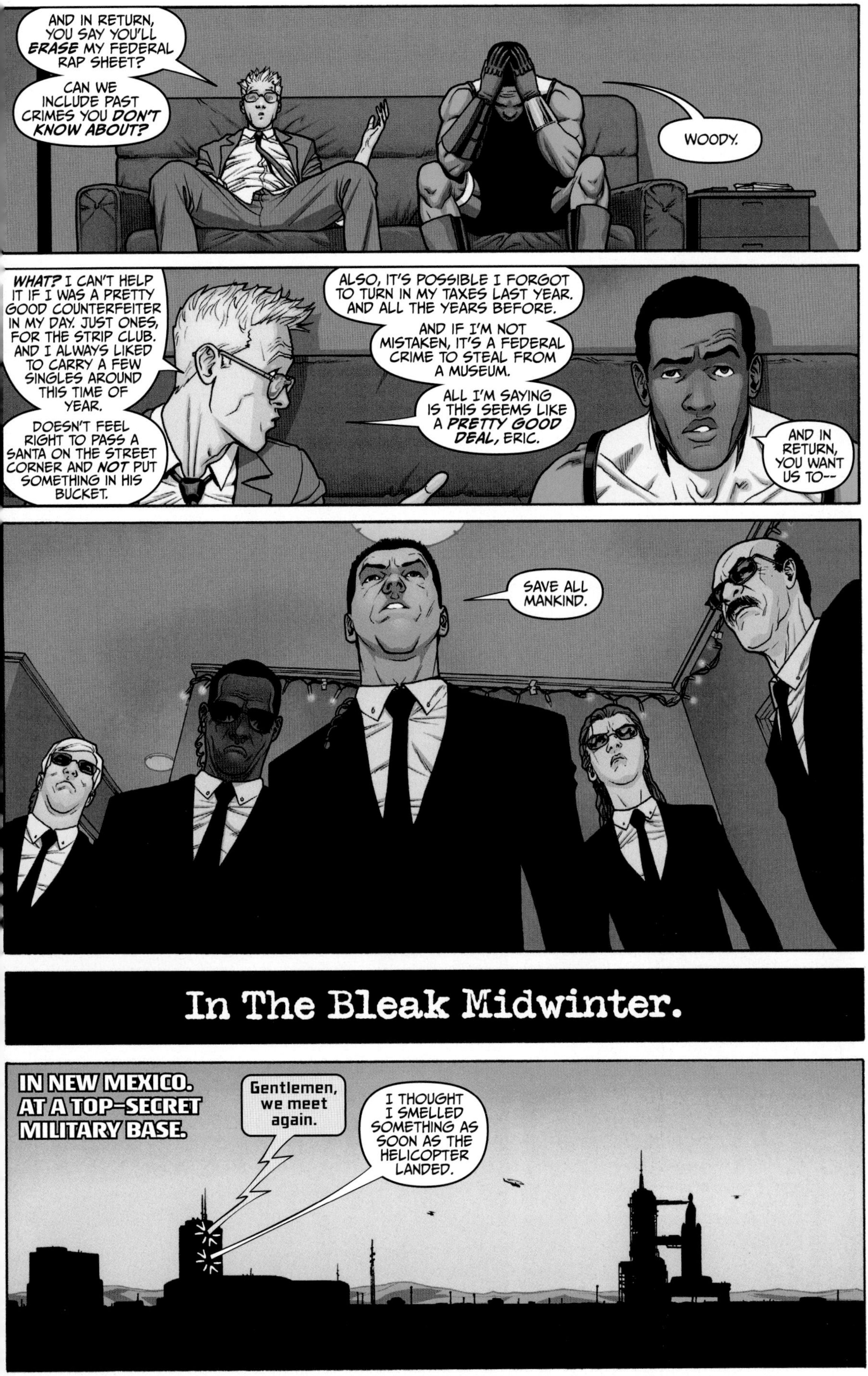

AND IN RETURN, YOU SAY YOU'LL ERASE MY FEDERAL RAP SHEET?
CAN WE INCLUDE PAST CRIMES YOU DON'T KNOW ABOUT?
WOODY.
WHAT? I CAN'T HELP IT IF I WAS A PRETTY GOOD COUNTERFEITER IN MY DAY. JUST ONES, FOR THE STRIP CLUB. AND I ALWAYS LIKED TO CARRY A FEW SINGLES AROUND THIS TIME OF YEAR.
DOESN'T FEEL RIGHT TO PASS A SANTA ON THE STREET CORNER AND NOT PUT SOMETHING IN HIS BUCKET.
ALSO, IT'S POSSIBLE I FORGOT TO TURN IN MY TAXES LAST YEAR. AND ALL THE YEARS BEFORE.
AND IF I'M NOT MISTAKEN, IT'S A FEDERAL CRIME TO STEAL FROM A MUSEUM.
ALL I'M SAYING IS THIS SEEMS LIKE A PRETTY GOOD DEAL, ERIC.
AND IN RETURN, YOU WANT US TO--
SAVE ALL MANKIND.
In The Bleak Midwinter.
IN NEW MEXICO. AT A TOP-SECRET MILITARY BASE.
Gentlemen, we meet again.
I THOUGHT I SMELLED SOMETHING AS SOON AS THE HELICOPTER LANDED.

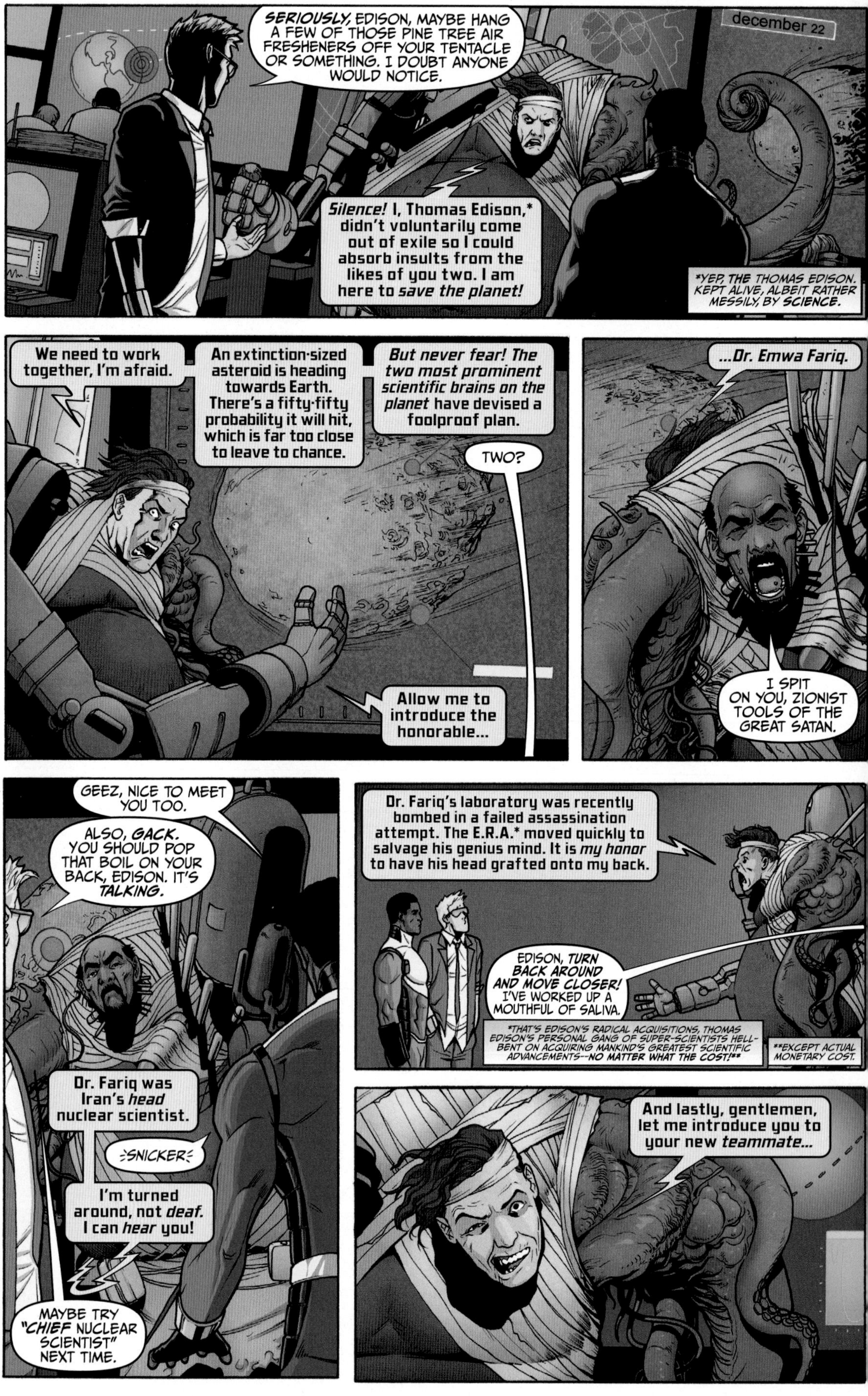
SERIOUSLY, EDISON, MAYBE HANG A FEW OF THOSE PINE TREE AIR FRESHENERS OFF YOUR TENTACLE OR SOMETHING. I DOUBT ANYONE WOULD NOTICE.
december 22
Silence! I, Thomas Edison,* didn't voluntarily come out of exile so I could absorb insults from the likes of you two. I am here to save the planet!
*YEP, THE THOMAS EDISON. KEPT ALIVE, ALBEIT RATHER MESSILY, BY SCIENCE.
We need to work together, I'm afraid.
An extinction-sized asteroid is heading towards Earth. There's a fifty-fifty probability it will hit, which is far too close to leave to chance.
But never fear! The two most prominent scientific brains on the planet have devised a foolproof plan.
TWO?
Allow me to introduce the honorable...
...Dr. Emwa Fariq.
I SPIT ON YOU, ZIONIST TOOLS OF THE GREAT SATAN.
GEEZ, NICE TO MEET YOU TOO.
ALSO, GACK. YOU SHOULD POP THAT BOIL ON YOUR BACK, EDISON. IT'S TALKING.
Dr. Fariq was Iran's head nuclear scientist.
SNICKER
I'm turned around, not deaf. I can hear you!
MAYBE TRY "CHIEF NUCLEAR SCIENTIST" NEXT TIME.
Dr. Fariq's laboratory was recently bombed in a failed assassination attempt. The E.R.A.* moved quickly to salvage his genius mind. It is my honor to have his head grafted onto my back.
EDISON, TURN BACK AROUND AND MOVE CLOSER! I'VE WORKED UP A MOUTHFUL OF SALIVA.
*THAT'S EDISON'S RADICAL ACQUISITIONS, THOMAS EDISON'S PERSONAL GANG OF SUPER-SCIENTISTS HELL-BENT ON ACQUIRING MANKIND'S GREATEST SCIENTIFIC ADVANCEMENTS--NO MATTER WHAT THE COST!**
**EXCEPT ACTUAL MONETARY COST.
And lastly, gentlemen, let me introduce you to your new teammate...

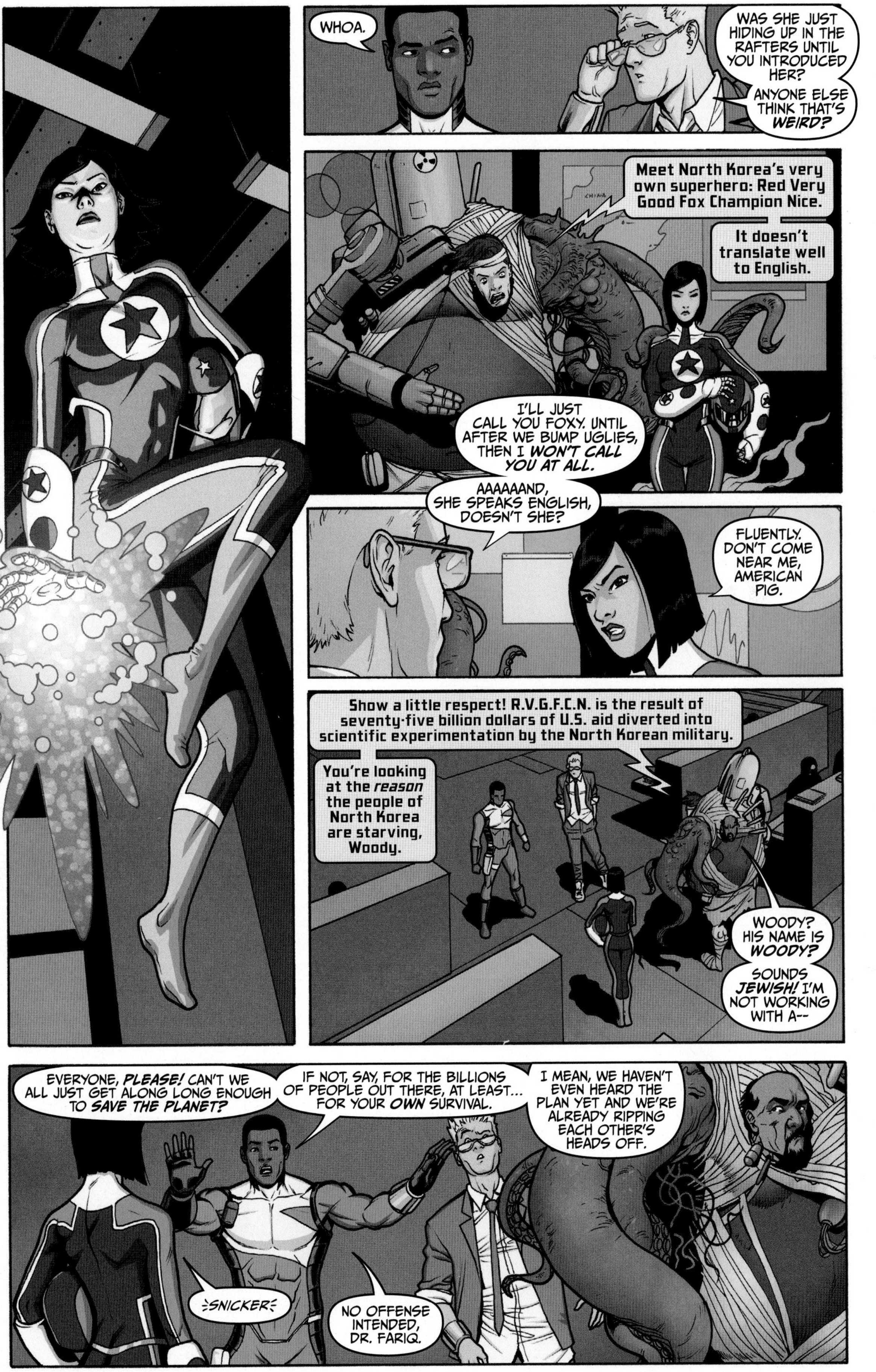
WHOA.
WAS SHE JUST HIDING UP IN THE RAFTERS UNTIL YOU INTRODUCED HER?
ANYONE ELSE THINK THAT'S *WEIRD?*
Meet North Korea's very own superhero: Red Very Good Fox Champion Nice.
It doesn't translate well to English.
I'LL JUST CALL YOU FOXY. UNTIL AFTER WE BUMP UGLIES, THEN I *WON'T CALL YOU AT ALL.*
AAAAAAND, SHE SPEAKS ENGLISH, DOESN'T SHE?
FLUENTLY. DON'T COME NEAR ME, AMERICAN PIG.
Show a little respect! R.V.G.F.C.N. is the result of seventy-five billion dollars of U.S. aid diverted into scientific experimentation by the North Korean military.
You're looking at the *reason* the people of North Korea are starving, Woody.
WOODY? HIS NAME IS *WOODY?*
SOUNDS *JEWISH!* I'M NOT WORKING WITH A--
EVERYONE, *PLEASE!* CAN'T WE ALL JUST GET ALONG LONG ENOUGH TO *SAVE THE PLANET?*
IF NOT, SAY, FOR THE BILLIONS OF PEOPLE OUT THERE, AT LEAST... FOR YOUR *OWN* SURVIVAL.
I MEAN, WE HAVEN'T EVEN HEARD THE PLAN YET AND WE'RE ALREADY RIPPING EACH OTHER'S HEADS OFF.
SNICKER
NO OFFENSE INTENDED, DR. FARIQ.

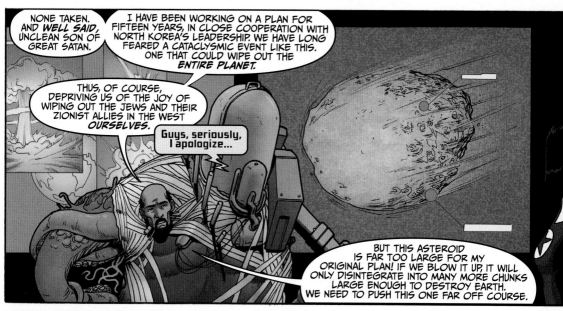

NONE TAKEN. AND **WELL SAID,** UNCLEAN SON OF GREAT SATAN.

I HAVE BEEN WORKING ON A PLAN FOR FIFTEEN YEARS, IN CLOSE COOPERATION WITH NORTH KOREA'S LEADERSHIP. WE HAVE LONG FEARED A CATACLYSMIC EVENT LIKE THIS. ONE THAT COULD WIPE OUT THE **ENTIRE PLANET.**

THUS, OF COURSE, DEPRIVING US OF THE JOY OF WIPING OUT THE JEWS AND THEIR ZIONIST ALLIES IN THE WEST **OURSELVES.**

Guys, seriously, I apologize...

BUT THIS ASTEROID IS FAR TOO LARGE FOR MY ORIGINAL PLAN! IF WE BLOW IT UP, IT WILL ONLY DISINTEGRATE INTO MANY MORE CHUNKS LARGE ENOUGH TO DESTROY EARTH. WE NEED TO PUSH THIS ONE FAR OFF COURSE.

R.V.G.F.C.N., who has spent the last seven years training for this day, will use her anti-gravity powers to *slow the asteroid to a complete stop.*

That's where the three of you come in.

Using my teleportation technology, we will instantly place Dr. Fariq's shuttle into deep space near the path of the asteroid.

Quantum, you will use your powers to place a protective force field around the asteroid. Woody, you will then use your powers to blast the asteroid.

Instead of disintegrating, the blast should bounce off Quantum's shield, thus creating the momentum to *push the asteroid away.*

ARE YOU SHOWING SLIDES? I CAN'T SEE THE SLIDES.

YOU KNOW WHAT? I'M *NOT EVEN GOING TO TRY* TO CONTAIN MY EXCITEMENT HERE.

I'M GOING TO **SPACE.** THAT'S THE *COOLEST* CHRISTMAS GIFT ANYONE'S EVER GIVEN ME.

DO YOU THINK I CAN KEEP THIS COFFEE MUG WHEN WE'RE DONE?

MUG? I WOULD PREFER TO KEEP *FROM DYING,* THANK YOU VERY MUCH. *NO WAY* AM I GETTING TELEPORTED NEAR THE PATH OF A GIANT ASTEROID. SORRY.

THE ALTERNATIVE JUST MIGHT BE PERISHING IN A TWO-THOUSAND-DEGREE CLOUD OF FIRE ALONG WITH THE REST OF EARTH'S INHABITANTS.

I HEAR SPACE IS NICE THIS TIME OF YEAR.

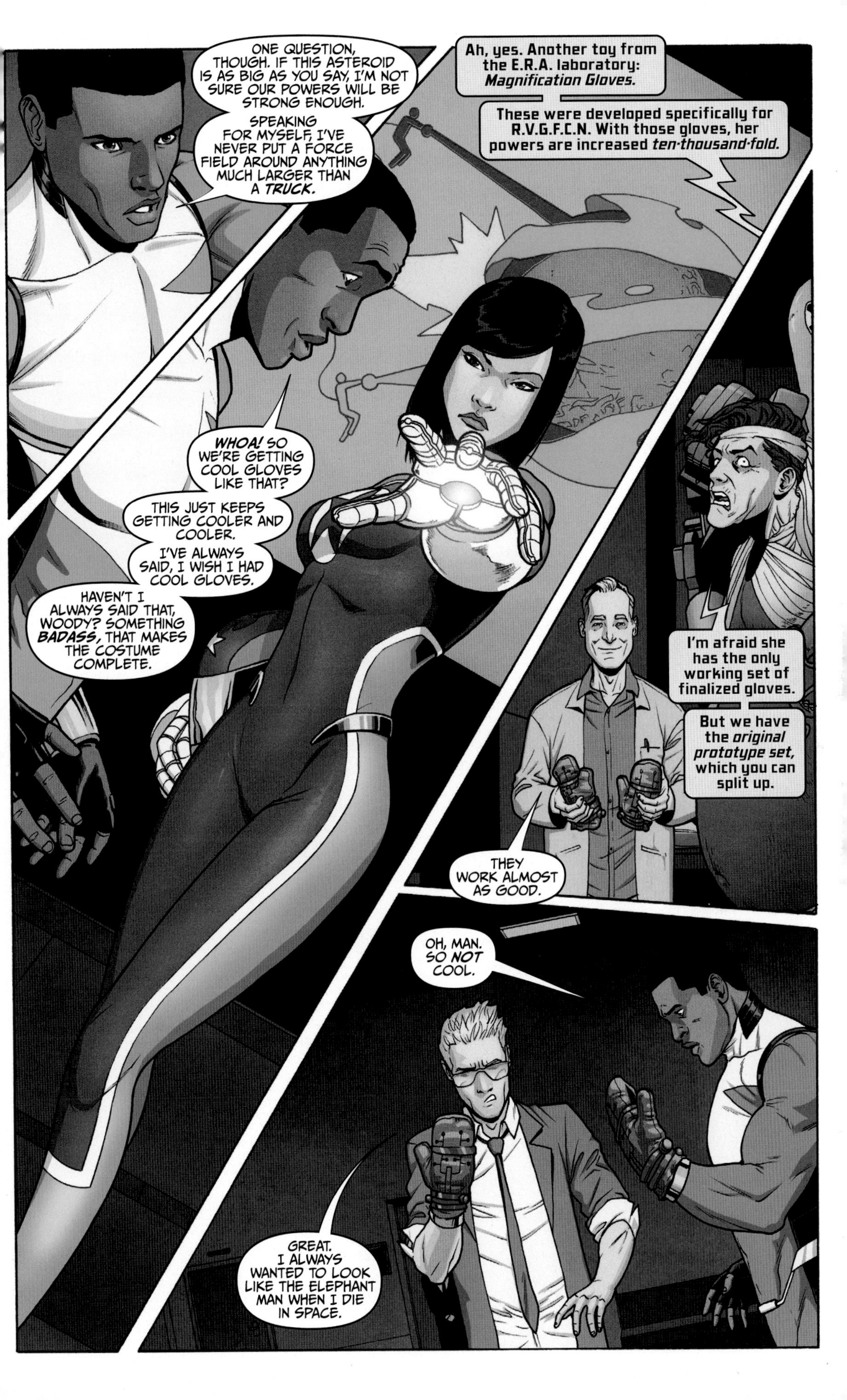

ONE QUESTION, THOUGH. IF THIS ASTEROID IS AS BIG AS YOU SAY, I'M NOT SURE OUR POWERS WILL BE STRONG ENOUGH.
SPEAKING FOR MYSELF, I'VE NEVER PUT A FORCE FIELD AROUND ANYTHING MUCH LARGER THAN A TRUCK.
Ah, yes. Another toy from the E.R.A. laboratory: Magnification Gloves.
These were developed specifically for R.V.G.F.C.N. With those gloves, her powers are increased ten·thousand·fold.
WHOA! SO WE'RE GETTING COOL GLOVES LIKE THAT?
THIS JUST KEEPS GETTING COOLER AND COOLER.
I'VE ALWAYS SAID, I WISH I HAD COOL GLOVES.
HAVEN'T I ALWAYS SAID THAT, WOODY? SOMETHING BADASS, THAT MAKES THE COSTUME COMPLETE.
I'm afraid she has the only working set of finalized gloves.
But we have the original prototype set, which you can split up.
THEY WORK ALMOST AS GOOD.
OH, MAN. SO NOT COOL.
GREAT. I ALWAYS WANTED TO LOOK LIKE THE ELEPHANT MAN WHEN I DIE IN SPACE.

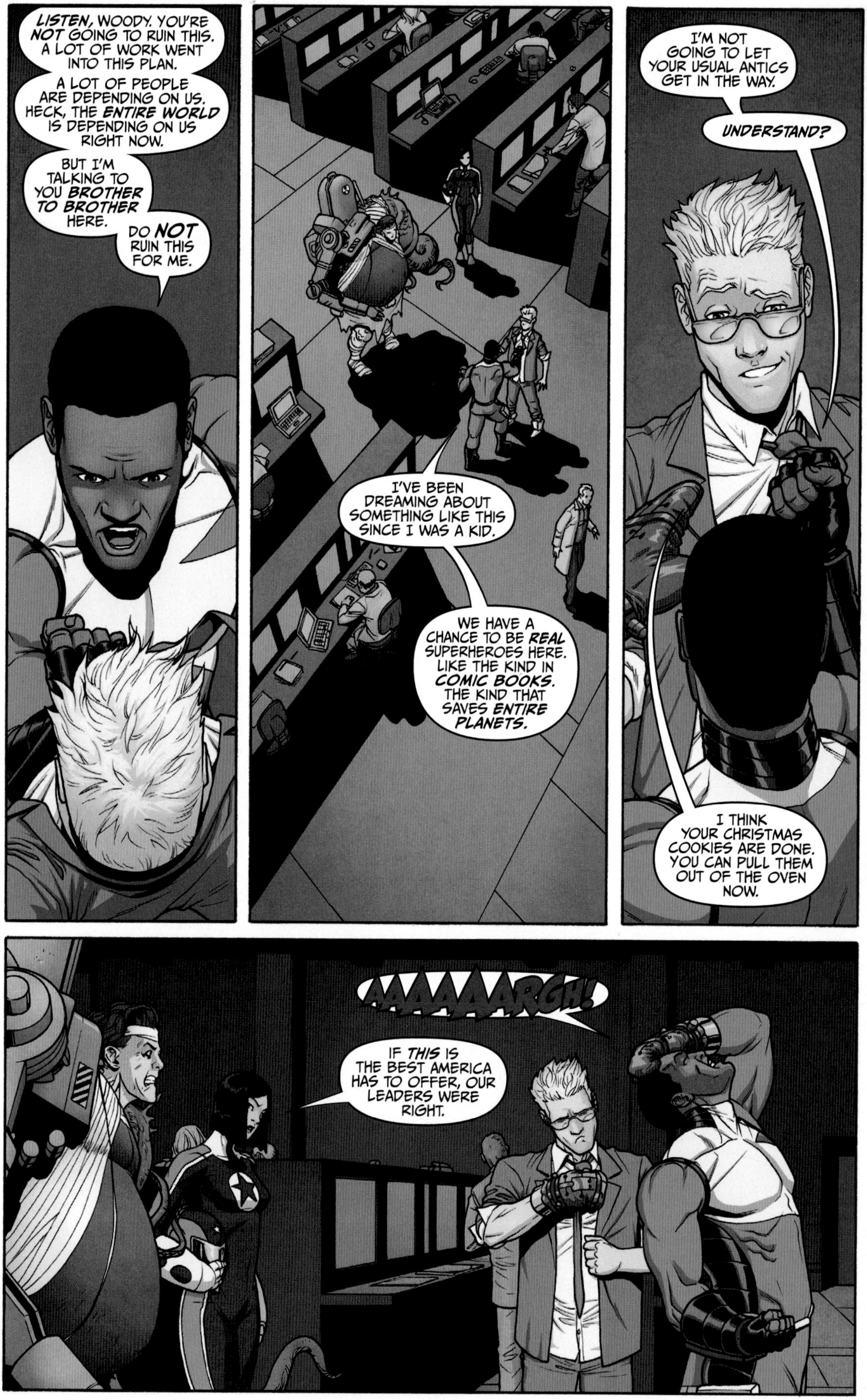
LISTEN, WOODY. YOU'RE NOT GOING TO RUIN THIS. A LOT OF WORK WENT INTO THIS PLAN.
A LOT OF PEOPLE ARE DEPENDING ON US. HECK, THE ENTIRE WORLD IS DEPENDING ON US RIGHT NOW.
BUT I'M TALKING TO YOU BROTHER TO BROTHER HERE.
DO NOT RUIN THIS FOR ME.
I'VE BEEN DREAMING ABOUT SOMETHING LIKE THIS SINCE I WAS A KID.
WE HAVE A CHANCE TO BE REAL SUPERHEROES HERE. LIKE THE KIND IN COMIC BOOKS. THE KIND THAT SAVES ENTIRE PLANETS.
I'M NOT GOING TO LET YOUR USUAL ANTICS GET IN THE WAY.
UNDERSTAND?
I THINK YOUR CHRISTMAS COOKIES ARE DONE. YOU CAN PULL THEM OUT OF THE OVEN NOW.
AAAAAARGH!
IF THIS IS THE BEST AMERICA HAS TO OFFER, OUR LEADERS WERE RIGHT.

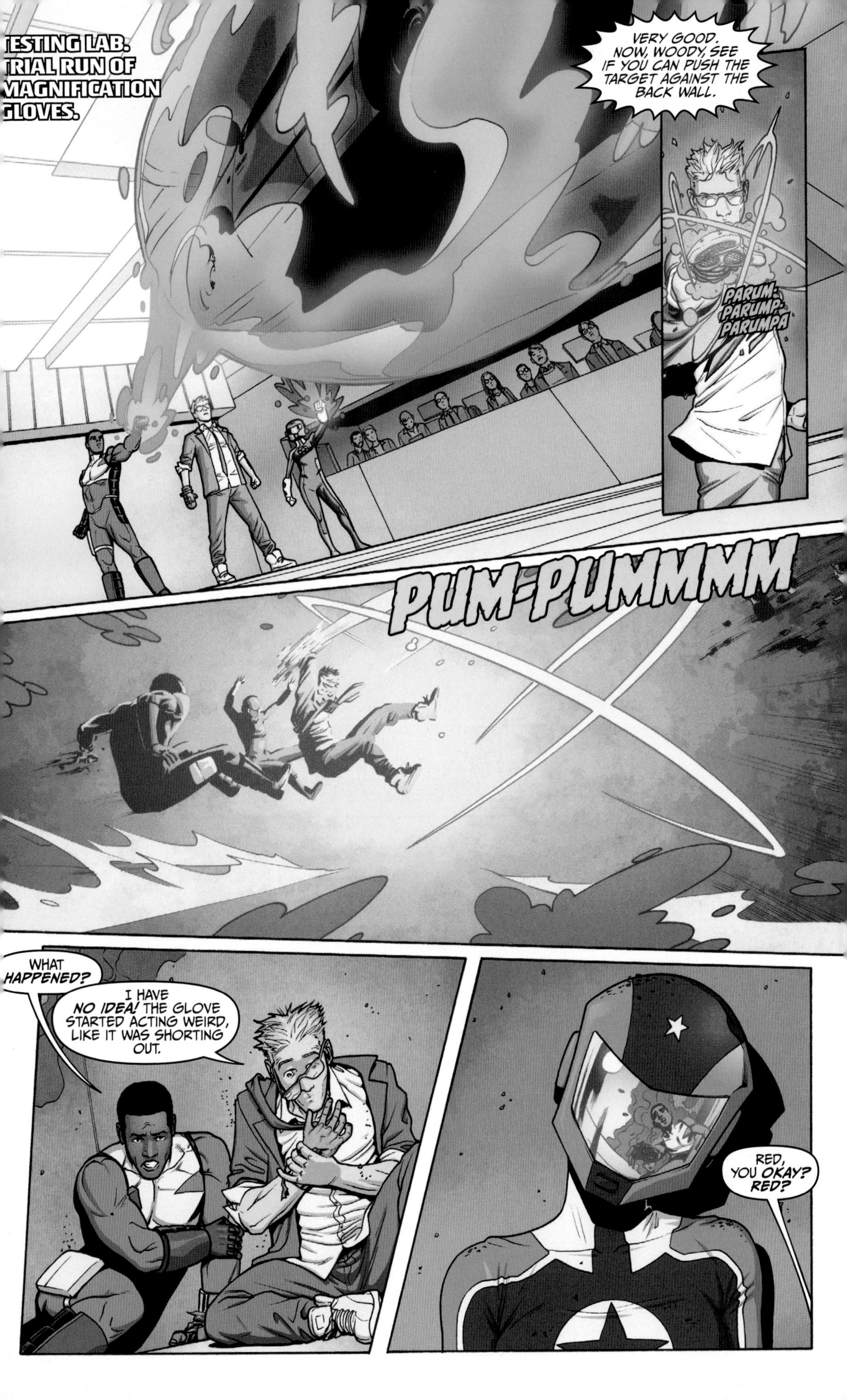

TESTING LAB. TRIAL RUN OF MAGNIFICATION GLOVES.
VERY GOOD. NOW, WOODY, SEE IF YOU CAN PUSH THE TARGET AGAINST THE BACK WALL.
PARUM-PARUMP-PARUMPA
PUM-PUMMMM
WHAT HAPPENED?
I HAVE NO IDEA! THE GLOVE STARTED ACTING WEIRD, LIKE IT WAS SHORTING OUT.
RED, YOU OKAY? RED?

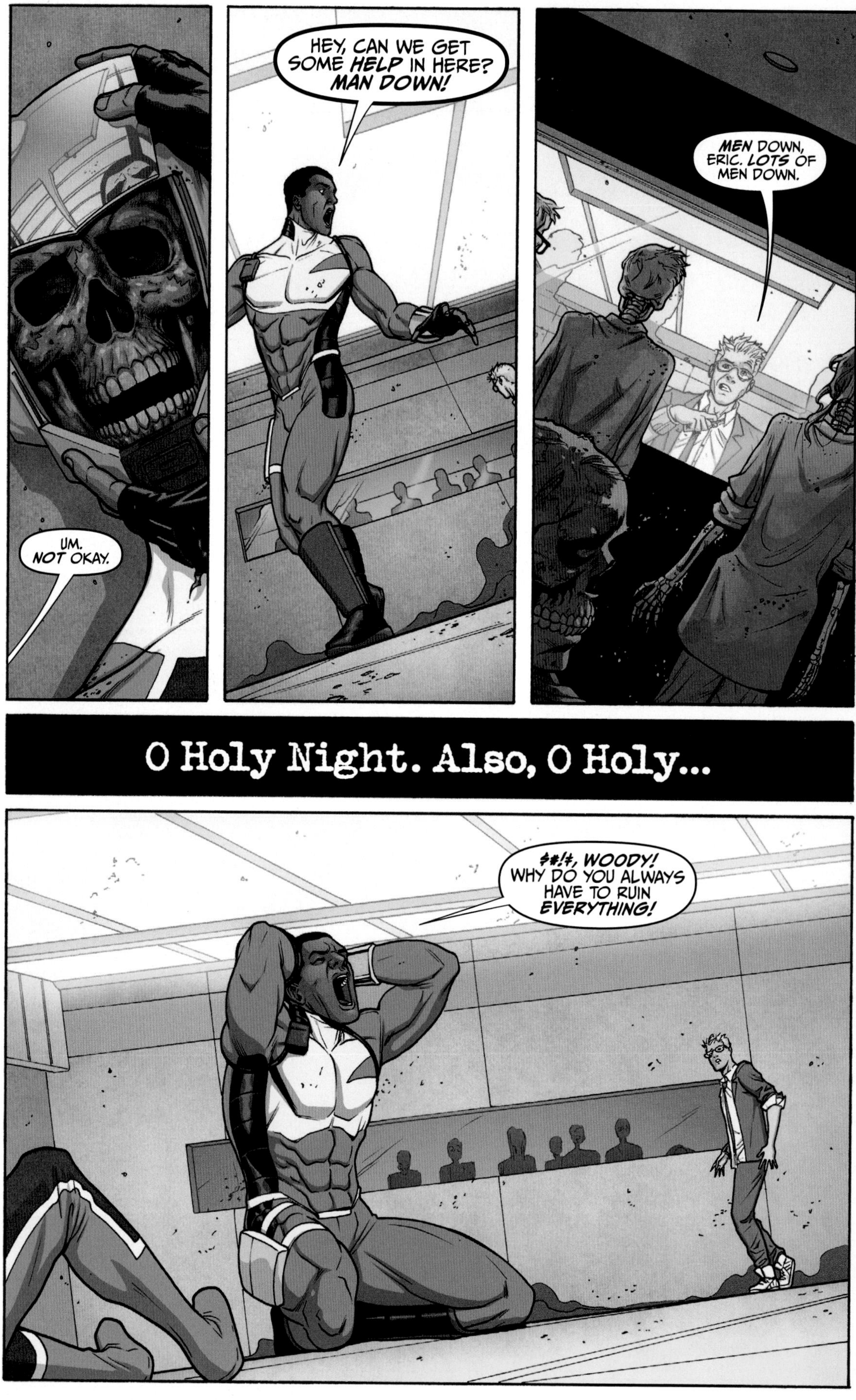
UM. NOT OKAY.
HEY, CAN WE GET SOME HELP IN HERE? MAN DOWN!
MEN DOWN, ERIC. LOTS OF MEN DOWN.
O Holy Night. Also, O Holy...
$#!*, WOODY! WHY DO YOU ALWAYS HAVE TO RUIN EVERYTHING!

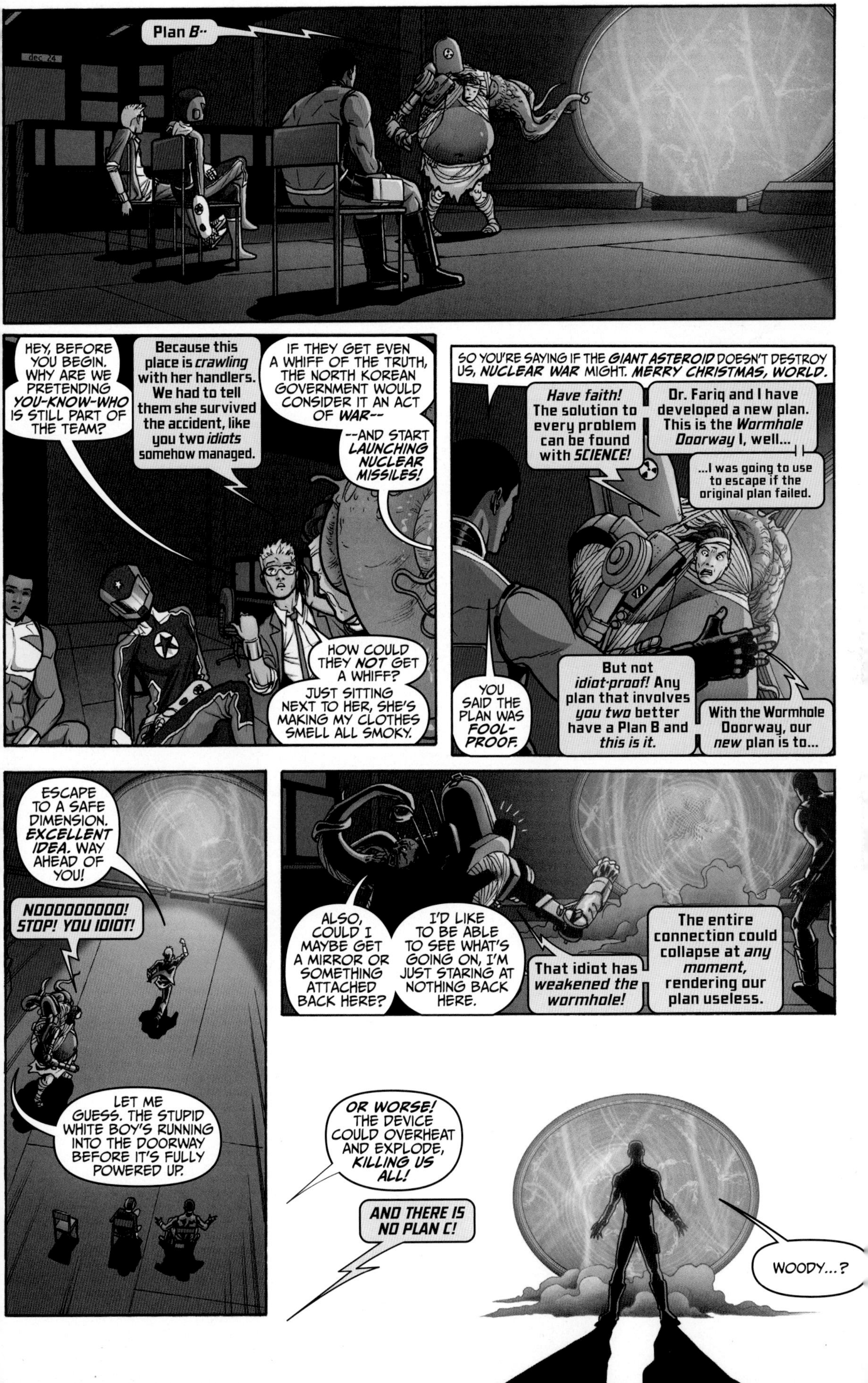
Plan B--
dec 24
HEY, BEFORE YOU BEGIN. WHY ARE WE PRETENDING YOU-KNOW-WHO IS STILL PART OF THE TEAM?
Because this place is crawling with her handlers. We had to tell them she survived the accident, like you two idiots somehow managed.
IF THEY GET EVEN A WHIFF OF THE TRUTH, THE NORTH KOREAN GOVERNMENT WOULD CONSIDER IT AN ACT OF WAR--
--AND START LAUNCHING NUCLEAR MISSILES!
HOW COULD THEY NOT GET A WHIFF?
JUST SITTING NEXT TO HER, SHE'S MAKING MY CLOTHES SMELL ALL SMOKY.
SO YOU'RE SAYING IF THE GIANT ASTEROID DOESN'T DESTROY US, NUCLEAR WAR MIGHT. MERRY CHRISTMAS, WORLD.
Have faith! The solution to every problem can be found with SCIENCE!
Dr. Fariq and I have developed a new plan. This is the Wormhole Doorway I, well...
...I was going to use to escape if the original plan failed.
YOU SAID THE PLAN WAS FOOL-PROOF.
But not idiot-proof! Any plan that involves you two better have a Plan B and this is it.
With the Wormhole Doorway, our new plan is to...
ESCAPE TO A SAFE DIMENSION. EXCELLENT IDEA. WAY AHEAD OF YOU!
NOOOOOOOOO! STOP! YOU IDIOT!
LET ME GUESS. THE STUPID WHITE BOY'S RUNNING INTO THE DOORWAY BEFORE IT'S FULLY POWERED UP.
ALSO, COULD I MAYBE GET A MIRROR OR SOMETHING ATTACHED BACK HERE?
I'D LIKE TO BE ABLE TO SEE WHAT'S GOING ON, I'M JUST STARING AT NOTHING BACK HERE.
That idiot has weakened the wormhole!
The entire connection could collapse at any moment, rendering our plan useless.
OR WORSE! THE DEVICE COULD OVERHEAT AND EXPLODE, KILLING US ALL!
AND THERE IS NO PLAN C!
WOODY...?

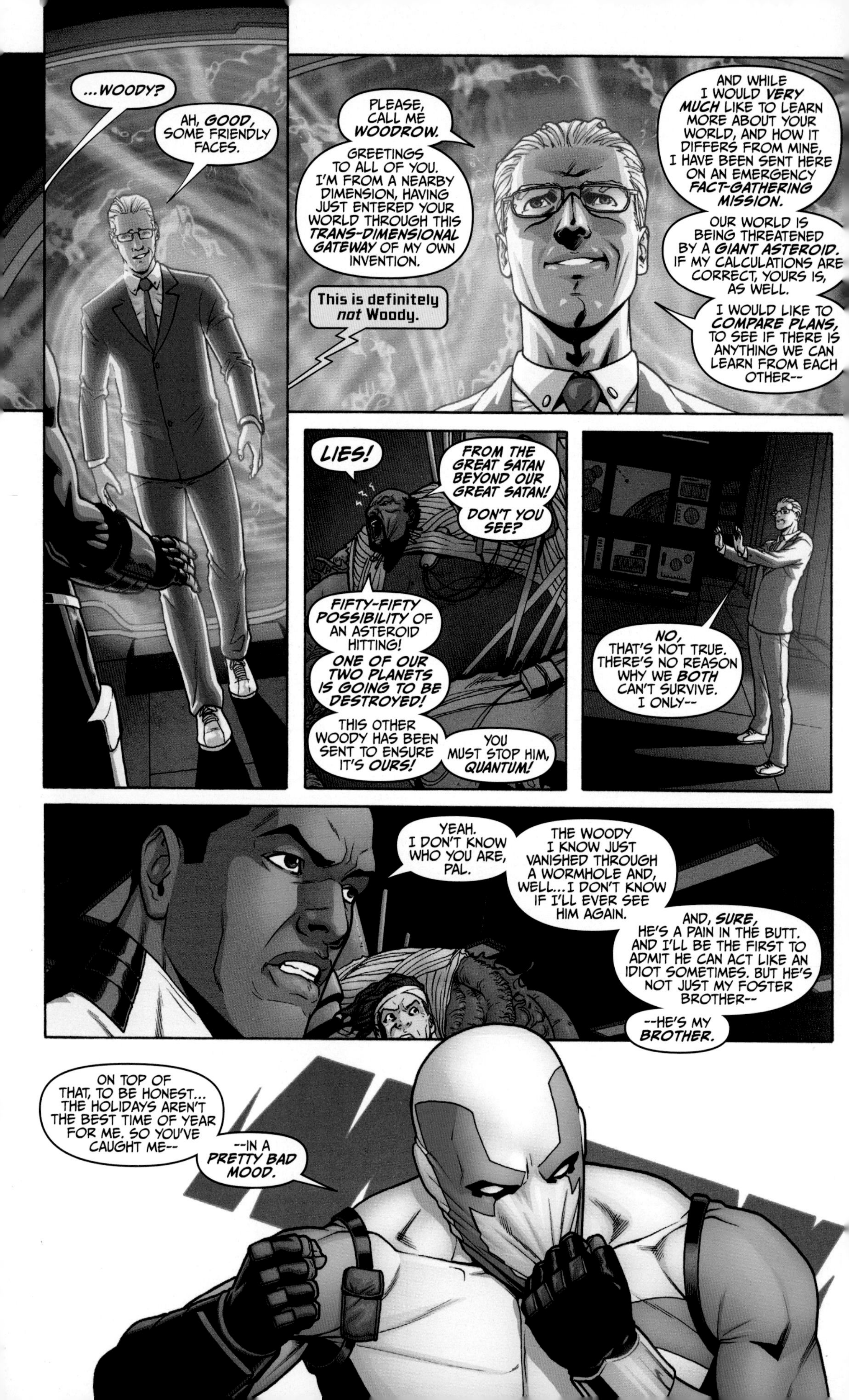
...WOODY?
AH, GOOD, SOME FRIENDLY FACES.
PLEASE, CALL ME WOODROW.
GREETINGS TO ALL OF YOU. I'M FROM A NEARBY DIMENSION, HAVING JUST ENTERED YOUR WORLD THROUGH THIS TRANS-DIMENSIONAL GATEWAY OF MY OWN INVENTION.
This is definitely not Woody.
AND WHILE I WOULD VERY MUCH LIKE TO LEARN MORE ABOUT YOUR WORLD, AND HOW IT DIFFERS FROM MINE, I HAVE BEEN SENT HERE ON AN EMERGENCY FACT-GATHERING MISSION.
OUR WORLD IS BEING THREATENED BY A GIANT ASTEROID. IF MY CALCULATIONS ARE CORRECT, YOURS IS, AS WELL.
I WOULD LIKE TO COMPARE PLANS, TO SEE IF THERE IS ANYTHING WE CAN LEARN FROM EACH OTHER--
LIES!
FROM THE GREAT SATAN BEYOND OUR GREAT SATAN!
DON'T YOU SEE?
FIFTY-FIFTY POSSIBILITY OF AN ASTEROID HITTING!
ONE OF OUR TWO PLANETS IS GOING TO BE DESTROYED!
THIS OTHER WOODY HAS BEEN SENT TO ENSURE IT'S OURS!
YOU MUST STOP HIM, QUANTUM!
NO, THAT'S NOT TRUE. THERE'S NO REASON WHY WE BOTH CAN'T SURVIVE. I ONLY--
YEAH. I DON'T KNOW WHO YOU ARE, PAL.
THE WOODY I KNOW JUST VANISHED THROUGH A WORMHOLE AND, WELL...I DON'T KNOW IF I'LL EVER SEE HIM AGAIN.
AND, SURE, HE'S A PAIN IN THE BUTT. AND I'LL BE THE FIRST TO ADMIT HE CAN ACT LIKE AN IDIOT SOMETIMES. BUT HE'S NOT JUST MY FOSTER BROTHER--
--HE'S MY BROTHER.
ON TOP OF THAT, TO BE HONEST... THE HOLIDAYS AREN'T THE BEST TIME OF YEAR FOR ME. SO YOU'VE CAUGHT ME--
--IN A PRETTY BAD MOOD.

You Better Watch Out. You Better Not Cry.

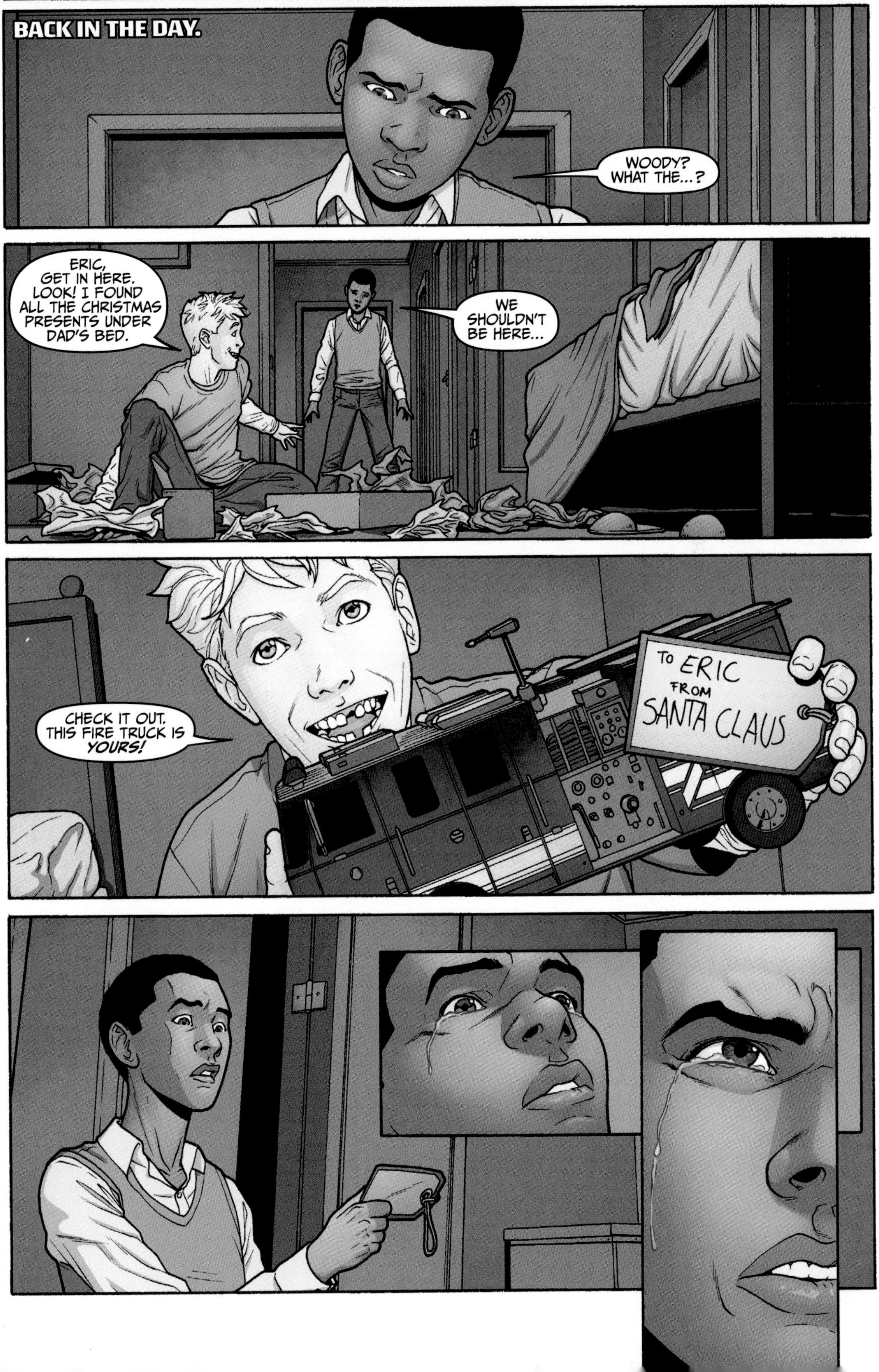
BACK IN THE DAY.
WOODY? WHAT THE...?
ERIC, GET IN HERE. LOOK! I FOUND ALL THE CHRISTMAS PRESENTS UNDER DAD'S BED.
WE SHOULDN'T BE HERE...
CHECK IT OUT. THIS FIRE TRUCK IS YOURS!
TO ERIC FROM SANTA CLAUS

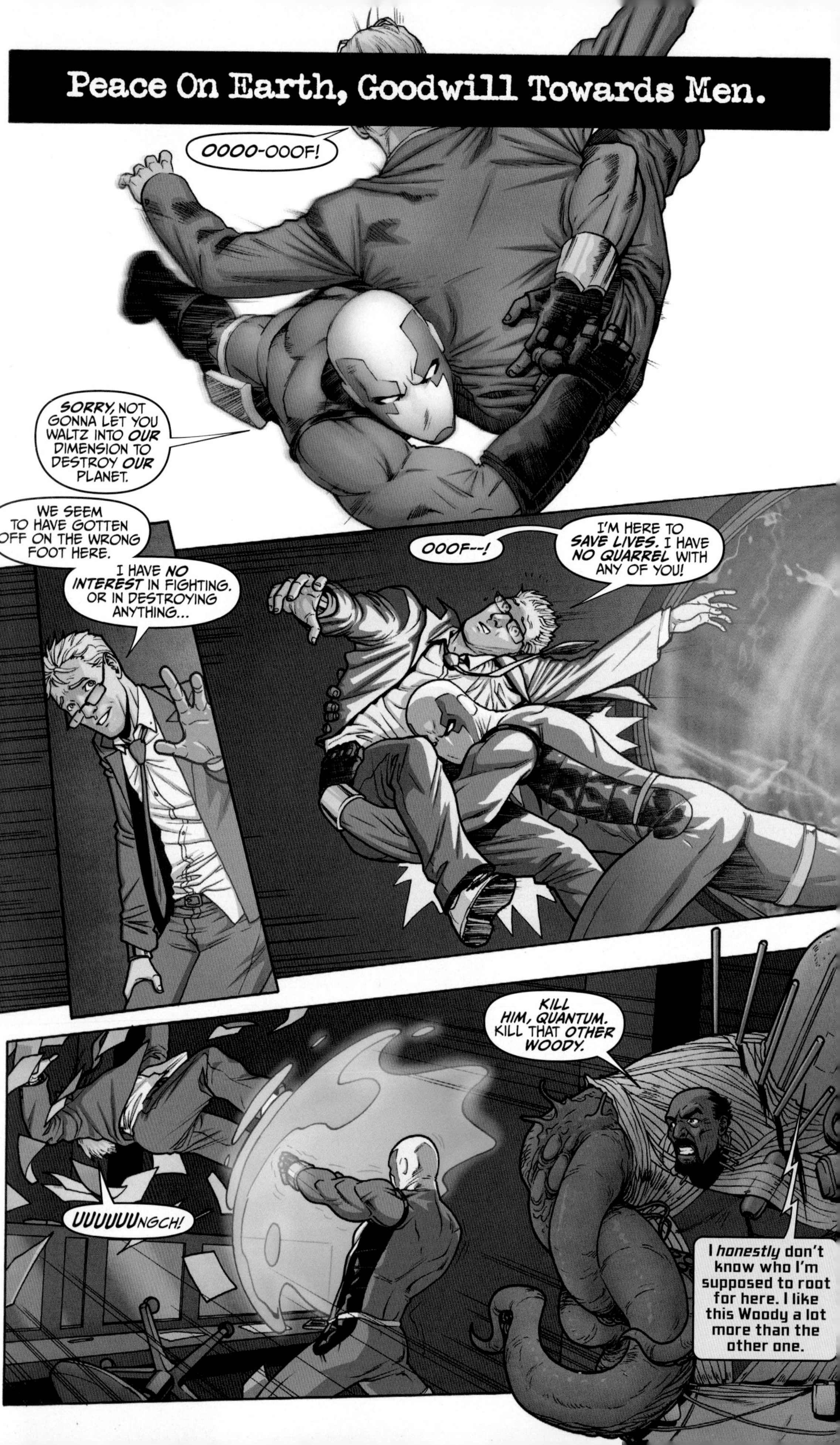
Peace On Earth, Goodwill Towards Men.
OOOO-OOOF!
SORRY, NOT GONNA LET YOU WALTZ INTO OUR DIMENSION TO DESTROY OUR PLANET.
WE SEEM TO HAVE GOTTEN OFF ON THE WRONG FOOT HERE.
I HAVE NO INTEREST IN FIGHTING. OR IN DESTROYING ANYTHING...
OOOF--!
I'M HERE TO SAVE LIVES. I HAVE NO QUARREL WITH ANY OF YOU!
KILL HIM, QUANTUM. KILL THAT OTHER WOODY.
UUUUUUNGCH!
I honestly don't know who I'm supposed to root for here. I like this Woody a lot more than the other one.

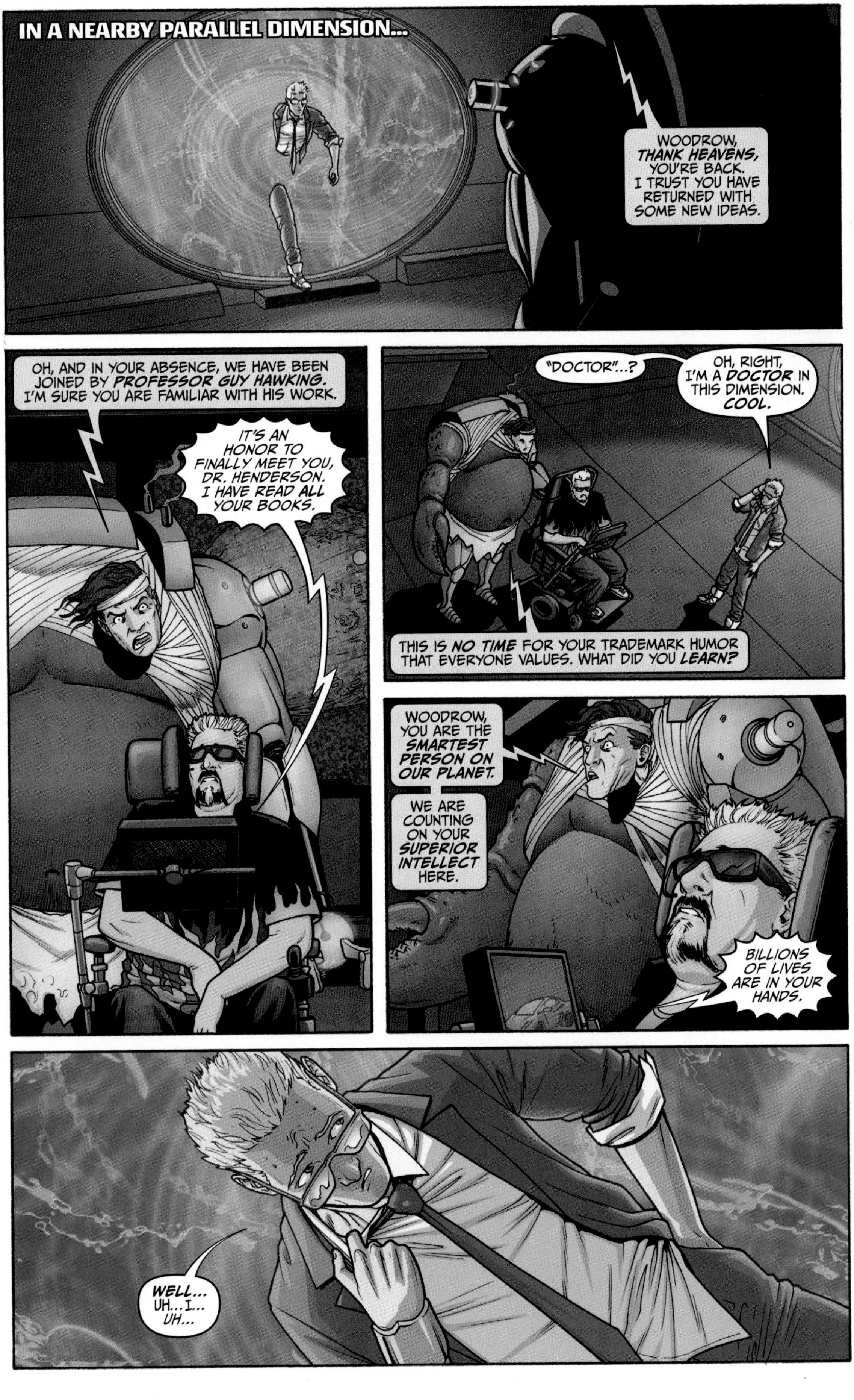
IN A NEARBY PARALLEL DIMENSION...
WOODROW, THANK HEAVENS, YOU'RE BACK. I TRUST YOU HAVE RETURNED WITH SOME NEW IDEAS.
OH, AND IN YOUR ABSENCE, WE HAVE BEEN JOINED BY PROFESSOR GUY HAWKING. I'M SURE YOU ARE FAMILIAR WITH HIS WORK.
IT'S AN HONOR TO FINALLY MEET YOU, DR. HENDERSON. I HAVE READ ALL YOUR BOOKS.
"DOCTOR"...?
OH, RIGHT, I'M A DOCTOR IN THIS DIMENSION. COOL.
THIS IS NO TIME FOR YOUR TRADEMARK HUMOR THAT EVERYONE VALUES. WHAT DID YOU LEARN?
WOODROW, YOU ARE THE SMARTEST PERSON ON OUR PLANET.
WE ARE COUNTING ON YOUR SUPERIOR INTELLECT HERE.
BILLIONS OF LIVES ARE IN YOUR HANDS.
WELL... UH... I... UH...

Better Not Pout, I'm Telling You Why.

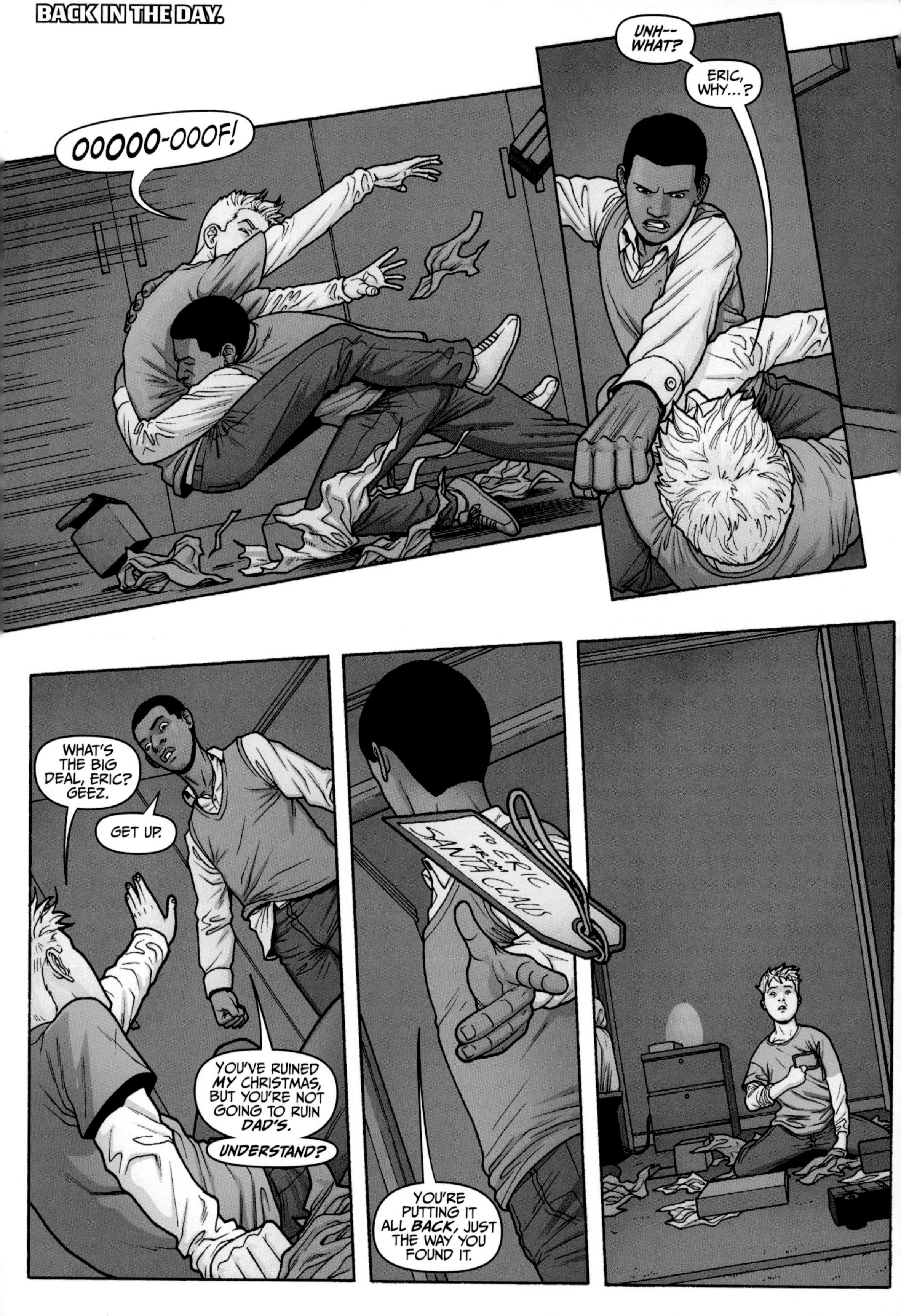
BACK IN THE DAY.
OOOOO-OOOF!
UNH-- WHAT?
ERIC, WHY...?
WHAT'S THE BIG DEAL, ERIC? GEEZ.
GET UP.
YOU'VE RUINED MY CHRISTMAS, BUT YOU'RE NOT GOING TO RUIN DAD'S.
UNDERSTAND?
TO ERIC FROM SANTA CLAUS
YOU'RE PUTTING IT ALL BACK, JUST THE WAY YOU FOUND IT.

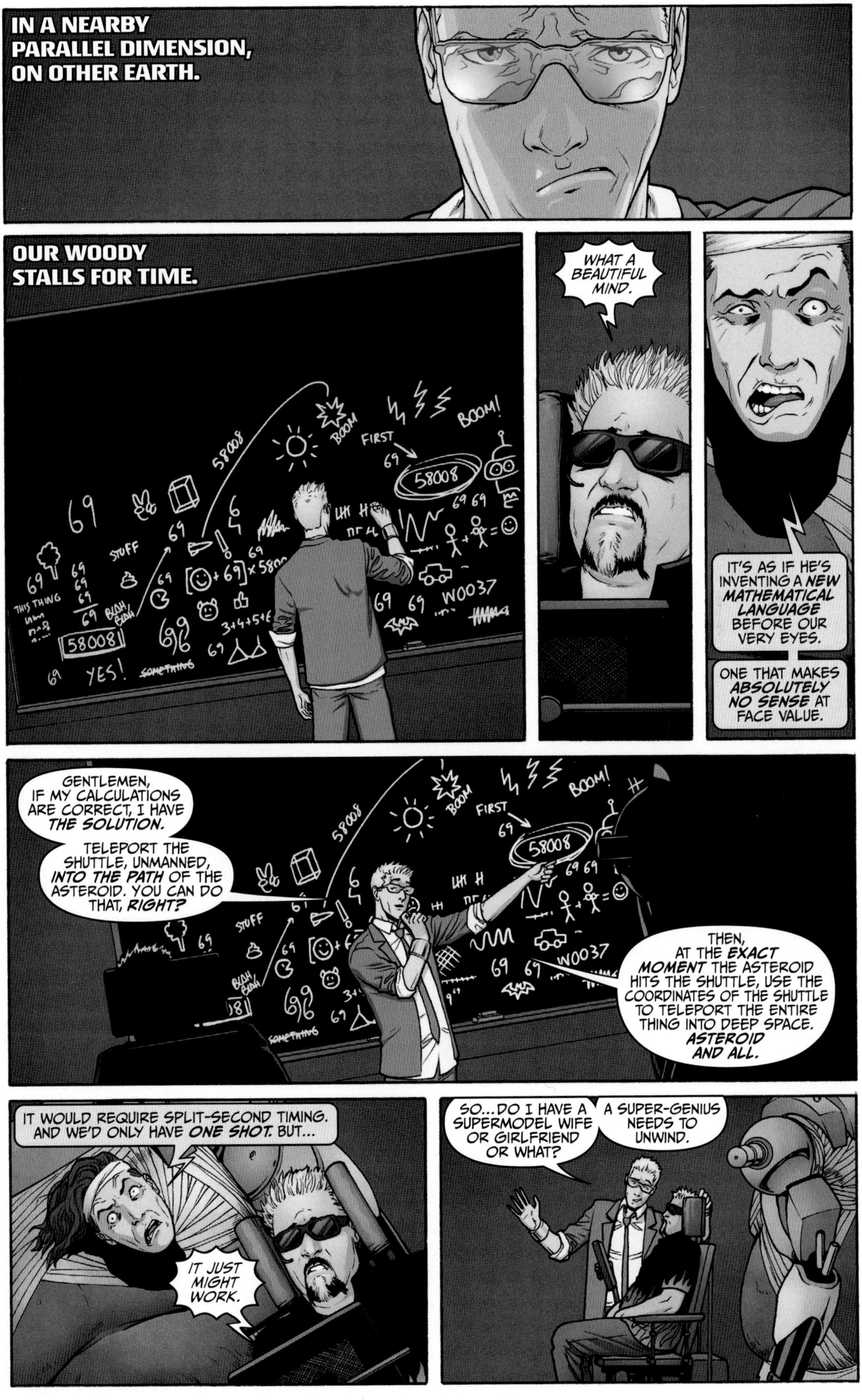
IN A NEARBY PARALLEL DIMENSION, ON OTHER EARTH.
OUR WOODY STALLS FOR TIME.
WHAT A BEAUTIFUL MIND.
IT'S AS IF HE'S INVENTING A NEW MATHEMATICAL LANGUAGE BEFORE OUR VERY EYES.
ONE THAT MAKES ABSOLUTELY NO SENSE AT FACE VALUE.
GENTLEMEN, IF MY CALCULATIONS ARE CORRECT, I HAVE THE SOLUTION.
TELEPORT THE SHUTTLE, UNMANNED, INTO THE PATH OF THE ASTEROID. YOU CAN DO THAT, RIGHT?
THEN, AT THE EXACT MOMENT THE ASTEROID HITS THE SHUTTLE, USE THE COORDINATES OF THE SHUTTLE TO TELEPORT THE ENTIRE THING INTO DEEP SPACE. ASTEROID AND ALL.
IT WOULD REQUIRE SPLIT-SECOND TIMING. AND WE'D ONLY HAVE ONE SHOT. BUT...
IT JUST MIGHT WORK.
SO...DO I HAVE A SUPERMODEL WIFE OR GIRLFRIEND OR WHAT?
A SUPER-GENIUS NEEDS TO UNWIND.

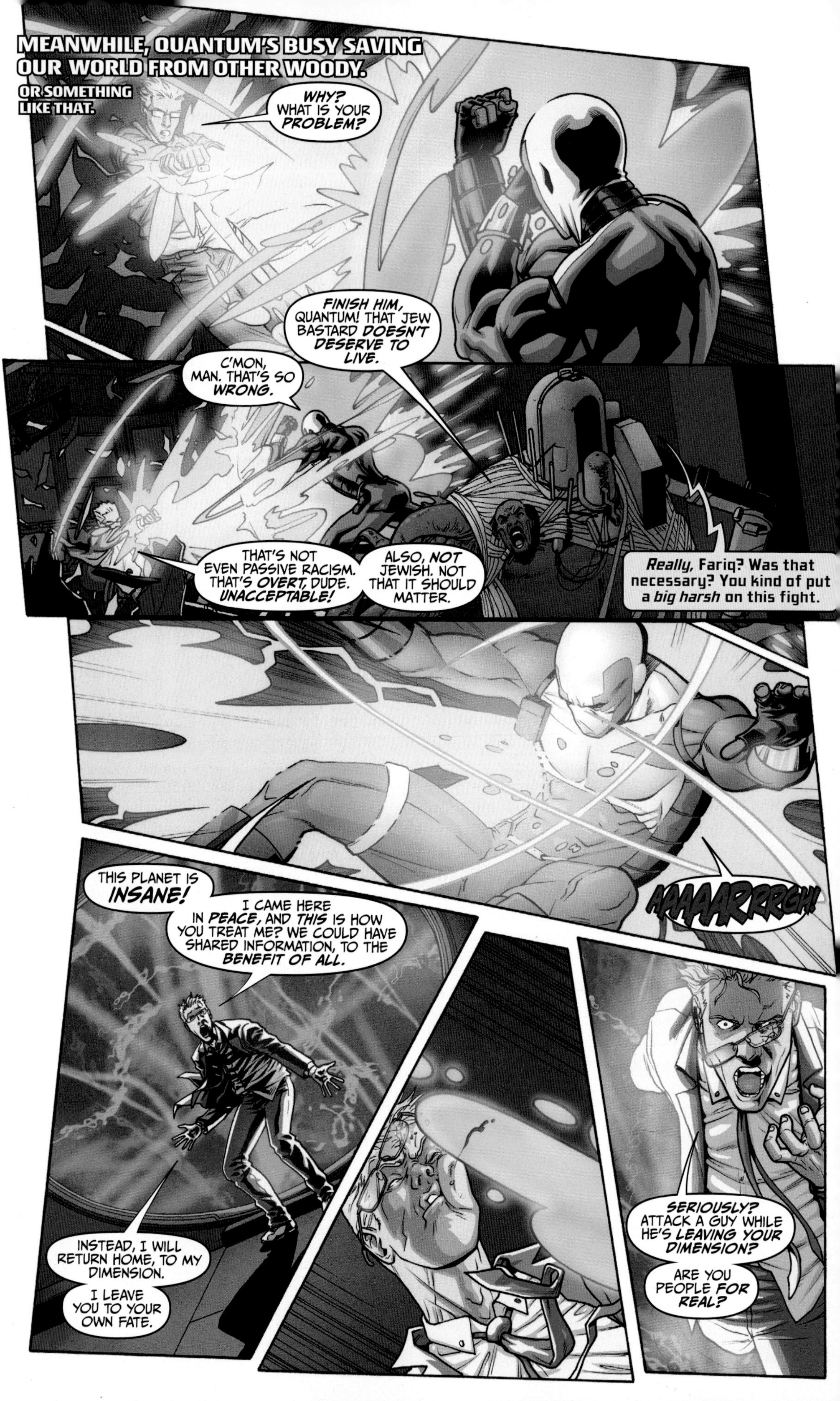

MEANWHILE, QUANTUM'S BUSY SAVING OUR WORLD FROM OTHER WOODY.
OR SOMETHING LIKE THAT.
WHY? WHAT IS YOUR PROBLEM?
FINISH HIM, QUANTUM! THAT JEW BASTARD DOESN'T DESERVE TO LIVE.
C'MON, MAN. THAT'S SO WRONG.
THAT'S NOT EVEN PASSIVE RACISM. THAT'S OVERT, DUDE. UNACCEPTABLE!
ALSO, NOT JEWISH. NOT THAT IT SHOULD MATTER.
Really, Fariq? Was that necessary? You kind of put a big harsh on this fight.
AAAAARRRGH!
THIS PLANET IS INSANE!
I CAME HERE IN PEACE, AND THIS IS HOW YOU TREAT ME? WE COULD HAVE SHARED INFORMATION, TO THE BENEFIT OF ALL.
INSTEAD, I WILL RETURN HOME, TO MY DIMENSION.
I LEAVE YOU TO YOUR OWN FATE.
SERIOUSLY? ATTACK A GUY WHILE HE'S LEAVING YOUR DIMENSION?
ARE YOU PEOPLE FOR REAL?

IN A NEARBY PARALLEL DIMENSION, MINUTES AGO, WHILE QUANTUM AND OTHER WOODY WERE FIGHTING ON OUR PLANET. UH, MAYBE DON'T THINK ABOUT IT TOO HARD.

SO, ARE *YOU* THE IDIOT ONE HERE? ALWAYS GETTING US INTO TROUBLE?

I DON'T KNOW WHAT YOU'RE TALKING ABOUT. *TROUBLE?*

JUST KIDDING. NICE CHAT, BRO.

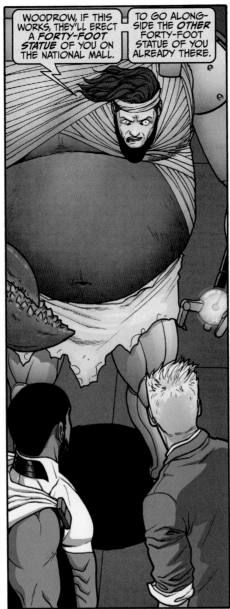

WOODROW, IF THIS WORKS, THEY'LL ERECT A *FORTY-FOOT STATUE* OF YOU ON THE NATIONAL MALL.

TO GO ALONG-SIDE THE *OTHER* FORTY-FOOT STATUE OF YOU ALREADY THERE.

UH, DIDN'T WORK.

IN FACT, IT BROKE THE ASTEROID INTO MANY PIECES. *ALL THOSE PIECES* ARE LARGE ENOUGH TO DESTROY EARTH.

IT'S ASSURED THAT AT LEAST ONE WILL BE A DIRECT HIT.

THE PIECES ARE TRAVELING *MUCH FASTER* NOW, SO THE COUNTDOWN IS BEING RESET ACCORDINGLY.

ALSO, WE WERE CONFUSED BY THIS NUMBER HE KEPT GIVING US.

IT DIDN'T SEEM TO FIT *ANYWHERE*, BUT ONE OF OUR ENGINEERS *DID* NOTICE THAT IT SPELLS *BOOBS* UPSIDE-DOWN.

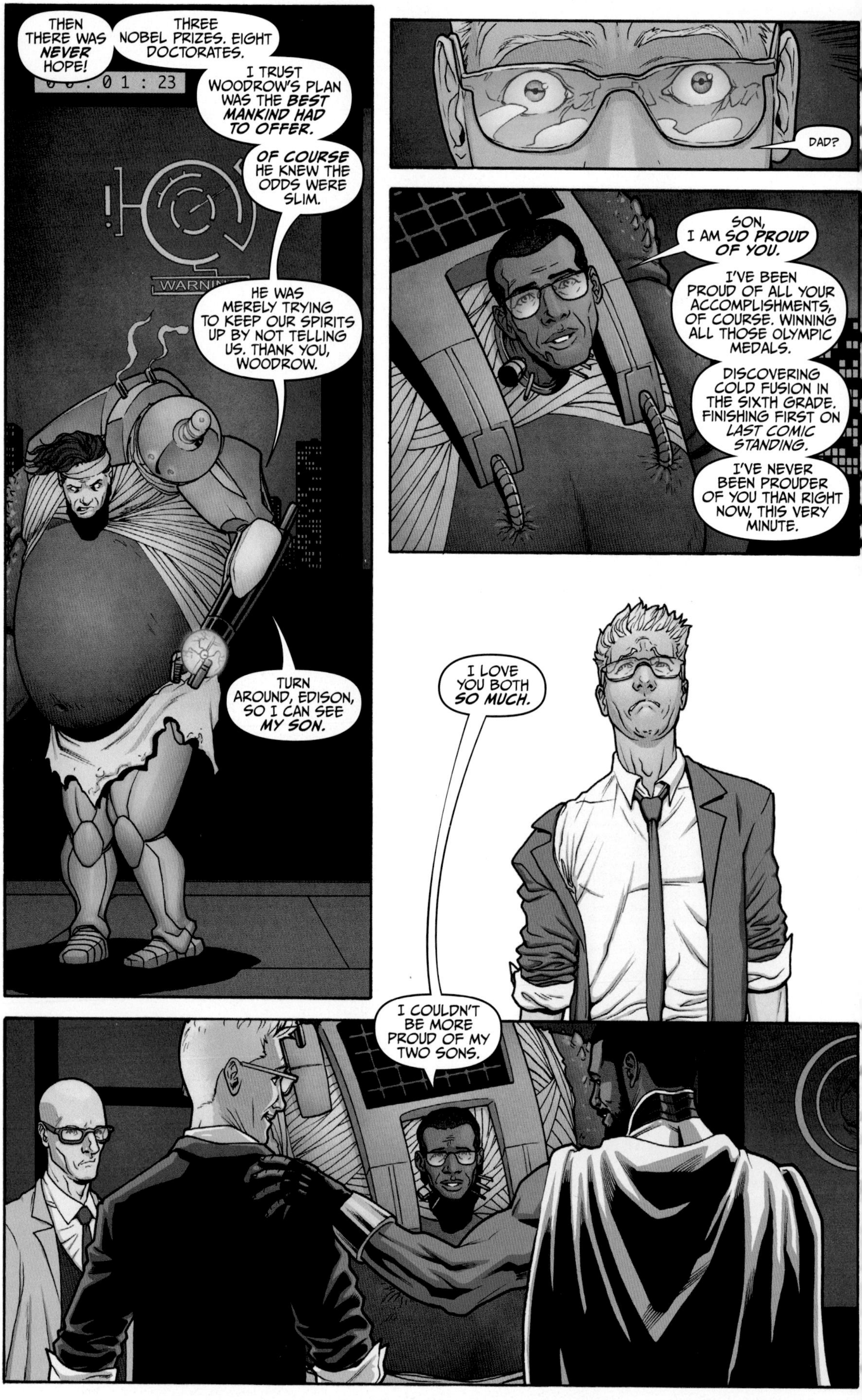
THEN THERE WAS NEVER HOPE!
THREE NOBEL PRIZES. EIGHT DOCTORATES.
00.01 : 23
I TRUST WOODROW'S PLAN WAS THE BEST MANKIND HAD TO OFFER.
OF COURSE HE KNEW THE ODDS WERE SLIM.
WARNING
HE WAS MERELY TRYING TO KEEP OUR SPIRITS UP BY NOT TELLING US. THANK YOU, WOODROW.
TURN AROUND, EDISON, SO I CAN SEE MY SON.
DAD?
SON, I AM SO PROUD OF YOU.
I'VE BEEN PROUD OF ALL YOUR ACCOMPLISHMENTS, OF COURSE. WINNING ALL THOSE OLYMPIC MEDALS.
DISCOVERING COLD FUSION IN THE SIXTH GRADE. FINISHING FIRST ON LAST COMIC STANDING.
I'VE NEVER BEEN PROUDER OF YOU THAN RIGHT NOW, THIS VERY MINUTE.
I LOVE YOU BOTH SO MUCH.
I COULDN'T BE MORE PROUD OF MY TWO SONS.

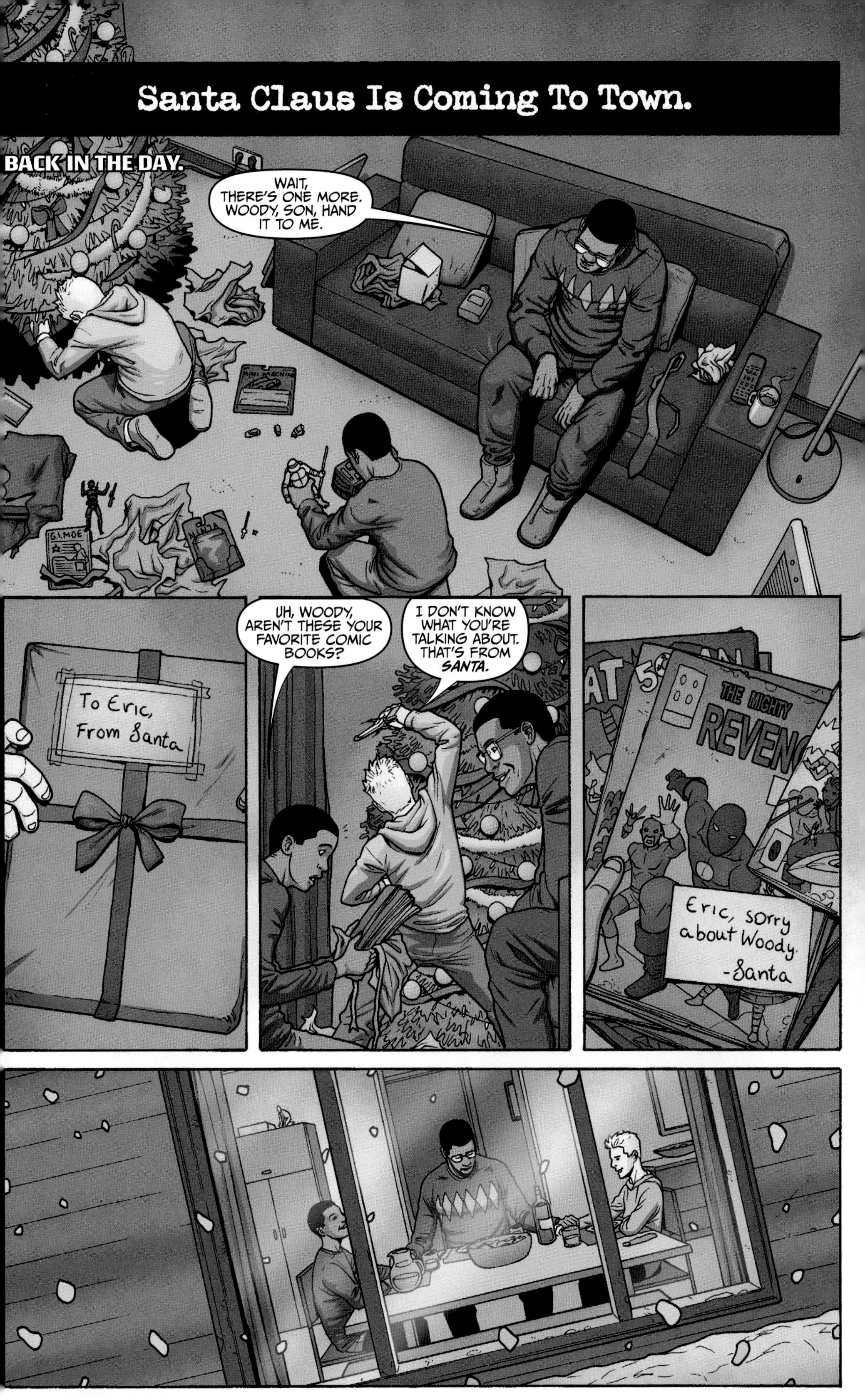
Santa Claus Is Coming To Town.
BACK IN THE DAY.
WAIT, THERE'S ONE MORE. WOODY, SON, HAND IT TO ME.
To Eric, From Santa
UH, WOODY, AREN'T THESE YOUR FAVORITE COMIC BOOKS?
I DON'T KNOW WHAT YOU'RE TALKING ABOUT. THAT'S FROM SANTA.
THE MIGHTY
Eric, sorry about Woody. -Santa

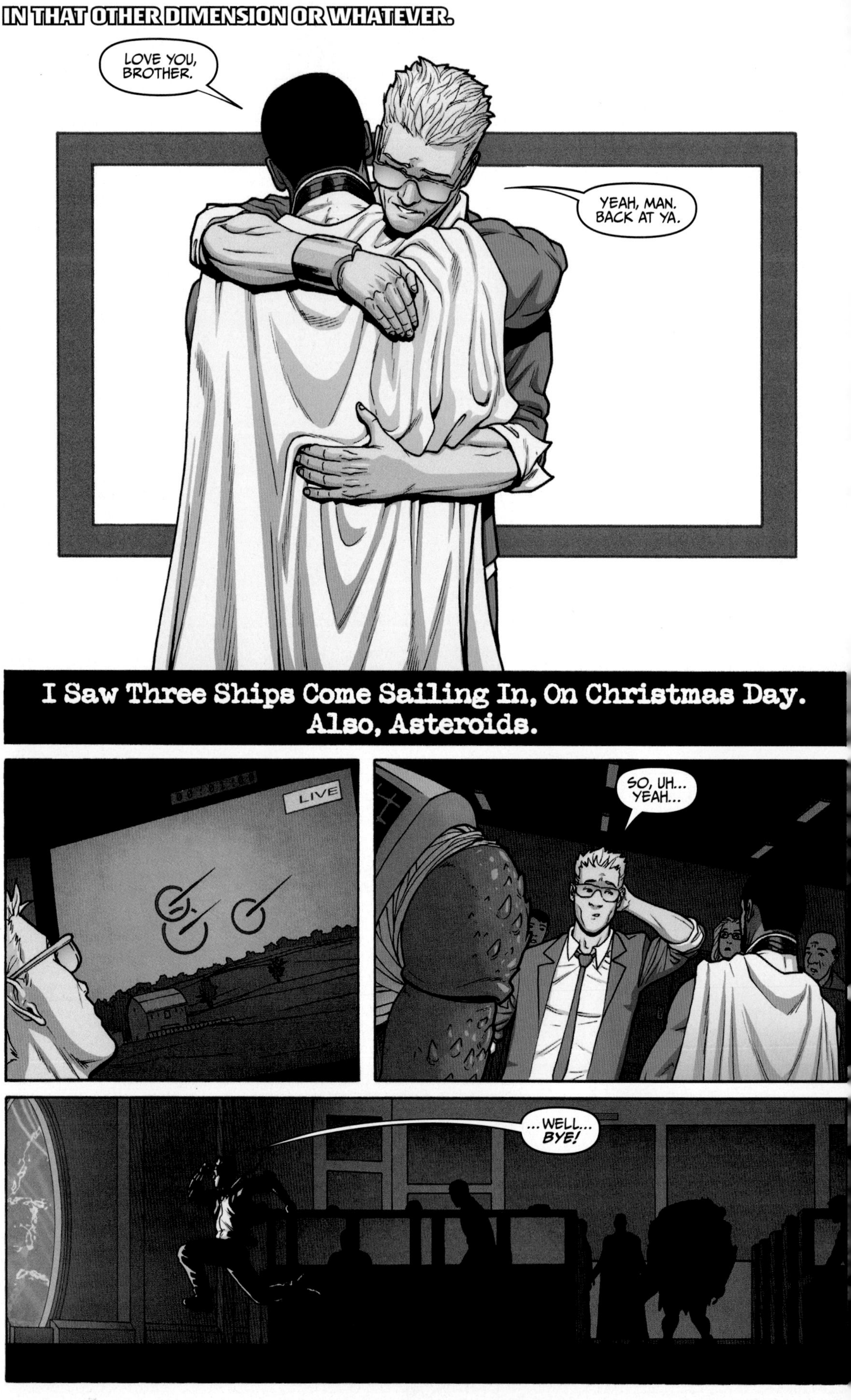
IN THAT OTHER DIMENSION OR WHATEVER.
LOVE YOU, BROTHER.
YEAH, MAN. BACK AT YA.
I Saw Three Ships Come Sailing In, On Christmas Day. Also, Asteroids.
LIVE
SO, UH... YEAH...
...WELL... BYE!

There's No Place Like Home For The Holidays.

WE MIGHT AS WELL STAY FOR THE REUNION.

BROTHER! FATHER! THE HYPER-AGGRESSIVE BUFFOONS IN THAT PARALLEL DIMENSION WERE *NO HELP* WHATSOEVER!

SO, WHAT DID I MISS HERE?

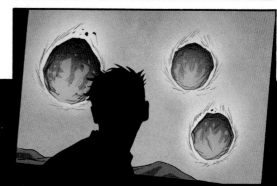

REUNION OVER.

OH...

Ding Dong, Merrily On High.

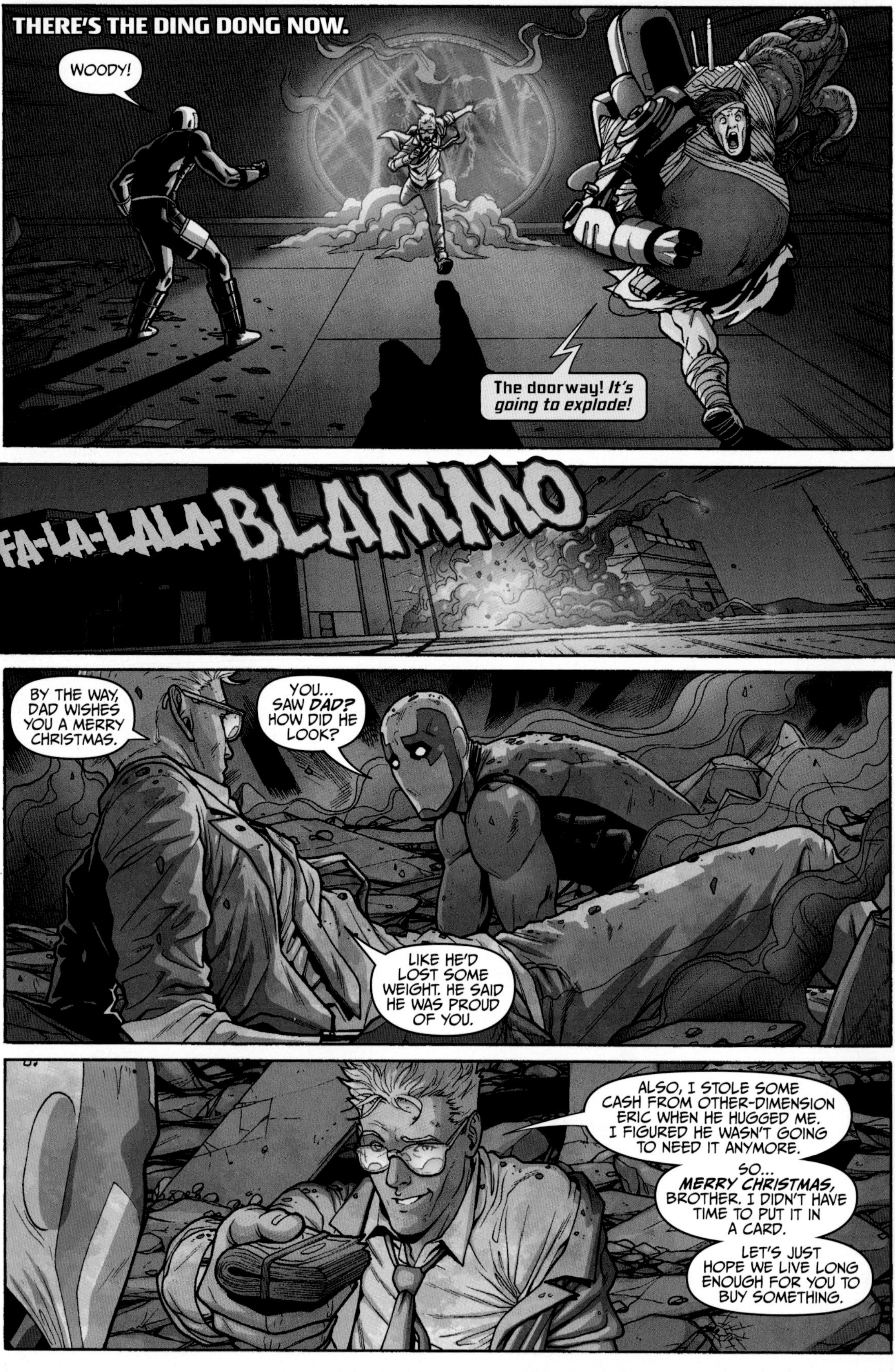
THERE'S THE DING DONG NOW.
WOODY!
The doorway! *It's going to explode!*
FA-LA-LALA-BLAMMO
BY THE WAY, DAD WISHES YOU A MERRY CHRISTMAS.
YOU... SAW *DAD?* HOW DID HE LOOK?
LIKE HE'D LOST SOME WEIGHT. HE SAID HE WAS PROUD OF YOU.
ALSO, I STOLE SOME CASH FROM OTHER-DIMENSION ERIC WHEN HE HUGGED ME. I FIGURED HE WASN'T GOING TO NEED IT ANYMORE.
SO... *MERRY CHRISTMAS,* BROTHER. I DIDN'T HAVE TIME TO PUT IT IN A CARD.
LET'S JUST HOPE WE LIVE LONG ENOUGH FOR YOU TO BUY SOMETHING.

Star Of Wonder, Star Of Night.

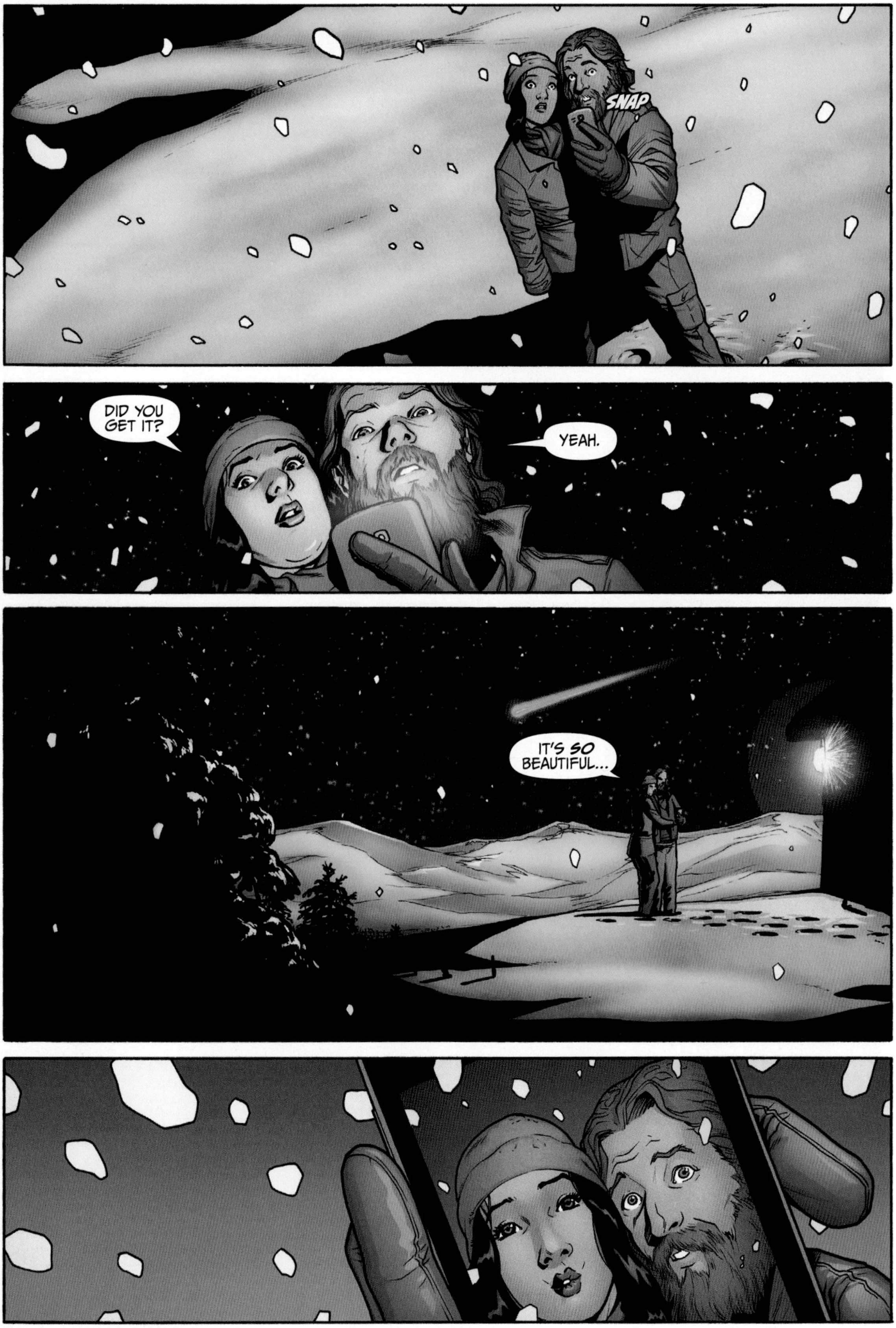
SNAP
DID YOU GET IT?
YEAH.
IT'S SO BEAUTIFUL...

The asteroid passed by Earth hours ago, everyone. Our planet has been *spared*.

Good work, team.

Now, it's *possible* our actions didn't have anything to do with this. In which case...

...we simply got *lucky*.

ALTHOUGH OUR ACTIONS MOST CERTAINLY *DESTROYED THAT OTHER PLANET.*

But I think it's best we not think too much on that fact and enjoy this moment.

WHAT DO WE DO WITH *HER?*

Leave that to *us*. It was always meant to be a suicide mission anyway.

OH, *HEY,* THERE'S SOME INFORMATION YOU LEFT OUT OF THE ORIGINAL BRIEFING.

WE SHOULD JUST PUT HER IN THE *SUICIDE SHUTTLE* AND SHOOT HER OFF INTO SPACE. TELL HER HANDLERS THAT EVERYTHING WORKED AS PLANNED.

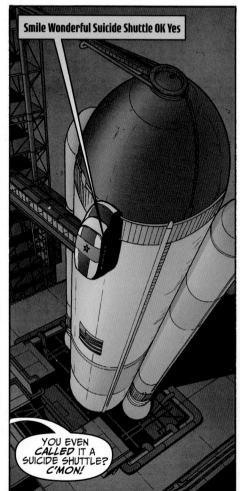

Smile Wonderful Suicide Shuttle OK Yes

YOU EVEN *CALLED* IT A SUICIDE SHUTTLE? *C'MON!*

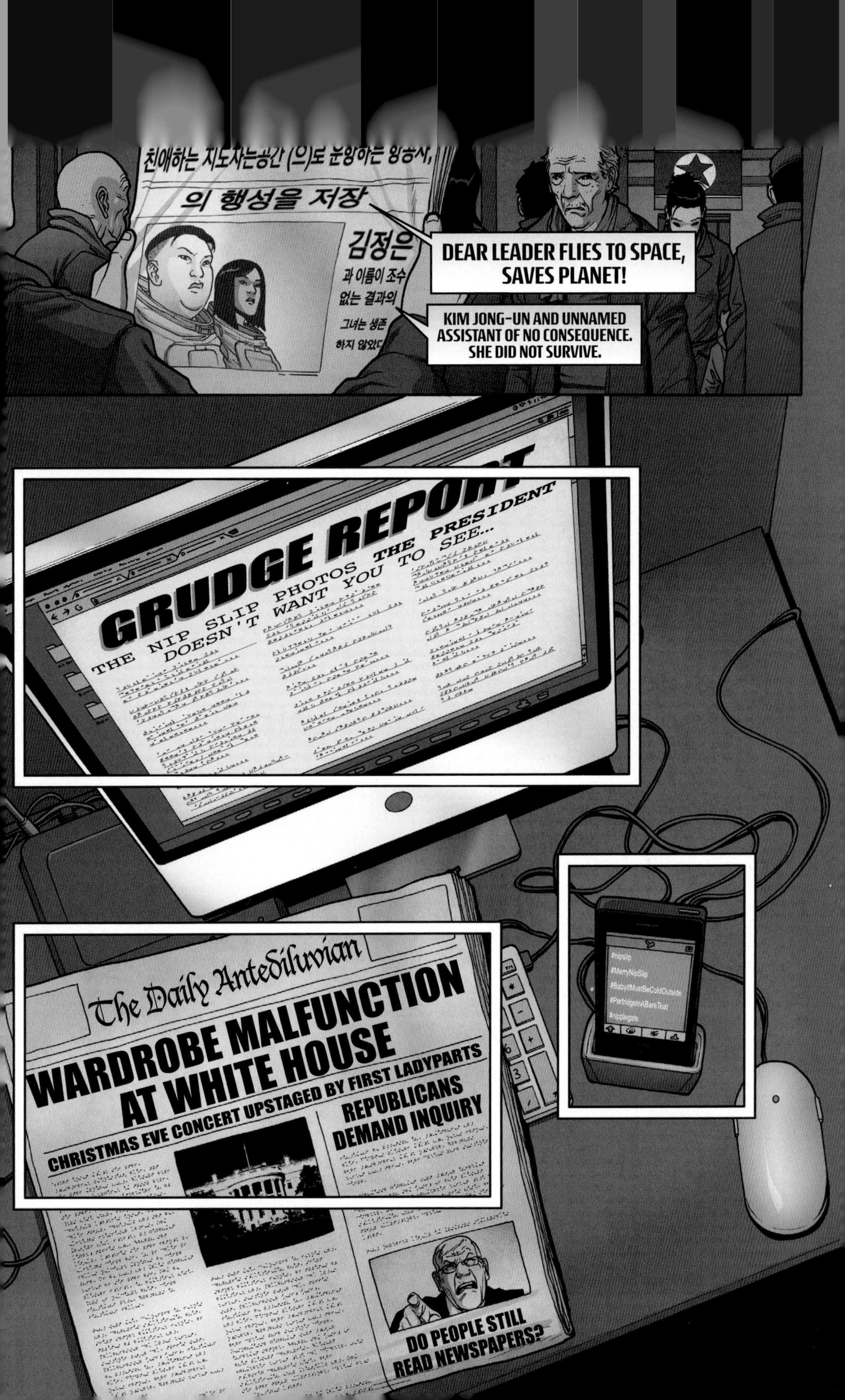
의 행성을 저장
김정은
과 이름이 조수
없는 결과의
그녀는 생존
하지 않았다
DEAR LEADER FLIES TO SPACE, SAVES PLANET!
KIM JONG-UN AND UNNAMED ASSISTANT OF NO CONSEQUENCE. SHE DID NOT SURVIVE.
GRUDGE REPORT
THE NIP SLIP PHOTOS THE PRESIDENT DOESN'T WANT YOU TO SEE...
#nipslip
#MerryNipSlip
#BabyItMustBeColdOutside
#PartridgeInABareTeat
#nipplegate
The Daily Antediluvian
WARDROBE MALFUNCTION AT WHITE HOUSE
CHRISTMAS EVE CONCERT UPSTAGED BY FIRST LADYPARTS
REPUBLICANS DEMAND INQUIRY
DO PEOPLE STILL READ NEWSPAPERS?

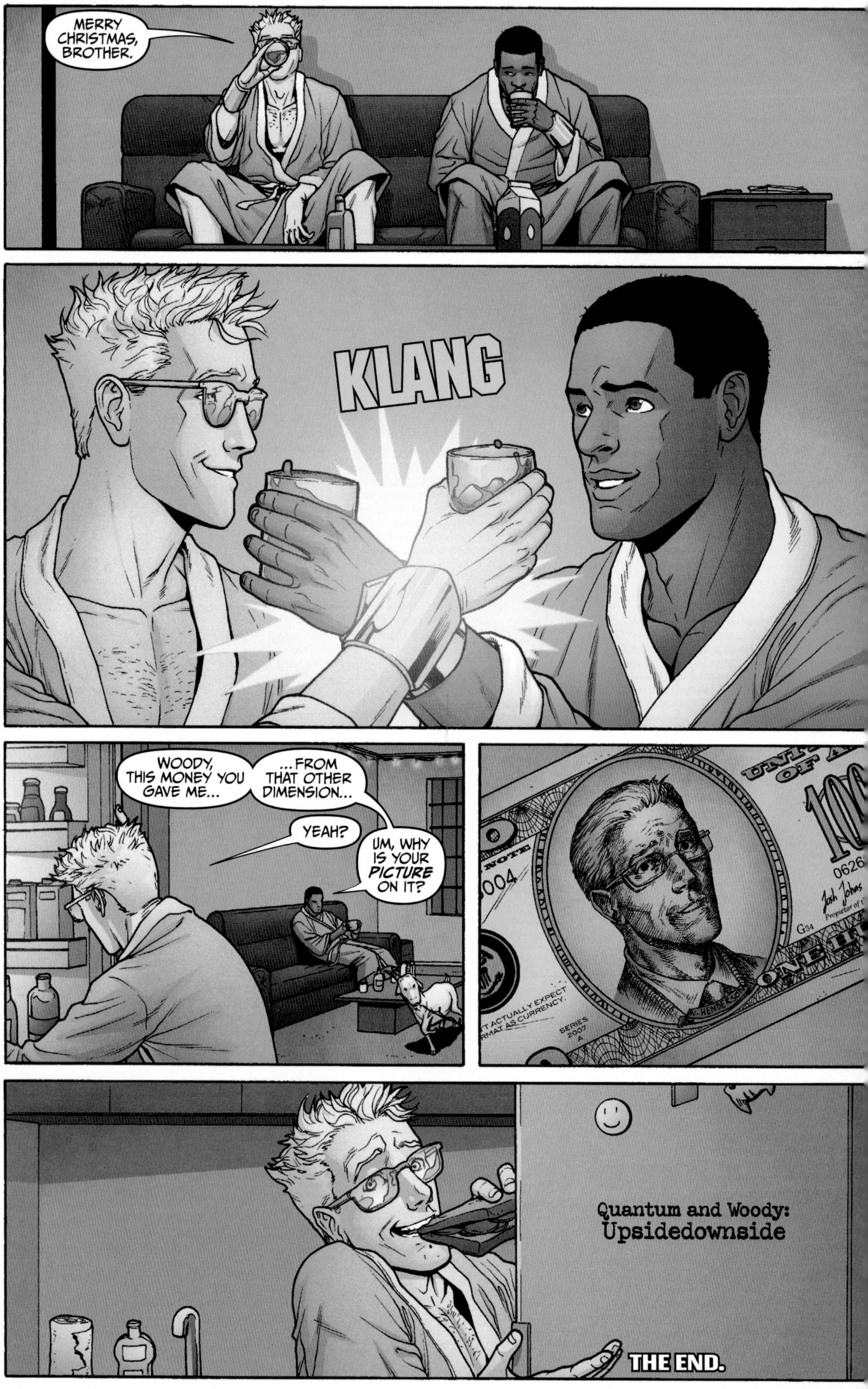

MERRY CHRISTMAS, BROTHER.
KLANG
WOODY, THIS MONEY YOU GAVE ME...
...FROM THAT OTHER DIMENSION...
YEAH?
UM, WHY IS YOUR PICTURE ON IT?
SERIES 2007 A
Quantum and Woody: Upsidedownside
THE END.

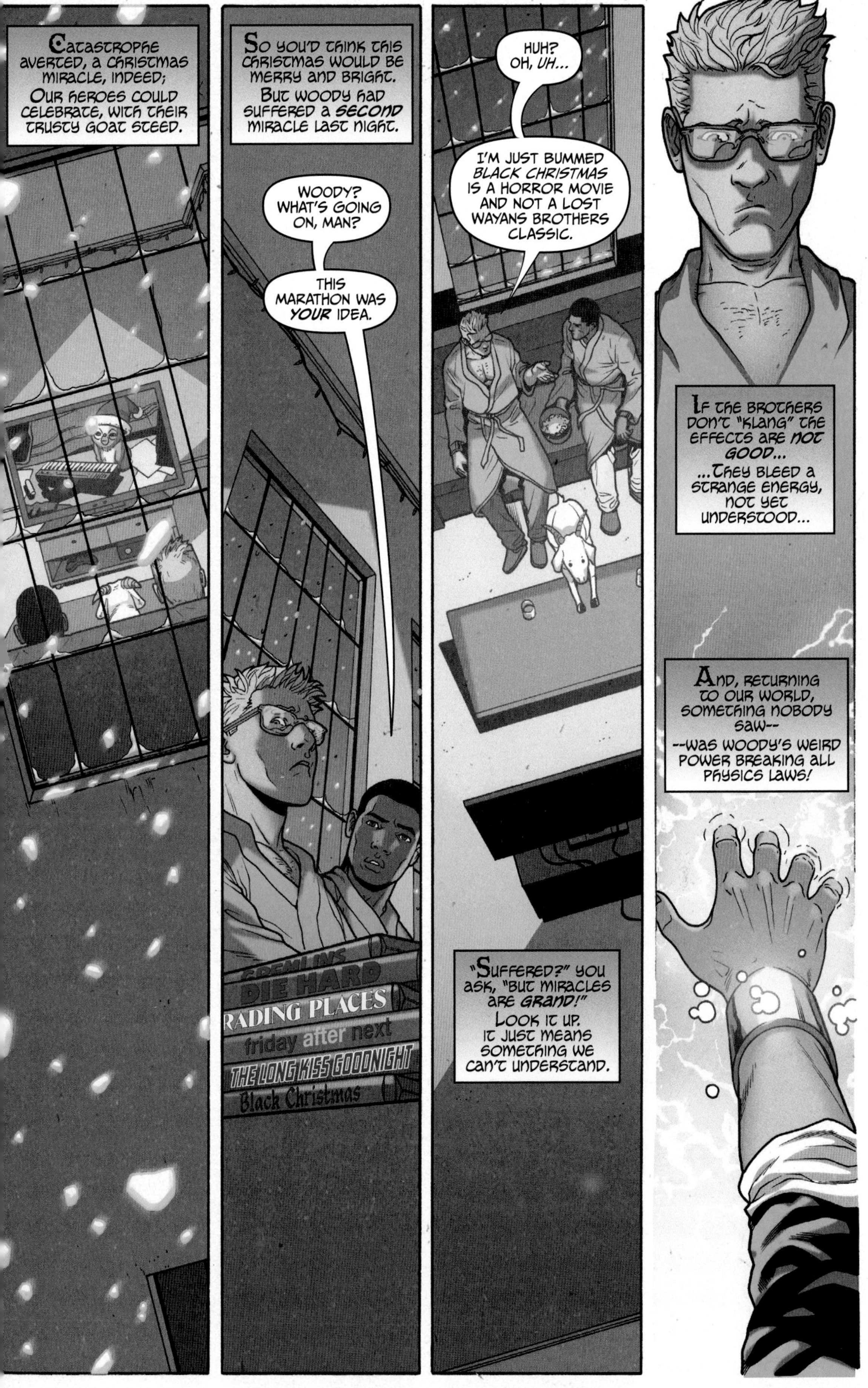
Catastrophe averted, a Christmas miracle, indeed;
Our heroes could celebrate, with their trusty goat steed.
So you'd think this Christmas would be merry and bright.
But Woody had suffered a *second* miracle last night.
WOODY? WHAT'S GOING ON, MAN?
THIS MARATHON WAS *YOUR* IDEA.
GREMLINS
DIE HARD
TRADING PLACES
friday after next
THE LONG KISS GOODNIGHT
Black Christmas
HUH? OH, *UH*...
I'M JUST BUMMED *BLACK CHRISTMAS* IS A HORROR MOVIE AND NOT A LOST WAYANS BROTHERS CLASSIC.
"Suffered?" you ask, "but miracles are *grand!*"
Look it up. It just means something we can't understand.
If the brothers don't "klang" the effects are *not good*...
...They bleed a strange energy, not yet understood...
And, returning to our world, something nobody saw--
--was Woody's weird power breaking all physics laws!

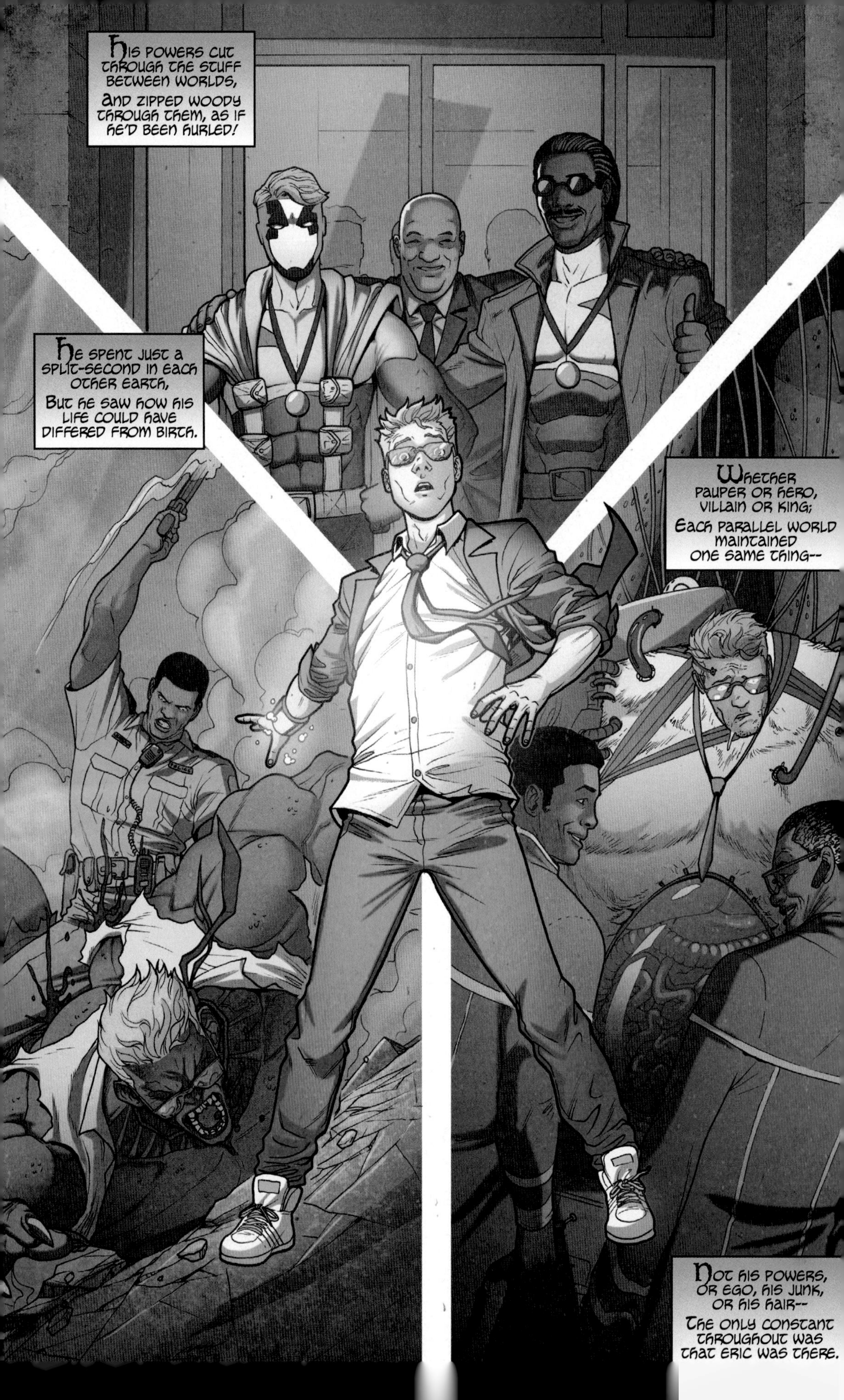
His powers cut through the stuff between worlds,
and zipped Woody through them, as if he'd been hurled!
He spent just a split-second in each other Earth,
But he saw how his life could have differed from birth.
Whether pauper or hero, villain or king;
Each parallel world maintained one same thing--
Not his powers, or ego, his junk, or his hair--
The only constant throughout was that Eric was there.

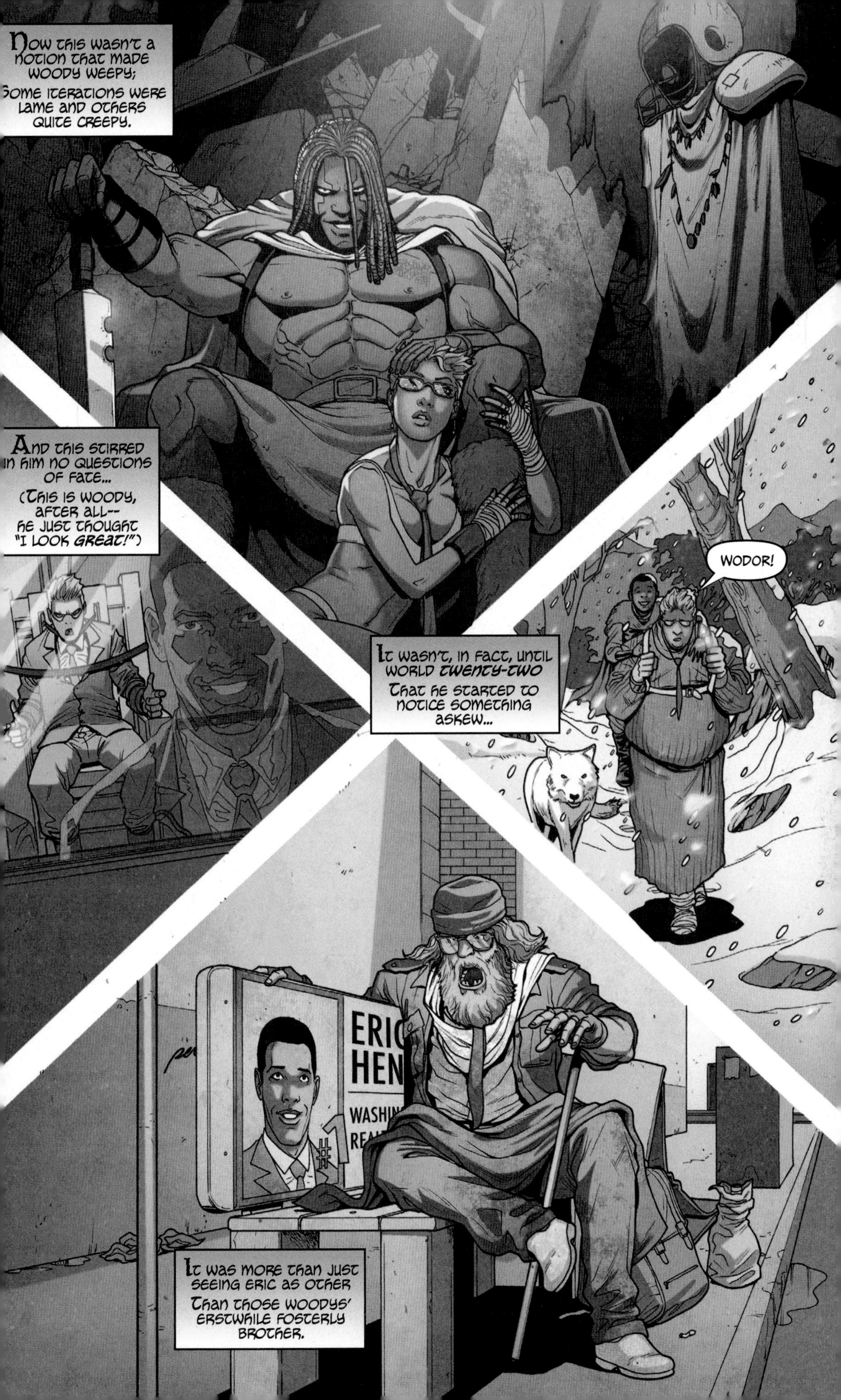

Now this wasn't a notion that made Woody weepy;
Some iterations were lame and others quite creepy.
And this stirred in him no questions of fate...
(This is Woody, after all-- he just thought "I look great!")
It wasn't, in fact, until world twenty-two
That he started to notice something askew...
WODOR!
ERIC
HEN
WASHIN
It was more than just seeing Eric as other
Than those Woodys' erstwhile fosterly brother.

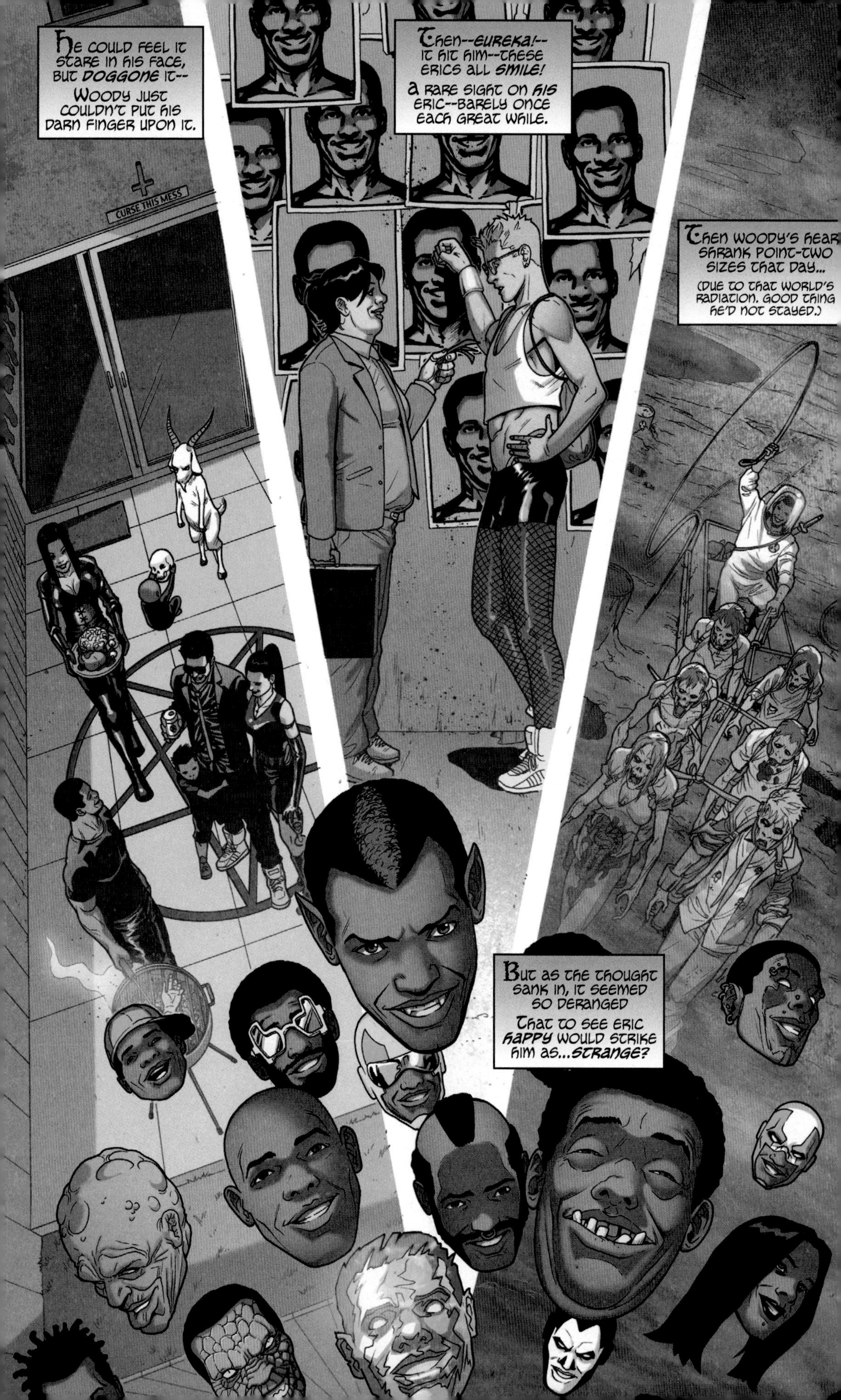

He could feel it stare in his face, but DOGGONE it--
Woody just couldn't put his darn finger upon it.
CURSE THIS MESS
Then--EUREKA!--it hit him--these Erics all SMILE!
A rare sight on HIS Eric--barely once each great while.
Then Woody's hear shrank point-two sizes that day...
(Due to that world's radiation. Good thing he'd not stayed.)
But as the thought sank in, it seemed so deranged
That to see Eric HAPPY would strike him as...STRANGE?

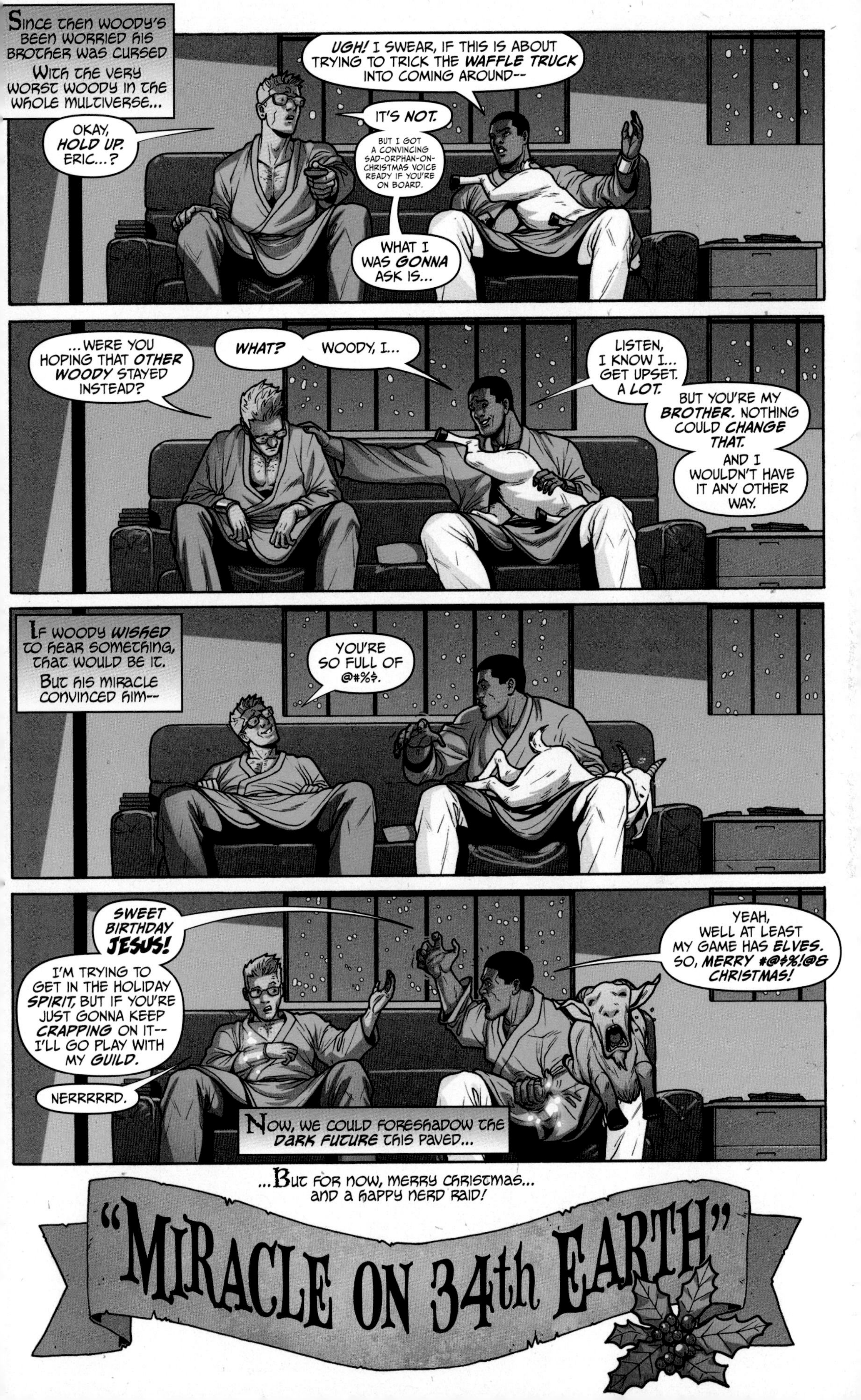
Since then Woody's been worried his brother was cursed
With the very worst Woody in the whole multiverse...
UGH! I SWEAR, IF THIS IS ABOUT TRYING TO TRICK THE WAFFLE TRUCK INTO COMING AROUND--
OKAY, HOLD UP. ERIC...?
IT'S NOT.
BUT I GOT A CONVINCING SAD-ORPHAN-ON-CHRISTMAS VOICE READY IF YOU'RE ON BOARD.
WHAT I WAS GONNA ASK IS...
...WERE YOU HOPING THAT OTHER WOODY STAYED INSTEAD?
WHAT?
WOODY, I...
LISTEN, I KNOW I... GET UPSET. A LOT.
BUT YOU'RE MY BROTHER. NOTHING COULD CHANGE THAT.
AND I WOULDN'T HAVE IT ANY OTHER WAY.
If Woody wished to hear something, that would be it.
But his miracle convinced him--
YOU'RE SO FULL OF @#%$.
SWEET BIRTHDAY JESUS!
I'M TRYING TO GET IN THE HOLIDAY SPIRIT, BUT IF YOU'RE JUST GONNA KEEP CRAPPING ON IT-- I'LL GO PLAY WITH MY GUILD.
NERRRRRD.
YEAH, WELL AT LEAST MY GAME HAS ELVES. SO, MERRY #@$%!@& CHRISTMAS!
Now, we could foreshadow the dark future this paved...
...But for now, merry Christmas... and a happy nerd raid!
"MIRACLE ON 34th EARTH"

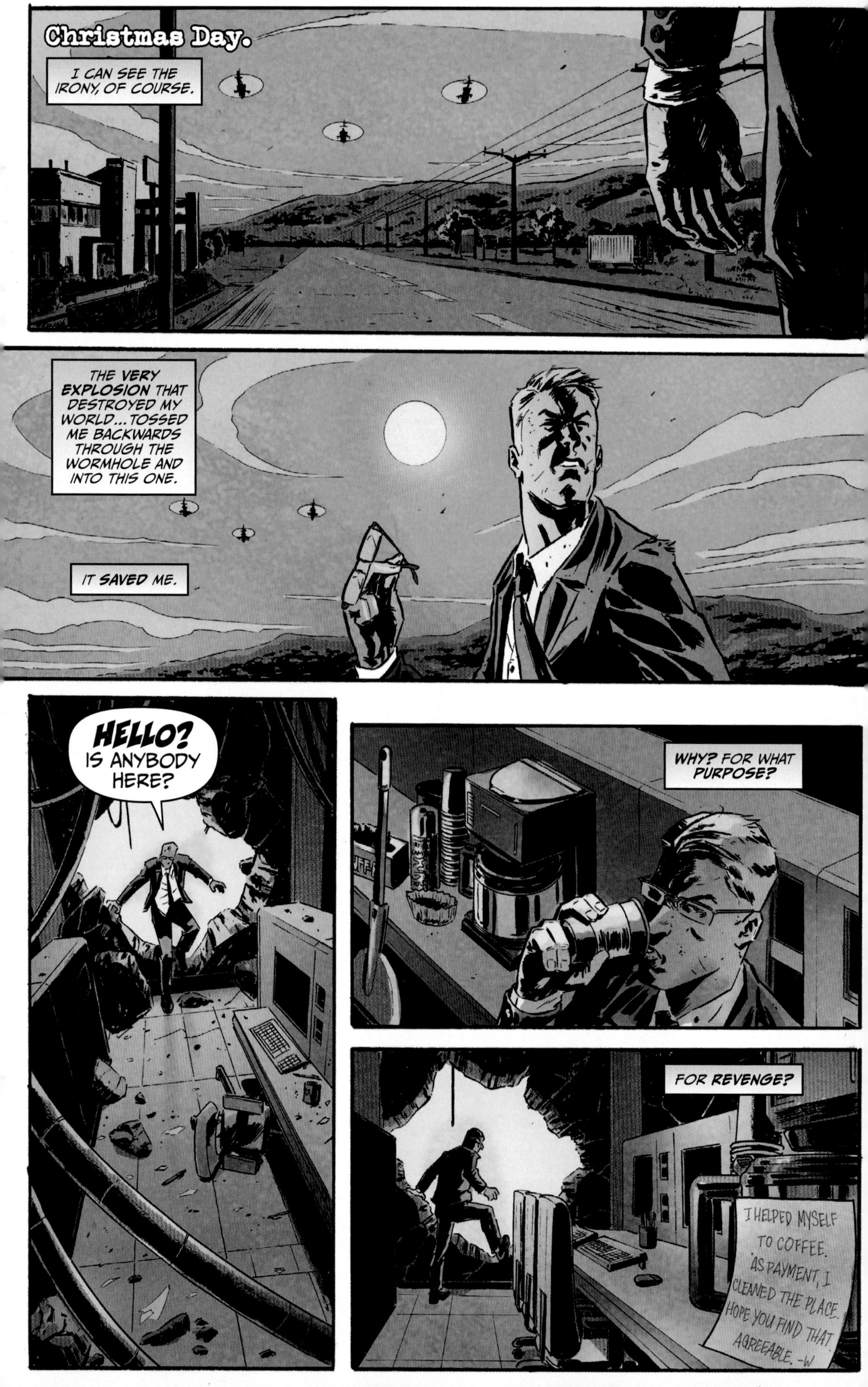
Christmas Day.
I CAN SEE THE IRONY, OF COURSE.
THE VERY EXPLOSION THAT DESTROYED MY WORLD...TOSSED ME BACKWARDS THROUGH THE WORMHOLE AND INTO THIS ONE.
IT SAVED ME.
HELLO? IS ANYBODY HERE?
WHY? FOR WHAT PURPOSE?
FOR REVENGE?
I HELPED MYSELF TO COFFEE. AS PAYMENT, I CLEANED THE PLACE. HOPE YOU FIND THAT AGREEABLE. -W

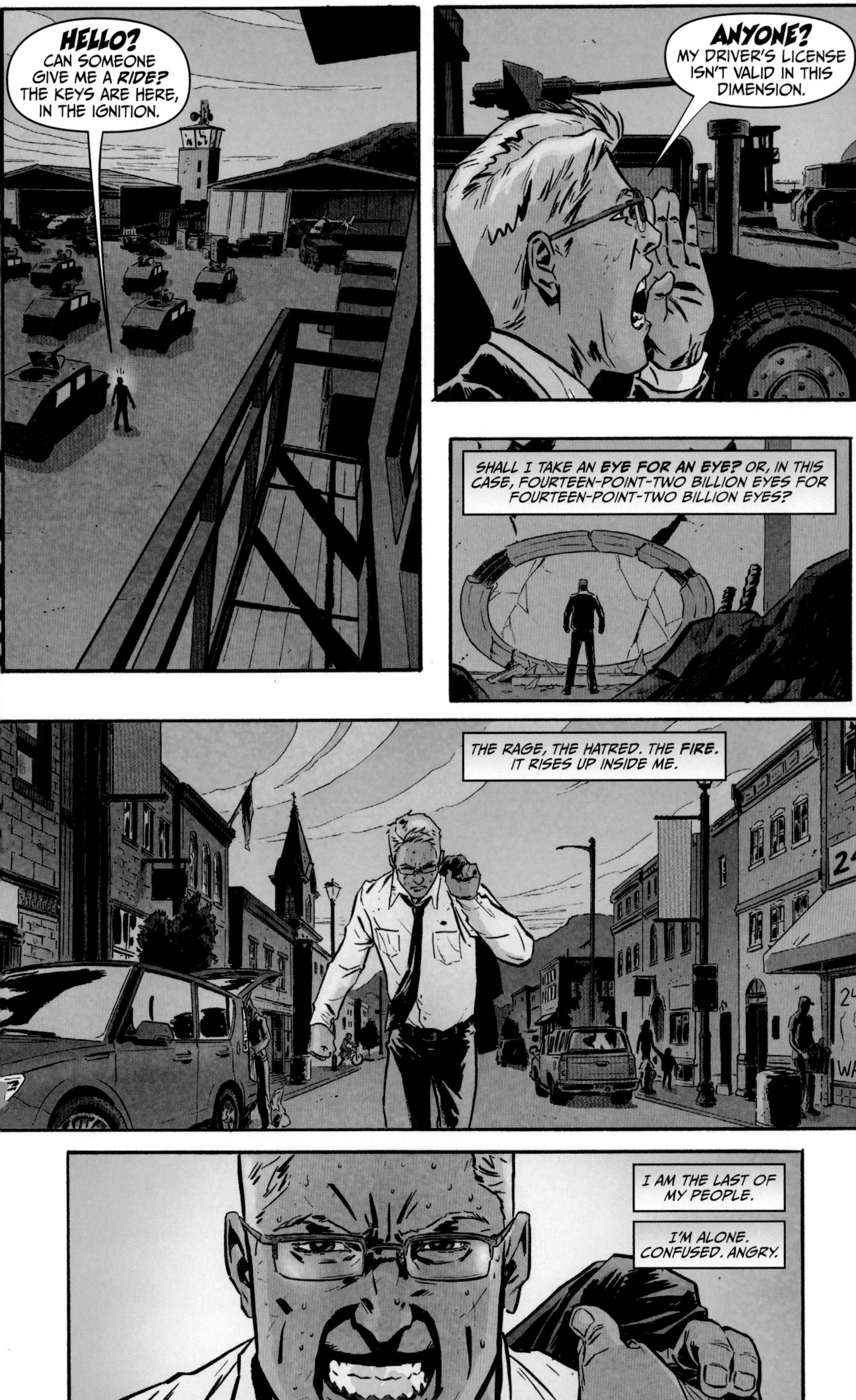
HELLO? CAN SOMEONE GIVE ME A RIDE? THE KEYS ARE HERE, IN THE IGNITION.
ANYONE? MY DRIVER'S LICENSE ISN'T VALID IN THIS DIMENSION.
SHALL I TAKE AN EYE FOR AN EYE? OR, IN THIS CASE, FOURTEEN-POINT-TWO BILLION EYES FOR FOURTEEN-POINT-TWO BILLION EYES?
THE RAGE, THE HATRED. THE FIRE. IT RISES UP INSIDE ME.
24
I AM THE LAST OF MY PEOPLE.
I'M ALONE. CONFUSED. ANGRY.

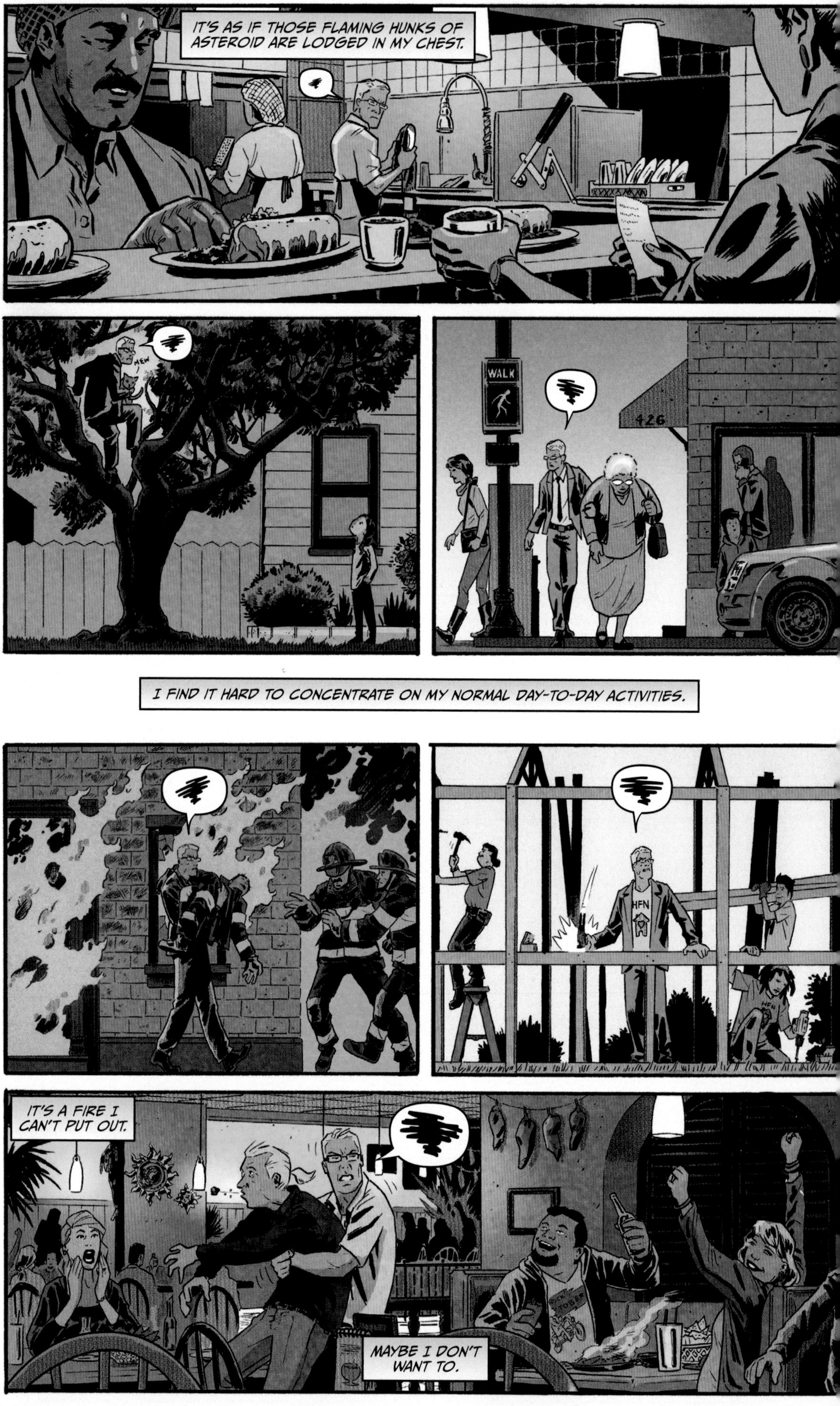
IT'S AS IF THOSE FLAMING HUNKS OF ASTEROID ARE LODGED IN MY CHEST.
MEW
WALK
426
I FIND IT HARD TO CONCENTRATE ON MY NORMAL DAY-TO-DAY ACTIVITIES.
HFN
IT'S A FIRE I CAN'T PUT OUT.
MAYBE I DON'T WANT TO.

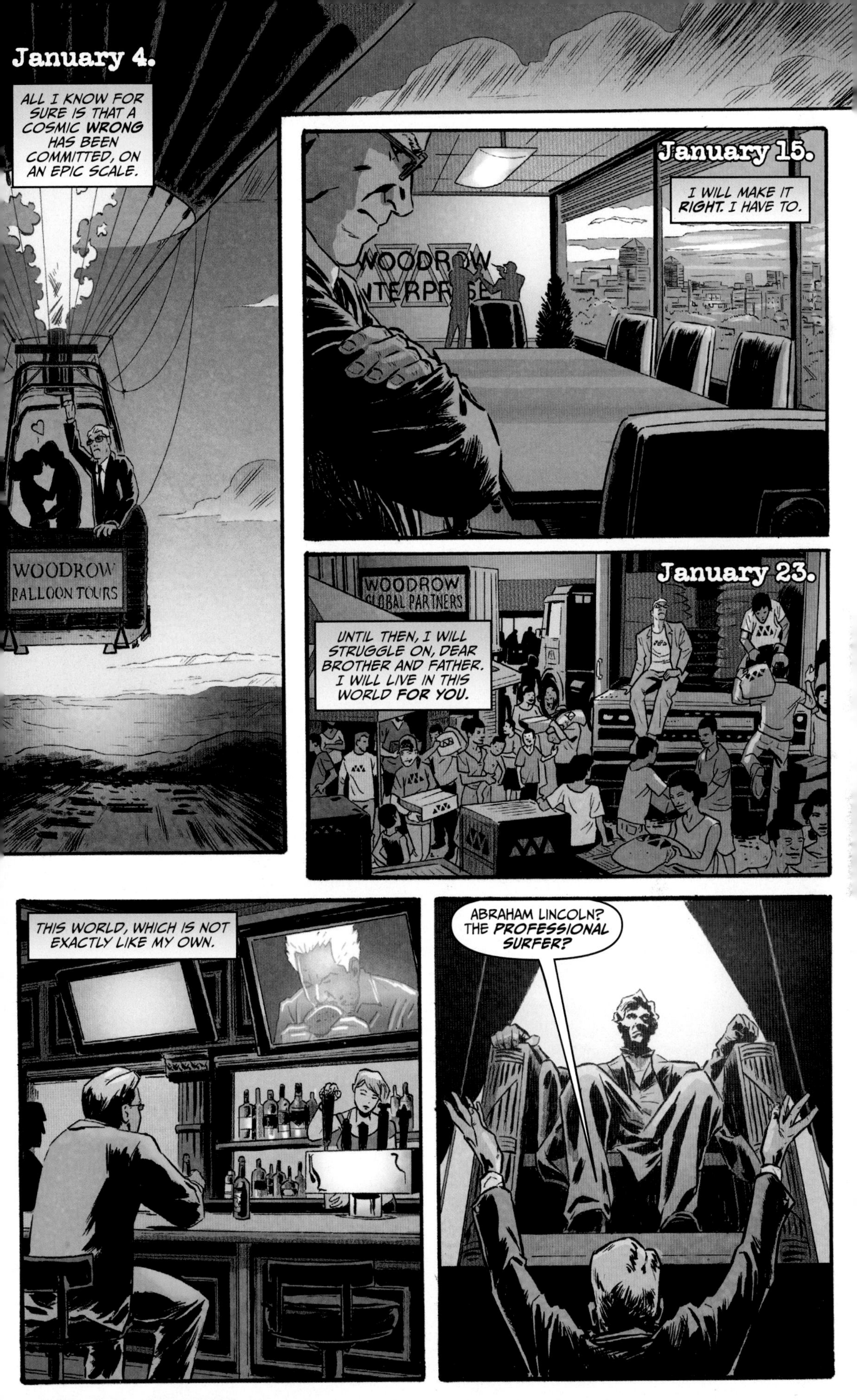
January 4.
ALL I KNOW FOR SURE IS THAT A COSMIC WRONG HAS BEEN COMMITTED, ON AN EPIC SCALE.
WOODROW BALLOON TOURS
January 15.
I WILL MAKE IT RIGHT. I HAVE TO.
WOODROW ENTERPRISE
January 23.
WOODROW GLOBAL PARTNERS
UNTIL THEN, I WILL STRUGGLE ON, DEAR BROTHER AND FATHER. I WILL LIVE IN THIS WORLD FOR YOU.
THIS WORLD, WHICH IS NOT EXACTLY LIKE MY OWN.
ABRAHAM LINCOLN? THE PROFESSIONAL SURFER?

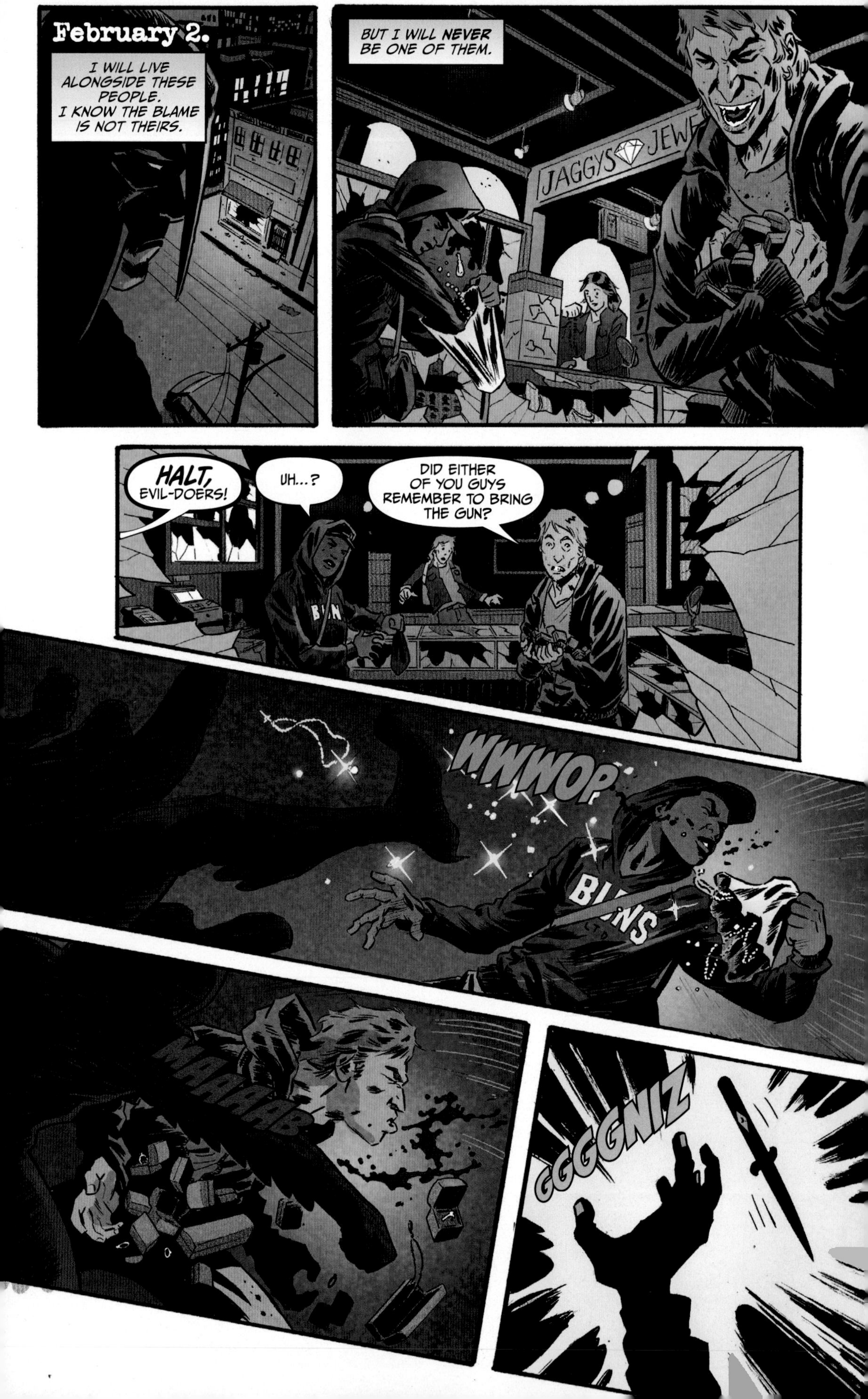
February 2.
I WILL LIVE ALONGSIDE THESE PEOPLE. I KNOW THE BLAME IS NOT THEIRS.
BUT I WILL NEVER BE ONE OF THEM.
JAGGYS JEWE
HALT, EVIL-DOERS!
UH...?
DID EITHER OF YOU GUYS REMEMBER TO BRING THE GUN?
WWWOP
GGGGNIZ

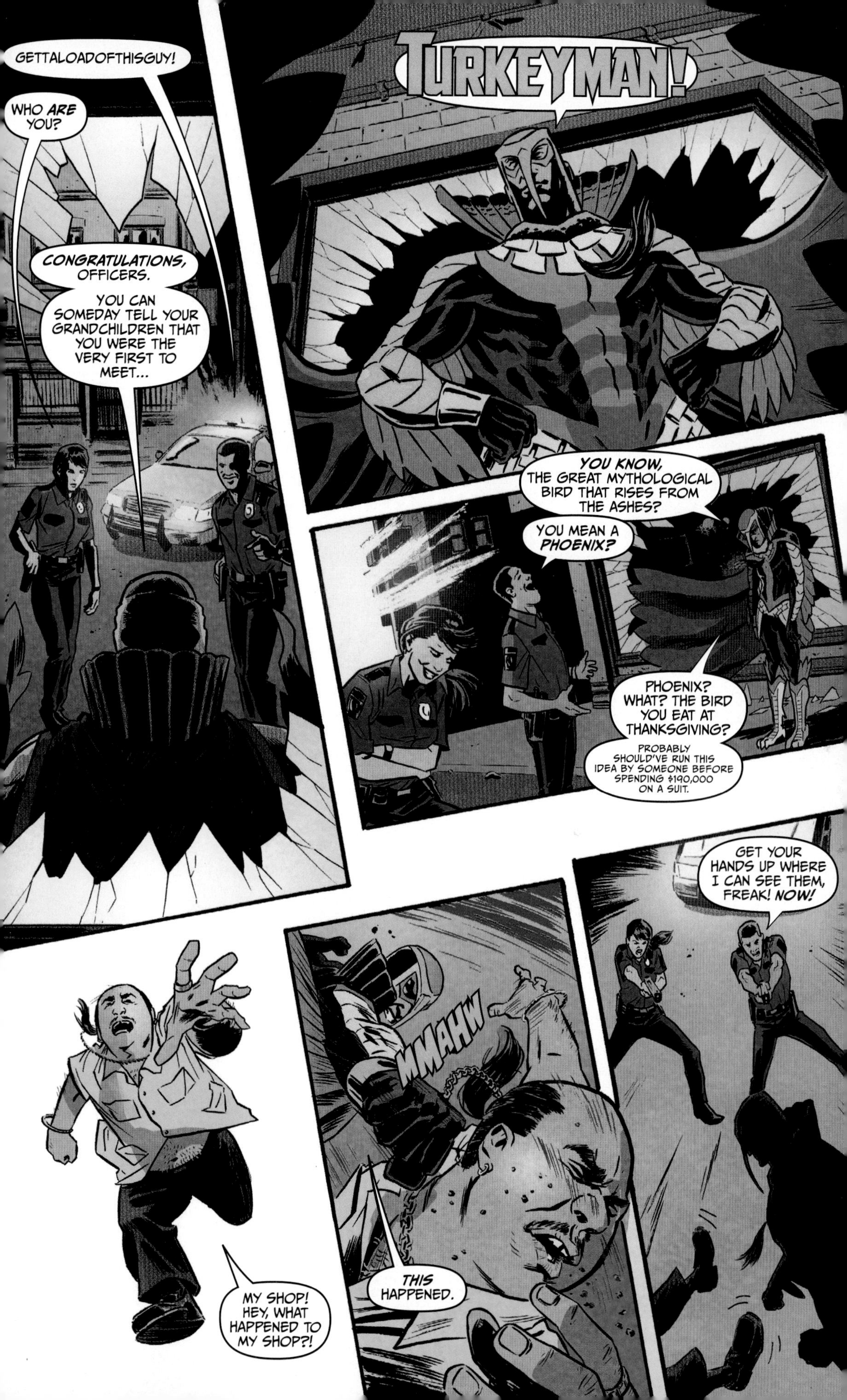
GETTALOADOFTHISGUY!
WHO *ARE* YOU?
CONGRATULATIONS, OFFICERS.
YOU CAN SOMEDAY TELL YOUR GRANDCHILDREN THAT YOU WERE THE VERY FIRST TO MEET...
TURKEYMAN!
YOU KNOW, THE GREAT MYTHOLOGICAL BIRD THAT RISES FROM THE ASHES?
YOU MEAN A *PHOENIX?*
PHOENIX? WHAT? THE BIRD YOU EAT AT THANKSGIVING?
PROBABLY SHOULD'VE RUN THIS IDEA BY SOMEONE BEFORE SPENDING $190,000 ON A SUIT.
GET YOUR HANDS UP WHERE I CAN SEE THEM, FREAK! *NOW!*
MMAHW
THIS HAPPENED.
MY SHOP! HEY, WHAT HAPPENED TO MY SHOP?!

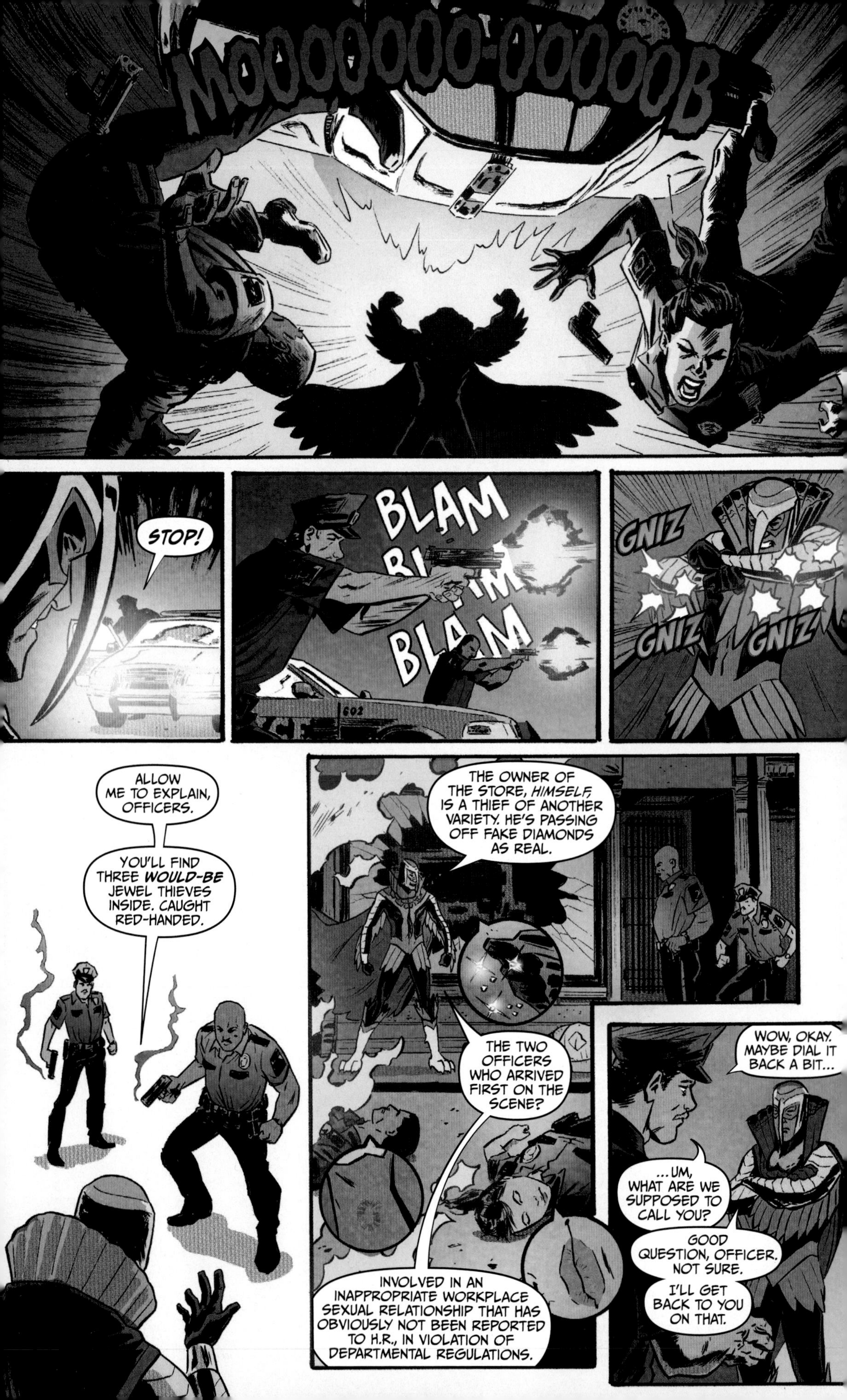
MOOOOOOO-OOOOOB
STOP!
BLAM
BLAM
BLAM
GNIZ
GNIZ
GNIZ
ALLOW ME TO EXPLAIN, OFFICERS.
YOU'LL FIND THREE WOULD-BE JEWEL THIEVES INSIDE. CAUGHT RED-HANDED.
THE OWNER OF THE STORE, HIMSELF, IS A THIEF OF ANOTHER VARIETY. HE'S PASSING OFF FAKE DIAMONDS AS REAL.
THE TWO OFFICERS WHO ARRIVED FIRST ON THE SCENE?
INVOLVED IN AN INAPPROPRIATE WORKPLACE SEXUAL RELATIONSHIP THAT HAS OBVIOUSLY NOT BEEN REPORTED TO H.R., IN VIOLATION OF DEPARTMENTAL REGULATIONS.
WOW, OKAY. MAYBE DIAL IT BACK A BIT...
...UM, WHAT ARE WE SUPPOSED TO CALL YOU?
GOOD QUESTION, OFFICER. NOT SURE.
I'LL GET BACK TO YOU ON THAT.

PHOENIX-MAN IT IS.

LET'S SEE. PHOENIX. YEAH, DARN. LOOKS LIKE THAT NAME'S ALREADY BEING USED.

DARK PHOENIX. TAKEN.

CAPTAIN PHOENIX. TAKEN.

MR. PHOENIX. NOPE, TAKEN.

PHOENIX-MAN? WAIT. OKAY, THIS ONE MIGHT WORK. *GOOD.*

YOU HEAR THAT, *QUANTUM?*

PHOENIX-MAN IS COMING FOR YOU.

I WILL TREAT YOU AS RUDELY AS YOU TREATED ME AND MY PLANET.

OTHER EARTH, HEAR MY PROMISE. I WILL HOLD HIM ACCOUNTABLE FOR HIS TREACHERY.

JUST AS SOON AS MY SCHEDULE OPENS UP A BIT. I HAVE THE CLEAN-WATER INITIATIVE TO OVERSEE IN ZAIRE. THE CHARITY BALL LATER THIS MONTH. EBOLA TO ERADICATE.

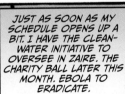

I WOULD PROBABLY USE A COLLOQUIAL SAYING HERE ABOUT REVENGE BEING BETTER THE LONGER YOU WAIT, BUT WE DIDN'T HAVE A SAYING LIKE THAT ON MY PLANET.

THE WOODROW FOUNDATION

I WILL DESTROY QUANTUM AND ALL HE HOLDS DEAR.

WELL, THERE'S NO RUSH FOR THIS, I GUESS.

"A WOODY RISES"

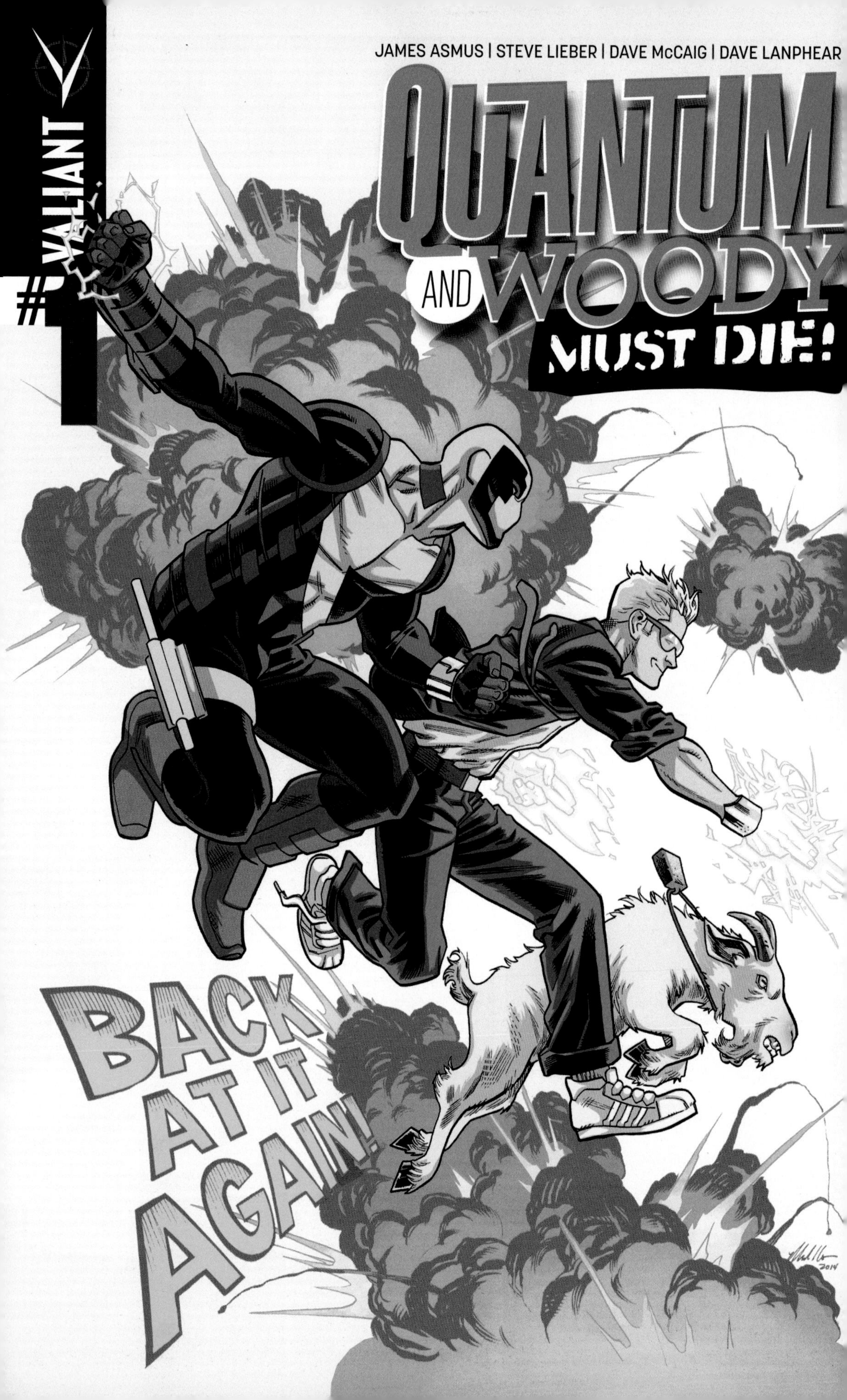

#1
VALIANT
JAMES ASMUS | STEVE LIEBER | DAVE McCAIG | DAVE LANPHEAR
QUANTUM AND WOODY
MUST DIE!
BACK AT IT AGAIN!

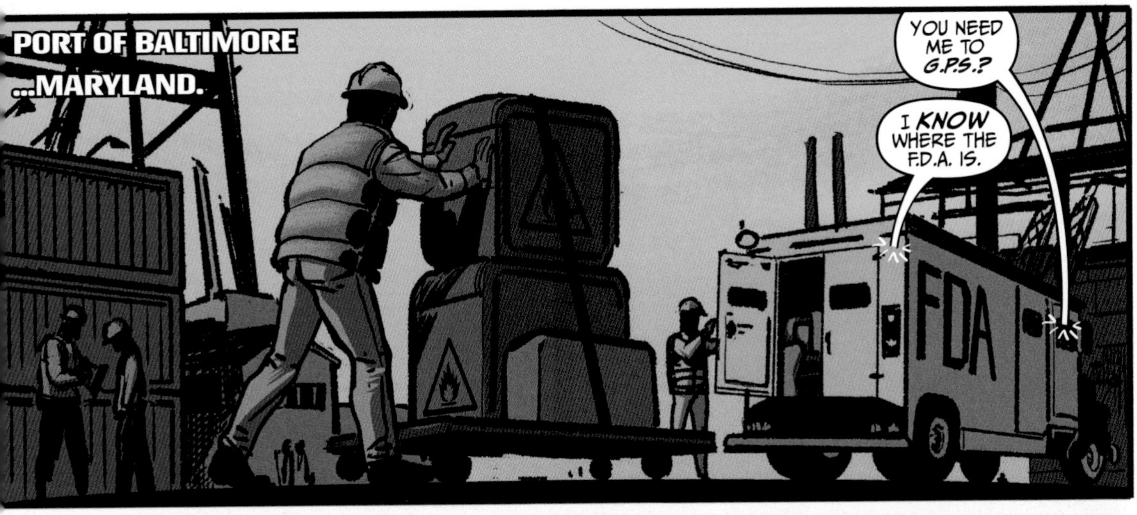
PORT OF BALTIMORE
...MARYLAND.
YOU NEED ME TO G.P.S.?
I KNOW WHERE THE F.D.A. IS.
FDA

Partners 'n Crime.

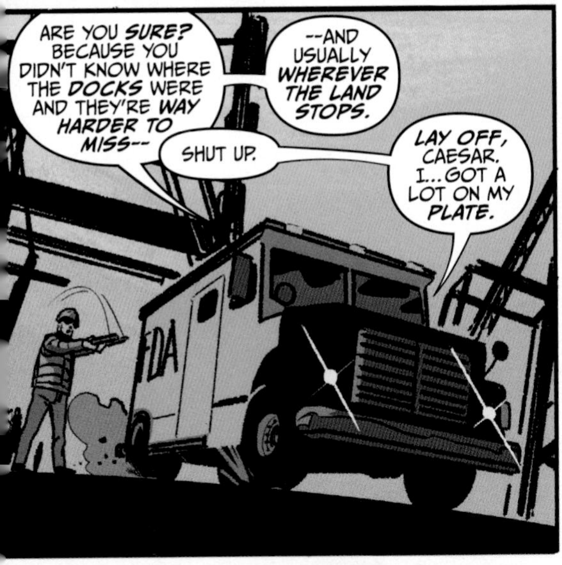
ARE YOU SURE? BECAUSE YOU DIDN'T KNOW WHERE THE DOCKS WERE AND THEY'RE WAY HARDER TO MISS--
--AND USUALLY WHEREVER THE LAND STOPS.
SHUT UP.
LAY OFF, CAESAR. I...GOT A LOT ON MY PLATE.
FDA

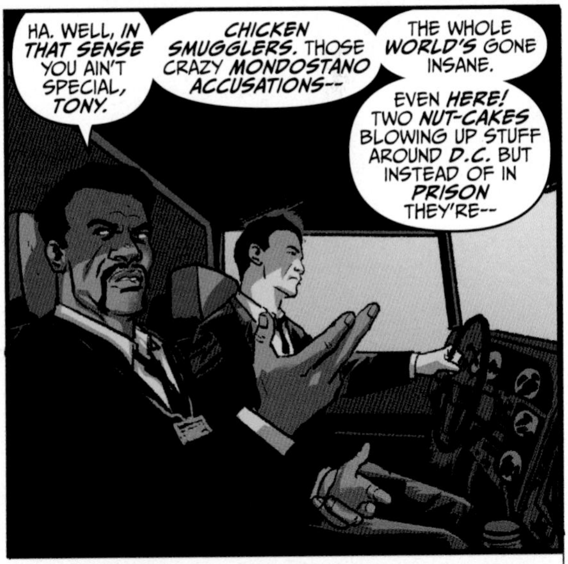
HA. WELL, IN THAT SENSE YOU AIN'T SPECIAL, TONY.
CHICKEN SMUGGLERS. THOSE CRAZY MONDOSTANO ACCUSATIONS--
THE WHOLE WORLD'S GONE INSANE.
EVEN HERE! TWO NUT-CAKES BLOWING UP STUFF AROUND D.C. BUT INSTEAD OF IN PRISON THEY'RE--

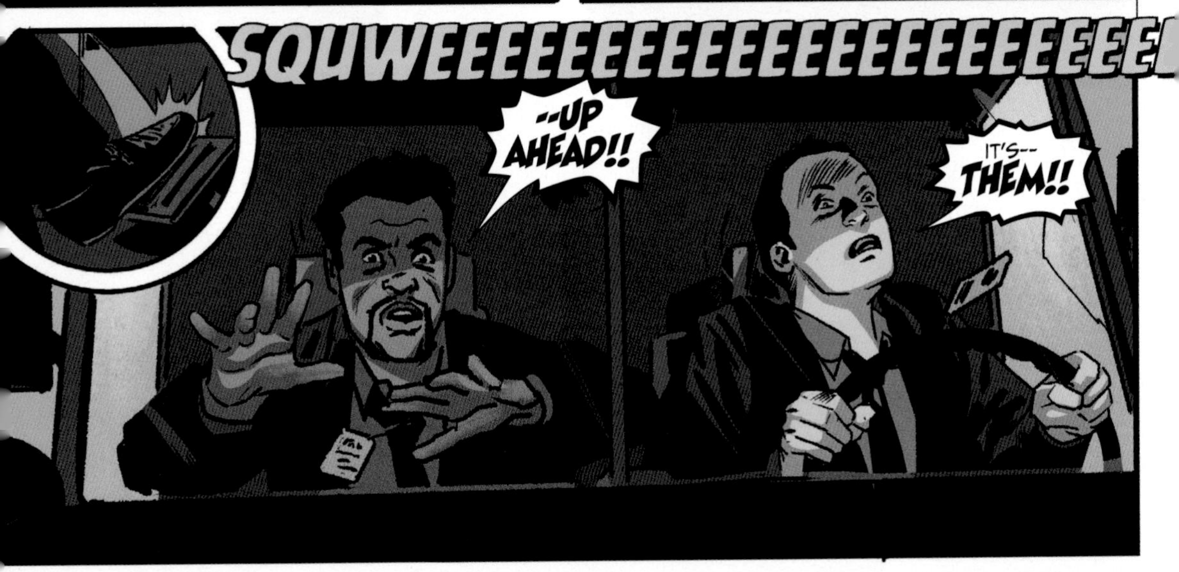
SQUWEEEEEEEEEEEEEEEEEEEEEE
--UP AHEAD!!
IT'S-- THEM!!

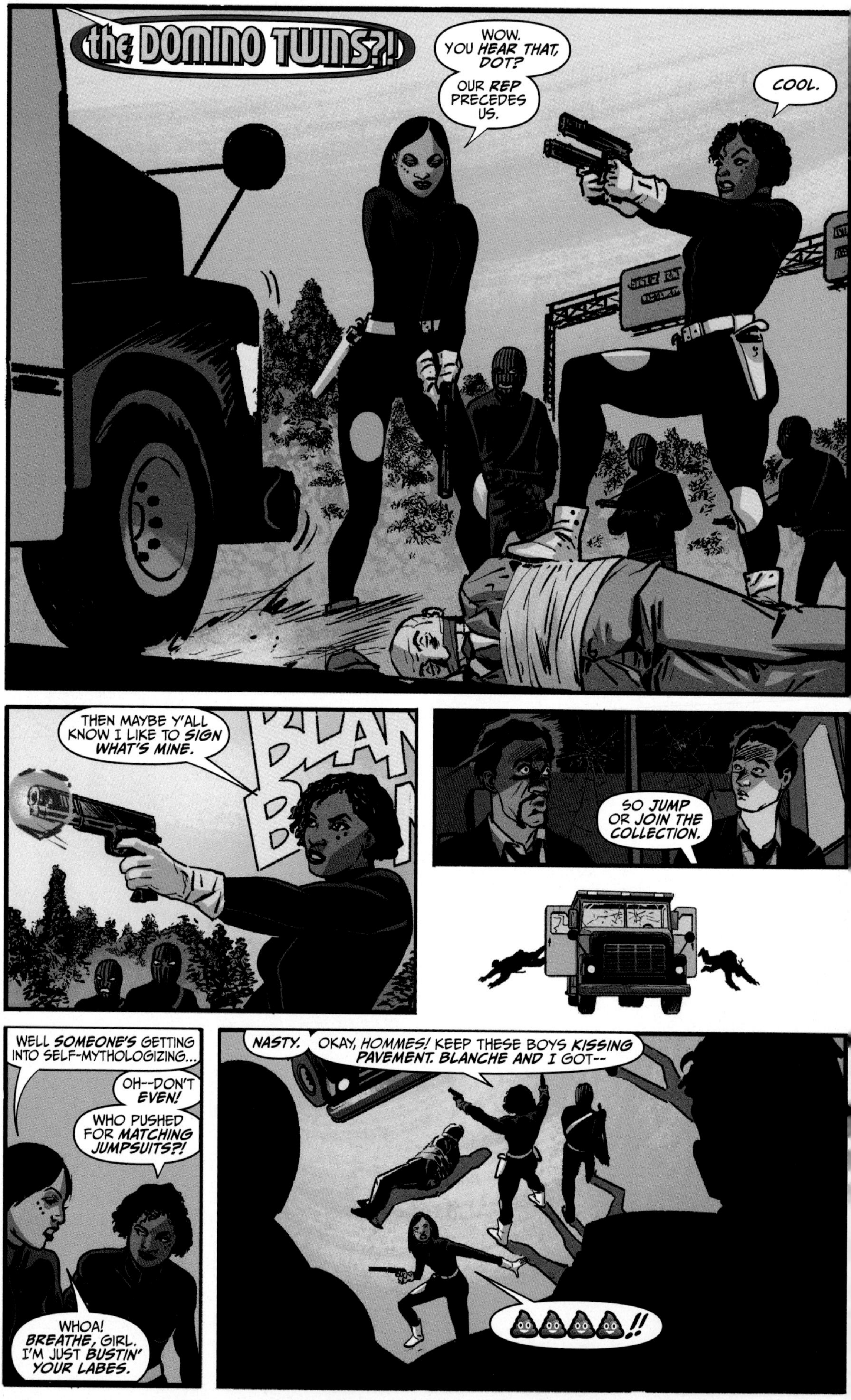
the DOMINO TWINS?!
WOW. YOU HEAR THAT, DOT?
OUR REP PRECEDES US.
COOL.
THEN MAYBE Y'ALL KNOW I LIKE TO SIGN WHAT'S MINE.
SO JUMP OR JOIN THE COLLECTION.
WELL SOMEONE'S GETTING INTO SELF-MYTHOLOGIZING...
OH--DON'T EVEN!
WHO PUSHED FOR MATCHING JUMPSUITS?!
WHOA! BREATHE, GIRL. I'M JUST BUSTIN' YOUR LABES.
NASTY.
OKAY, HOMMES! KEEP THESE BOYS KISSING PAVEMENT. BLANCHE AND I GOT--
💩💩💩💩!!

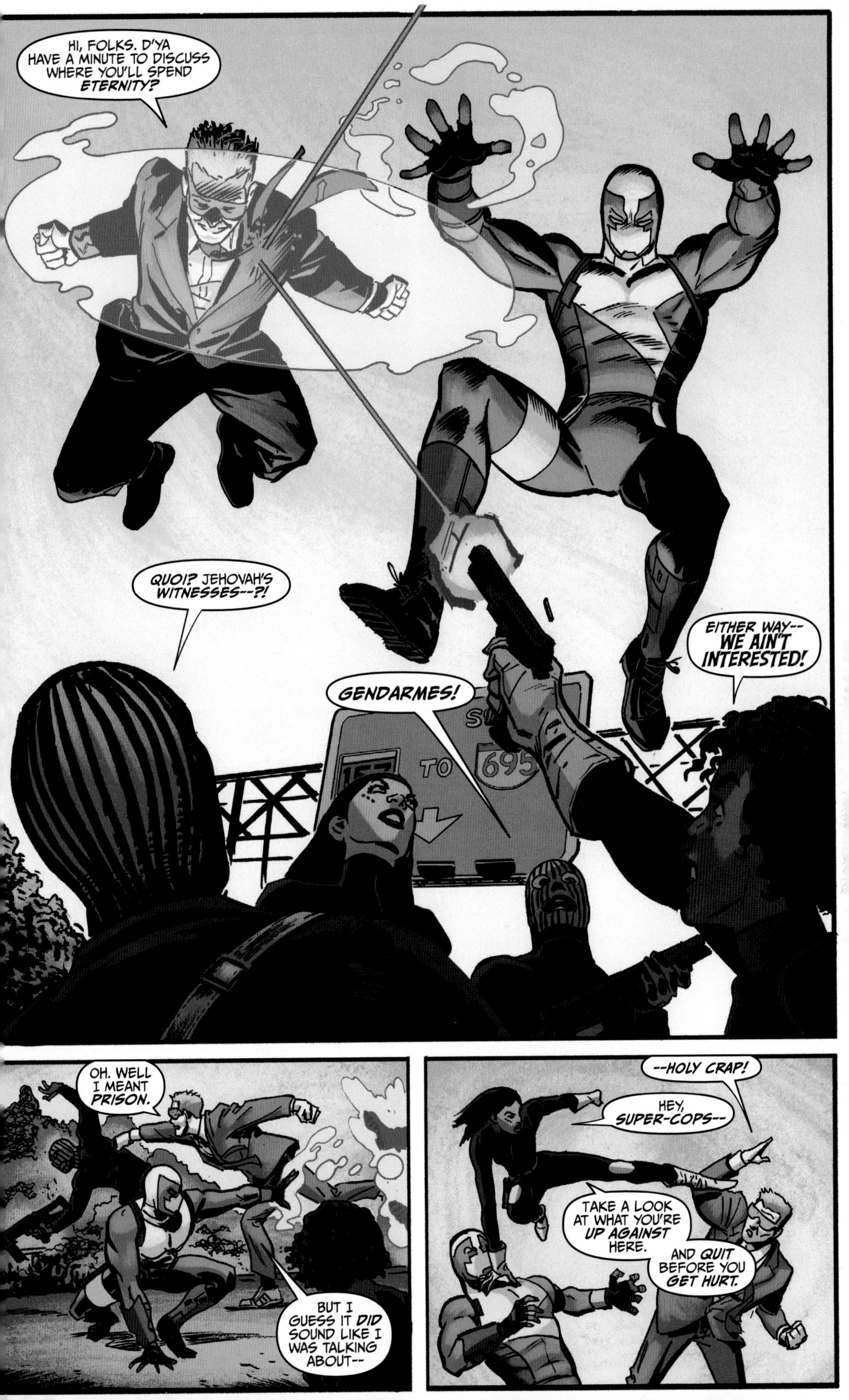
HI, FOLKS. D'YA HAVE A MINUTE TO DISCUSS WHERE YOU'LL SPEND *ETERNITY?*
QUOI? JEHOVAH'S *WITNESSES--?!*
GENDARMES!
EITHER WAY-- **WE AIN'T INTERESTED!**
TO 695
OH. WELL I MEANT *PRISON.*
BUT I GUESS IT *DID* SOUND LIKE I WAS TALKING ABOUT--
--HOLY CRAP!
HEY, *SUPER-COPS--*
TAKE A LOOK AT WHAT YOU'RE *UP AGAINST* HERE.
AND *QUIT* BEFORE YOU *GET HURT.*

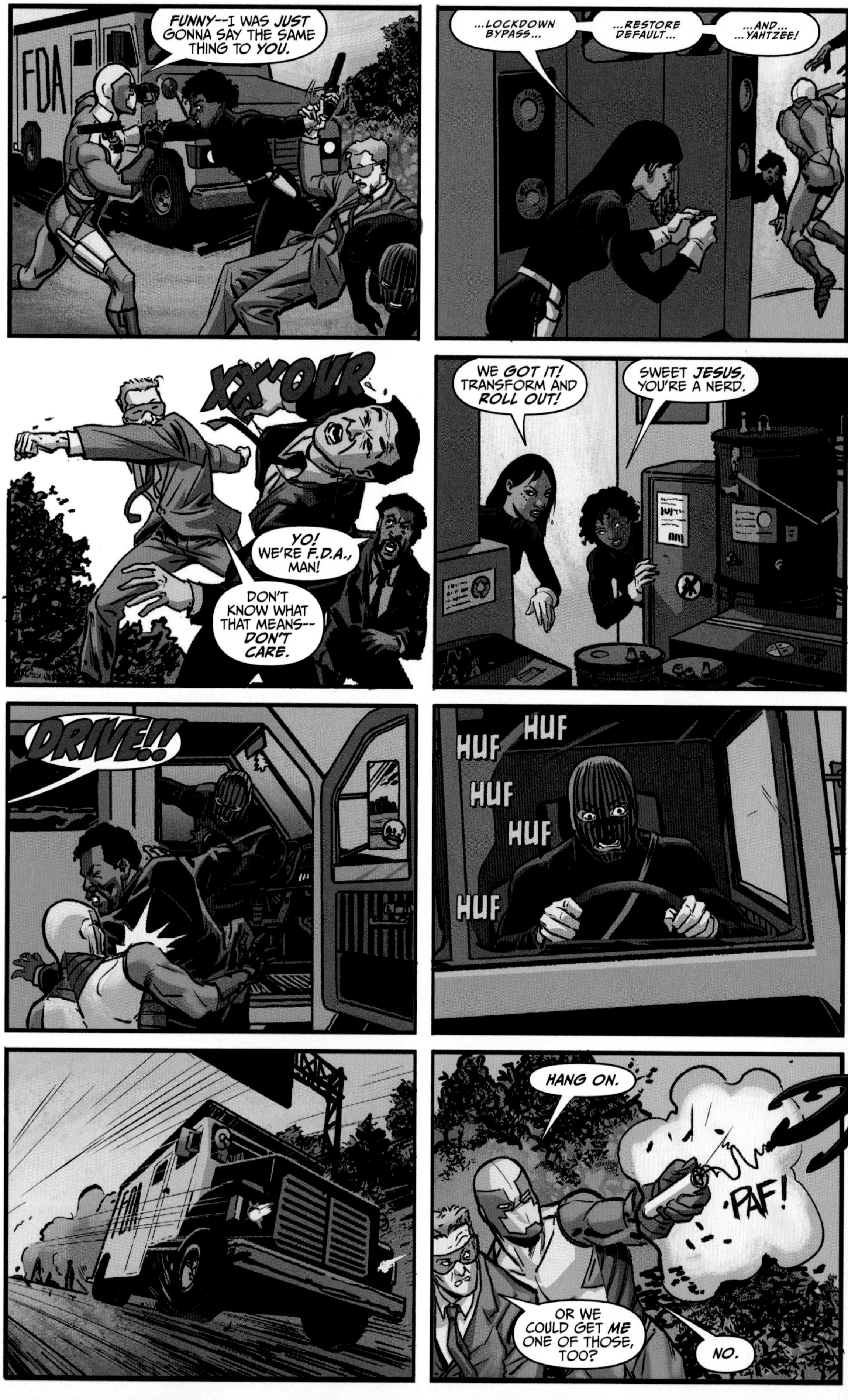
FUNNY--I WAS JUST GONNA SAY THE SAME THING TO YOU.
FDA
...LOCKDOWN BYPASS...
...RESTORE DEFAULT...
...AND... ...YAHTZEE!
XX'OUR
YO! WE'RE F.D.A., MAN!
DON'T KNOW WHAT THAT MEANS-- DON'T CARE.
WE GOT IT! TRANSFORM AND ROLL OUT!
SWEET JESUS, YOU'RE A NERD.
DRIVE!!
HUF
HUF
HUF
HUF
HUF
FDA
HANG ON.
PAF!
OR WE COULD GET ME ONE OF THOSE, TOO?
NO.

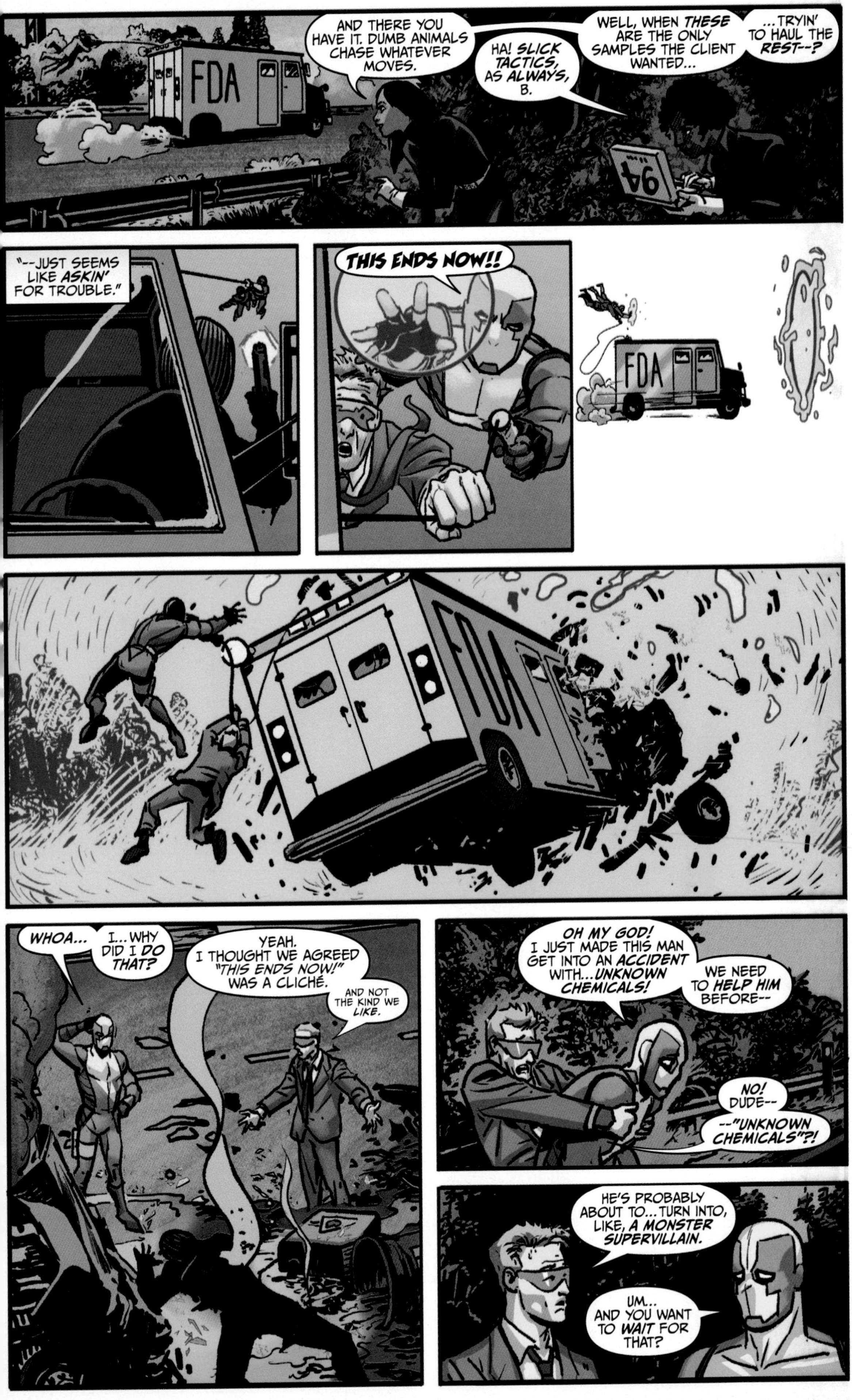
AND THERE YOU HAVE IT. DUMB ANIMALS CHASE WHATEVER MOVES.
HA! SLICK TACTICS, AS ALWAYS, B.
WELL, WHEN THESE ARE THE ONLY SAMPLES THE CLIENT WANTED...
...TRYIN' TO HAUL THE REST--?
"--JUST SEEMS LIKE ASKIN' FOR TROUBLE."
THIS ENDS NOW!!
FDA
WHOA...
I...WHY DID I DO THAT?
YEAH. I THOUGHT WE AGREED "THIS ENDS NOW!" WAS A CLICHÉ.
AND NOT THE KIND WE LIKE.
OH MY GOD! I JUST MADE THIS MAN GET INTO AN ACCIDENT WITH...UNKNOWN CHEMICALS!
WE NEED TO HELP HIM BEFORE--
NO! DUDE--
--"UNKNOWN CHEMICALS"?!
HE'S PROBABLY ABOUT TO...TURN INTO, LIKE, A MONSTER SUPERVILLAIN.
UM... AND YOU WANT TO WAIT FOR THAT?

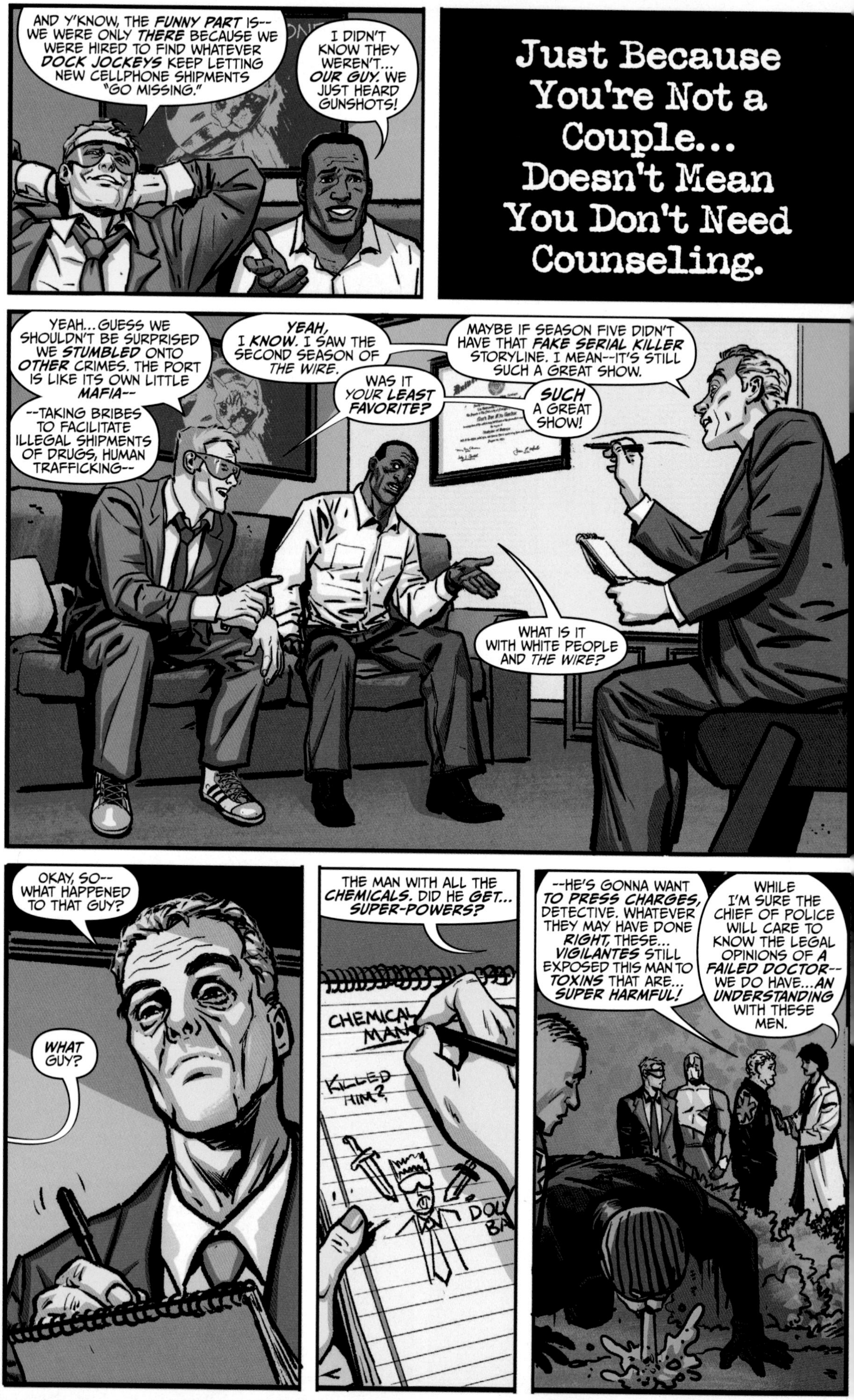
AND Y'KNOW, THE FUNNY PART IS-- WE WERE ONLY THERE BECAUSE WE WERE HIRED TO FIND WHATEVER DOCK JOCKEYS KEEP LETTING NEW CELLPHONE SHIPMENTS "GO MISSING."
I DIDN'T KNOW THEY WEREN'T... OUR GUY. WE JUST HEARD GUNSHOTS!
Just Because You're Not a Couple... Doesn't Mean You Don't Need Counseling.
YEAH... GUESS WE SHOULDN'T BE SURPRISED WE STUMBLED ONTO OTHER CRIMES. THE PORT IS LIKE ITS OWN LITTLE MAFIA--
--TAKING BRIBES TO FACILITATE ILLEGAL SHIPMENTS OF DRUGS, HUMAN TRAFFICKING--
YEAH, I KNOW. I SAW THE SECOND SEASON OF THE WIRE.
WAS IT YOUR LEAST FAVORITE?
MAYBE IF SEASON FIVE DIDN'T HAVE THAT FAKE SERIAL KILLER STORYLINE. I MEAN--IT'S STILL SUCH A GREAT SHOW.
SUCH A GREAT SHOW!
WHAT IS IT WITH WHITE PEOPLE AND THE WIRE?
OKAY, SO-- WHAT HAPPENED TO THAT GUY?
WHAT GUY?
THE MAN WITH ALL THE CHEMICALS. DID HE GET... SUPER-POWERS?
CHEMICAL MAN
KILLED HIM?
--HE'S GONNA WANT TO PRESS CHARGES, DETECTIVE. WHATEVER THEY MAY HAVE DONE RIGHT, THESE... VIGILANTES STILL EXPOSED THIS MAN TO TOXINS THAT ARE... SUPER HARMFUL!
WHILE I'M SURE THE CHIEF OF POLICE WILL CARE TO KNOW THE LEGAL OPINIONS OF A FAILED DOCTOR-- WE DO HAVE... AN UNDERSTANDING WITH THESE MEN.

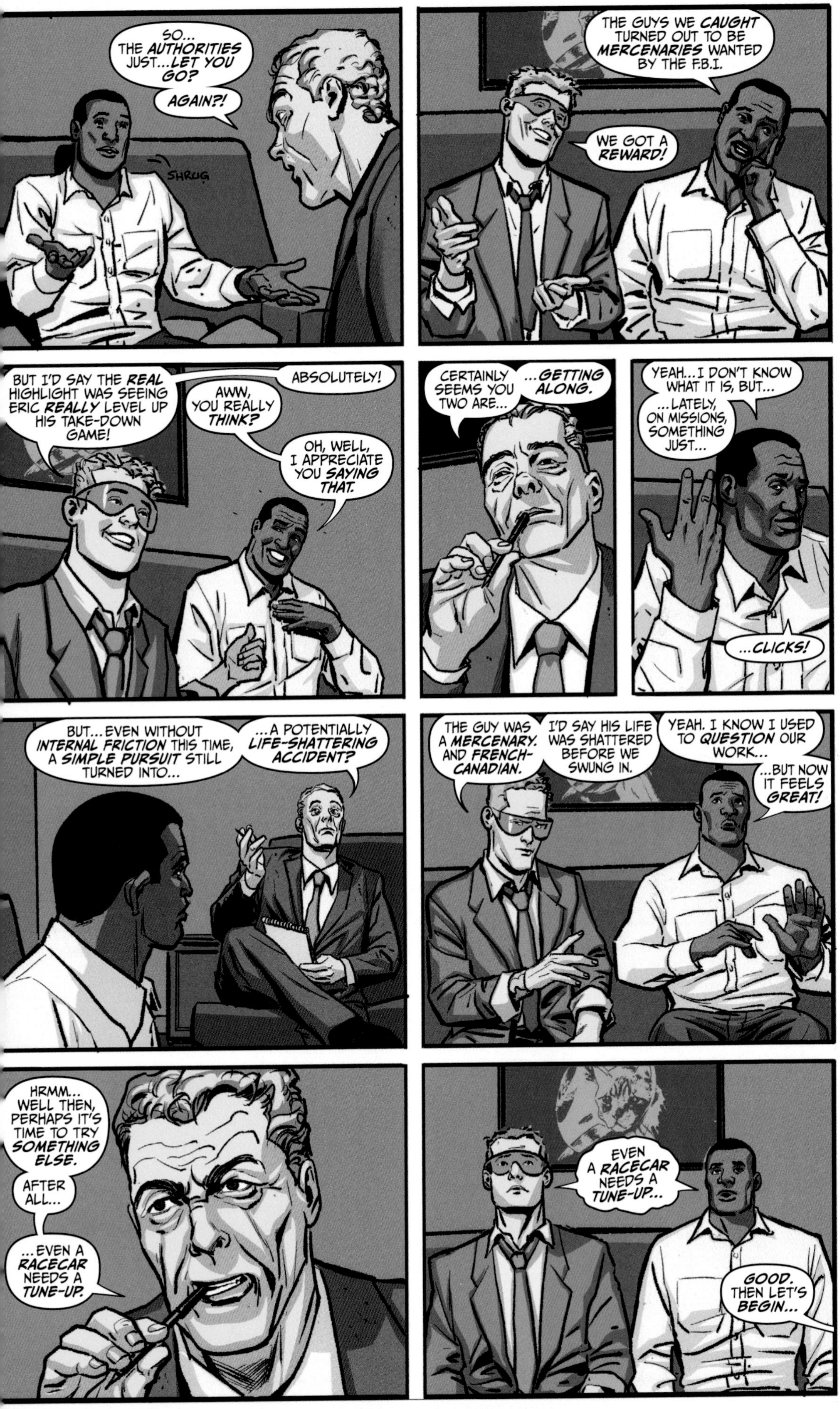
SO... THE AUTHORITIES JUST...LET YOU GO?
AGAIN?!
SHRUG
THE GUYS WE CAUGHT TURNED OUT TO BE MERCENARIES WANTED BY THE F.B.I.
WE GOT A REWARD!
BUT I'D SAY THE REAL HIGHLIGHT WAS SEEING ERIC REALLY LEVEL UP HIS TAKE-DOWN GAME!
ABSOLUTELY!
AWW, YOU REALLY THINK?
OH, WELL, I APPRECIATE YOU SAYING THAT.
CERTAINLY SEEMS YOU TWO ARE...
...GETTING ALONG.
YEAH...I DON'T KNOW WHAT IT IS, BUT...
...LATELY, ON MISSIONS, SOMETHING JUST...
...CLICKS!
BUT...EVEN WITHOUT INTERNAL FRICTION THIS TIME, A SIMPLE PURSUIT STILL TURNED INTO...
...A POTENTIALLY LIFE-SHATTERING ACCIDENT?
THE GUY WAS A MERCENARY. AND FRENCH-CANADIAN.
I'D SAY HIS LIFE WAS SHATTERED BEFORE WE SWUNG IN.
YEAH. I KNOW I USED TO QUESTION OUR WORK...
...BUT NOW IT FEELS GREAT!
HRMM... WELL THEN, PERHAPS IT'S TIME TO TRY SOMETHING ELSE.
AFTER ALL...
...EVEN A RACECAR NEEDS A TUNE-UP.
EVEN A RACECAR NEEDS A TUNE-UP...
GOOD. THEN LET'S BEGIN...

All Your Old Favorites, Together Again for the First Time.

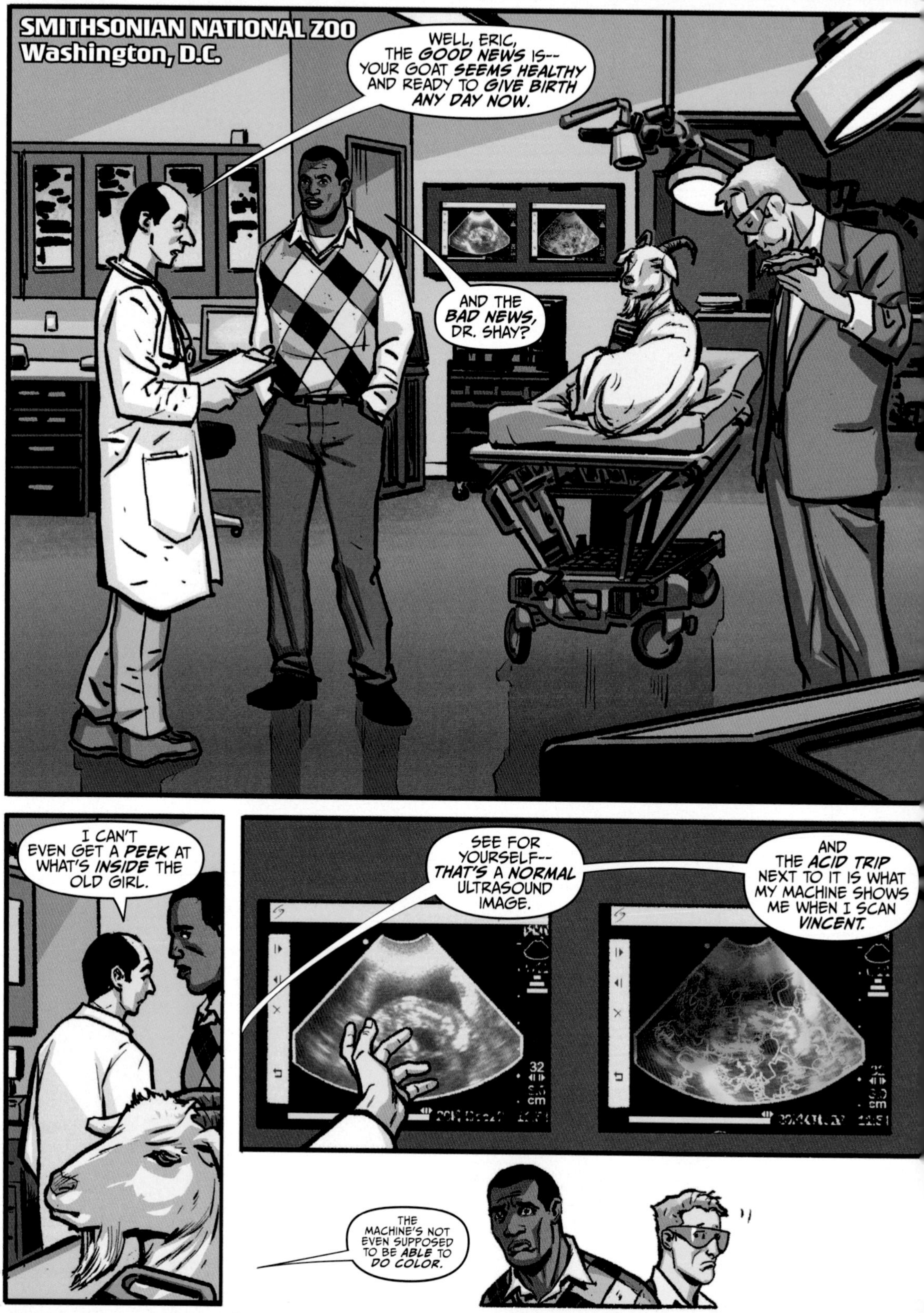
SMITHSONIAN NATIONAL ZOO
Washington, D.C.
WELL, ERIC, THE GOOD NEWS IS-- YOUR GOAT SEEMS HEALTHY AND READY TO GIVE BIRTH ANY DAY NOW.
AND THE BAD NEWS, DR. SHAY?
I CAN'T EVEN GET A PEEK AT WHAT'S INSIDE THE OLD GIRL.
SEE FOR YOURSELF-- THAT'S A NORMAL ULTRASOUND IMAGE.
AND THE ACID TRIP NEXT TO IT IS WHAT MY MACHINE SHOWS ME WHEN I SCAN VINCENT.
THE MACHINE'S NOT EVEN SUPPOSED TO BE ABLE TO DO COLOR.

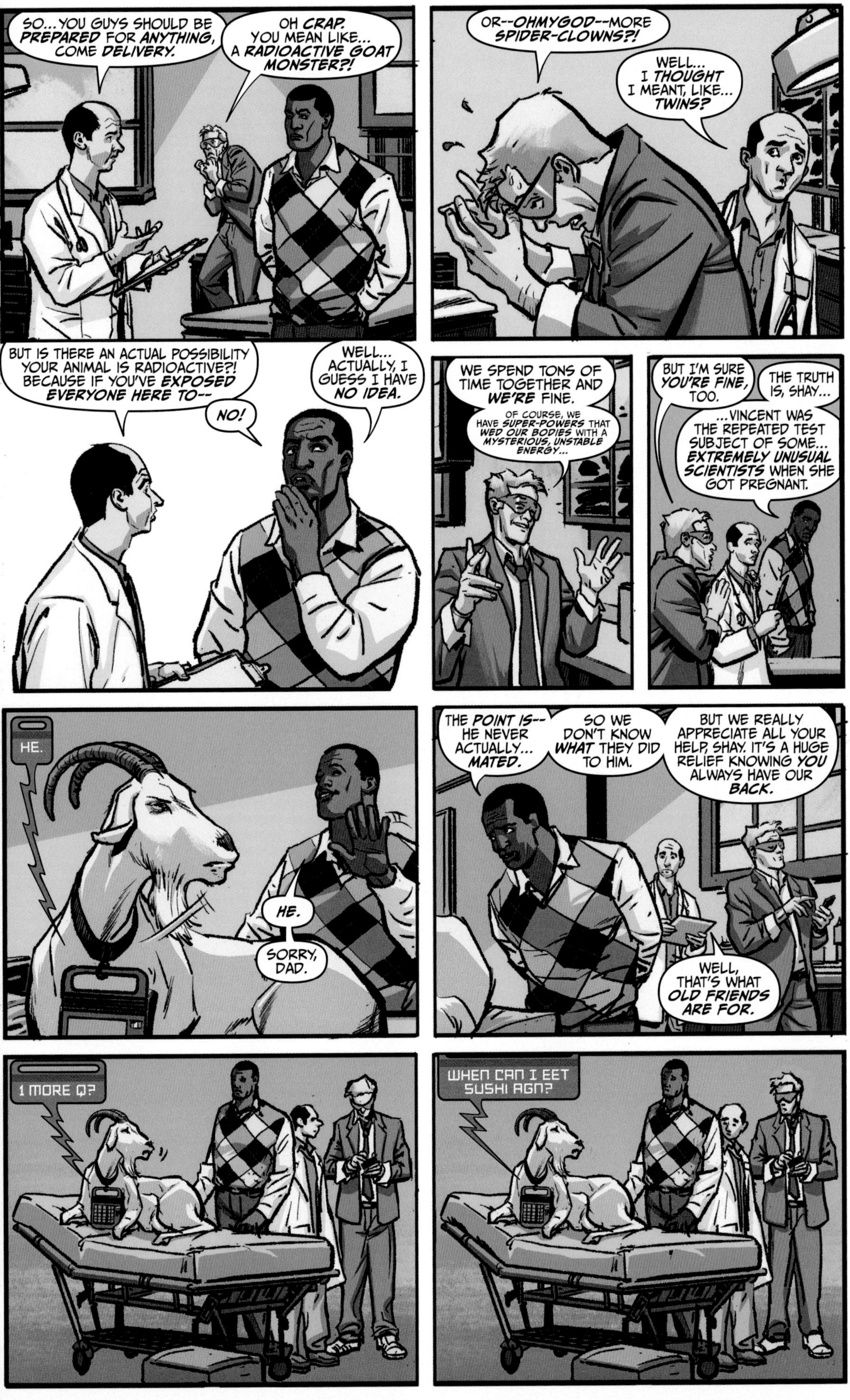
SO...YOU GUYS SHOULD BE PREPARED FOR ANYTHING, COME DELIVERY.
OH CRAP. YOU MEAN LIKE... A RADIOACTIVE GOAT MONSTER?!
OR--OHMYGOD--MORE SPIDER-CLOWNS?!
WELL... I THOUGHT I MEANT, LIKE... TWINS?
BUT IS THERE AN ACTUAL POSSIBILITY YOUR ANIMAL IS RADIOACTIVE?! BECAUSE IF YOU'VE EXPOSED EVERYONE HERE TO--
NO!
WELL... ACTUALLY, I GUESS I HAVE NO IDEA.
WE SPEND TONS OF TIME TOGETHER AND WE'RE FINE.
OF COURSE, WE HAVE SUPER-POWERS THAT WED OUR BODIES WITH A MYSTERIOUS, UNSTABLE ENERGY...
BUT I'M SURE YOU'RE FINE, TOO.
THE TRUTH IS, SHAY...
...VINCENT WAS THE REPEATED TEST SUBJECT OF SOME... EXTREMELY UNUSUAL SCIENTISTS WHEN SHE GOT PREGNANT.
HE.
HE.
SORRY, DAD.
THE POINT IS-- HE NEVER ACTUALLY... MATED.
SO WE DON'T KNOW WHAT THEY DID TO HIM.
BUT WE REALLY APPRECIATE ALL YOUR HELP, SHAY. IT'S A HUGE RELIEF KNOWING YOU ALWAYS HAVE OUR BACK.
WELL, THAT'S WHAT OLD FRIENDS ARE FOR.
1 MORE Q?
WHEN CAN I EET SUSHI AGN?

ERIC. GOAT. ...WOODY. YOU KNOW WHAT YOU'D LIKE?

VEGEEZ.

I'LL JUST GET MY USUAL.

KIM!

HOW'S MY FAVORITE *ASIAN* SENSATION?

"ASIAN"? REALLY?

ARE YOU... *NOT* ASIAN?

BECAUSE I'LL BE HONEST-- IF YOU'RE, LIKE, *SAMOAN* OR SOMETHING WEIRD--

--IT'S MUCH HOTTER TO JUST LET PEOPLE THINK YOU'RE ASIAN.

IT'S *REDUCTIVE.* ASIA IS A *CONTINENT.* MADE UP OF OVER FORTY-NINE NATIONS AND COUNTLESS DISTINCT CULTURES, ETHNICITIES, AND HISTORIES.

YEAH. I *KNOW.* Y'KNOW... I'M NOT AN *IDIOT,* KIM.

I JUST... Y'KNOW... MIGHT BE A BIT HAZY ON TELLING THEM APART.

OKAY. SO YOU WERE JUST SAYING WE *"ALL LOOK ALIKE"* IN YOUR *WHITE EYES.*

THAT IS *NOT* WHAT I MEANT! I KNOW LUCY LIU FROM BAI LING. I'M JUST SAYING, IF I HAD TO MATCH A RANDOM PERSON TO EACH COUNTRY MY SCORE WOULD BE...

...*LAOS-Y.*

...GET IT?

LIKE *"LOUSY"?*

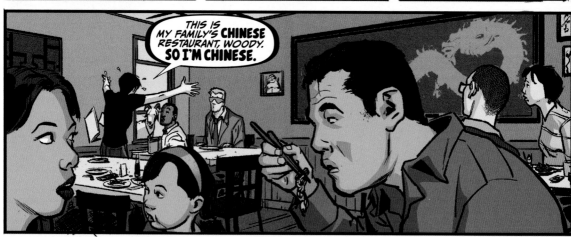

THIS IS MY FAMILY'S *CHINESE* RESTAURANT, WOODY. **SO I'M CHINESE.**

WELL, NOW YOU'RE PRACTICALLY *BEGGING* ME TO STEREOTYPE.

I APOLOGIZE, ON BEHALF OF MY BROTHER, FOR EVERYTHING ABOUT HIM.

AT LEAST GIMME *SOME* POINTS FOR *KNOWING* LAOS IS A COUNTRY. BESIDES! IF YOU WANNA GET *PICKY*--I AT LEAST NARROWED DOWN YOUR IDENTITY. CALLING ME "WHITE" WHITTLES ME TO A WHOPPING FIVE OUT OF SEVEN *CONTINENTS.*

NORTH AMERICA. EUROPE. AUSTRALIA.

SOUTH AFRICA. THE ARCTIC.

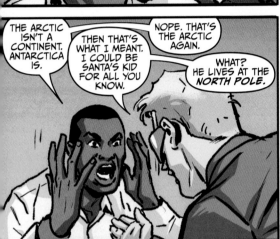

THE ARCTIC ISN'T A CONTINENT. ANTARCTICA IS.

THEN THAT'S WHAT I MEANT. I COULD BE SANTA'S KID FOR ALL YOU KNOW.

NOPE. THAT'S THE ARCTIC AGAIN.

WHAT? HE LIVES AT THE *NORTH POLE.*

THAT'S *THE ARCTIC!* ANTARCTICA IS ON THE *BOTTOM.* AND SANTA DOESN'T *HAVE* CHILDREN.

WHY ARE YOU BOTH TALKING LIKE SANTA *IS REAL?!*

· · ·

OH YEAH-- AND *I'M* THE MONSTER HERE.

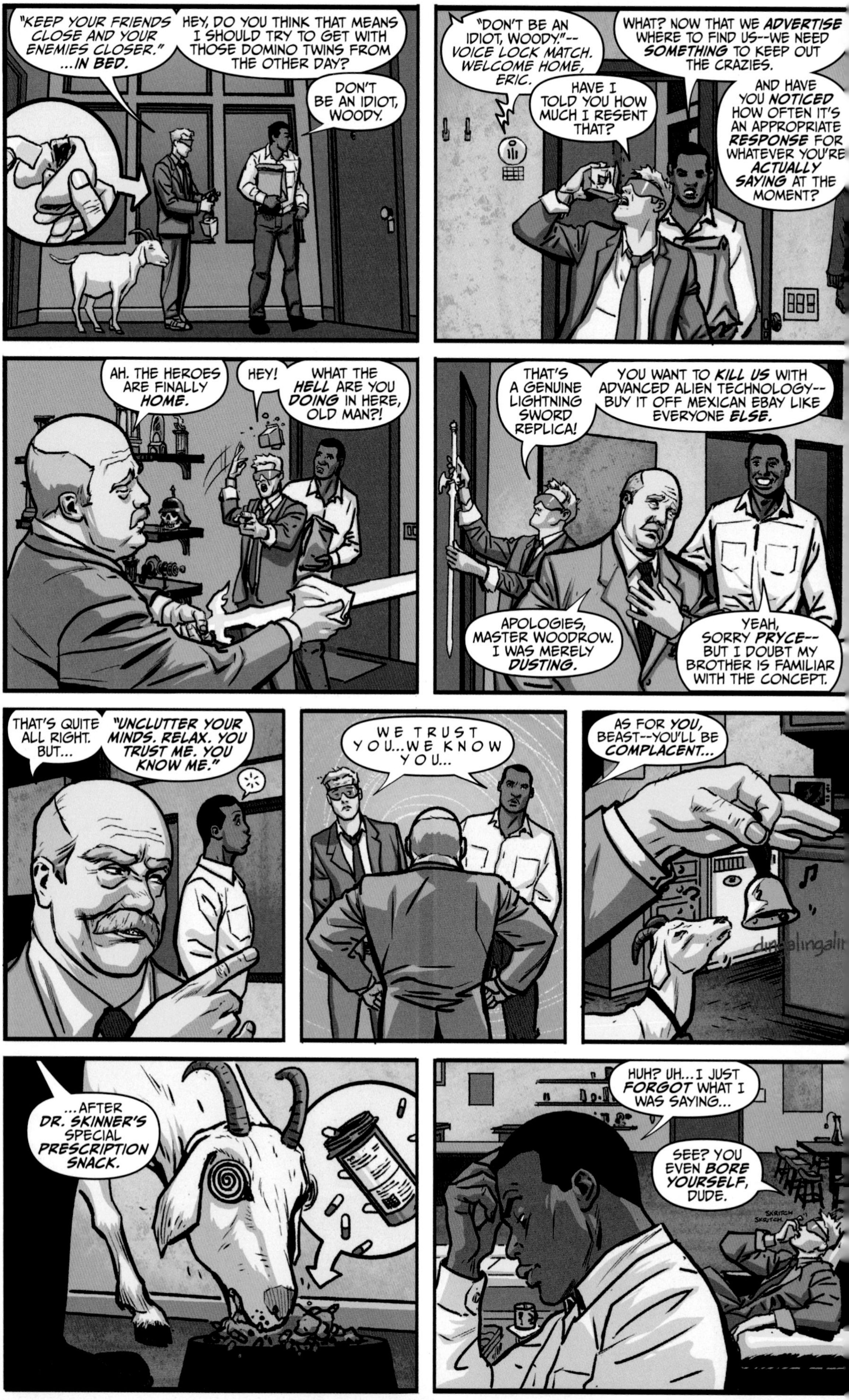

"KEEP YOUR FRIENDS CLOSE AND YOUR ENEMIES CLOSER." ...IN BED.
HEY, DO YOU THINK THAT MEANS I SHOULD TRY TO GET WITH THOSE DOMINO TWINS FROM THE OTHER DAY?
DON'T BE AN IDIOT, WOODY.
"DON'T BE AN IDIOT, WOODY."-- VOICE LOCK MATCH. WELCOME HOME, ERIC.
HAVE I TOLD YOU HOW MUCH I RESENT THAT?
WHAT? NOW THAT WE ADVERTISE WHERE TO FIND US--WE NEED SOMETHING TO KEEP OUT THE CRAZIES.
AND HAVE YOU NOTICED HOW OFTEN IT'S AN APPROPRIATE RESPONSE FOR WHATEVER YOU'RE ACTUALLY SAYING AT THE MOMENT?
AH. THE HEROES ARE FINALLY HOME.
HEY!
WHAT THE HELL ARE YOU DOING IN HERE, OLD MAN?!
THAT'S A GENUINE LIGHTNING SWORD REPLICA!
YOU WANT TO KILL US WITH ADVANCED ALIEN TECHNOLOGY-- BUY IT OFF MEXICAN EBAY LIKE EVERYONE ELSE.
APOLOGIES, MASTER WOODROW. I WAS MERELY DUSTING.
YEAH, SORRY PRYCE-- BUT I DOUBT MY BROTHER IS FAMILIAR WITH THE CONCEPT.
THAT'S QUITE ALL RIGHT. BUT...
"UNCLUTTER YOUR MINDS. RELAX. YOU TRUST ME. YOU KNOW ME."
WE TRUST YOU...WE KNOW YOU...
AS FOR YOU, BEAST--YOU'LL BE COMPLACENT...
...AFTER DR. SKINNER'S SPECIAL PRESCRIPTION SNACK.
HUH? UH...I JUST FORGOT WHAT I WAS SAYING...
SEE? YOU EVEN BORE YOURSELF, DUDE.
SKRITCH SKRITCH

EMILE COCTEAU? MY NAME IS DOCTOR HENRIK SKINNER.

ACCORDING TO YOUR *CHART,* I SEE *HALF* THE CHEMICAL COMPOUNDS YOU WERE EXPOSED TO ARE STILL... *EXPERIMENTAL...*

BUT UNLIKE IN THE *MOVIES*-- THIS ACCIDENT *DIDN'T* GIVE YOU *SUPER-POWERS?*

NON. ONLY *SEVEN* TYPES OF CANCER.

NOW YOU MAY EITHER GIVE ME MORE *MORPHINE,* GET OUT--

--OR MAKE ONE MORE *JOKE* AND I'LL *DROWN YOU IN* MY *BEDPAN.*

I DON'T *MEAN* IT AS A JOKE.

TWO MEN *DID THIS* TO YOU. *QUANTUM AND WOODY.*

YET THE AUTHORITIES LET *THEM* RUN AROUND WITH *IMPUNITY* WHILE *YOUR* ONLY OPTIONS ARE AN *EARLY GRAVE* OR A *LIFE* IN PRISON.

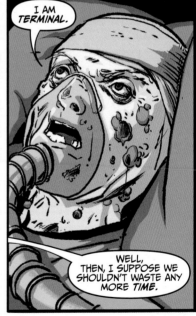

I AM *TERMINAL.*

WELL, THEN, I SUPPOSE WE SHOULDN'T WASTE ANY MORE *TIME.*

BECAUSE *QUANTUM AND WOODY* RUINED *MY LIFE,* TOO.

AND I BELIEVE WE CAN *HELP EACH OTHER* END THEIR REIGN OF TERROR-- *FOREVER!*

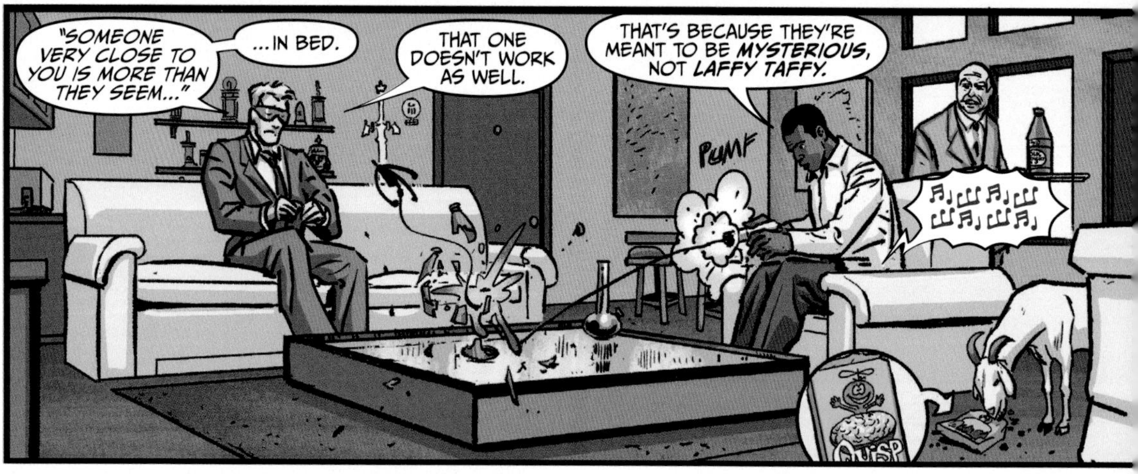
"SOMEONE VERY CLOSE TO YOU IS MORE THAN THEY SEEM..."
...IN BED.
THAT ONE DOESN'T WORK AS WELL.
THAT'S BECAUSE THEY'RE MEANT TO BE *MYSTERIOUS*, NOT *LAFFY TAFFY*.
PUMF

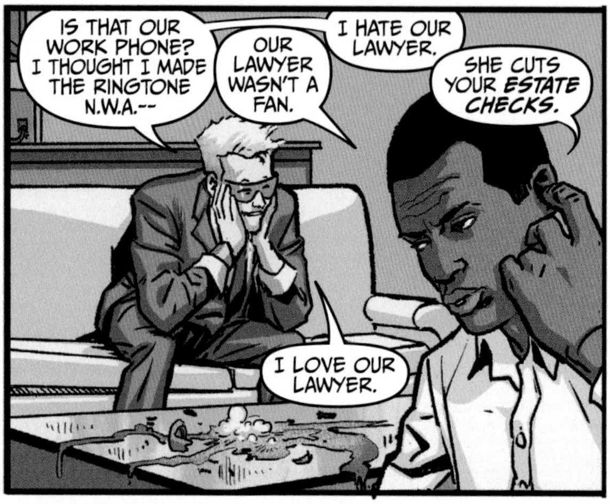
IS THAT OUR WORK PHONE? I THOUGHT I MADE THE RINGTONE N.W.A.--
OUR LAWYER WASN'T A FAN.
I HATE OUR LAWYER.
SHE CUTS YOUR *ESTATE CHECKS.*
I LOVE OUR LAWYER.

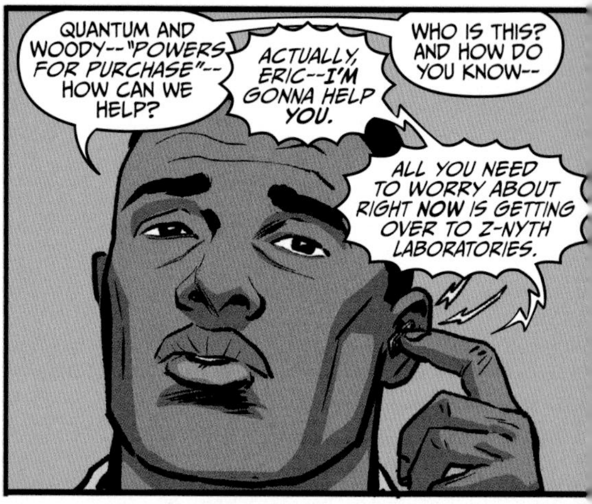
QUANTUM AND WOODY--"POWERS FOR PURCHASE"--HOW CAN WE HELP?
ACTUALLY, ERIC--*I'M* GONNA HELP *YOU*.
WHO IS THIS? AND HOW DO YOU KNOW--
ALL YOU NEED TO WORRY ABOUT RIGHT *NOW* IS GETTING OVER TO Z-NYTH LABORATORIES.

Better Dying Through Chemistry.

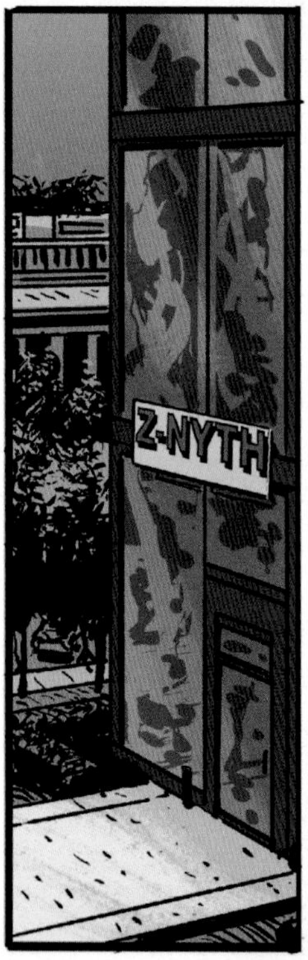
Z-NYTH

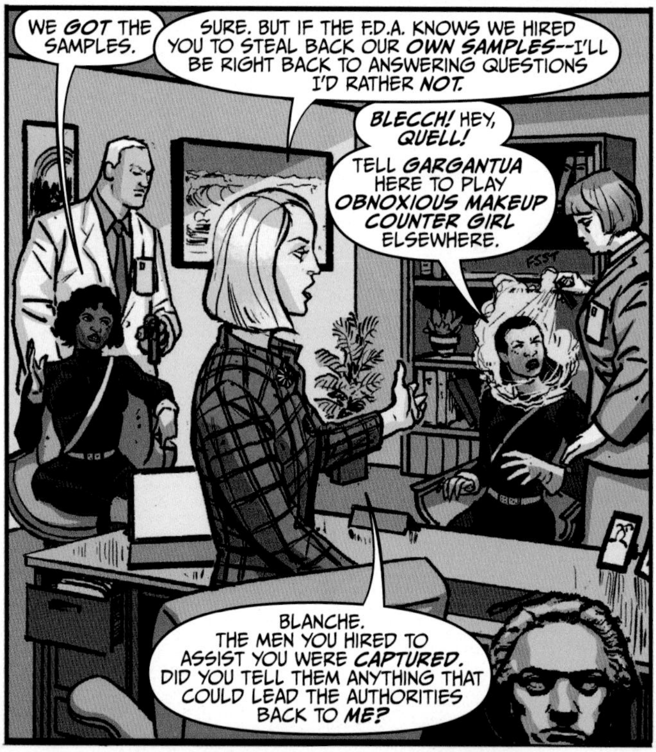
WE *GOT* THE SAMPLES.
SURE. BUT IF THE F.D.A. KNOWS WE HIRED YOU TO STEAL BACK OUR *OWN SAMPLES*--I'LL BE RIGHT BACK TO ANSWERING QUESTIONS I'D RATHER *NOT*.
BLECCH! HEY, *QUELL!*
TELL *GARGANTUA* HERE TO PLAY *OBNOXIOUS MAKEUP COUNTER GIRL* ELSEWHERE.
FSST
BLANCHE. THE MEN YOU HIRED TO ASSIST YOU WERE *CAPTURED*. DID YOU TELL THEM ANYTHING THAT COULD LEAD THE AUTHORITIES BACK TO *ME?*

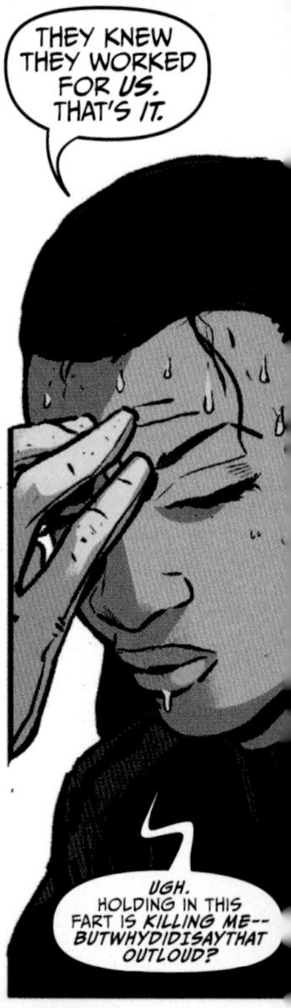
THEY KNEW THEY WORKED FOR *US*. THAT'S *IT*.
UGH. HOLDING IN THIS FART IS *KILLING ME*-- *BUTWHYDIDISAYTHAT OUTLOUD?*

THAT SPRAY WAS A FAST-ACTING INHALANT VARIATION ON SODIUM PENTOTHAL, BY THE WAY. DON'T WORRY. NO SIDE EFFECTS.
SIMPLEST WAY TO KNOW WHETHER YOU COVERED OUR TRACKS. SEEMS YOU'RE A COUPLE OF SMART COOKIES, AFTER ALL.
YOU DRUGGED US?!
I SHOULD BE MAD...
...BUT NOW I WANT MATCHING "SMART COOKIE" NECKLACES.
CORRECTION. ONLY THE INTENDED SIDE EFFECT OF TOTAL CANDOR. BUT NOW THAT WE'RE FRIENDS AGAIN-- I'LL EVEN SHOW YOU MY CLUBHOUSE.
YOU WERE PROBABLY WONDERING WHY I HAD YOU STEAL OUR OWN COMPOUNDS.
YOU DIDN'T PAY US TO WONDER. JUST TO RETRIEVE--
I WONDERED!
...SORRY. THAT JUST CAME OUT.
THE F.D.A. GRABBED THOSE DURING A SURPRISE INSPECTION OF OUR GUAM FACILITY.
NEEDLESS TO SAY, IT'S A COMPOUND WE HADN'T INTENDED TO SHARE WITH THEM.
R-AND-D IN THE PHARMACEUTICAL INDUSTRY IS, FRANKLY, NUT-BALLS.
CREATING CURES ON MONDAY, DISEASES ON TUESDAY, AND ON WEDNESDAY-- WE JUST MIX A BUNCH OF 💩💩💩💩 TOGETHER AND SHOOT IT INTO RATS.
BUT OCCASIONALLY A DRUG OR TREATMENT WE TEST YIELDS... UNEXPECTED SIDE EFFECTS.
MAN-BOOBS?
WELL...YES. BUT MORE EXCITINGLY-- REMARKABLE SPIKES IN STRENGTH, REFLEXES, BIO-ELECTRIC PRODUCTION-- EVEN THE OCCASIONAL WHOLLY NEW PHYSIOLOGICAL ABILITY.
YOU'RE SAYING YOU ACCIDENTALLY DISCOVERED... DRUGS THAT GIVE PEOPLE SUPER-POWERS?
NO. WE FOUND A FEW COMPOUNDS GIVE ONE IN A MILLION PEOPLE ABILITIES.
THE REAL WORK IS HARVESTING THE NEUROCHEMICALS THESE OUTLIERS PRODUCE THAT ACTUALLY MANIFEST THE POWERS. THAT WE CAN SELL.
SWEET SHEBA...
I KNOW. IN FACT, I IMAGINE THIS IS HOW PEOPLE IN THE MAKEUP INDUSTRY FELT WHEN THEY REALIZED WHALE FAT MADE A FANTASTIC DIFFERENCE IN THEIR PRODUCTS.
NO ONE WANTS TO KILL WHALES. BUT THE MONEY IS BONKERS.
THIS...IS A WHOLE BOND VILLAIN THING, ISN'T IT?
YOU'RE SHOWING US THIS BECAUSE YOU'RE ABOUT TO KILL US TO BURY YOUR CONNECTION TO THE THEFT?
SEE? SMART COOKIES.

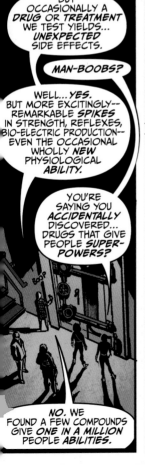

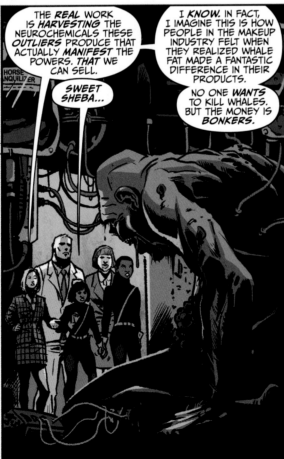

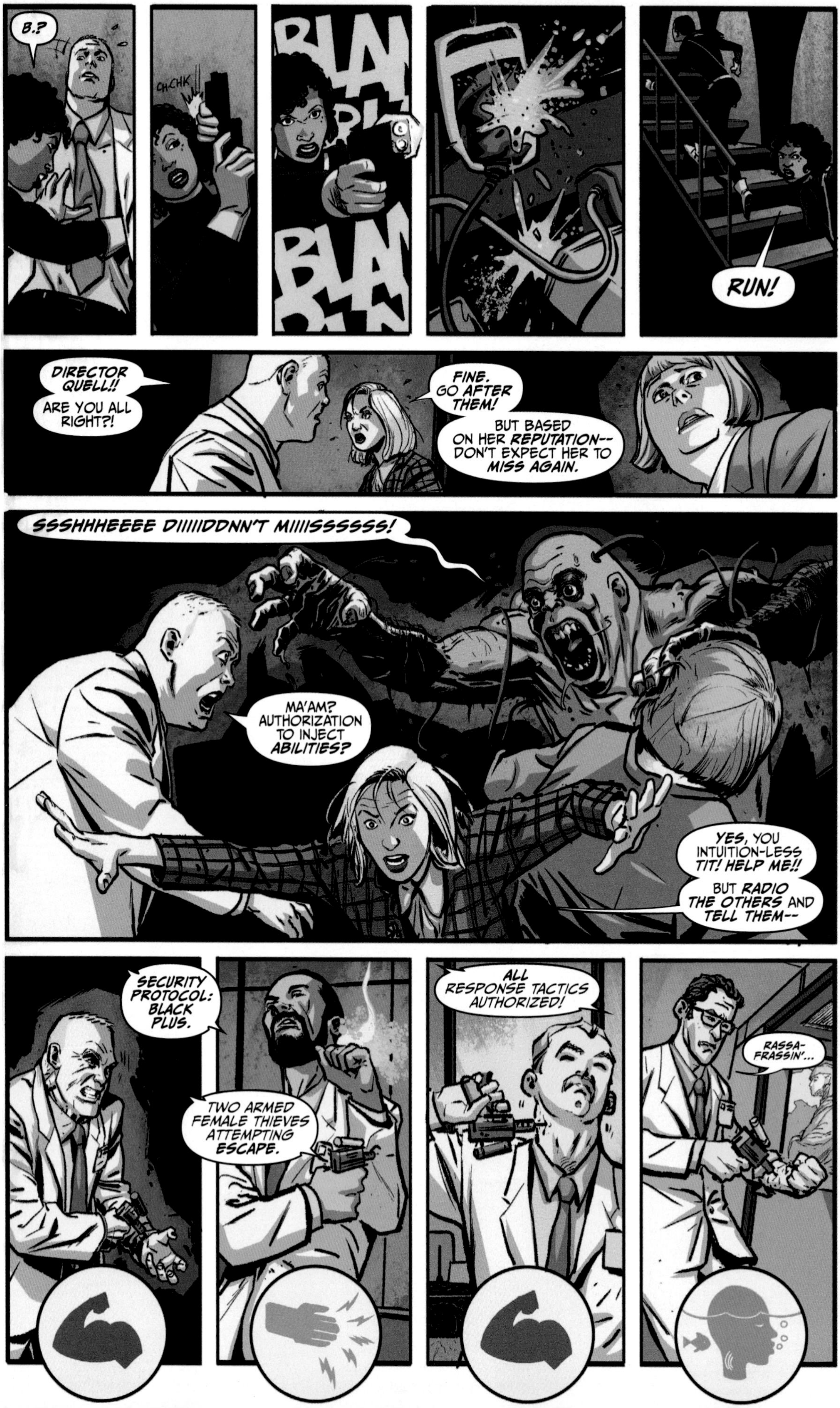

B.?
CH-CHK
BLAM
BLAM
RUN!
DIRECTOR QUELL!!
ARE YOU ALL RIGHT?!
FINE. GO AFTER THEM!
BUT BASED ON HER REPUTATION-- DON'T EXPECT HER TO MISS AGAIN.
SSSHHHEEEE DIIIIDDNN'T MIIIISSSSSS!
MA'AM? AUTHORIZATION TO INJECT ABILITIES?
YES, YOU INTUITION-LESS TIT! HELP ME!!
BUT RADIO THE OTHERS AND TELL THEM--
SECURITY PROTOCOL: BLACK PLUS.
TWO ARMED FEMALE THIEVES ATTEMPTING ESCAPE.
ALL RESPONSE TACTICS AUTHORIZED!
RASSA-FRASSIN'...

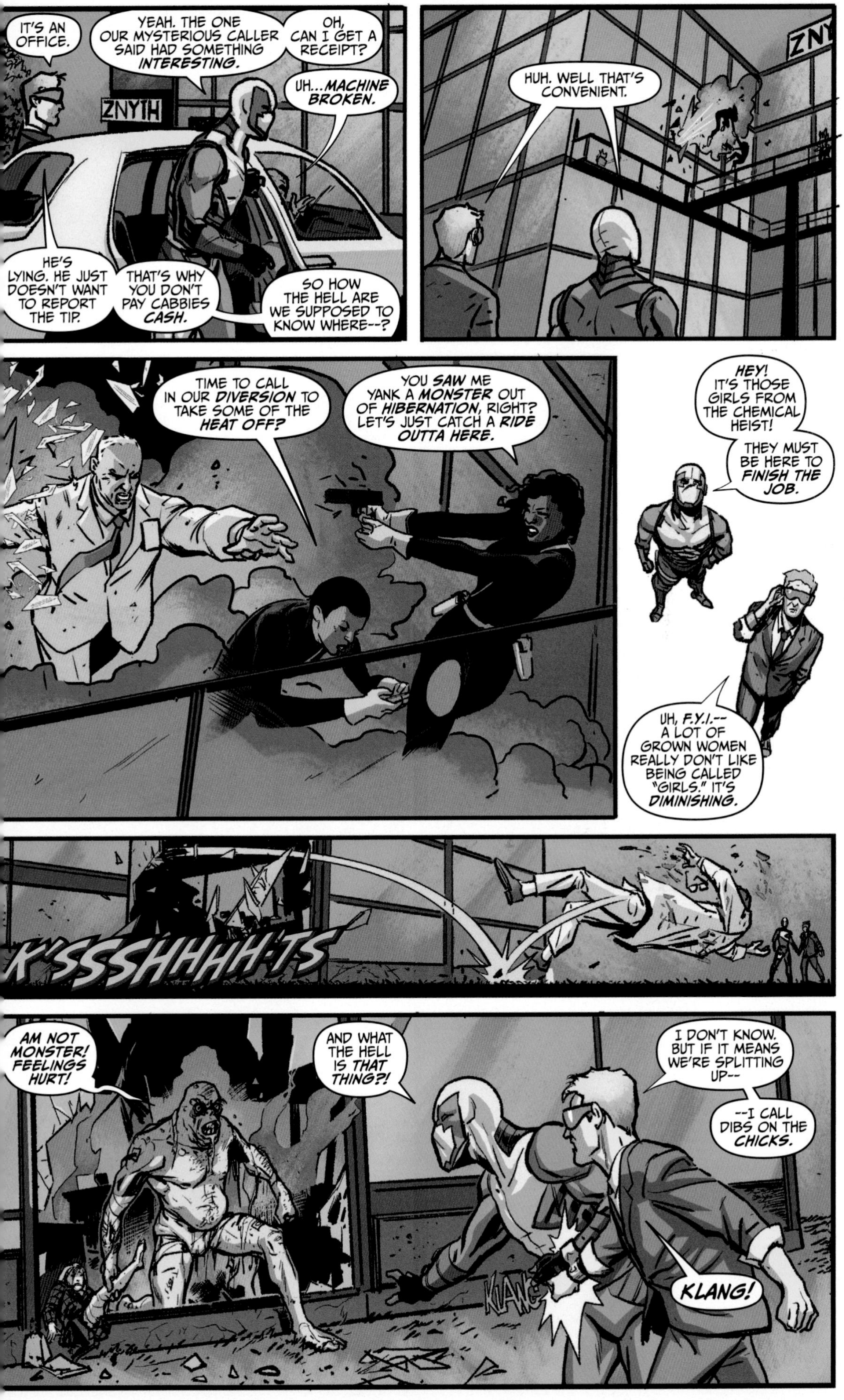
IT'S AN OFFICE.
YEAH. THE ONE OUR MYSTERIOUS CALLER SAID HAD SOMETHING INTERESTING.
OH, CAN I GET A RECEIPT?
UH...MACHINE BROKEN.
ZNY1H
HE'S LYING. HE JUST DOESN'T WANT TO REPORT THE TIP.
THAT'S WHY YOU DON'T PAY CABBIES CASH.
SO HOW THE HELL ARE WE SUPPOSED TO KNOW WHERE--?
ZNY
HUH. WELL THAT'S CONVENIENT.
TIME TO CALL IN OUR DIVERSION TO TAKE SOME OF THE HEAT OFF?
YOU SAW ME YANK A MONSTER OUT OF HIBERNATION, RIGHT? LET'S JUST CATCH A RIDE OUTTA HERE.
HEY! IT'S THOSE GIRLS FROM THE CHEMICAL HEIST!
THEY MUST BE HERE TO FINISH THE JOB.
UH, F.Y.I.-- A LOT OF GROWN WOMEN REALLY DON'T LIKE BEING CALLED "GIRLS." IT'S DIMINISHING.
K'SSSHHHH-TS
AM NOT MONSTER! FEELINGS HURT!
AND WHAT THE HELL IS THAT THING?!
I DON'T KNOW. BUT IF IT MEANS WE'RE SPLITTING UP--
--I CALL DIBS ON THE CHICKS.
KLANG
KLANG!

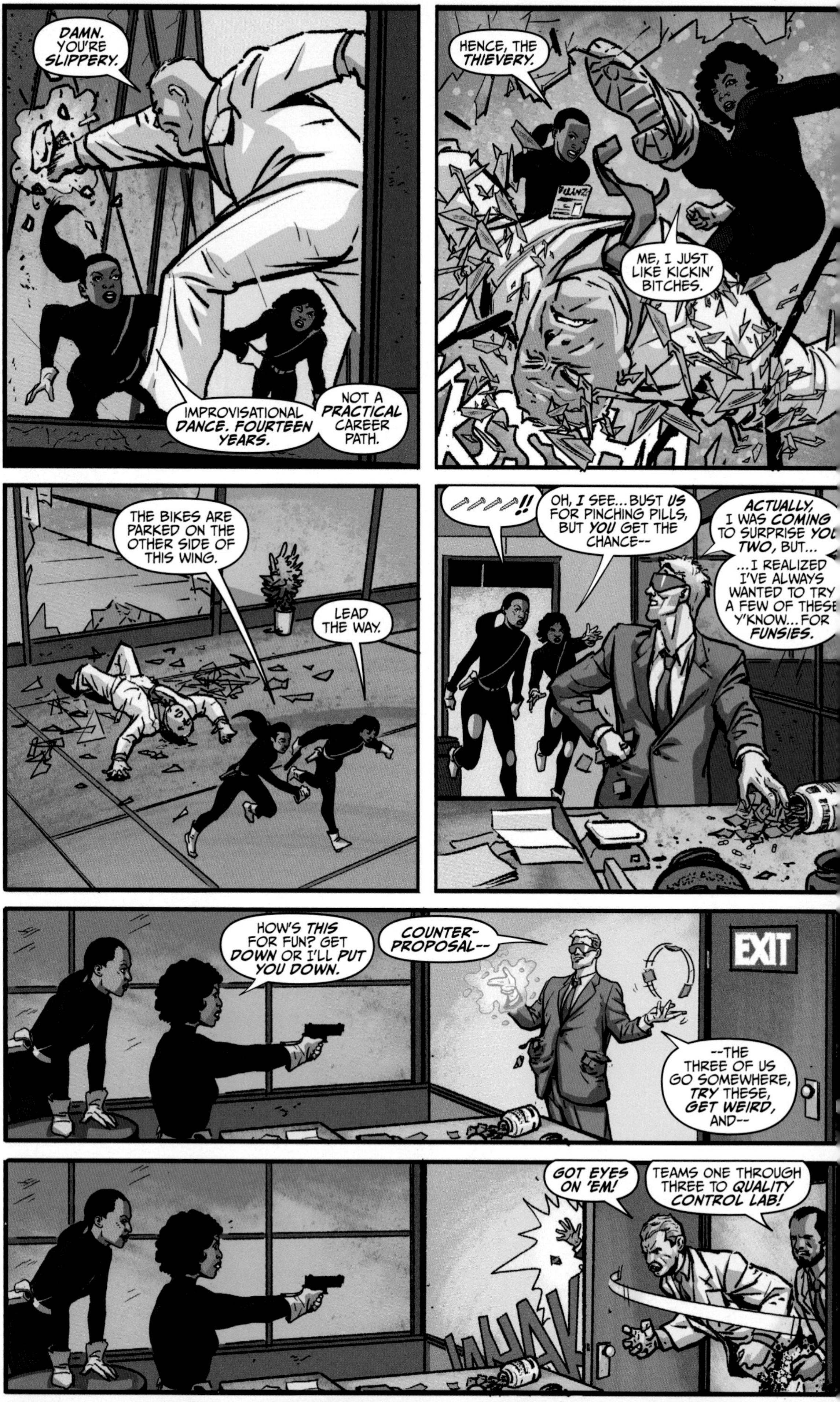
DAMN. YOU'RE SLIPPERY.
IMPROVISATIONAL DANCE. FOURTEEN YEARS.
NOT A PRACTICAL CAREER PATH.
HENCE, THE THIEVERY.
ME, I JUST LIKE KICKIN' BITCHES.
THE BIKES ARE PARKED ON THE OTHER SIDE OF THIS WING.
LEAD THE WAY.
!!
OH, I SEE... BUST US FOR PINCHING PILLS, BUT YOU GET THE CHANCE--
ACTUALLY, I WAS COMING TO SURPRISE YOU TWO, BUT...
...I REALIZED I'VE ALWAYS WANTED TO TRY A FEW OF THESE Y'KNOW... FOR FUNSIES.
HOW'S THIS FOR FUN? GET DOWN OR I'LL PUT YOU DOWN.
COUNTER-PROPOSAL--
EXIT
--THE THREE OF US GO SOMEWHERE, TRY THESE, GET WEIRD, AND--
GOT EYES ON 'EM!
TEAMS ONE THROUGH THREE TO QUALITY CONTROL LAB!

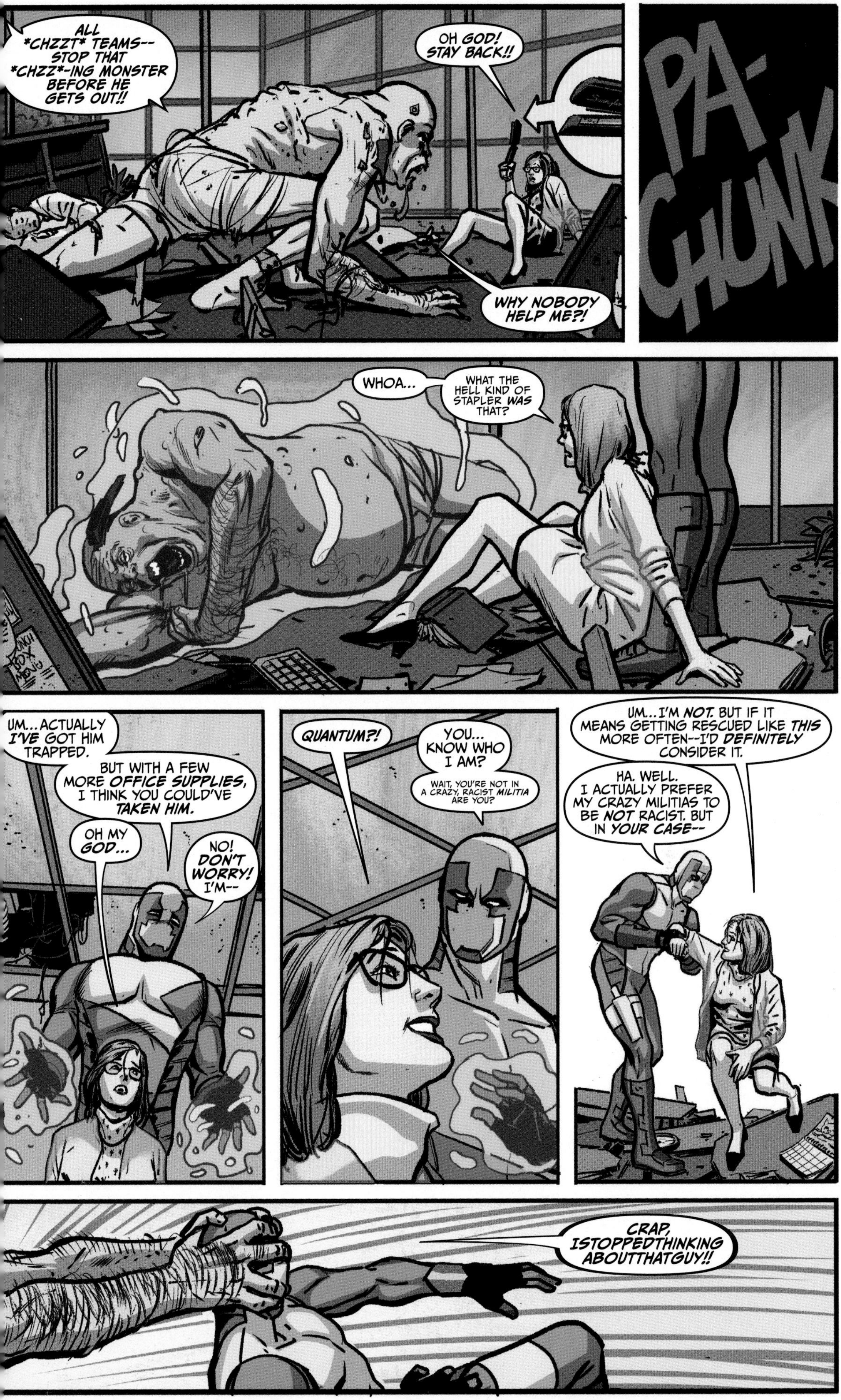
ALL *CHZZT* TEAMS-- STOP THAT *CHZZ*-ING MONSTER BEFORE HE GETS OUT!!
OH GOD! STAY BACK!!
WHY NOBODY HELP ME?!
PA-CHUNK
WHOA...
WHAT THE HELL KIND OF STAPLER WAS THAT?
UM...ACTUALLY I'VE GOT HIM TRAPPED.
BUT WITH A FEW MORE OFFICE SUPPLIES, I THINK YOU COULD'VE TAKEN HIM.
OH MY GOD...
NO! DON'T WORRY! I'M--
QUANTUM?!
YOU... KNOW WHO I AM?
WAIT, YOU'RE NOT IN A CRAZY, RACIST MILITIA ARE YOU?
UM...I'M NOT. BUT IF IT MEANS GETTING RESCUED LIKE THIS MORE OFTEN--I'D DEFINITELY CONSIDER IT.
HA. WELL. I ACTUALLY PREFER MY CRAZY MILITIAS TO BE NOT RACIST. BUT IN YOUR CASE--
CRAP, ISTOPPEDTHINKING ABOUTTHATGUY!!

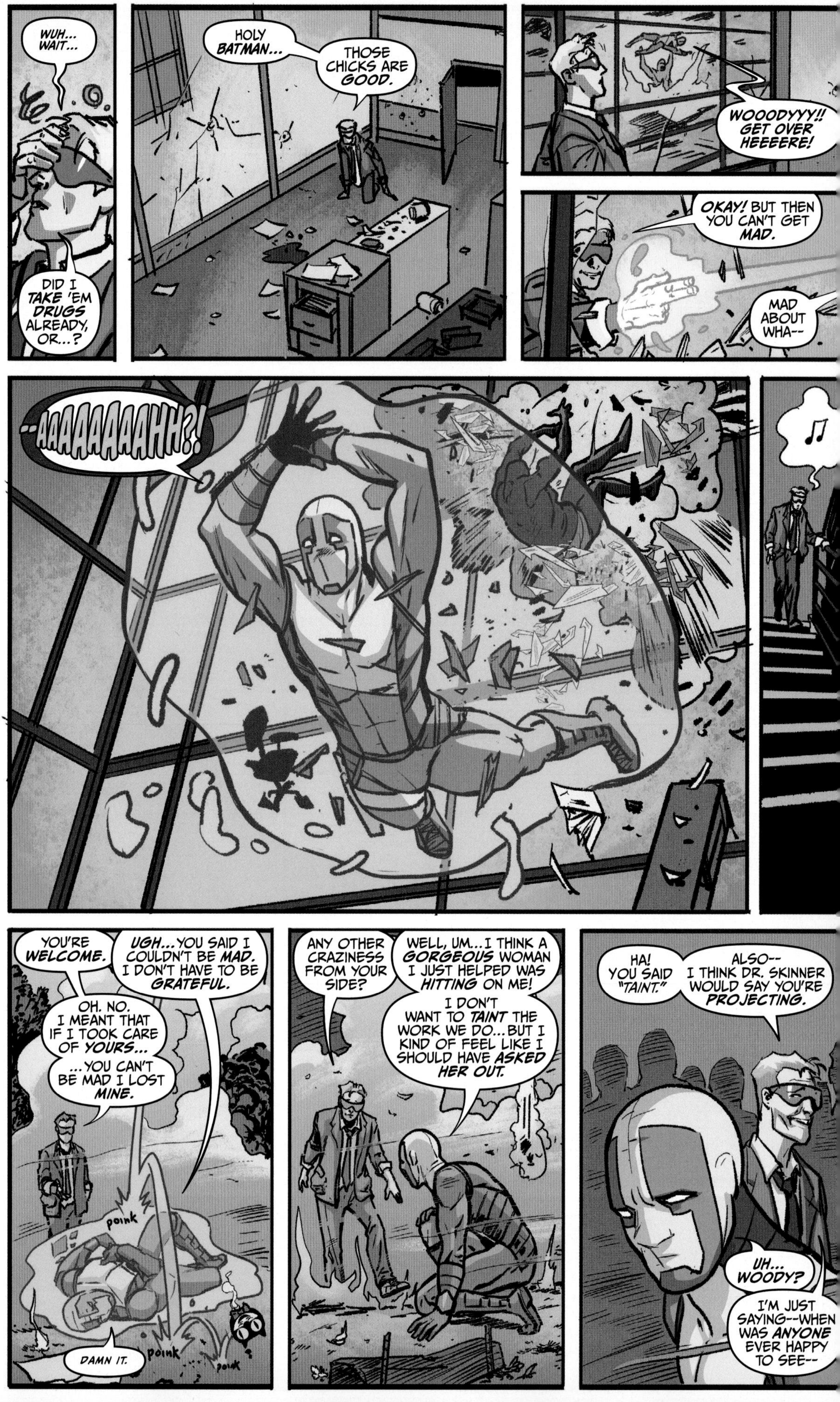
WUH... WAIT...
DID I TAKE 'EM DRUGS ALREADY, OR...?
HOLY BATMAN...
THOSE CHICKS ARE GOOD.
WOOODYYY!! GET OVER HEEEERE!
OKAY! BUT THEN YOU CAN'T GET MAD.
MAD ABOUT WHA--
--AAAAAAAAHH?!
♫
YOU'RE WELCOME.
UGH... YOU SAID I COULDN'T BE MAD. I DON'T HAVE TO BE GRATEFUL.
OH. NO. I MEANT THAT IF I TOOK CARE OF YOURS...
...YOU CAN'T BE MAD I LOST MINE.
poink
poink
poink
DAMN IT.
ANY OTHER CRAZINESS FROM YOUR SIDE?
WELL, UM... I THINK A GORGEOUS WOMAN I JUST HELPED WAS HITTING ON ME!
I DON'T WANT TO TAINT THE WORK WE DO... BUT I KIND OF FEEL LIKE I SHOULD HAVE ASKED HER OUT.
HA! YOU SAID "TAINT."
ALSO-- I THINK DR. SKINNER WOULD SAY YOU'RE PROJECTING.
UH... WOODY?
I'M JUST SAYING--WHEN WAS ANYONE EVER HAPPY TO SEE--

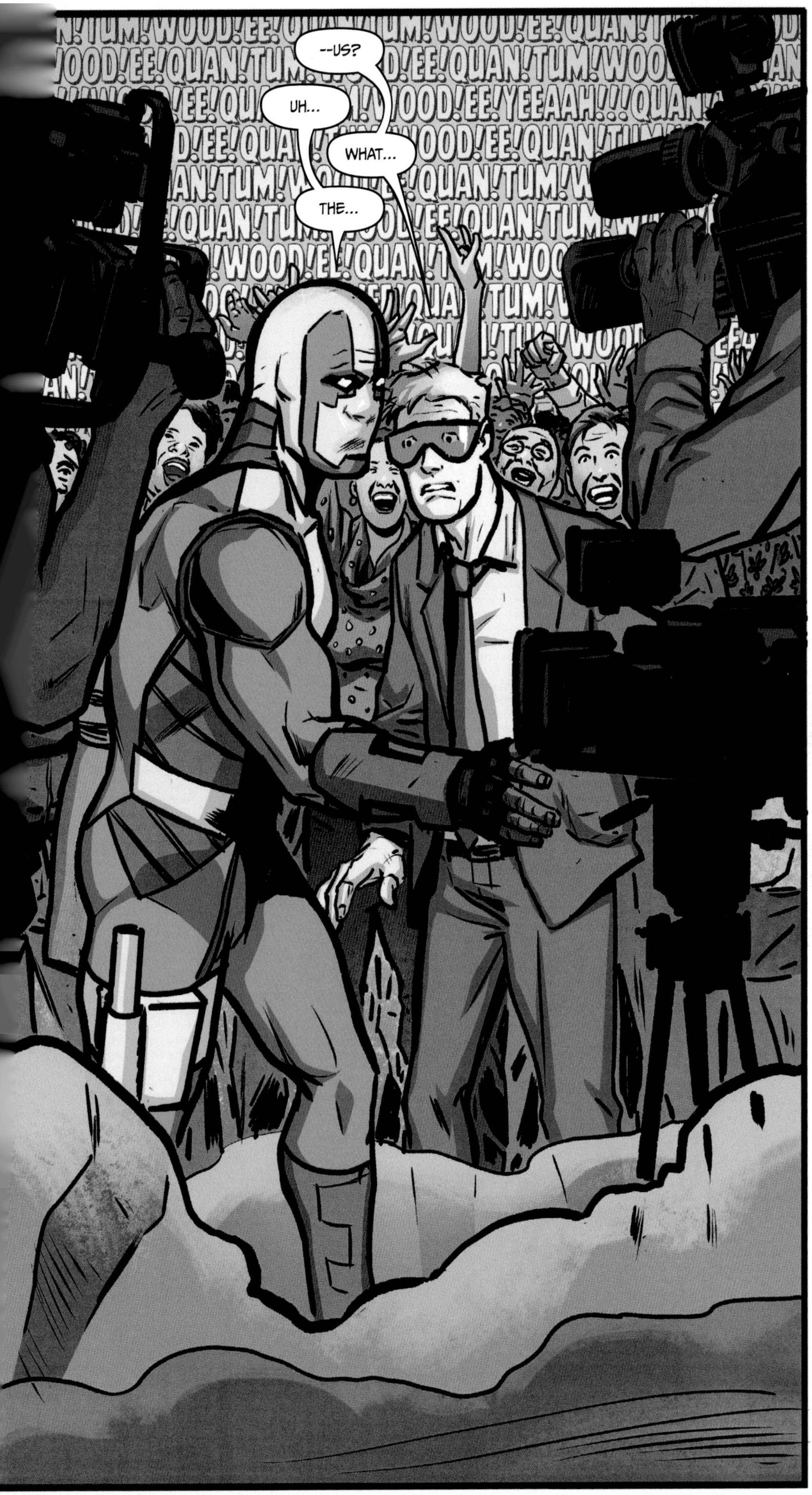

--US?
UH...
WHAT...
THE...
QUAN! TUM! WOOD! EE! QUAN! TUM! WOOD! EE! YEEAAH!!!

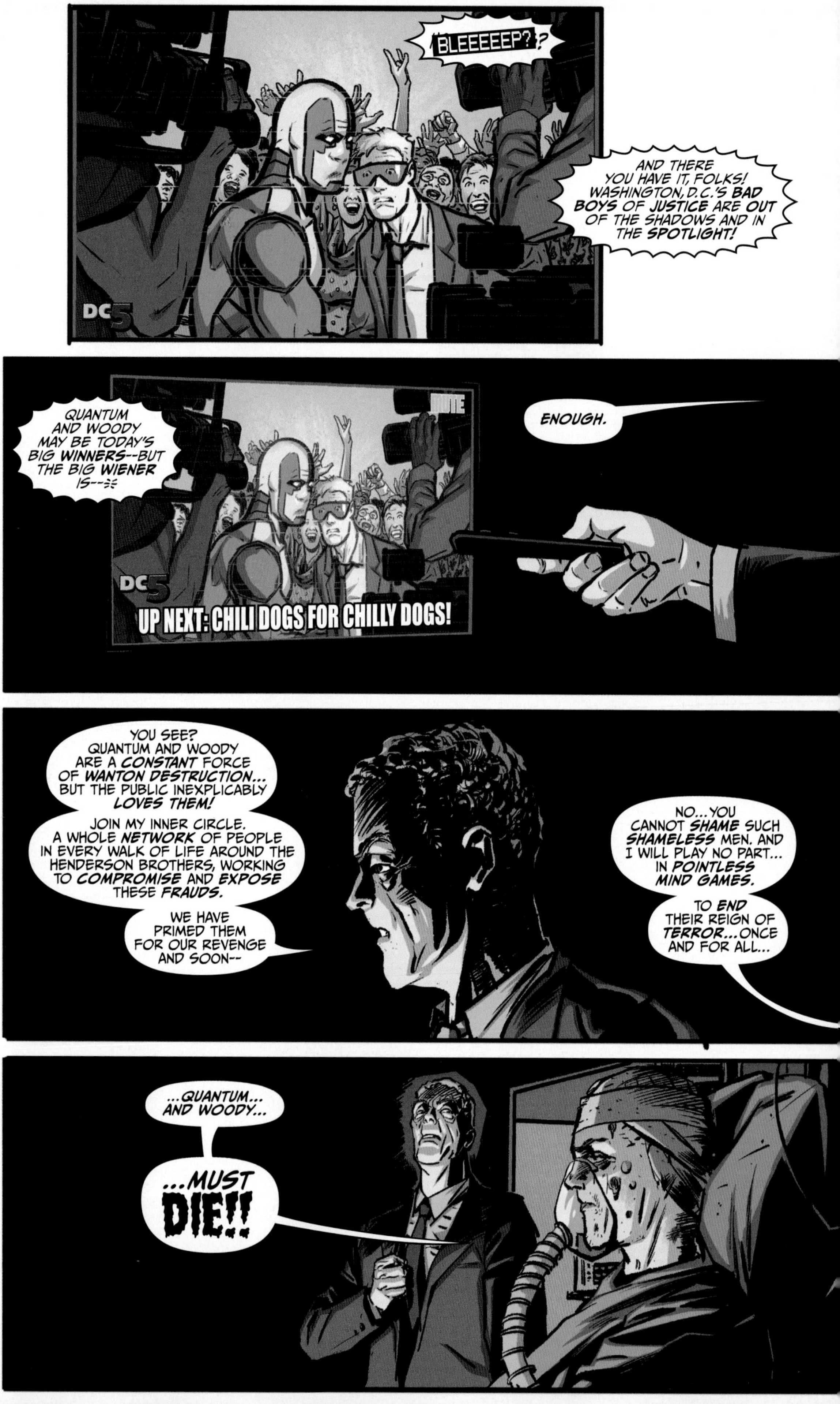
BLEEEEEP?
AND THERE YOU HAVE IT, FOLKS! WASHINGTON, D.C.'S BAD BOYS OF JUSTICE ARE OUT OF THE SHADOWS AND IN THE SPOTLIGHT!
DC5
QUANTUM AND WOODY MAY BE TODAY'S BIG WINNERS--BUT THE BIG WIENER IS--
MUTE
ENOUGH.
DC5
UP NEXT: CHILI DOGS FOR CHILLY DOGS!
YOU SEE? QUANTUM AND WOODY ARE A CONSTANT FORCE OF WANTON DESTRUCTION... BUT THE PUBLIC INEXPLICABLY LOVES THEM!
JOIN MY INNER CIRCLE. A WHOLE NETWORK OF PEOPLE IN EVERY WALK OF LIFE AROUND THE HENDERSON BROTHERS, WORKING TO COMPROMISE AND EXPOSE THESE FRAUDS.
WE HAVE PRIMED THEM FOR OUR REVENGE AND SOON--
NO...YOU CANNOT SHAME SUCH SHAMELESS MEN. AND I WILL PLAY NO PART... IN POINTLESS MIND GAMES.
TO END THEIR REIGN OF TERROR...ONCE AND FOR ALL...
...QUANTUM... AND WOODY...
...MUST DIE!!

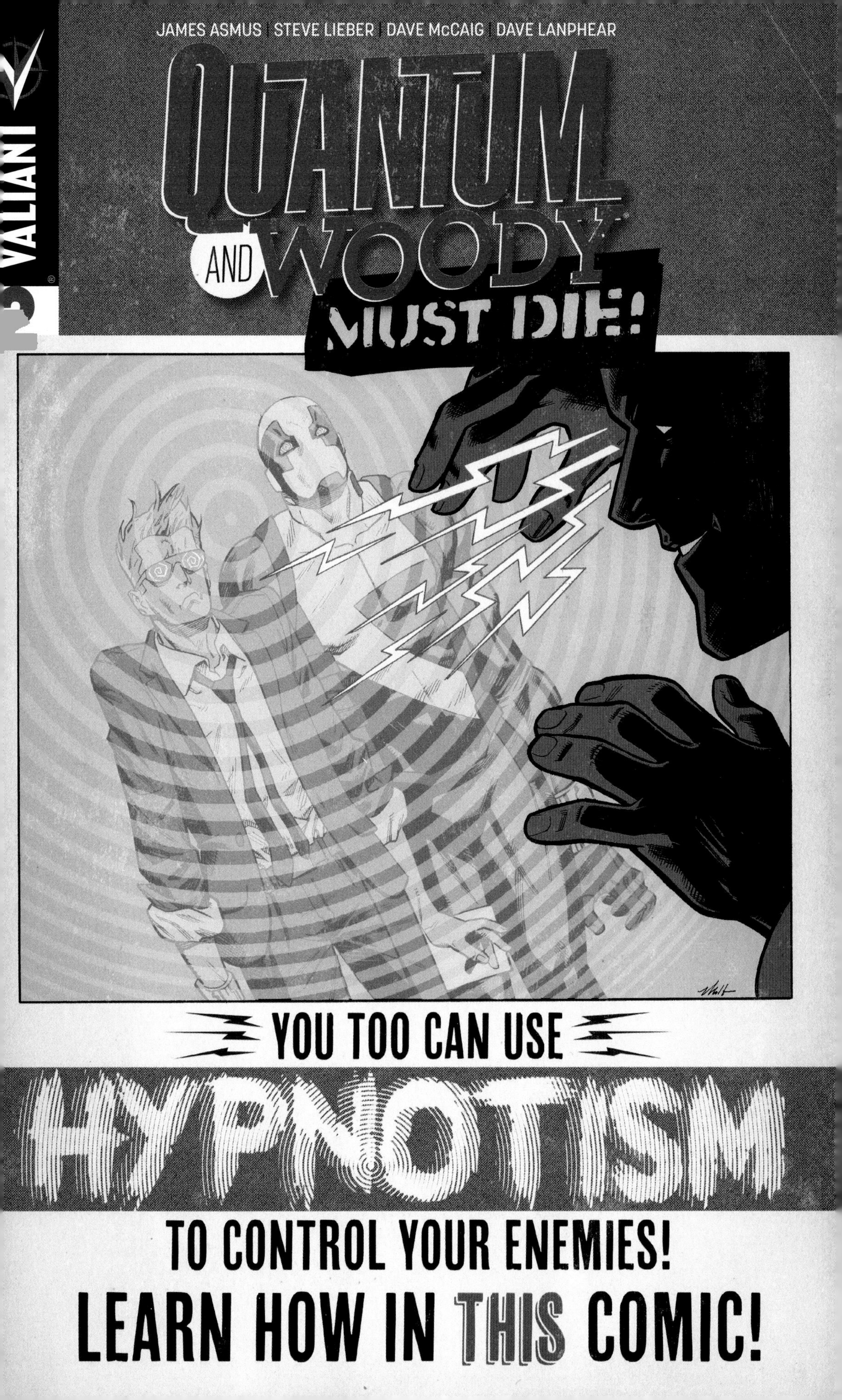

VALIANT
JAMES ASMUS | STEVE LIEBER | DAVE McCAIG | DAVE LANPHEAR
QUANTUM AND WOODY MUST DIE!
YOU TOO CAN USE
HYPNOTISM
TO CONTROL YOUR ENEMIES!
LEARN HOW IN THIS COMIC!

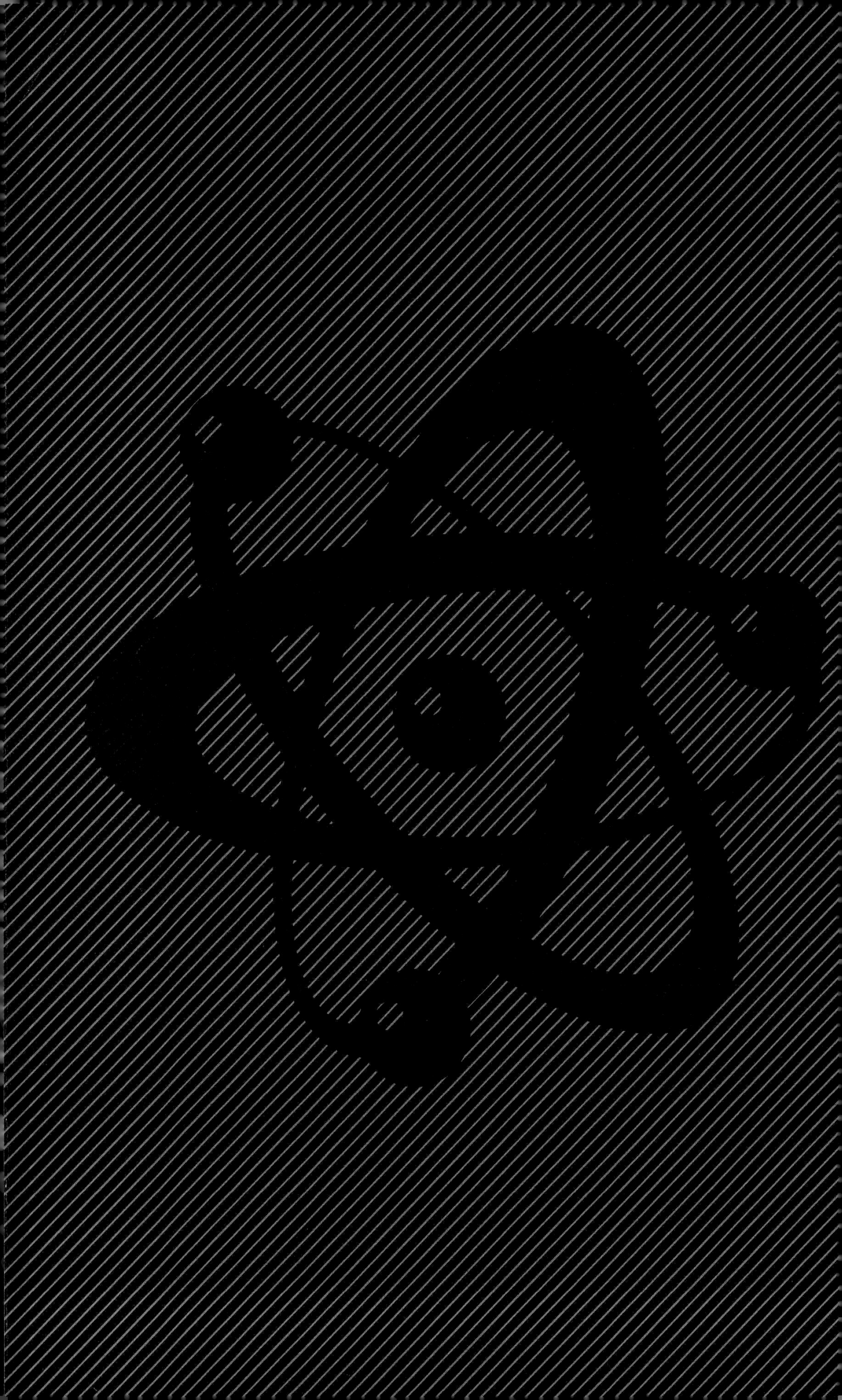

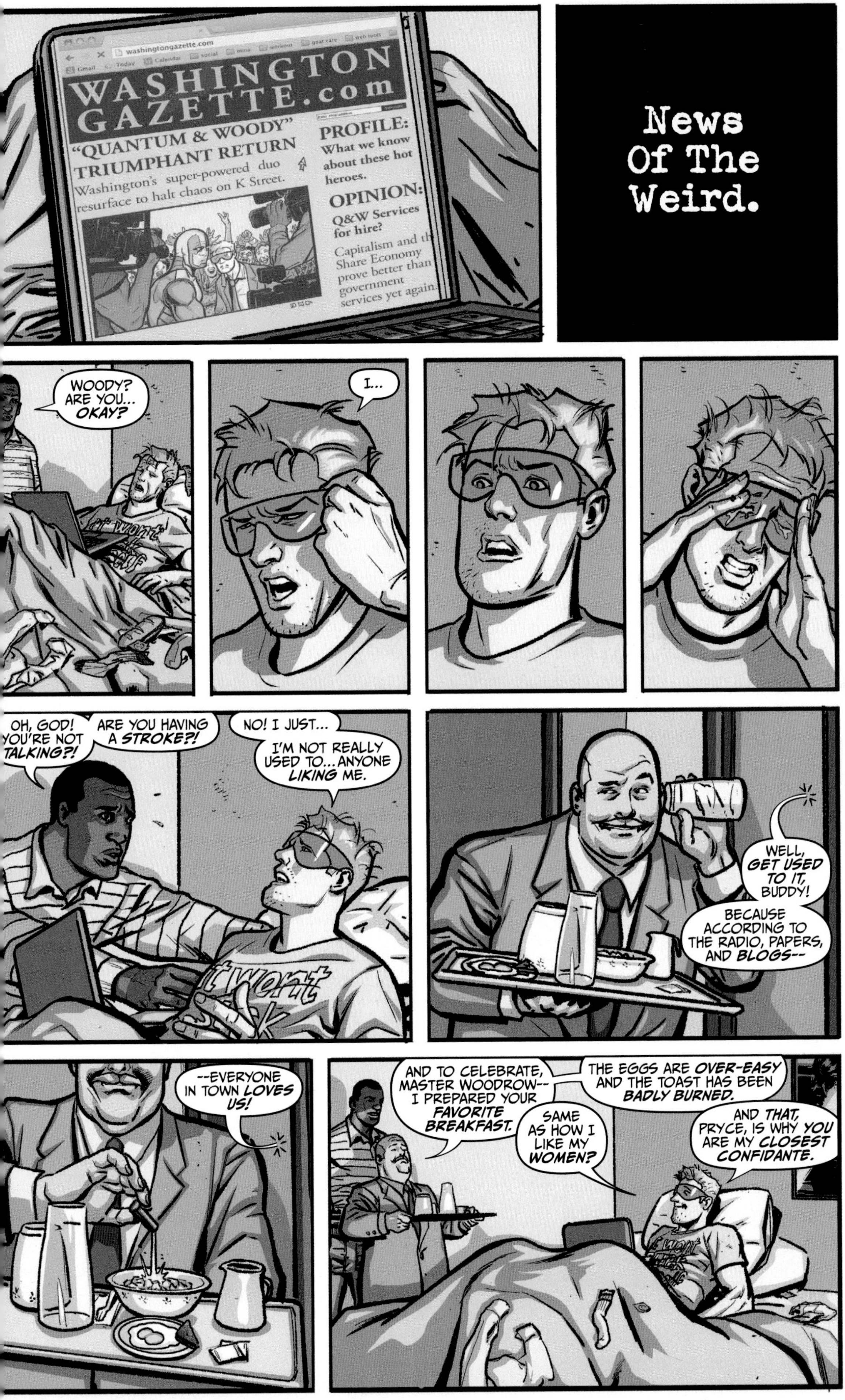
washingtongazette.com
WASHINGTON GAZETTE.com
“QUANTUM & WOODY” TRIUMPHANT RETURN
Washington's super-powered duo resurface to halt chaos on K Street.
PROFILE: What we know about these hot heroes.
OPINION: Q&W Services for hire?
Capitalism and th Share Economy prove better than government services yet again.
News Of The Weird.
WOODY? ARE YOU... OKAY?
I...
OH, GOD! YOU'RE NOT TALKING?!
ARE YOU HAVING A STROKE?!
NO! I JUST...
I'M NOT REALLY USED TO... ANYONE LIKING ME.
WELL, GET USED TO IT, BUDDY!
BECAUSE ACCORDING TO THE RADIO, PAPERS, AND BLOGS--
--EVERYONE IN TOWN LOVES US!
AND TO CELEBRATE, MASTER WOODROW-- I PREPARED YOUR FAVORITE BREAKFAST.
THE EGGS ARE OVER-EASY AND THE TOAST HAS BEEN BADLY BURNED.
SAME AS HOW I LIKE MY WOMEN?
AND THAT, PRYCE, IS WHY YOU ARE MY CLOSEST CONFIDANTE.

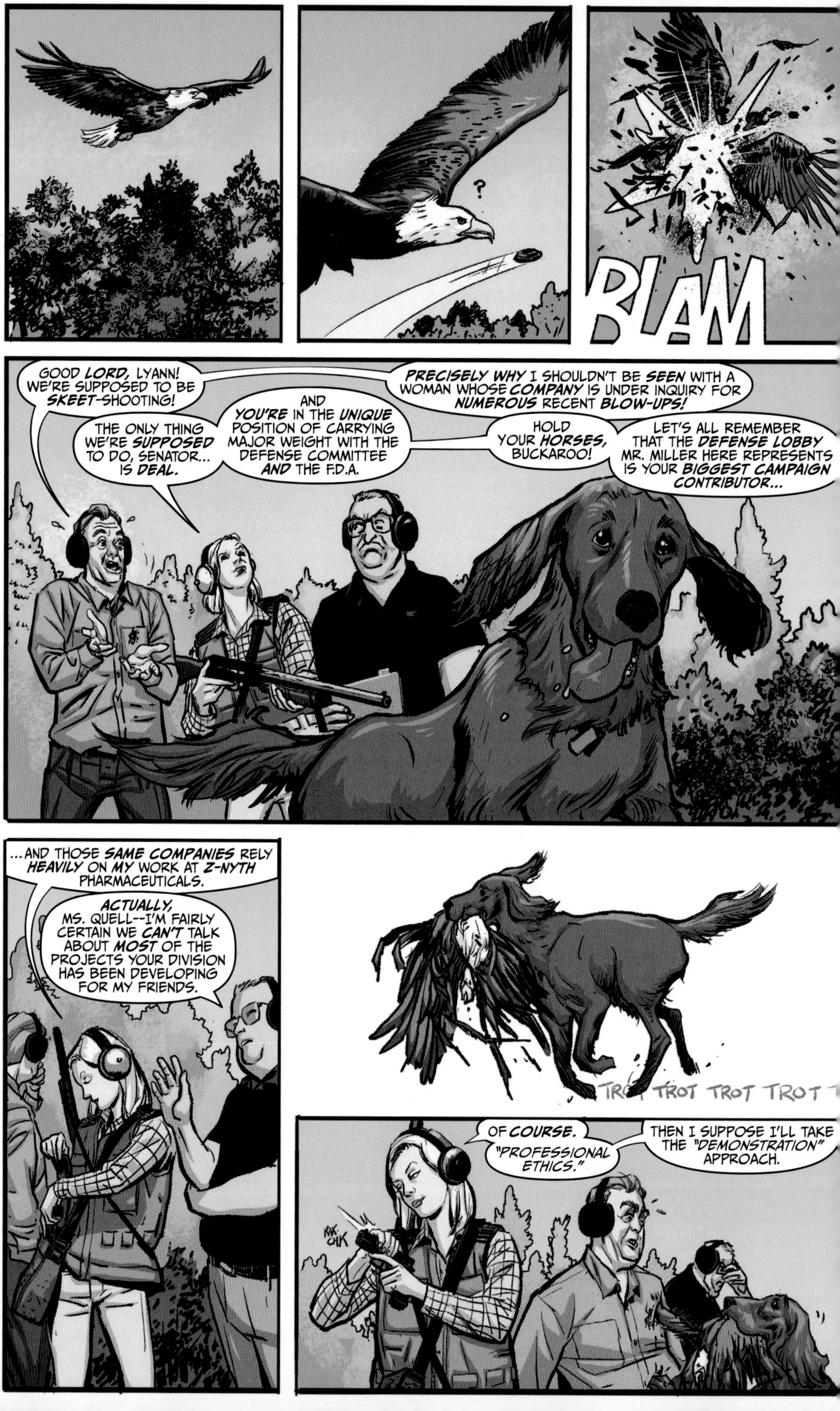
?
BLAM
GOOD LORD, LYANN! WE'RE SUPPOSED TO BE SKEET-SHOOTING!
THE ONLY THING WE'RE SUPPOSED TO DO, SENATOR... IS DEAL.
AND YOU'RE IN THE UNIQUE POSITION OF CARRYING MAJOR WEIGHT WITH THE DEFENSE COMMITTEE AND THE F.D.A.
PRECISELY WHY I SHOULDN'T BE SEEN WITH A WOMAN WHOSE COMPANY IS UNDER INQUIRY FOR NUMEROUS RECENT BLOW-UPS!
HOLD YOUR HORSES, BUCKAROO!
LET'S ALL REMEMBER THAT THE DEFENSE LOBBY MR. MILLER HERE REPRESENTS IS YOUR BIGGEST CAMPAIGN CONTRIBUTOR...
...AND THOSE SAME COMPANIES RELY HEAVILY ON MY WORK AT Z-NYTH PHARMACEUTICALS.
ACTUALLY, MS. QUELL--I'M FAIRLY CERTAIN WE CAN'T TALK ABOUT MOST OF THE PROJECTS YOUR DIVISION HAS BEEN DEVELOPING FOR MY FRIENDS.
TROT TROT TROT TROT
OF COURSE. "PROFESSIONAL ETHICS."
THEN I SUPPOSE I'LL TAKE THE "DEMONSTRATION" APPROACH.
KAK-CHK

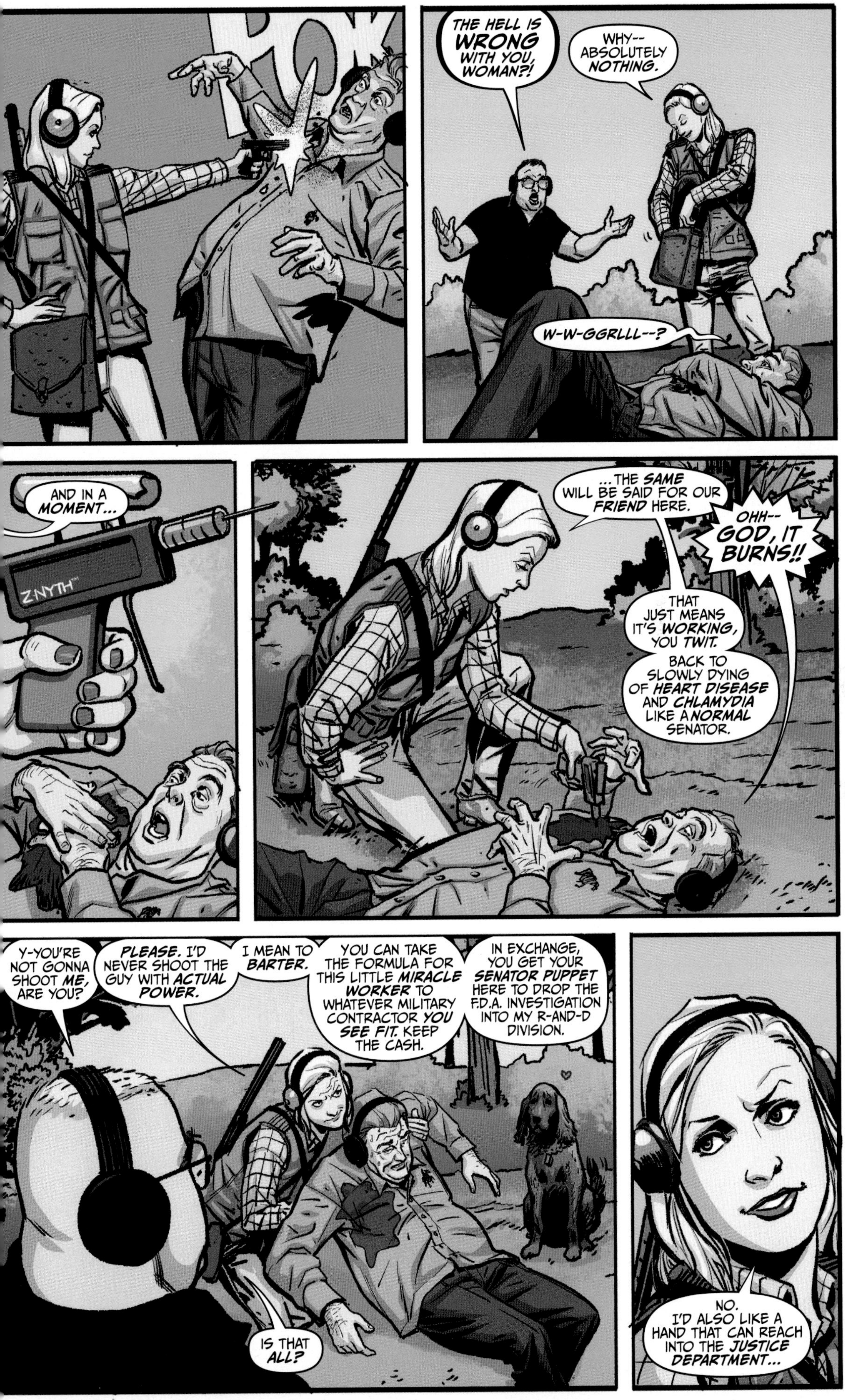
BLAM
THE HELL IS WRONG WITH YOU, WOMAN?!
WHY-- ABSOLUTELY NOTHING.
W-W-GGRLLL--?
AND IN A MOMENT...
Z·NYTH™
...THE SAME WILL BE SAID FOR OUR FRIEND HERE.
OHH-- GOD, IT BURNS!!
THAT JUST MEANS IT'S WORKING, YOU TWIT.
BACK TO SLOWLY DYING OF HEART DISEASE AND CHLAMYDIA LIKE A NORMAL SENATOR.
Y-YOU'RE NOT GONNA SHOOT ME, ARE YOU?
PLEASE. I'D NEVER SHOOT THE GUY WITH ACTUAL POWER.
I MEAN TO BARTER.
YOU CAN TAKE THE FORMULA FOR THIS LITTLE MIRACLE WORKER TO WHATEVER MILITARY CONTRACTOR YOU SEE FIT. KEEP THE CASH.
IN EXCHANGE, YOU GET YOUR SENATOR PUPPET HERE TO DROP THE F.D.A. INVESTIGATION INTO MY R-AND-D DIVISION.
IS THAT ALL?
NO. I'D ALSO LIKE A HAND THAT CAN REACH INTO THE JUSTICE DEPARTMENT...

I'm Sorry. Your Time Is Up.

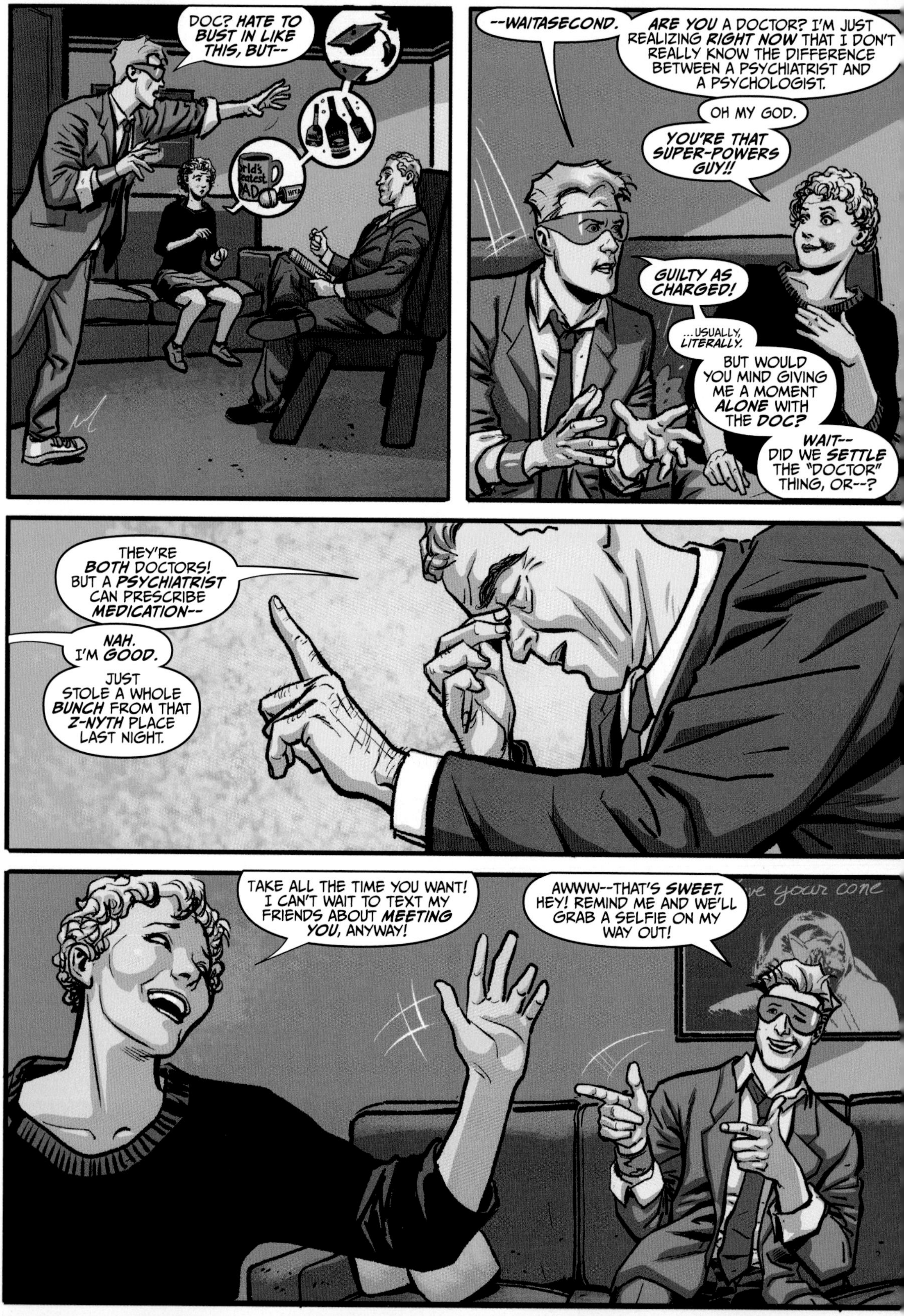
DOC? HATE TO BUST IN LIKE THIS, BUT--
--WAITASECOND.
ARE YOU A DOCTOR? I'M JUST REALIZING RIGHT NOW THAT I DON'T REALLY KNOW THE DIFFERENCE BETWEEN A PSYCHIATRIST AND A PSYCHOLOGIST.
OH MY GOD.
YOU'RE THAT SUPER-POWERS GUY!!
GUILTY AS CHARGED!
...USUALLY, LITERALLY.
BUT WOULD YOU MIND GIVING ME A MOMENT ALONE WITH THE DOC?
WAIT-- DID WE SETTLE THE "DOCTOR" THING, OR--?
THEY'RE BOTH DOCTORS! BUT A PSYCHIATRIST CAN PRESCRIBE MEDICATION--
NAH. I'M GOOD.
JUST STOLE A WHOLE BUNCH FROM THAT Z-NYTH PLACE LAST NIGHT.
TAKE ALL THE TIME YOU WANT! I CAN'T WAIT TO TEXT MY FRIENDS ABOUT MEETING YOU, ANYWAY!
AWWW--THAT'S SWEET. HEY! REMIND ME AND WE'LL GRAB A SELFIE ON MY WAY OUT!

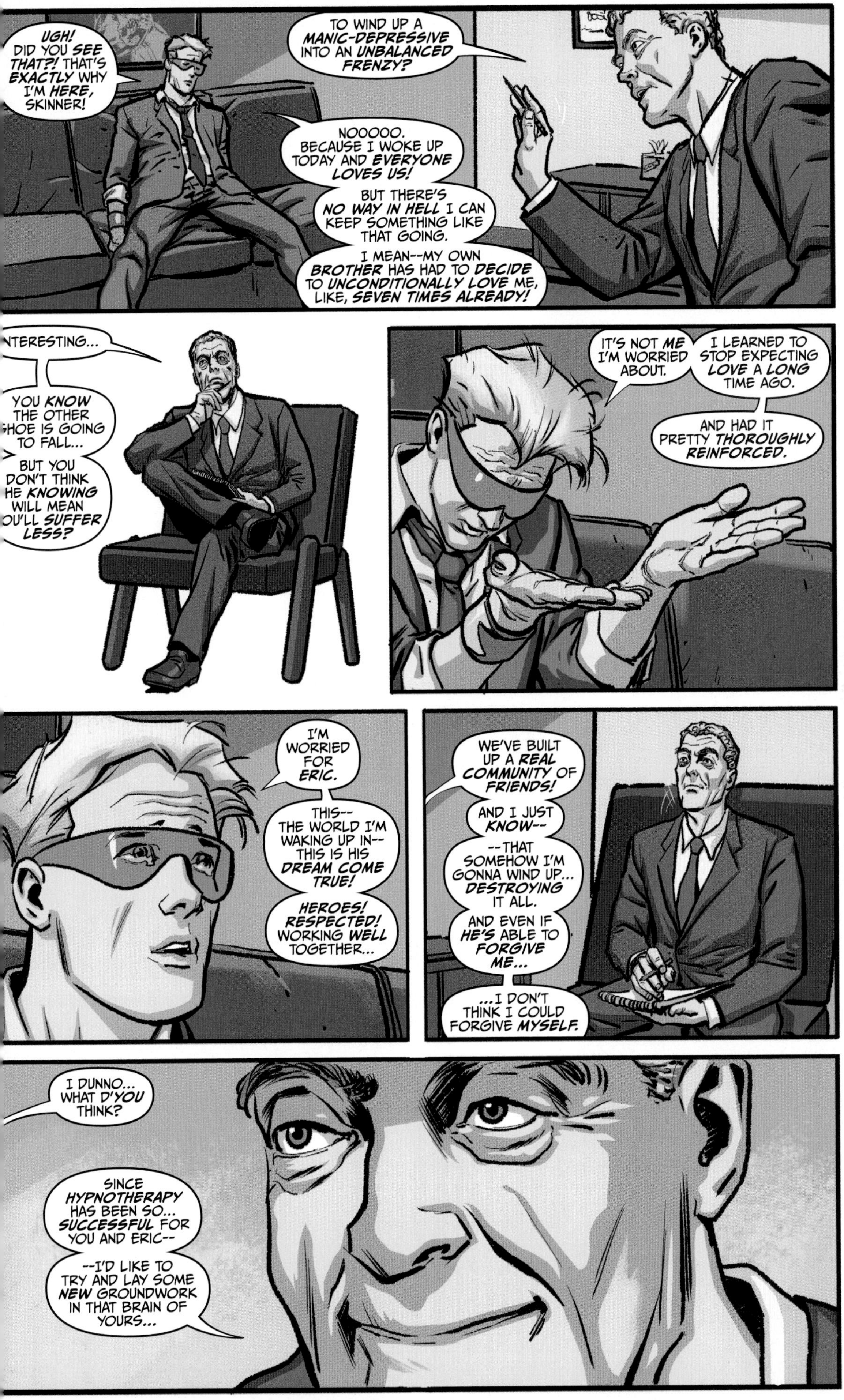
UGH! DID YOU SEE THAT?! THAT'S EXACTLY WHY I'M HERE, SKINNER!
TO WIND UP A MANIC-DEPRESSIVE INTO AN UNBALANCED FRENZY?
NOOOOO. BECAUSE I WOKE UP TODAY AND EVERYONE LOVES US!
BUT THERE'S NO WAY IN HELL I CAN KEEP SOMETHING LIKE THAT GOING.
I MEAN--MY OWN BROTHER HAS HAD TO DECIDE TO UNCONDITIONALLY LOVE ME, LIKE, SEVEN TIMES ALREADY!
NTERESTING...
YOU KNOW THE OTHER HOE IS GOING TO FALL...
BUT YOU DON'T THINK HE KNOWING WILL MEAN OU'LL SUFFER LESS?
IT'S NOT ME I'M WORRIED ABOUT.
I LEARNED TO STOP EXPECTING LOVE A LONG TIME AGO.
AND HAD IT PRETTY THOROUGHLY REINFORCED.
I'M WORRIED FOR ERIC.
THIS-- THE WORLD I'M WAKING UP IN-- THIS IS HIS DREAM COME TRUE!
HEROES! RESPECTED! WORKING WELL TOGETHER...
WE'VE BUILT UP A REAL COMMUNITY OF FRIENDS!
AND I JUST KNOW--
--THAT SOMEHOW I'M GONNA WIND UP... DESTROYING IT ALL.
AND EVEN IF HE'S ABLE TO FORGIVE ME...
...I DON'T THINK I COULD FORGIVE MYSELF.
I DUNNO... WHAT D'YOU THINK?
SINCE HYPNOTHERAPY HAS BEEN SO... SUCCESSFUL FOR YOU AND ERIC--
--I'D LIKE TO TRY AND LAY SOME NEW GROUNDWORK IN THAT BRAIN OF YOURS...

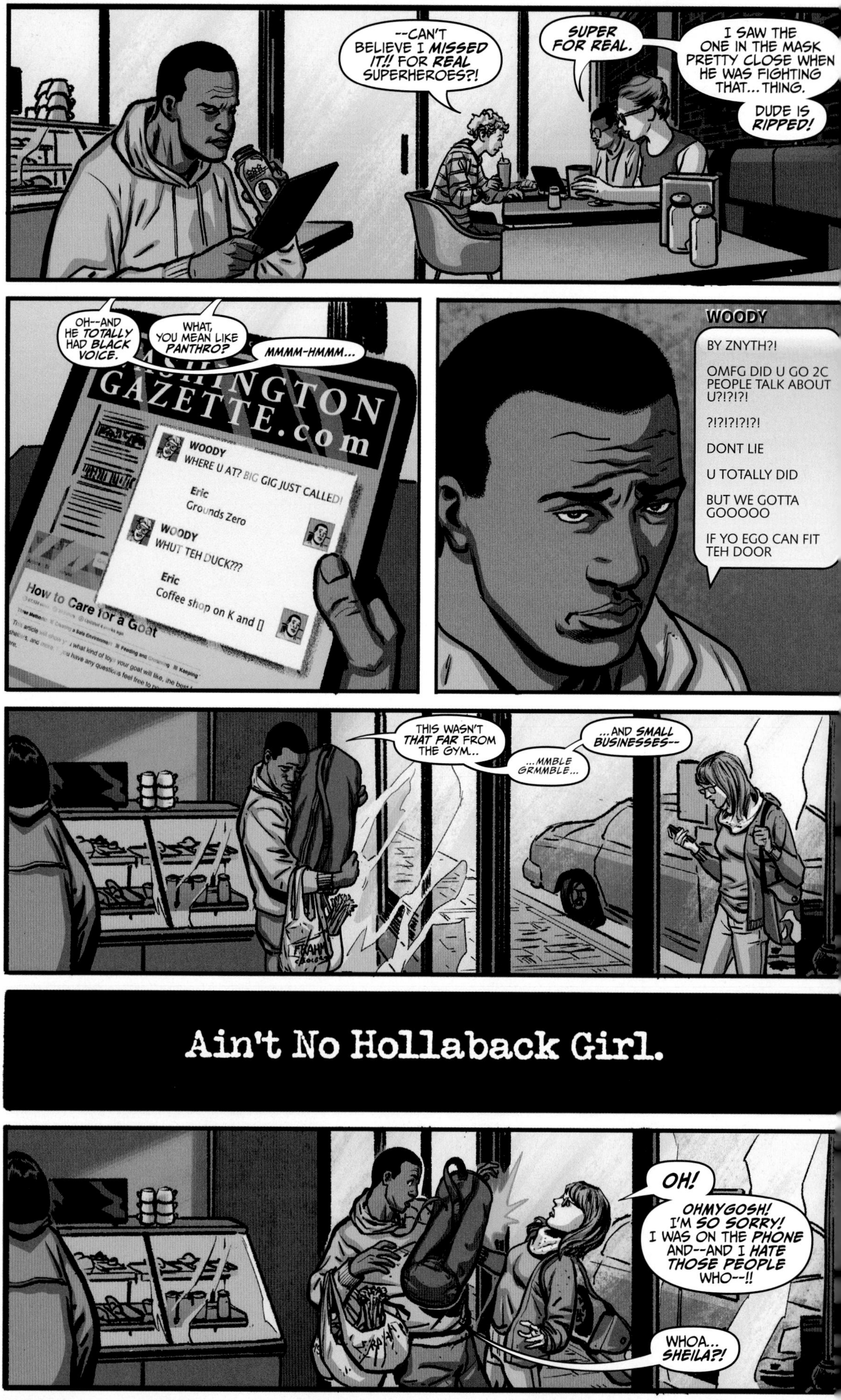
--CAN'T BELIEVE I MISSED IT!! FOR REAL SUPERHEROES?!
SUPER FOR REAL.
I SAW THE ONE IN THE MASK PRETTY CLOSE WHEN HE WAS FIGHTING THAT... THING.
DUDE IS RIPPED!
OH--AND HE TOTALLY HAD BLACK VOICE.
WHAT, YOU MEAN LIKE PANTHRO?
MMMM-HMMM...
GAZETTE.com
WOODY
WHERE U AT? BIG GIG JUST CALLED!
Eric
Grounds Zero
WOODY
WHUT TEH DUCK???
Eric
Coffee shop on K and []
How to Care for a Goat
WOODY
BY ZNYTH?!
OMFG DID U GO 2C PEOPLE TALK ABOUT U?!?!?!
?!?!?!?!?!
DONT LIE
U TOTALLY DID
BUT WE GOTTA GOOOOO
IF YO EGO CAN FIT TEH DOOR
THIS WASN'T THAT FAR FROM THE GYM...
...MMBLE GRMMBLE...
...AND SMALL BUSINESSES--
Ain't No Hollaback Girl.
OH!
OHMYGOSH! I'M SO SORRY! I WAS ON THE PHONE AND--AND I HATE THOSE PEOPLE WHO--!!
WHOA... SHEILA?!

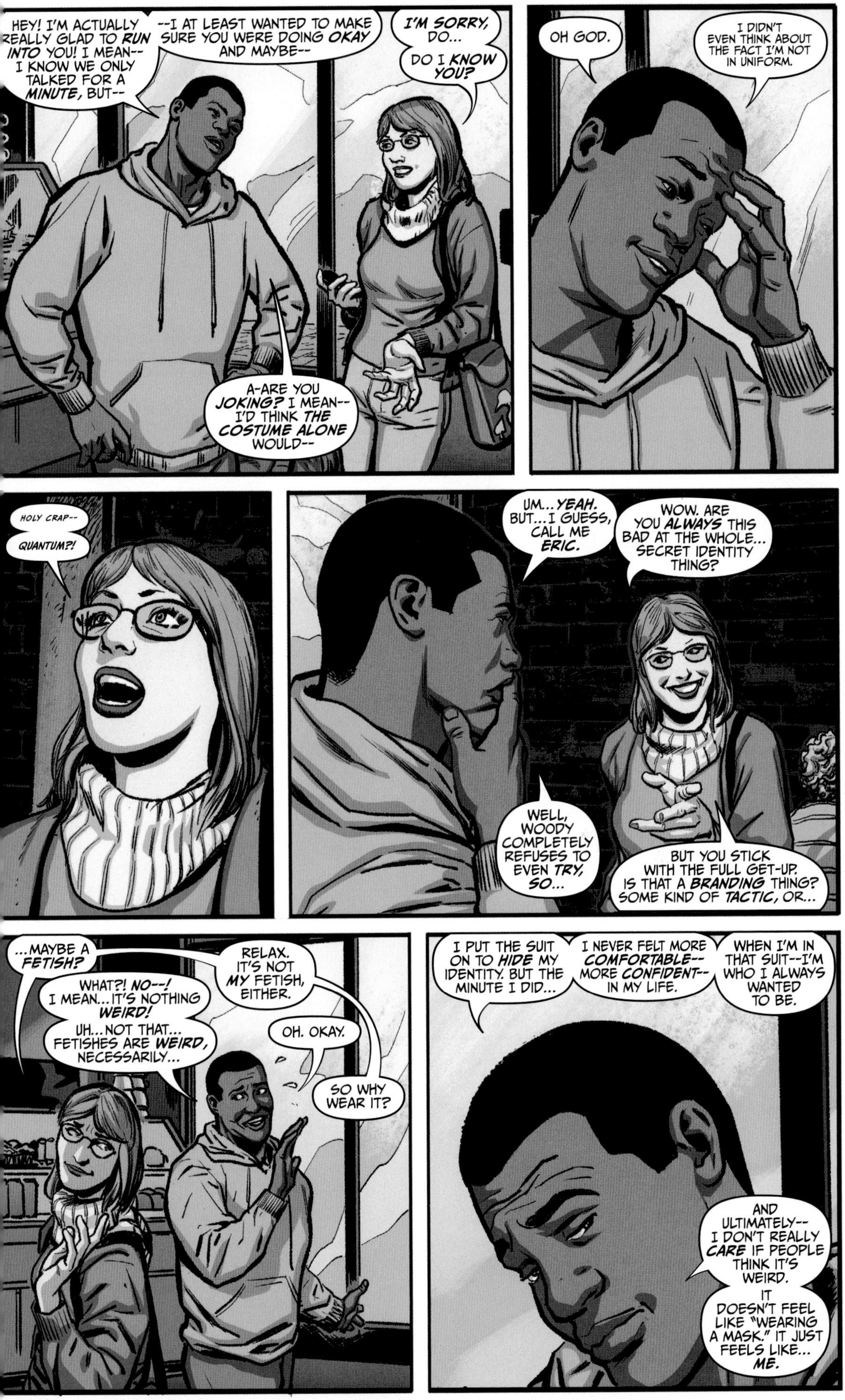
HEY! I'M ACTUALLY REALLY GLAD TO RUN INTO YOU! I MEAN-- I KNOW WE ONLY TALKED FOR A MINUTE, BUT--
--I AT LEAST WANTED TO MAKE SURE YOU WERE DOING OKAY AND MAYBE--
I'M SORRY, DO...
DO I KNOW YOU?
A-ARE YOU JOKING? I MEAN-- I'D THINK THE COSTUME ALONE WOULD--
OH GOD.
I DIDN'T EVEN THINK ABOUT THE FACT I'M NOT IN UNIFORM.
HOLY CRAP--
QUANTUM?!
UM...YEAH. BUT...I GUESS, CALL ME ERIC.
WOW. ARE YOU ALWAYS THIS BAD AT THE WHOLE... SECRET IDENTITY THING?
WELL, WOODY COMPLETELY REFUSES TO EVEN TRY, SO...
BUT YOU STICK WITH THE FULL GET-UP. IS THAT A BRANDING THING? SOME KIND OF TACTIC, OR...
...MAYBE A FETISH?
WHAT?! NO--! I MEAN...IT'S NOTHING WEIRD!
UH...NOT THAT... FETISHES ARE WEIRD, NECESSARILY...
RELAX. IT'S NOT MY FETISH, EITHER.
OH. OKAY.
SO WHY WEAR IT?
I PUT THE SUIT ON TO HIDE MY IDENTITY. BUT THE MINUTE I DID...
I NEVER FELT MORE COMFORTABLE-- MORE CONFIDENT-- IN MY LIFE.
WHEN I'M IN THAT SUIT--I'M WHO I ALWAYS WANTED TO BE.
AND ULTIMATELY-- I DON'T REALLY CARE IF PEOPLE THINK IT'S WEIRD.
IT DOESN'T FEEL LIKE "WEARING A MASK." IT JUST FEELS LIKE... ME.

SMEK! ♥

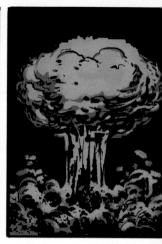

SORRY, I-- UM... THAT JUST STRUCK MORE OF A *CHORD* THAN I WAS EXPECTING...

♫

OH, *BALLS*. THE BOSS IS CALLING!

WAI--THA *WHUH...?*

NOT SPRINGSTEEN. MY *ACTUAL BOSS.*

DOUBLE *BALLS!* I GOTTA GO.

WAIT! BUT--

I'M *SORRY.* I WAS ONLY SUPPOSED TO BE GONE FOR A *MINUTE. SORRY!*

YOU WEREN'T ANSWERING MY *OFFICE CALLS,* SHEILA. IS THAT YOUR *RESIGNATION?*

I'D HOPE NOT. I'M NOT SURE YOUR *NEXT* JOB WOULD SO LIBERALLY COVER THE *TREATMENT* FOR YOUR... *CONDITION.*

NO, MA'AM.

IT'S NOT A *CONDITION.* I'M--

GOING TO CANCEL MY *AFTERNOON APPOINTMENTS.*

IT SEEMS THERE'S A BIT OF *PROPRIETARY EQUITY* OUT THERE I NEED TO... SHORE UP.

WELL, *THAT* FELT LIKE *MIXED SIGNALS.*

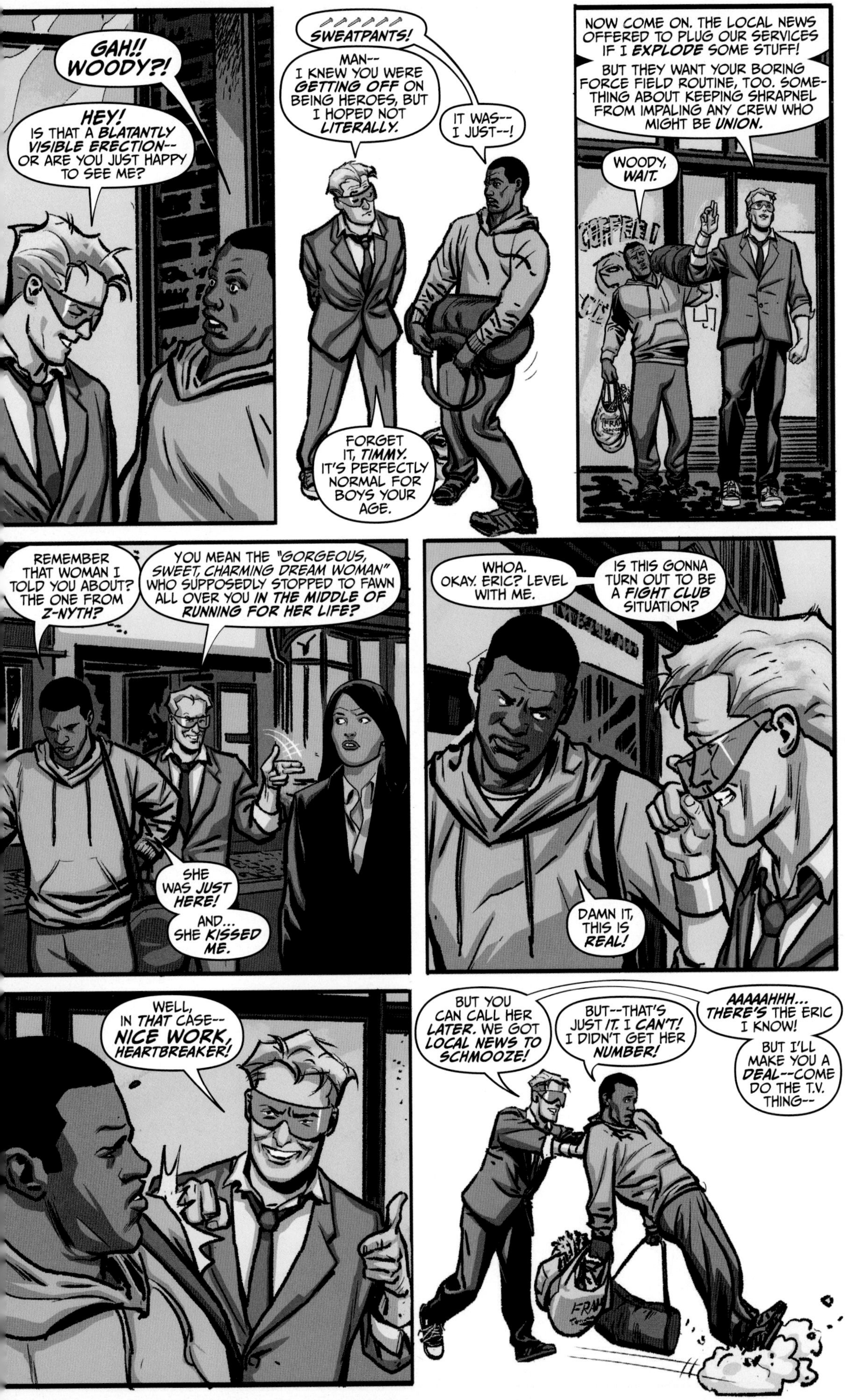
GAH!! WOODY?!
HEY! IS THAT A BLATANTLY VISIBLE ERECTION-- OR ARE YOU JUST HAPPY TO SEE ME?
SWEATPANTS!
MAN-- I KNEW YOU WERE GETTING OFF ON BEING HEROES, BUT I HOPED NOT LITERALLY.
IT WAS-- I JUST--!
FORGET IT, TIMMY. IT'S PERFECTLY NORMAL FOR BOYS YOUR AGE.
NOW COME ON. THE LOCAL NEWS OFFERED TO PLUG OUR SERVICES IF I EXPLODE SOME STUFF!
BUT THEY WANT YOUR BORING FORCE FIELD ROUTINE, TOO. SOMETHING ABOUT KEEPING SHRAPNEL FROM IMPALING ANY CREW WHO MIGHT BE UNION.
WOODY, WAIT.
REMEMBER THAT WOMAN I TOLD YOU ABOUT? THE ONE FROM Z-NYTH?
YOU MEAN THE "GORGEOUS, SWEET, CHARMING DREAM WOMAN" WHO SUPPOSEDLY STOPPED TO FAWN ALL OVER YOU IN THE MIDDLE OF RUNNING FOR HER LIFE?
SHE WAS JUST HERE!
AND... SHE KISSED ME.
WHOA. OKAY. ERIC? LEVEL WITH ME.
IS THIS GONNA TURN OUT TO BE A FIGHT CLUB SITUATION?
DAMN IT, THIS IS REAL!
WELL, IN THAT CASE-- NICE WORK, HEARTBREAKER!
BUT YOU CAN CALL HER LATER. WE GOT LOCAL NEWS TO SCHMOOZE!
BUT--THAT'S JUST IT. I CAN'T! I DIDN'T GET HER NUMBER!
AAAAAHHH... THERE'S THE ERIC I KNOW!
BUT I'LL MAKE YOU A DEAL--COME DO THE T.V. THING--

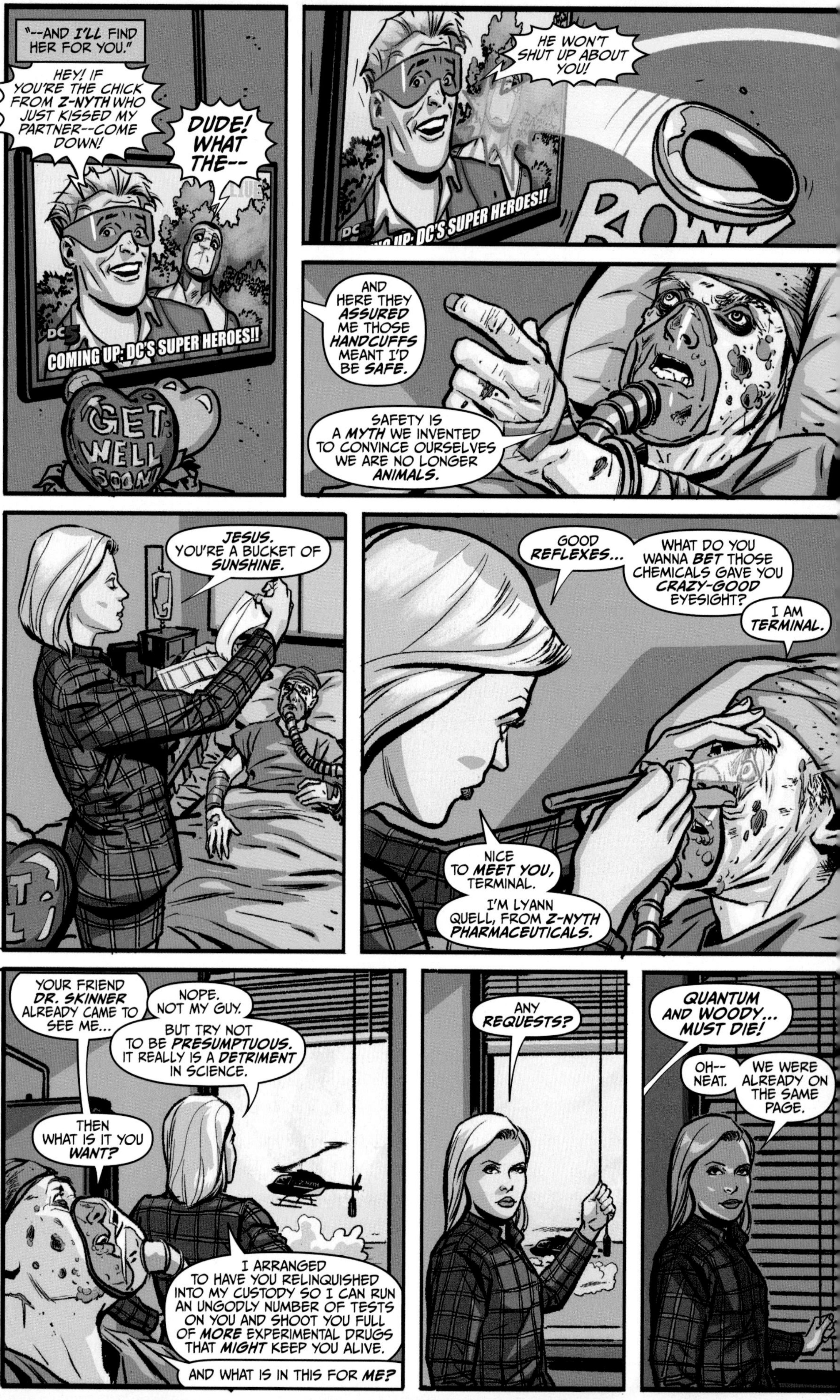
"--AND I'LL FIND HER FOR YOU."
HEY! IF YOU'RE THE CHICK FROM Z-NYTH WHO JUST KISSED MY PARTNER--COME DOWN!
DUDE! WHAT THE--
DC 5
COMING UP: DC'S SUPER HEROES!!
GET WELL SOON!
HE WON'T SHUT UP ABOUT YOU!
UP: DC'S SUPER HEROES!!
AND HERE THEY ASSURED ME THOSE HANDCUFFS MEANT I'D BE SAFE.
SAFETY IS A MYTH WE INVENTED TO CONVINCE OURSELVES WE ARE NO LONGER ANIMALS.
JESUS. YOU'RE A BUCKET OF SUNSHINE.
GOOD REFLEXES...
WHAT DO YOU WANNA BET THOSE CHEMICALS GAVE YOU CRAZY-GOOD EYESIGHT?
I AM TERMINAL.
NICE TO MEET YOU, TERMINAL.
I'M LYANN QUELL, FROM Z-NYTH PHARMACEUTICALS.
YOUR FRIEND DR. SKINNER ALREADY CAME TO SEE ME...
NOPE. NOT MY GUY.
BUT TRY NOT TO BE PRESUMPTUOUS. IT REALLY IS A DETRIMENT IN SCIENCE.
THEN WHAT IS IT YOU WANT?
I ARRANGED TO HAVE YOU RELINQUISHED INTO MY CUSTODY SO I CAN RUN AN UNGODLY NUMBER OF TESTS ON YOU AND SHOOT YOU FULL OF MORE EXPERIMENTAL DRUGS THAT MIGHT KEEP YOU ALIVE.
AND WHAT IS IN THIS FOR ME?
ANY REQUESTS?
QUANTUM AND WOODY... MUST DIE!
OH-- NEAT.
WE WERE ALREADY ON THE SAME PAGE.

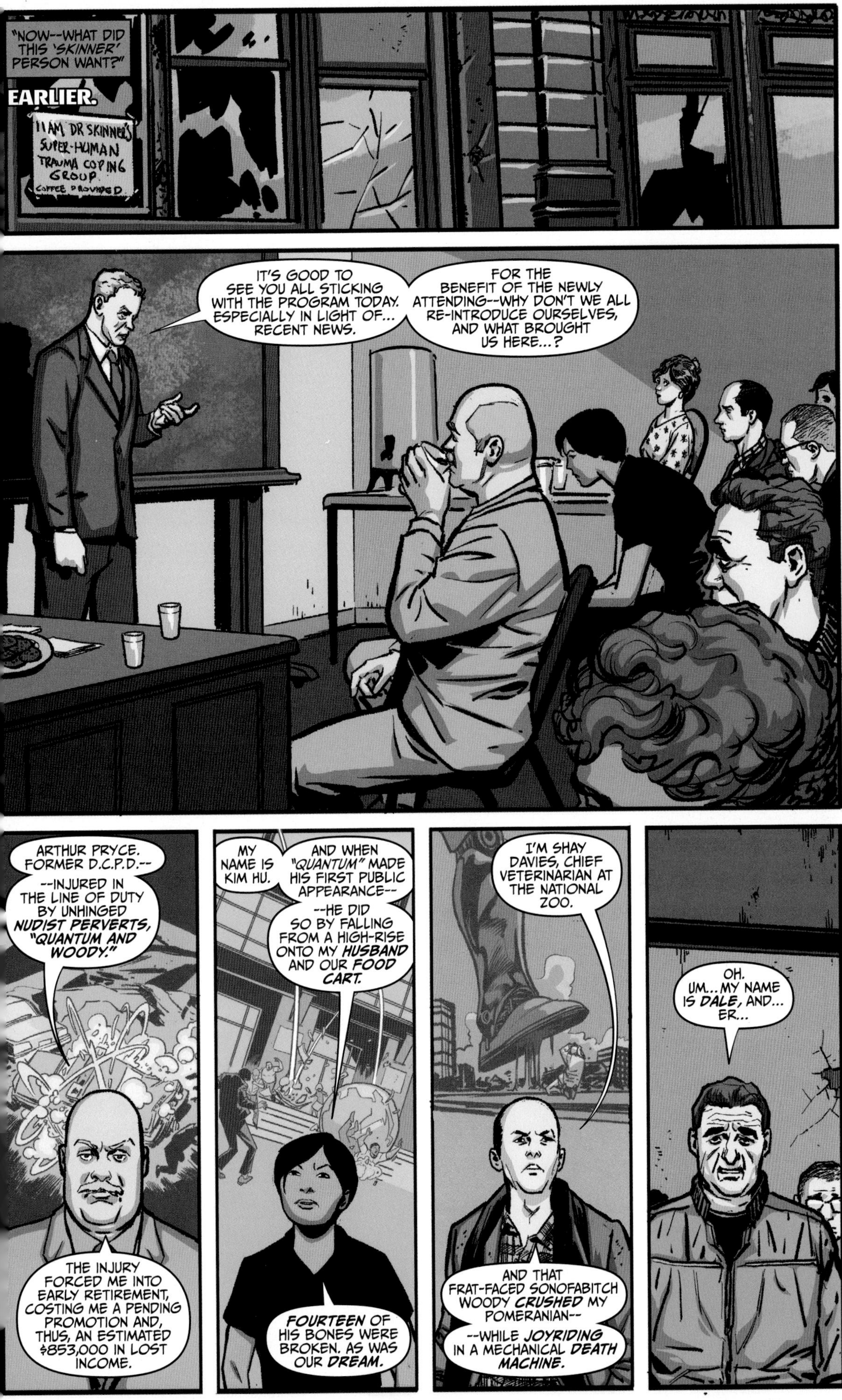
"NOW--WHAT DID THIS 'SKINNER' PERSON WANT?"
EARLIER.
11 AM DR SKINNER'S SUPER-HUMAN TRAUMA COPING GROUP COFFEE PROVIDED
IT'S GOOD TO SEE YOU ALL STICKING WITH THE PROGRAM TODAY. ESPECIALLY IN LIGHT OF... RECENT NEWS.
FOR THE BENEFIT OF THE NEWLY ATTENDING--WHY DON'T WE ALL RE-INTRODUCE OURSELVES, AND WHAT BROUGHT US HERE...?
ARTHUR PRYCE. FORMER D.C.P.D.--
--INJURED IN THE LINE OF DUTY BY UNHINGED NUDIST PERVERTS, "QUANTUM AND WOODY."
THE INJURY FORCED ME INTO EARLY RETIREMENT, COSTING ME A PENDING PROMOTION AND, THUS, AN ESTIMATED $853,000 IN LOST INCOME.
MY NAME IS KIM HU.
AND WHEN "QUANTUM" MADE HIS FIRST PUBLIC APPEARANCE--
--HE DID SO BY FALLING FROM A HIGH-RISE ONTO MY HUSBAND AND OUR FOOD CART.
FOURTEEN OF HIS BONES WERE BROKEN. AS WAS OUR DREAM.
I'M SHAY DAVIES, CHIEF VETERINARIAN AT THE NATIONAL ZOO.
AND THAT FRAT-FACED SONOFABITCH WOODY CRUSHED MY POMERANIAN--
--WHILE JOYRIDING IN A MECHANICAL DEATH MACHINE.
OH. UM...MY NAME IS DALE, AND... ER...

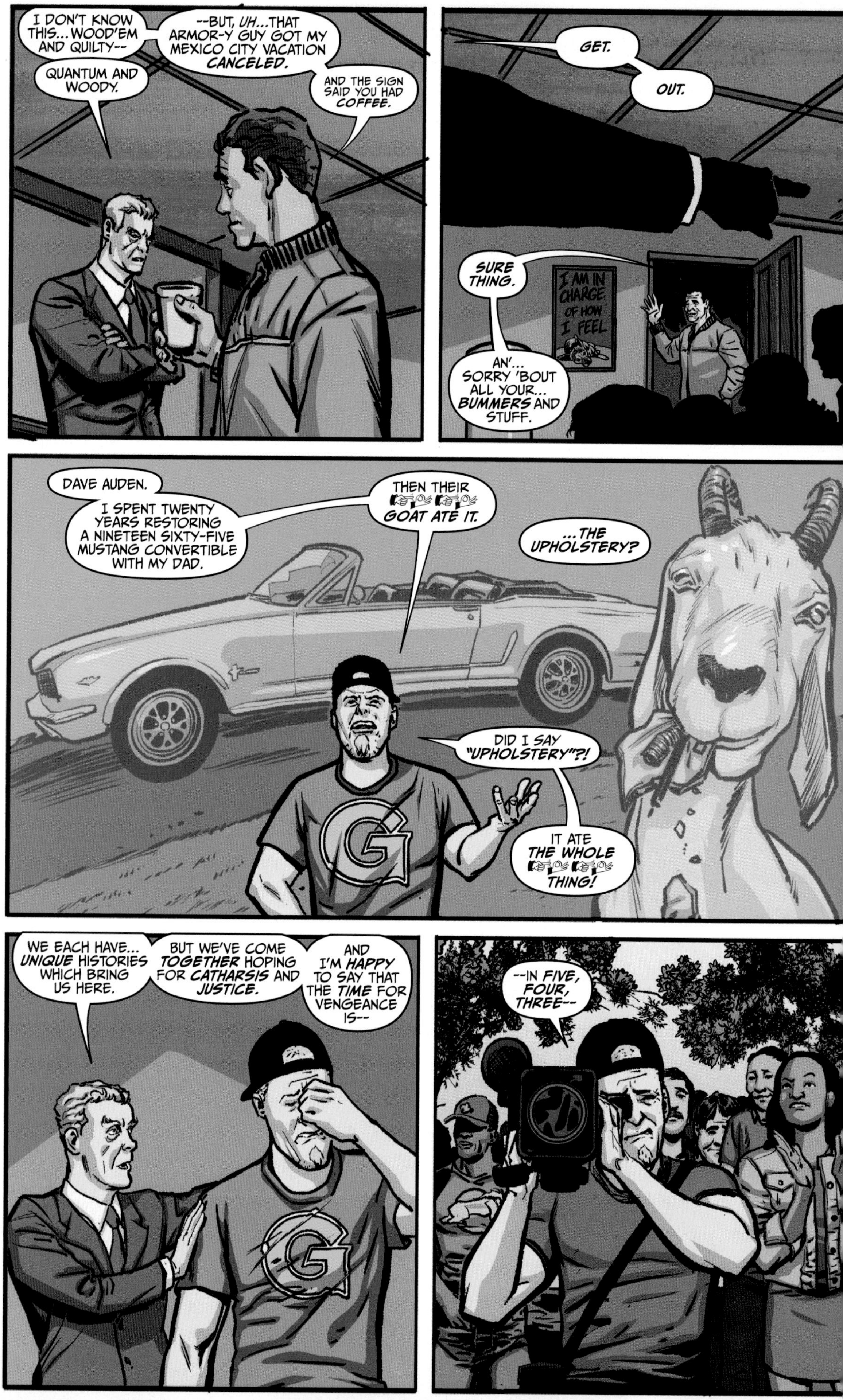
I DON'T KNOW THIS... WOOD'EM AND QUILTY--
QUANTUM AND WOODY.
--BUT, UH...THAT ARMOR-Y GUY GOT MY MEXICO CITY VACATION CANCELED.
AND THE SIGN SAID YOU HAD COFFEE.
GET.
OUT.
I AM IN CHARGE OF HOW I FEEL
SURE THING.
AN'... SORRY 'BOUT ALL YOUR... BUMMERS AND STUFF.
DAVE AUDEN.
I SPENT TWENTY YEARS RESTORING A NINETEEN SIXTY-FIVE MUSTANG CONVERTIBLE WITH MY DAD.
THEN THEIR GOAT ATE IT.
...THE UPHOLSTERY?
DID I SAY "UPHOLSTERY"?!
IT ATE THE WHOLE THING!
WE EACH HAVE... UNIQUE HISTORIES WHICH BRING US HERE.
BUT WE'VE COME TOGETHER HOPING FOR CATHARSIS AND JUSTICE.
AND I'M HAPPY TO SAY THAT THE TIME FOR VENGEANCE IS--
--IN FIVE, FOUR, THREE--

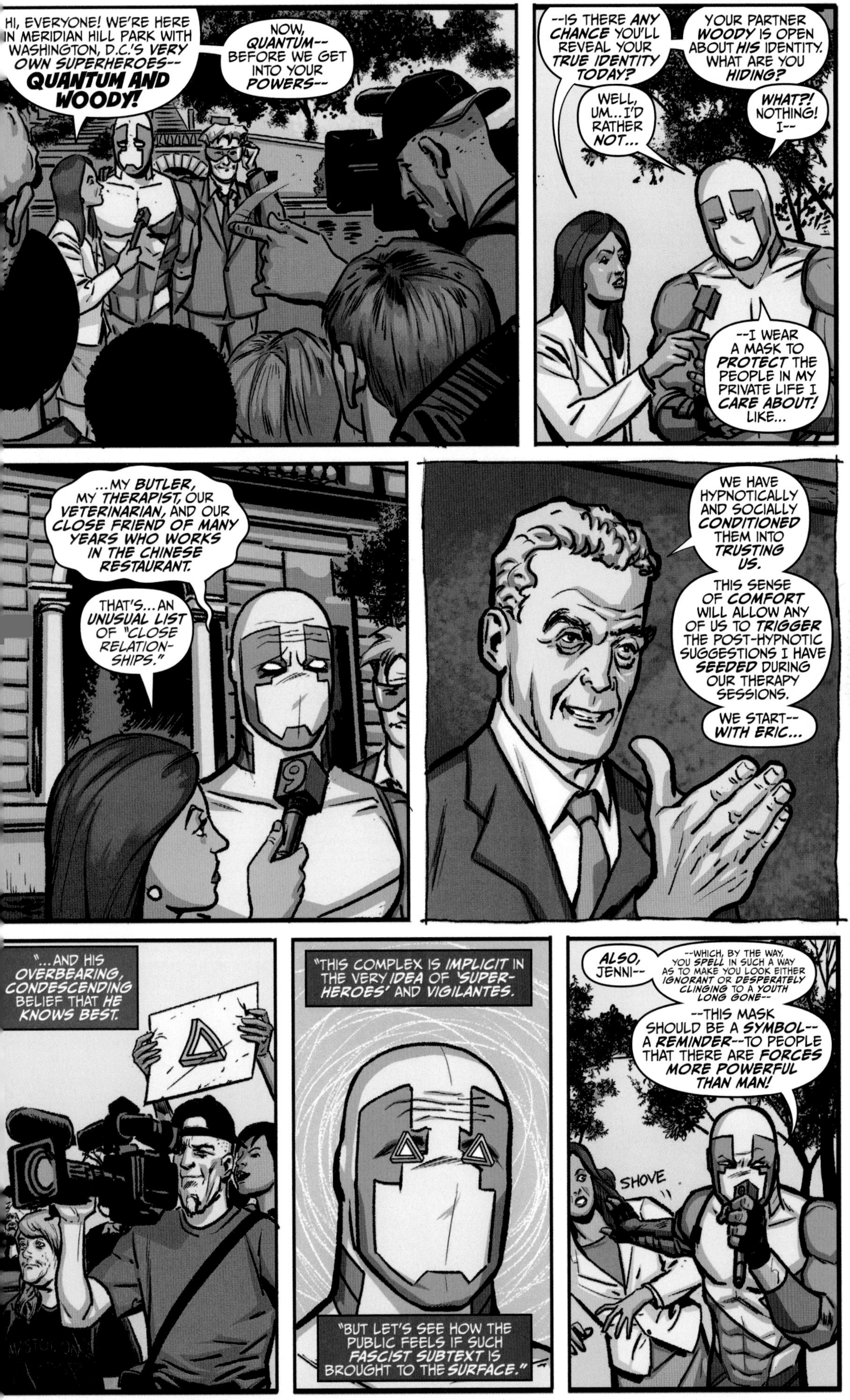

HI, EVERYONE! WE'RE HERE IN MERIDIAN HILL PARK WITH WASHINGTON, D.C.'S VERY OWN SUPERHEROES-- QUANTUM AND WOODY!
NOW, QUANTUM-- BEFORE WE GET INTO YOUR POWERS--
--IS THERE ANY CHANCE YOU'LL REVEAL YOUR TRUE IDENTITY TODAY?
WELL, UM...I'D RATHER NOT...
YOUR PARTNER WOODY IS OPEN ABOUT HIS IDENTITY. WHAT ARE YOU HIDING?
WHAT?! NOTHING! I--
--I WEAR A MASK TO PROTECT THE PEOPLE IN MY PRIVATE LIFE I CARE ABOUT! LIKE...
...MY BUTLER, MY THERAPIST, OUR VETERINARIAN, AND OUR CLOSE FRIEND OF MANY YEARS WHO WORKS IN THE CHINESE RESTAURANT.
THAT'S...AN UNUSUAL LIST OF "CLOSE RELATION-SHIPS."
9
WE HAVE HYPNOTICALLY AND SOCIALLY CONDITIONED THEM INTO TRUSTING US.
THIS SENSE OF COMFORT WILL ALLOW ANY OF US TO TRIGGER THE POST-HYPNOTIC SUGGESTIONS I HAVE SEEDED DURING OUR THERAPY SESSIONS.
WE START-- WITH ERIC...
"...AND HIS OVERBEARING, CONDESCENDING BELIEF THAT HE KNOWS BEST.
"THIS COMPLEX IS IMPLICIT IN THE VERY IDEA OF 'SUPER-HEROES' AND VIGILANTES.
"BUT LET'S SEE HOW THE PUBLIC FEELS IF SUCH FASCIST SUBTEXT IS BROUGHT TO THE SURFACE."
ALSO, JENNI--
--WHICH, BY THE WAY, YOU SPELL IN SUCH A WAY AS TO MAKE YOU LOOK EITHER IGNORANT OR DESPERATELY CLINGING TO A YOUTH LONG GONE--
--THIS MASK SHOULD BE A SYMBOL-- A REMINDER--TO PEOPLE THAT THERE ARE FORCES MORE POWERFUL THAN MAN!
SHOVE

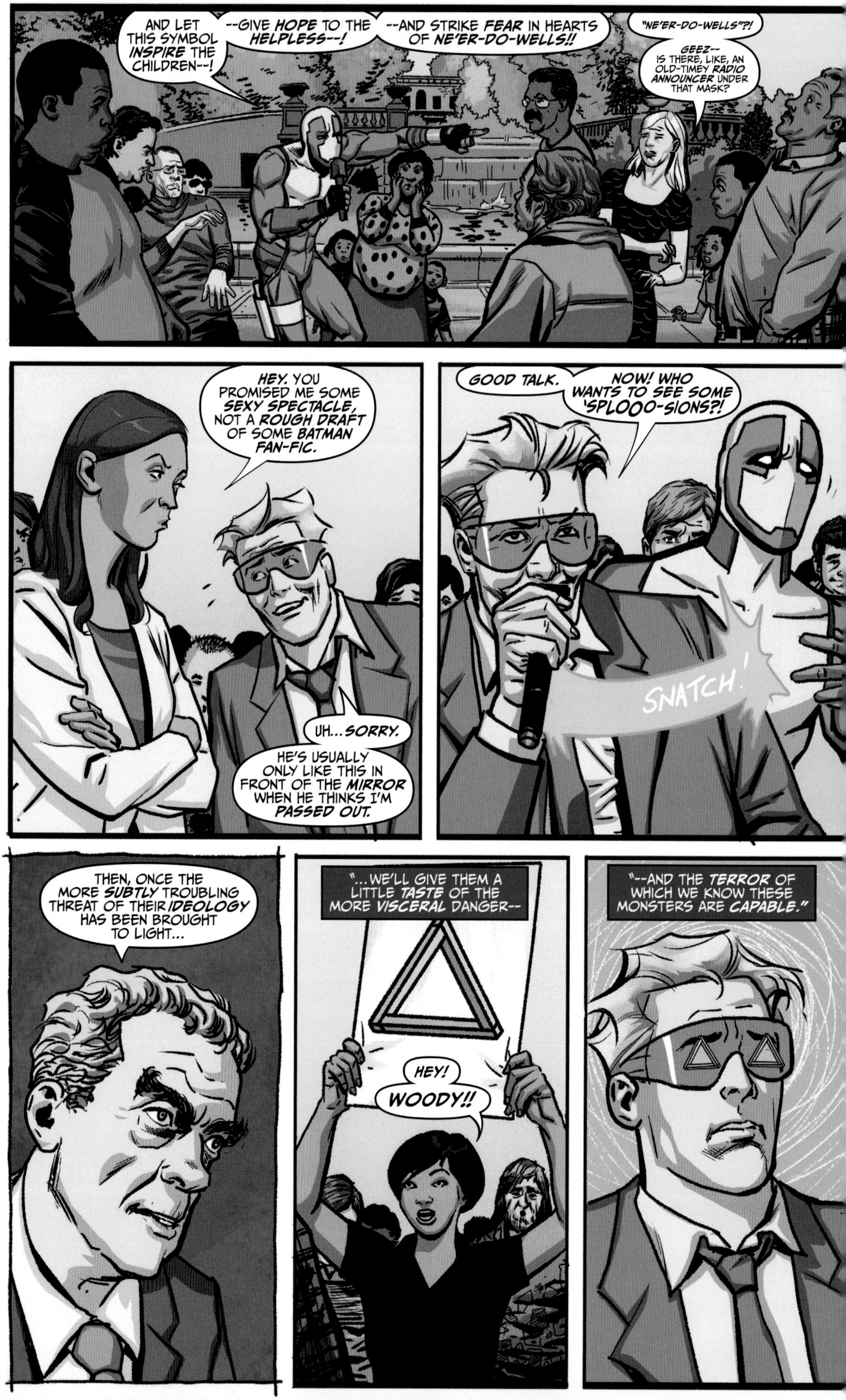
AND LET THIS SYMBOL INSPIRE THE CHILDREN--!
--GIVE HOPE TO THE HELPLESS--!
--AND STRIKE FEAR IN HEARTS OF NE'ER-DO-WELLS!!
"NE'ER-DO-WELLS"?!
GEEZ-- IS THERE, LIKE, AN OLD-TIMEY RADIO ANNOUNCER UNDER THAT MASK?
HEY. YOU PROMISED ME SOME SEXY SPECTACLE, NOT A ROUGH DRAFT OF SOME BATMAN FAN-FIC.
UH...SORRY.
HE'S USUALLY ONLY LIKE THIS IN FRONT OF THE MIRROR WHEN HE THINKS I'M PASSED OUT.
GOOD TALK.
NOW! WHO WANTS TO SEE SOME 'SPLOOO-SIONS?!
SNATCH!
THEN, ONCE THE MORE SUBTLY TROUBLING THREAT OF THEIR IDEOLOGY HAS BEEN BROUGHT TO LIGHT...
"...WE'LL GIVE THEM A LITTLE TASTE OF THE MORE VISCERAL DANGER--
HEY!
WOODY!!
"--AND THE TERROR OF WHICH WE KNOW THESE MONSTERS ARE CAPABLE."

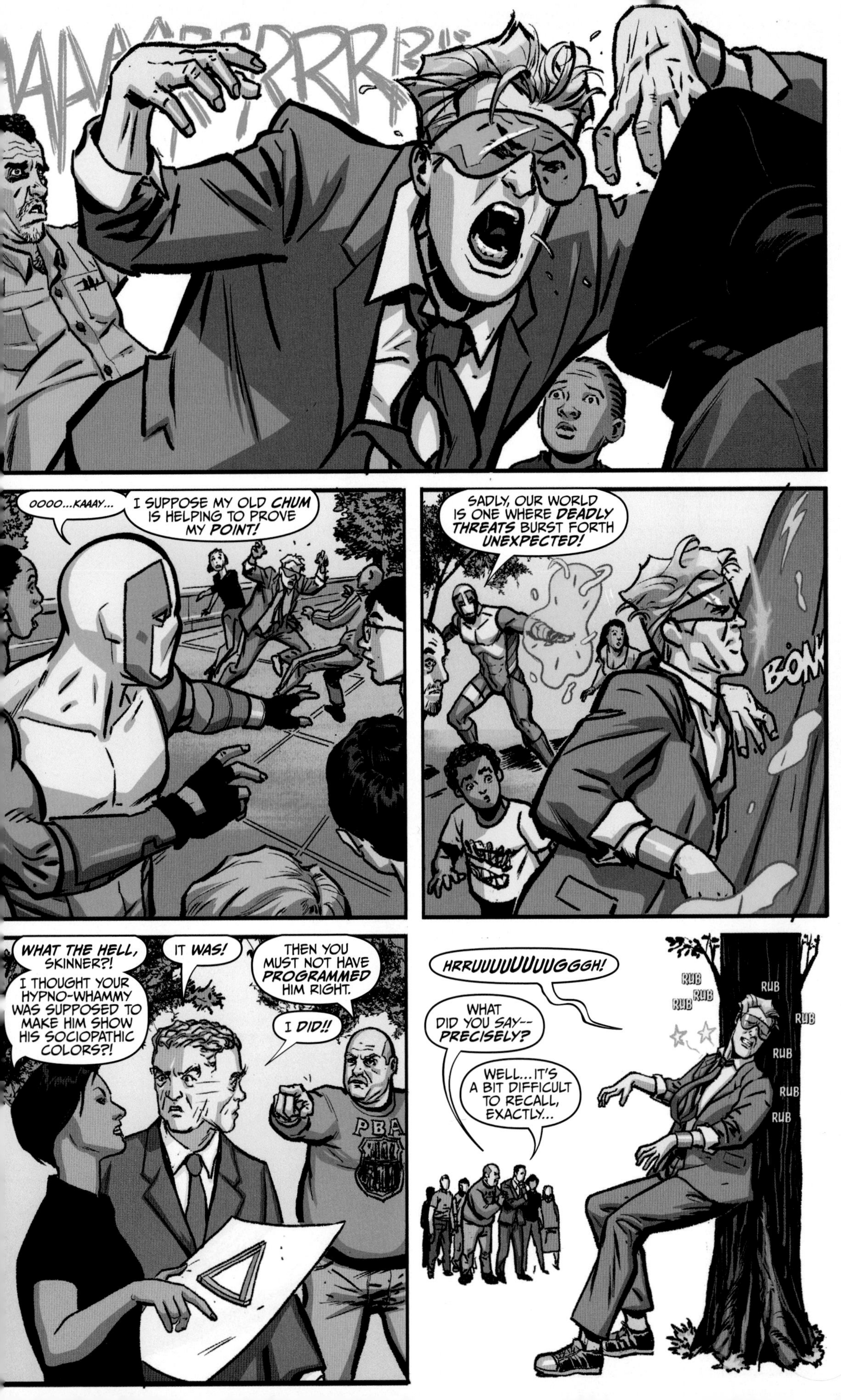

OOOO...KAAAY...
I SUPPOSE MY OLD CHUM IS HELPING TO PROVE MY POINT!
SADLY, OUR WORLD IS ONE WHERE DEADLY THREATS BURST FORTH UNEXPECTED!
WHAT THE HELL, SKINNER?!
I THOUGHT YOUR HYPNO-WHAMMY WAS SUPPOSED TO MAKE HIM SHOW HIS SOCIOPATHIC COLORS?!
IT WAS!
THEN YOU MUST NOT HAVE PROGRAMMED HIM RIGHT.
I DID!!
PBA
HRRUUUUUUUUGGGH!
RUB RUB RUB RUB RUB RUB RUB RUB
WHAT DID YOU SAY-- PRECISELY?
WELL...IT'S A BIT DIFFICULT TO RECALL, EXACTLY...

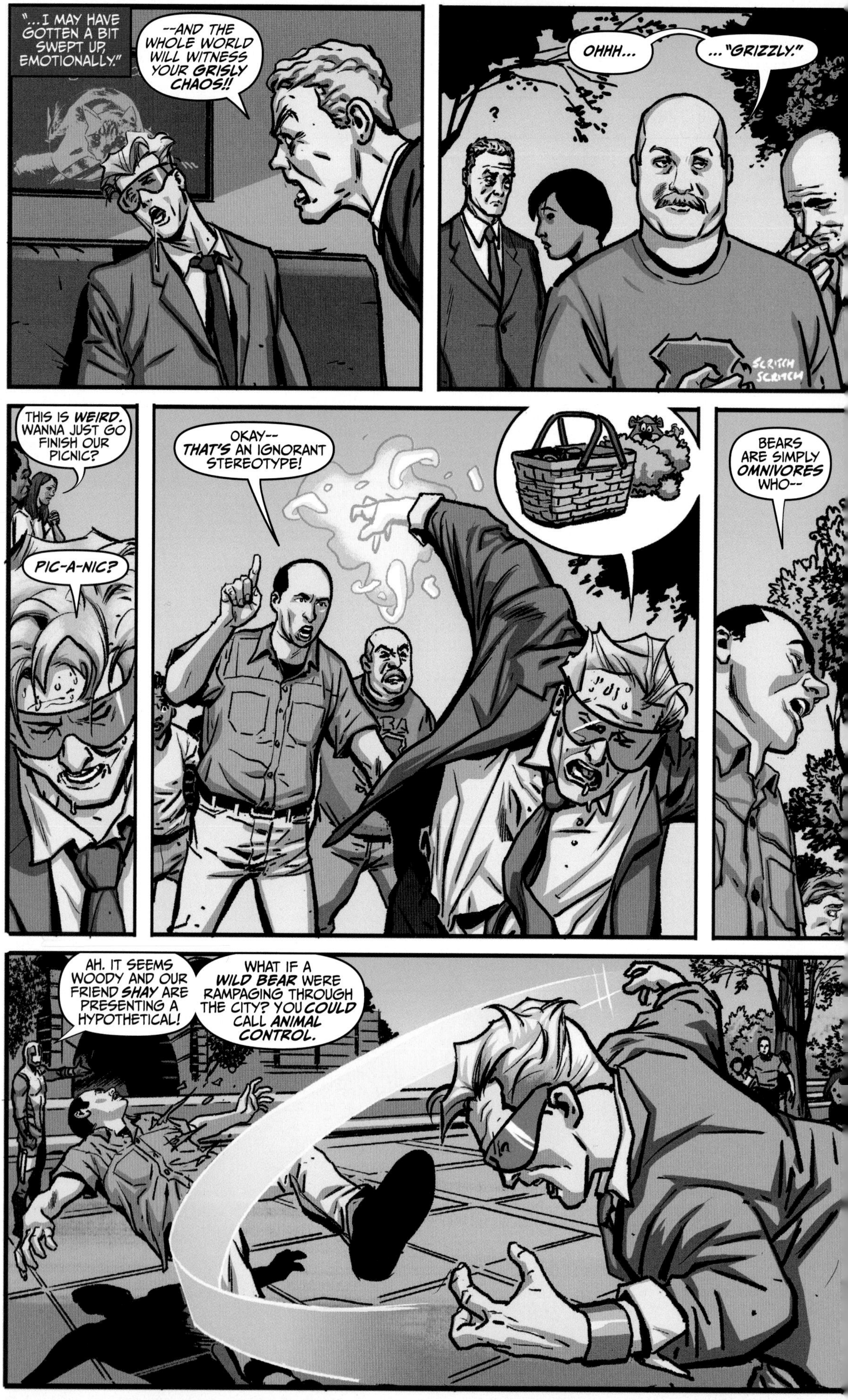
"...I MAY HAVE GOTTEN A BIT SWEPT UP, EMOTIONALLY."
--AND THE WHOLE WORLD WILL WITNESS YOUR GRISLY CHAOS!!
OHHH...
..."GRIZZLY."
?
SCRITCH SCRATCH
THIS IS WEIRD. WANNA JUST GO FINISH OUR PICNIC?
PIC-A-NIC?
OKAY-- THAT'S AN IGNORANT STEREOTYPE!
BEARS ARE SIMPLY OMNIVORES WHO--
AH. IT SEEMS WOODY AND OUR FRIEND SHAY ARE PRESENTING A HYPOTHETICAL!
WHAT IF A WILD BEAR WERE RAMPAGING THROUGH THE CITY? YOU COULD CALL ANIMAL CONTROL.

BUT! WHAT IF *THIS* ANIMAL WAS AN EXPERIMENT? SAY, *SMARTER* THAN THE AVERAGE BEAR--?

IS THAT YOUR *ONLY* FRAME OF *REFERENCE* FOR B--

OH, CRAP...

--OR A BEAR WITH *EXPLOSION* POWERS?

YOU MAY *LAUGH,* BUT THESE *FANTASTICAL DANGERS* ARE ON THE *RISE* ALL AROUND THE *WORLD.*

SO WHEN A SMART EXPLOSION-BEAR COMES FOR *YOUR* PICNIC, WILL YOU WANT *ANIMAL CONTROL*--

--OR *SOMEONE* WHO CAN DO *THIS?*

QUANTUM AND WOODY!

(HE'LL BE FINE.)

PROTECTION FOR YOUR PLEASURE!

WHAT THE--?!

HOLY SNEAK ATTA--

EEEOOOOOEEEEEOOOOOEEEEEOOOOEEEE

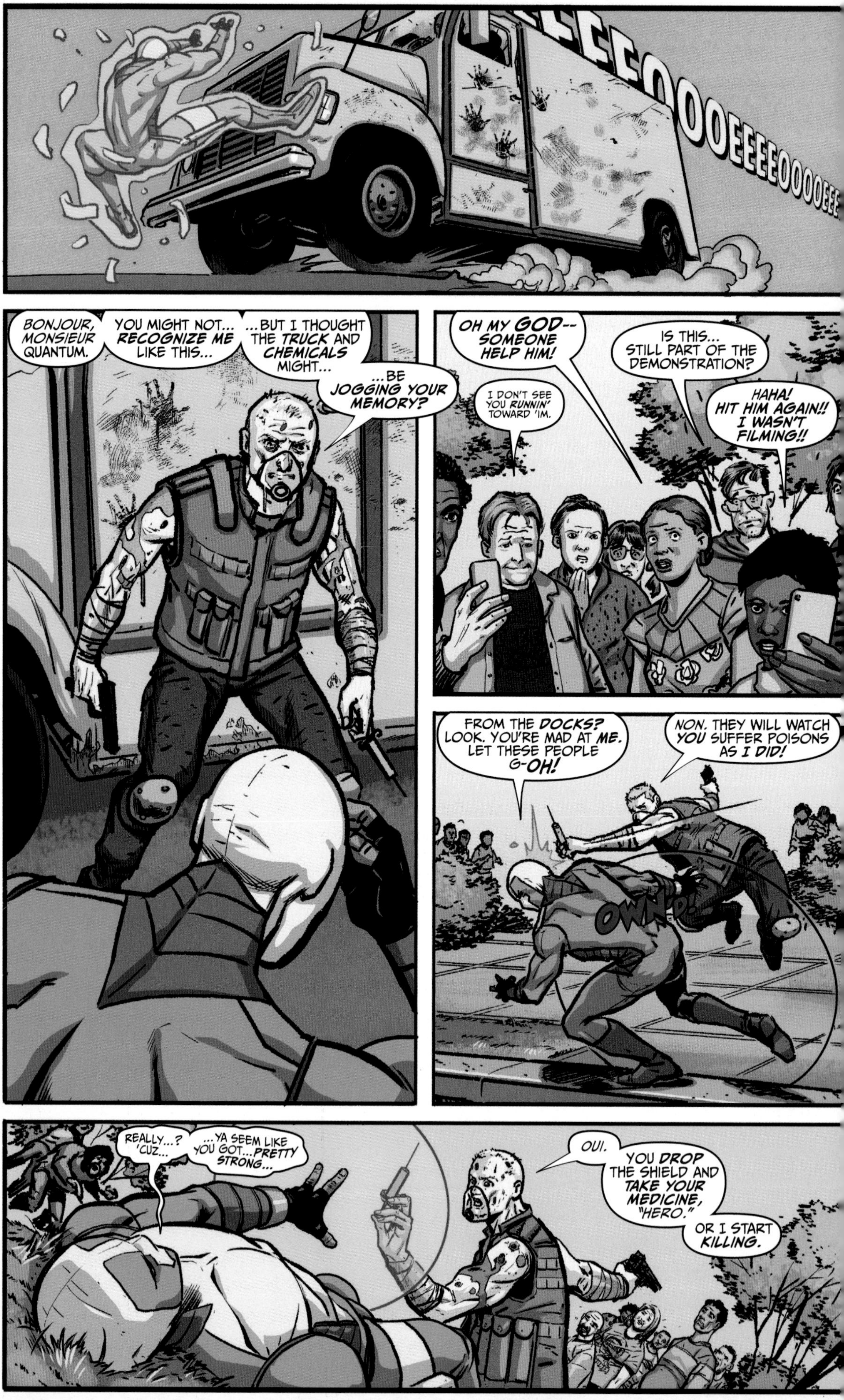
EEEEOOOEEEEOOOOEEE
BONJOUR, MONSIEUR QUANTUM.
YOU MIGHT NOT... RECOGNIZE ME LIKE THIS...
...BUT I THOUGHT THE TRUCK AND CHEMICALS MIGHT...
...BE JOGGING YOUR MEMORY?
OH MY GOD-- SOMEONE HELP HIM!
I DON'T SEE YOU RUNNIN' TOWARD 'IM.
IS THIS... STILL PART OF THE DEMONSTRATION?
HAHA! HIT HIM AGAIN!! I WASN'T FILMING!!
FROM THE DOCKS? LOOK. YOU'RE MAD AT ME. LET THESE PEOPLE G-OH!
NON. THEY WILL WATCH YOU SUFFER POISONS AS I DID!
OWND!
REALLY...? 'CUZ...
...YA SEEM LIKE YOU GOT...PRETTY STRONG...
OUI.
YOU DROP THE SHIELD AND TAKE YOUR MEDICINE, "HERO."
OR I START KILLING.

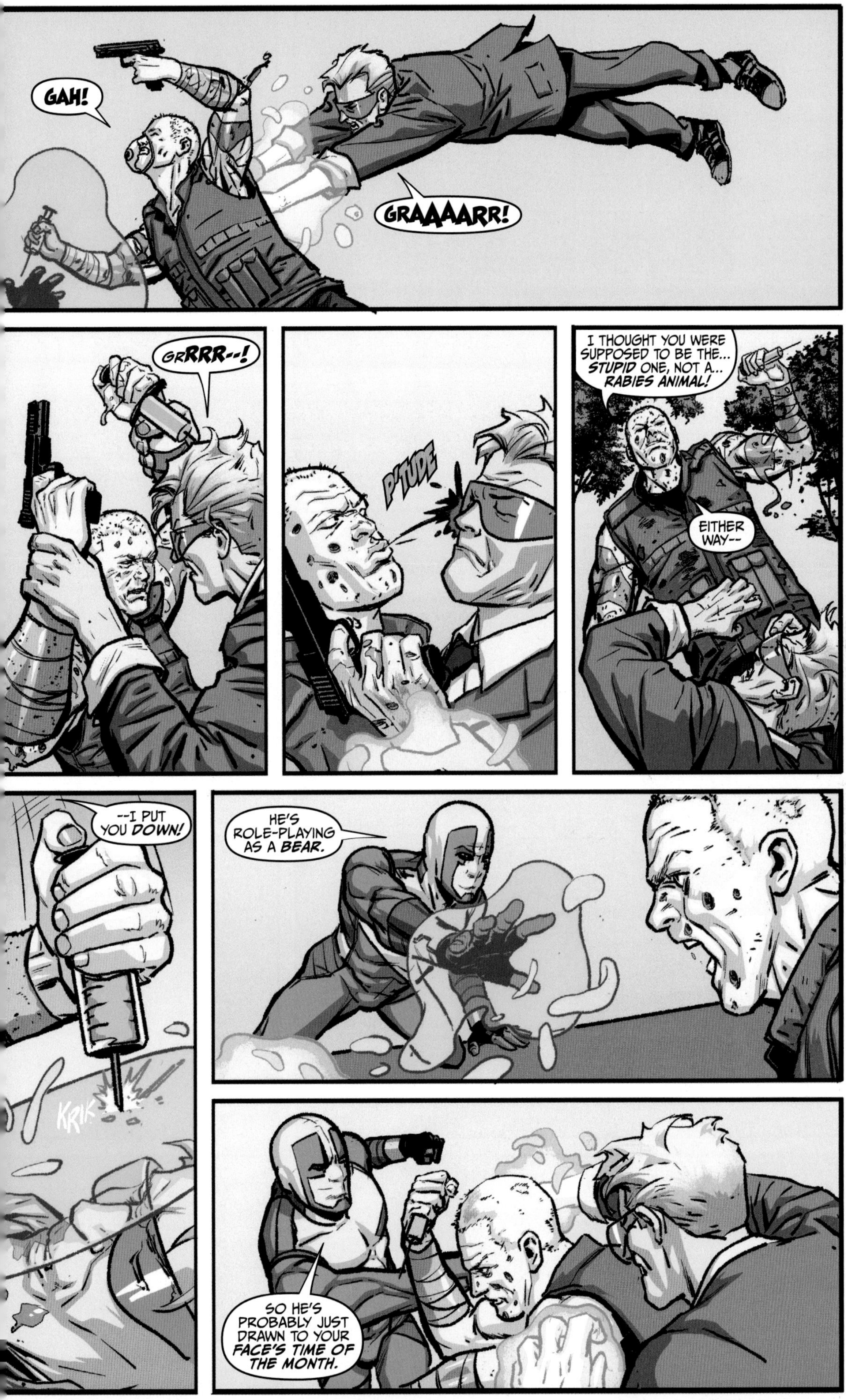
GAH!
GRAAAARR!
GRRRR--!
P'TUDE
I THOUGHT YOU WERE SUPPOSED TO BE THE... STUPID ONE, NOT A... RABIES ANIMAL!
EITHER WAY--
--I PUT YOU DOWN!
KRIK
HE'S ROLE-PLAYING AS A BEAR.
SO HE'S PROBABLY JUST DRAWN TO YOUR FACE'S TIME OF THE MONTH.

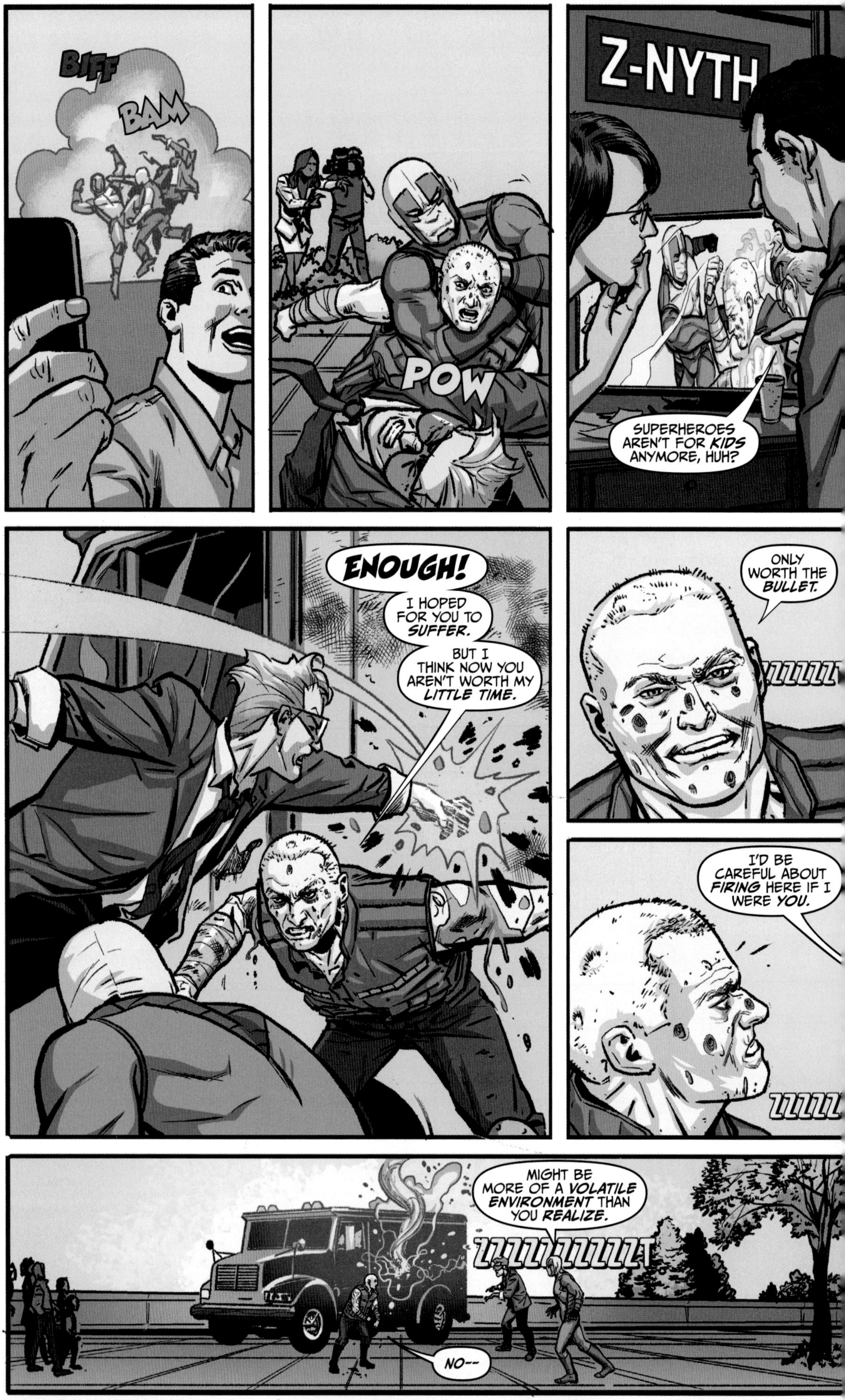
BIFF
BAM
POW
Z-NYTH
SUPERHEROES AREN'T FOR KIDS ANYMORE, HUH?
ENOUGH!
I HOPED FOR YOU TO SUFFER.
BUT I THINK NOW YOU AREN'T WORTH MY LITTLE TIME.
ONLY WORTH THE BULLET.
ZZZZZZ
I'D BE CAREFUL ABOUT FIRING HERE IF I WERE YOU.
ZZZZZ
MIGHT BE MORE OF A VOLATILE ENVIRONMENT THAN YOU REALIZE.
ZZZZZZZZZZZZT
NO--

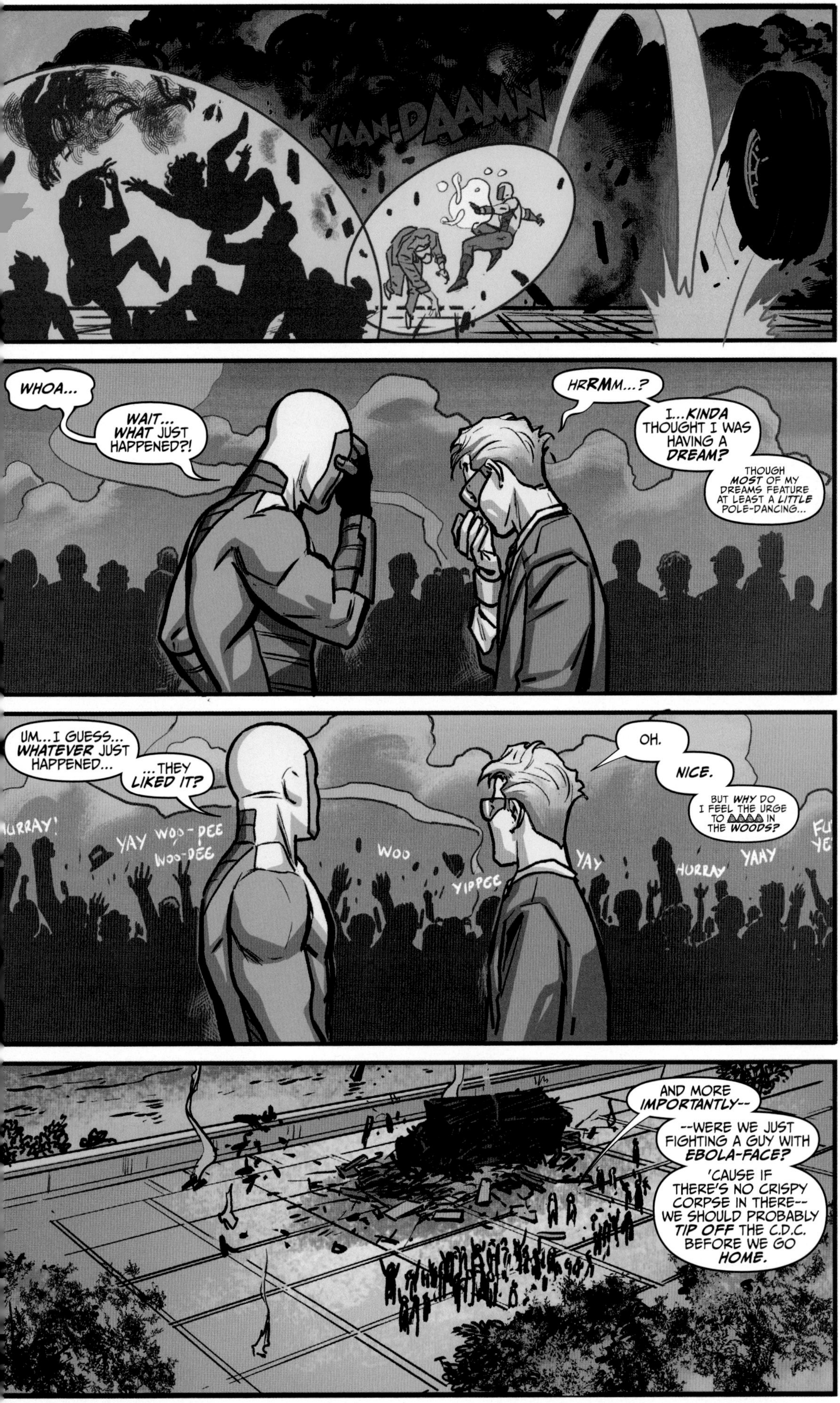
VAAN-DAAMN
WHOA...
WAIT... WHAT JUST HAPPENED?!
HRRMM...?
I...KINDA THOUGHT I WAS HAVING A DREAM?
THOUGH MOST OF MY DREAMS FEATURE AT LEAST A LITTLE POLE-DANCING...
UM...I GUESS... WHATEVER JUST HAPPENED...
...THEY LIKED IT?
OH.
NICE.
BUT WHY DO I FEEL THE URGE TO IN THE WOODS?
YAY
WOO-PEE
WOO-DEE
WOO
YIPPEE
YAY
HURRAY
YAHY
AND MORE IMPORTANTLY--
--WERE WE JUST FIGHTING A GUY WITH EBOLA-FACE?
'CAUSE IF THERE'S NO CRISPY CORPSE IN THERE-- WE SHOULD PROBABLY TIP OFF THE C.D.C. BEFORE WE GO HOME.

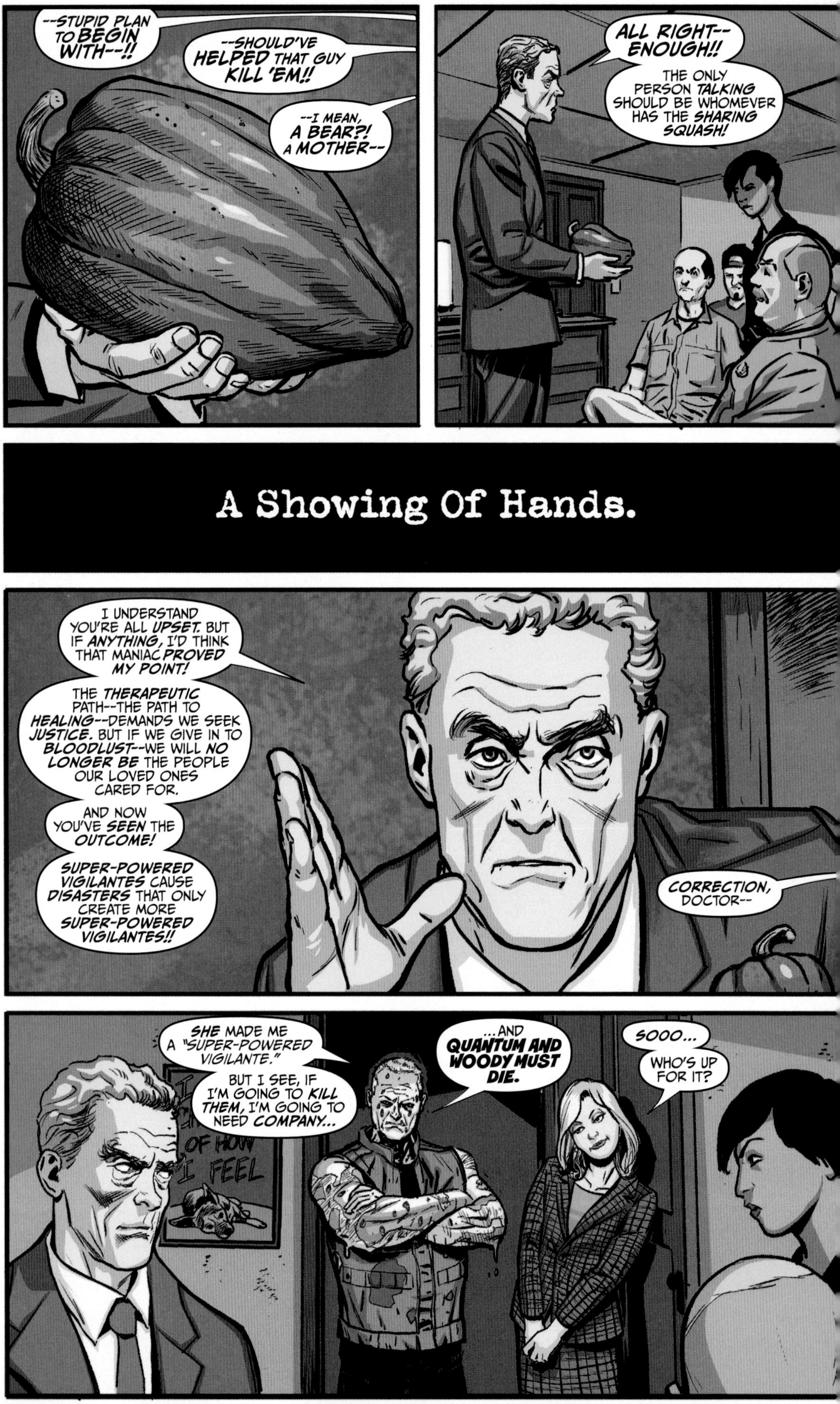
--STUPID PLAN TO BEGIN WITH--!!
--SHOULD'VE HELPED THAT GUY KILL 'EM!!
--I MEAN, A BEAR?! A MOTHER--
ALL RIGHT-- ENOUGH!!
THE ONLY PERSON TALKING SHOULD BE WHOMEVER HAS THE SHARING SQUASH!
A Showing Of Hands.
I UNDERSTAND YOU'RE ALL UPSET. BUT IF ANYTHING, I'D THINK THAT MANIAC PROVED MY POINT!
THE THERAPEUTIC PATH--THE PATH TO HEALING--DEMANDS WE SEEK JUSTICE. BUT IF WE GIVE IN TO BLOODLUST--WE WILL NO LONGER BE THE PEOPLE OUR LOVED ONES CARED FOR.
AND NOW YOU'VE SEEN THE OUTCOME!
SUPER-POWERED VIGILANTES CAUSE DISASTERS THAT ONLY CREATE MORE SUPER-POWERED VIGILANTES!!
CORRECTION, DOCTOR--
SHE MADE ME A "SUPER-POWERED VIGILANTE."
BUT I SEE, IF I'M GOING TO KILL THEM, I'M GOING TO NEED COMPANY...
...AND QUANTUM AND WOODY MUST DIE.
SOOO...
WHO'S UP FOR IT?

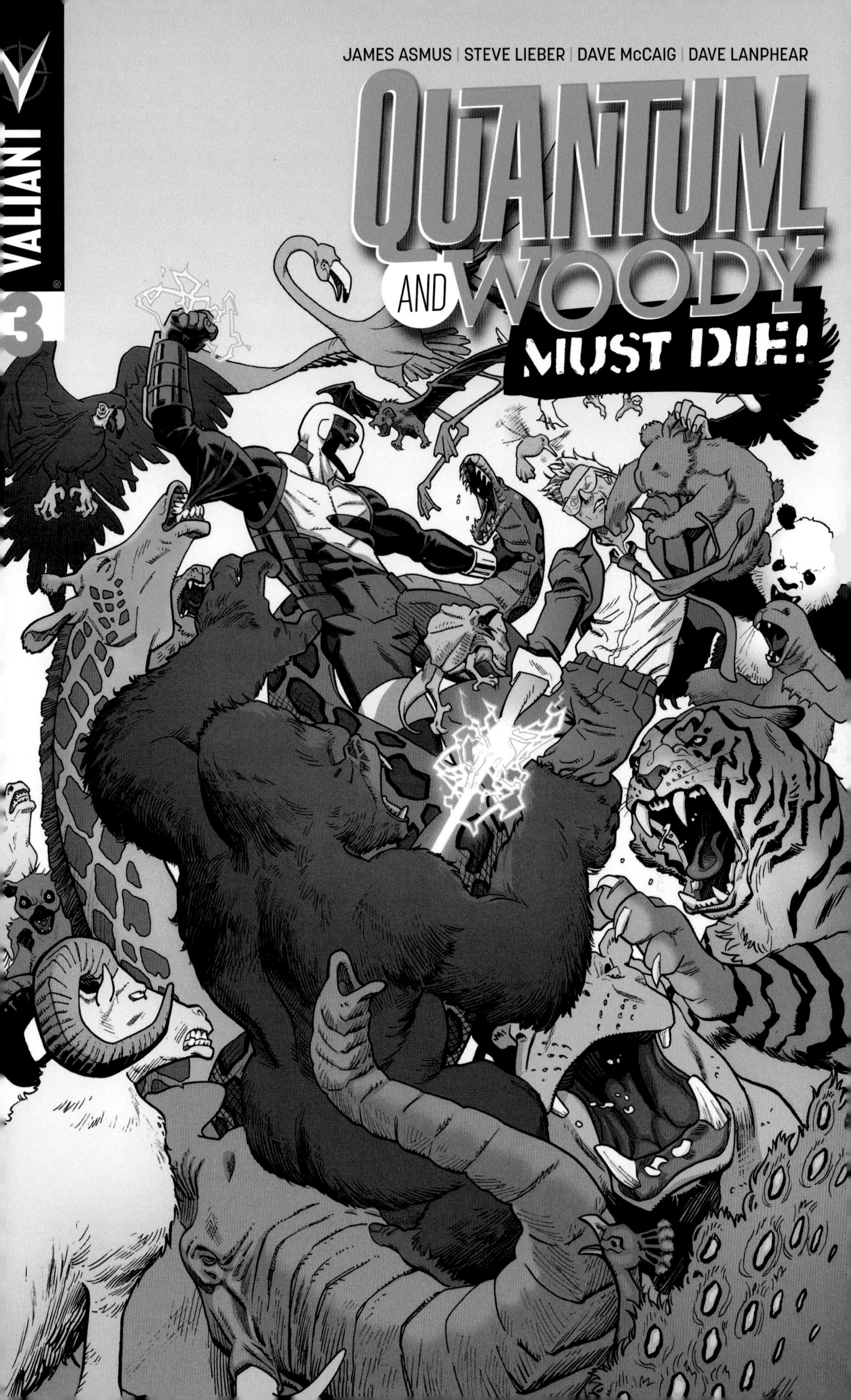
VALIANT
3
JAMES ASMUS | STEVE LIEBER | DAVE McCAIG | DAVE LANPHEAR
QUANTUM
AND
WOODY
MUST DIE!

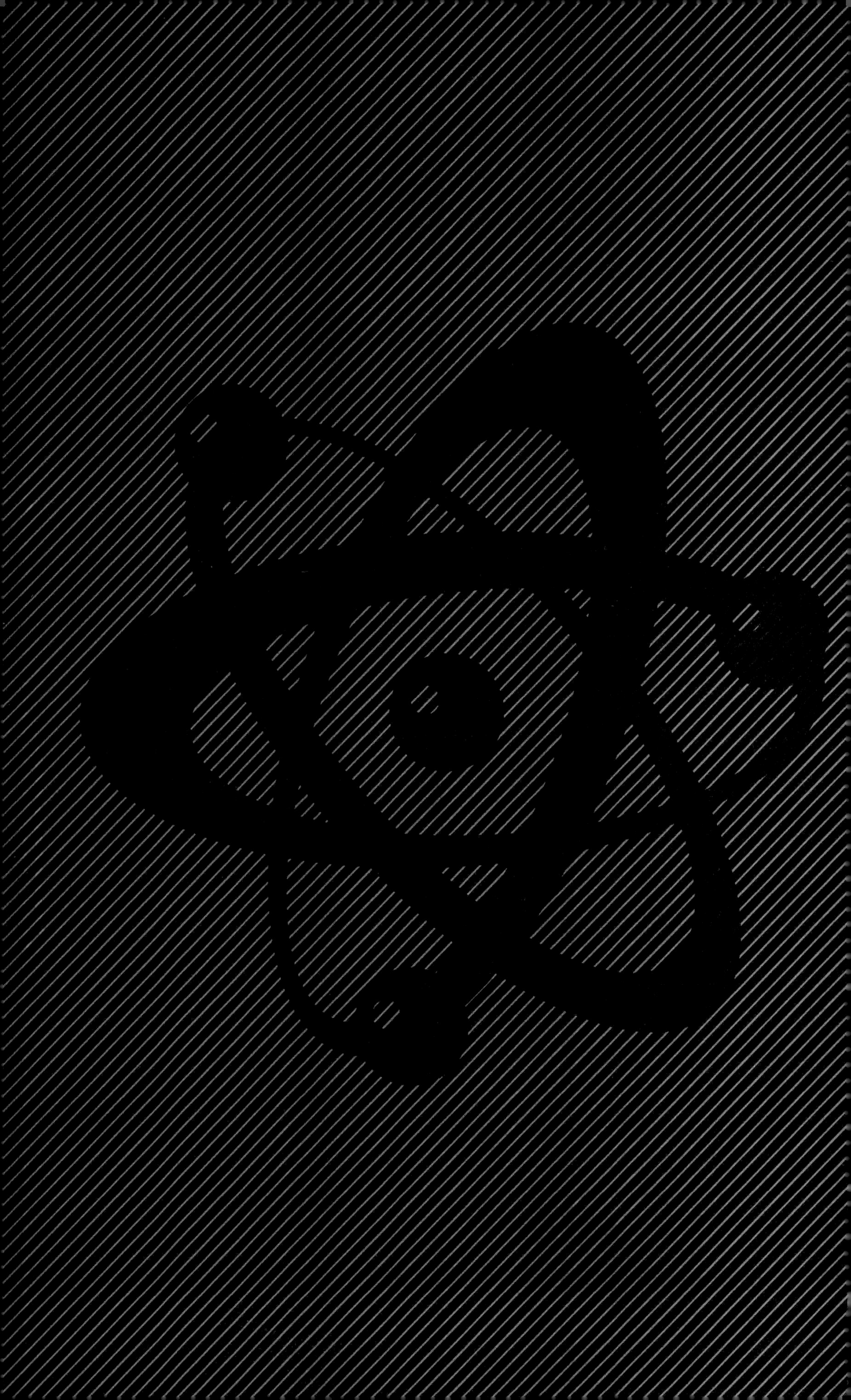

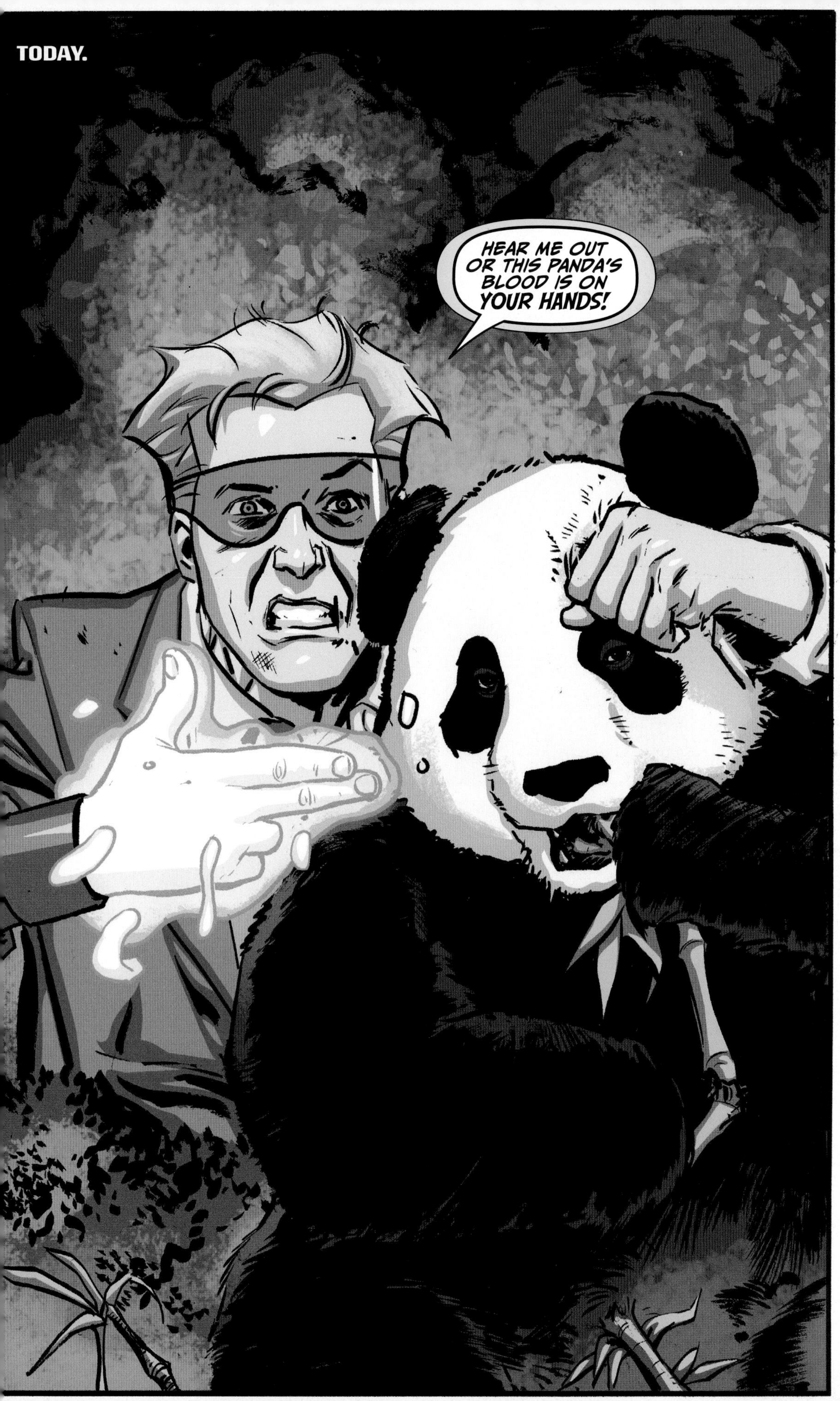
TODAY.
HEAR ME OUT OR THIS PANDA'S BLOOD IS ON YOUR HANDS!

Pride Parade Goeth Before the Fall.

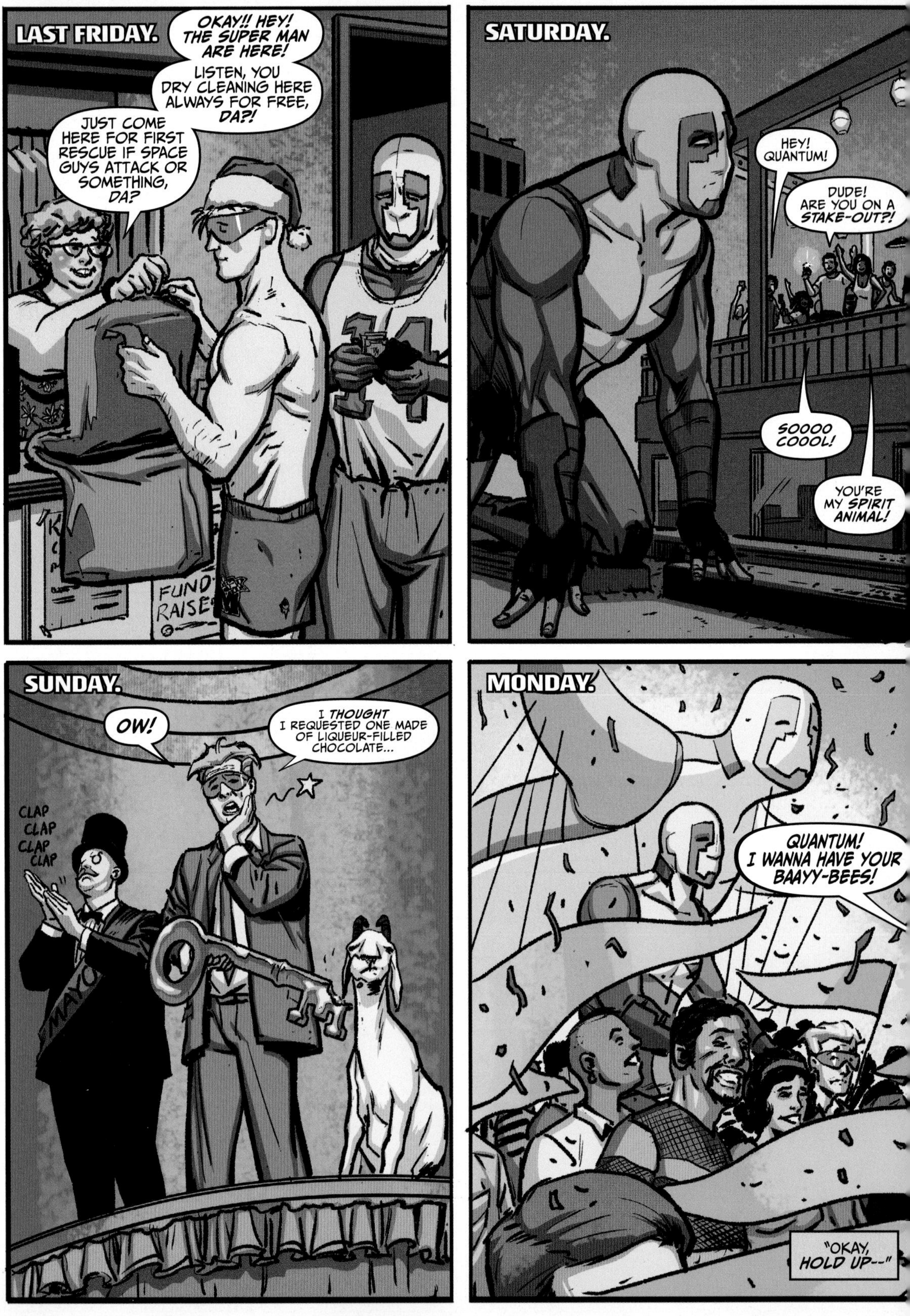
LAST FRIDAY.
OKAY!! HEY! THE SUPER MAN ARE HERE!
LISTEN, YOU DRY CLEANING HERE ALWAYS FOR FREE, DA?!
JUST COME HERE FOR FIRST RESCUE IF SPACE GUYS ATTACK OR SOMETHING, DA?
SATURDAY.
HEY! QUANTUM!
DUDE! ARE YOU ON A STAKE-OUT?!
SOOOO COOOL!
YOU'RE MY SPIRIT ANIMAL!
SUNDAY.
OW!
I THOUGHT I REQUESTED ONE MADE OF LIQUEUR-FILLED CHOCOLATE...
CLAP CLAP CLAP CLAP
MONDAY.
QUANTUM! I WANNA HAVE YOUR BAAYY-BEES!
"OKAY, HOLD UP--"

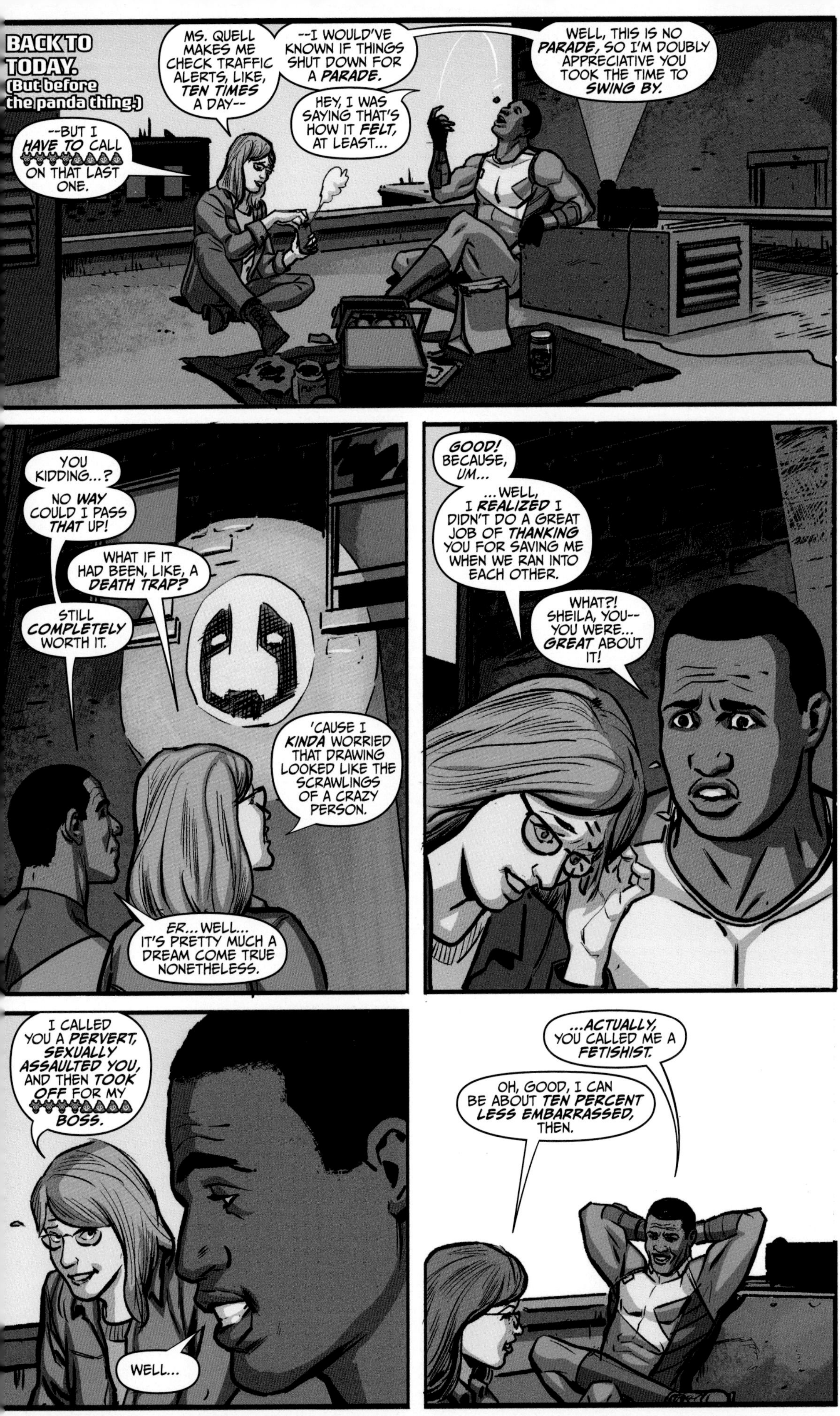
BACK TO TODAY.
(But before the panda thing.)
MS. QUELL MAKES ME CHECK TRAFFIC ALERTS, LIKE, TEN TIMES A DAY--
--I WOULD'VE KNOWN IF THINGS SHUT DOWN FOR A PARADE.
WELL, THIS IS NO PARADE, SO I'M DOUBLY APPRECIATIVE YOU TOOK THE TIME TO SWING BY.
HEY, I WAS SAYING THAT'S HOW IT FELT, AT LEAST...
--BUT I HAVE TO CALL ON THAT LAST ONE.
YOU KIDDING...?
NO WAY COULD I PASS THAT UP!
WHAT IF IT HAD BEEN, LIKE, A DEATH TRAP?
STILL COMPLETELY WORTH IT.
'CAUSE I KINDA WORRIED THAT DRAWING LOOKED LIKE THE SCRAWLINGS OF A CRAZY PERSON.
ER...WELL... IT'S PRETTY MUCH A DREAM COME TRUE NONETHELESS.
GOOD! BECAUSE, UM...
...WELL, I REALIZED I DIDN'T DO A GREAT JOB OF THANKING YOU FOR SAVING ME WHEN WE RAN INTO EACH OTHER.
WHAT?! SHEILA, YOU-- YOU WERE... GREAT ABOUT IT!
I CALLED YOU A PERVERT, SEXUALLY ASSAULTED YOU, AND THEN TOOK OFF FOR MY BOSS.
WELL...
...ACTUALLY, YOU CALLED ME A FETISHIST.
OH, GOOD, I CAN BE ABOUT TEN PERCENT LESS EMBARRASSED, THEN.

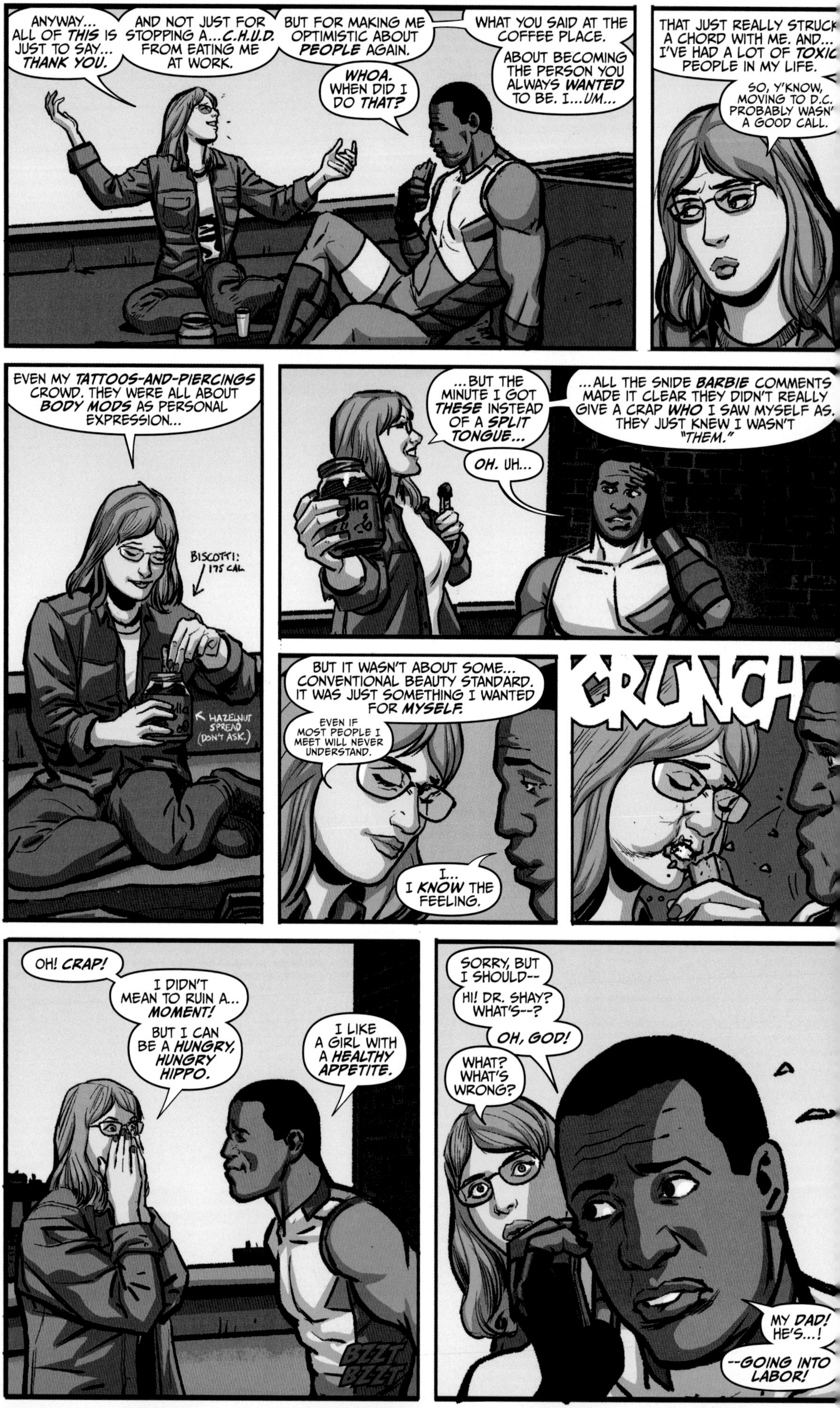
ANYWAY... ALL OF THIS IS JUST TO SAY... THANK YOU.
AND NOT JUST FOR STOPPING A... C.H.U.D. FROM EATING ME AT WORK.
BUT FOR MAKING ME OPTIMISTIC ABOUT PEOPLE AGAIN.
WHOA. WHEN DID I DO THAT?
WHAT YOU SAID AT THE COFFEE PLACE.
ABOUT BECOMING THE PERSON YOU ALWAYS WANTED TO BE. I... UM...
THAT JUST REALLY STRUCK A CHORD WITH ME. AND... I'VE HAD A LOT OF TOXIC PEOPLE IN MY LIFE.
SO, Y'KNOW, MOVING TO D.C. PROBABLY WASN' A GOOD CALL.
EVEN MY TATTOOS-AND-PIERCINGS CROWD. THEY WERE ALL ABOUT BODY MODS AS PERSONAL EXPRESSION...
BISCOTTI: 175 CAL
HAZELNUT SPREAD (DON'T ASK.)
...BUT THE MINUTE I GOT THESE INSTEAD OF A SPLIT TONGUE...
OH. UH...
...ALL THE SNIDE BARBIE COMMENTS MADE IT CLEAR THEY DIDN'T REALLY GIVE A CRAP WHO I SAW MYSELF AS. THEY JUST KNEW I WASN'T "THEM."
BUT IT WASN'T ABOUT SOME... CONVENTIONAL BEAUTY STANDARD. IT WAS JUST SOMETHING I WANTED FOR MYSELF.
EVEN IF MOST PEOPLE I MEET WILL NEVER UNDERSTAND.
I... I KNOW THE FEELING.
CRUNCH
OH! CRAP!
I DIDN'T MEAN TO RUIN A... MOMENT!
BUT I CAN BE A HUNGRY, HUNGRY HIPPO.
I LIKE A GIRL WITH A HEALTHY APPETITE.
BZZT BZZT
SORRY, BUT I SHOULD--
HI! DR. SHAY? WHAT'S--?
OH, GOD!
WHAT? WHAT'S WRONG?
MY DAD! HE'S...!
--GOING INTO LABOR!

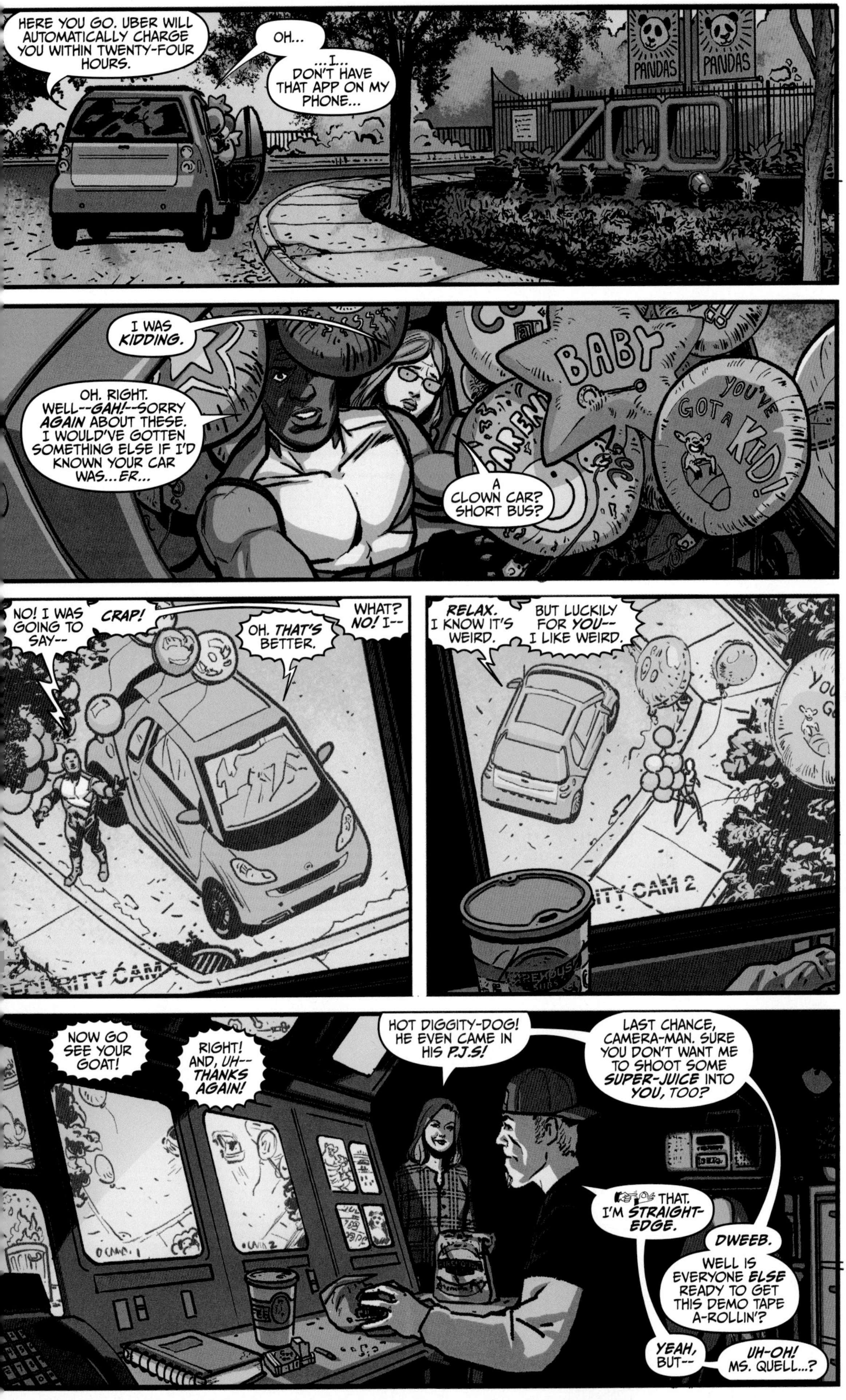
HERE YOU GO. UBER WILL AUTOMATICALLY CHARGE YOU WITHIN TWENTY-FOUR HOURS.
OH...
...I... DON'T HAVE THAT APP ON MY PHONE...
PANDAS
PANDAS
ZOO
I WAS *KIDDING.*
OH. RIGHT. WELL--*GAH!*--SORRY *AGAIN* ABOUT THESE. I WOULD'VE GOTTEN SOMETHING ELSE IF I'D KNOWN YOUR CAR WAS...*ER*...
A CLOWN CAR? SHORT BUS?
BABY
YOU'VE GOT A KID!
NO! I WAS GOING TO SAY--
CRAP!
WHAT? *NO!* I--
OH. *THAT'S* BETTER.
SECURITY CAM
RELAX. I KNOW IT'S WEIRD.
BUT LUCKILY FOR *YOU*--I LIKE WEIRD.
SECURITY CAM 2
NOW GO SEE YOUR GOAT!
RIGHT! AND, *UH*-- *THANKS AGAIN!*
HOT DIGGITY-DOG! HE EVEN CAME IN HIS *P.J.S!*
LAST CHANCE, CAMERA-MAN. SURE YOU DON'T WANT ME TO SHOOT SOME *SUPER-JUICE* INTO *YOU,* TOO?
THAT. I'M *STRAIGHT-EDGE.*
DWEEB.
WELL IS EVERYONE *ELSE* READY TO GET THIS DEMO TAPE A-ROLLIN'?
YEAH, BUT--
UH-OH! MS. QUELL...?

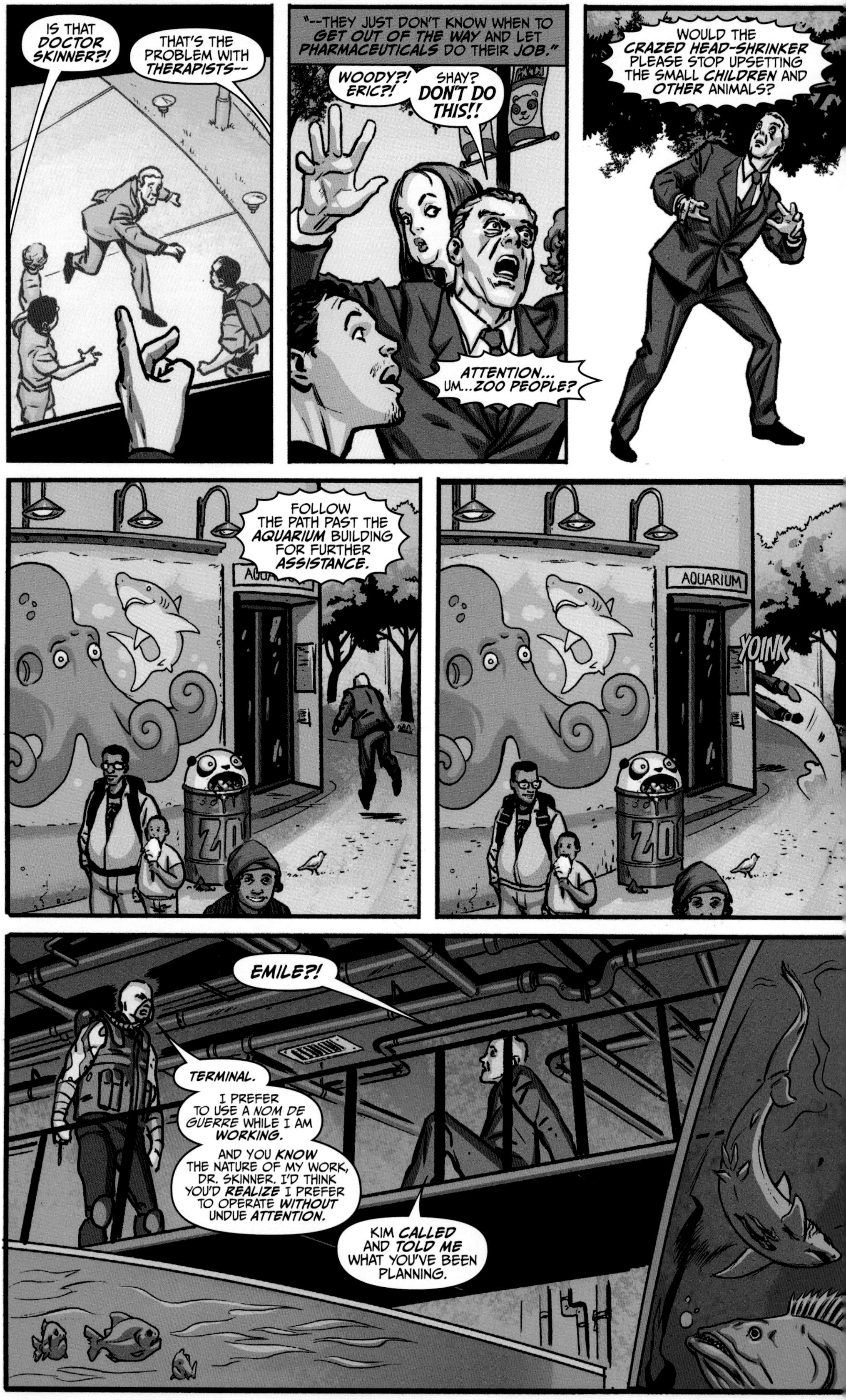
IS THAT DOCTOR SKINNER?!
THAT'S THE PROBLEM WITH THERAPISTS--
"--THEY JUST DON'T KNOW WHEN TO GET OUT OF THE WAY AND LET PHARMACEUTICALS DO THEIR JOB."
WOODY?! ERIC?!
SHAY? DON'T DO THIS!!
ATTENTION... UM...ZOO PEOPLE?
WOULD THE CRAZED HEAD-SHRINKER PLEASE STOP UPSETTING THE SMALL CHILDREN AND OTHER ANIMALS?
FOLLOW THE PATH PAST THE AQUARIUM BUILDING FOR FURTHER ASSISTANCE.
ZOO
AQUARIUM
YOINK
ZOO
EMILE?!
TERMINAL.
I PREFER TO USE A NOM DE GUERRE WHILE I AM WORKING.
AND YOU KNOW THE NATURE OF MY WORK, DR. SKINNER. I'D THINK YOU'D REALIZE I PREFER TO OPERATE WITHOUT UNDUE ATTENTION.
KIM CALLED AND TOLD ME WHAT YOU'VE BEEN PLANNING.

--THAT PSYCHO *PHARMA-LADY* JUST *LAUGHED* AND SAID, "THAT'S THE *TRIAL PHASE* FOR YA!"

I'M SPROUTING... *APPENDAGES!*

AND SHE *WON'T* EVEN LET ME USE THEM TO *STRANGLE QUANTUM AND WOODY!!*

EVERYONE *ELSE* RESPONDED TO THEIR INJECTIONS... *BETTER.*

PLEASE! THESE ARE *PEOPLE* YOU AND THAT...*DRUG WOMAN* ARE *USING!* MY *PATIENTS!* THEY NEED TO *HEAL,* NOT...*PERPETUATE* THE *CYCLE OF VIOLENCE!*

YOU'RE TURNING THEM INTO *MONSTERS?!* FOR *WHAT?!* QUANTUM AND WOODY ARE *RECKLESS*--BUT THEY AREN'T *MURDERERS!*

I AM THE MAN THEY *MURDERED!*

IF NOT FOR DIRECTOR QUELL AND *Z-NYTH,* I WOULD BE *DEAD*--FROM *THEIR CHAOS!*

SHE WANTED *TEST SUBJECTS* FOR HER... SUPER-POWER *BYPRODUCTS*--

--AND YOUR *PATIENTS* WANTED *REVENGE.*

WE ALREADY *TRIED YOUR WAY.*

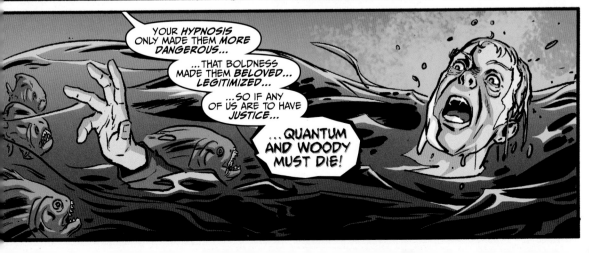

YOUR *HYPNOSIS* ONLY MADE THEM *MORE DANGEROUS...*

...THAT BOLDNESS MADE THEM *BELOVED...* *LEGITIMIZED...*

...SO IF ANY OF US ARE TO HAVE *JUSTICE...*

...*QUANTUM AND WOODY MUST DIE!*

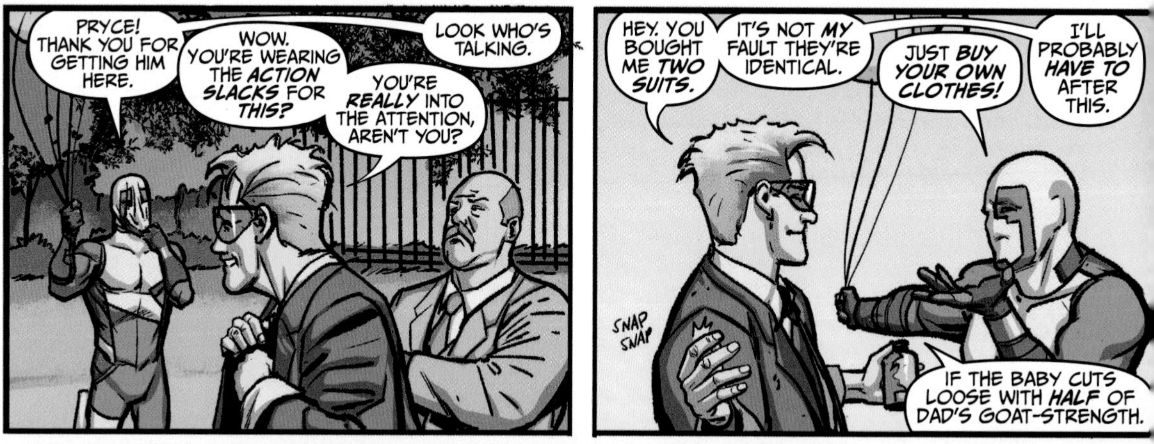
PRYCE! THANK YOU FOR GETTING HIM HERE.
WOW. YOU'RE WEARING THE ACTION SLACKS FOR THIS?
LOOK WHO'S TALKING.
YOU'RE REALLY INTO THE ATTENTION, AREN'T YOU?
HEY. YOU BOUGHT ME TWO SUITS.
IT'S NOT MY FAULT THEY'RE IDENTICAL.
JUST BUY YOUR OWN CLOTHES!
I'LL PROBABLY HAVE TO AFTER THIS.
SNAP SNAP
IF THE BABY CUTS LOOSE WITH HALF OF DAD'S GOAT-STRENGTH.

Endangered Animals.

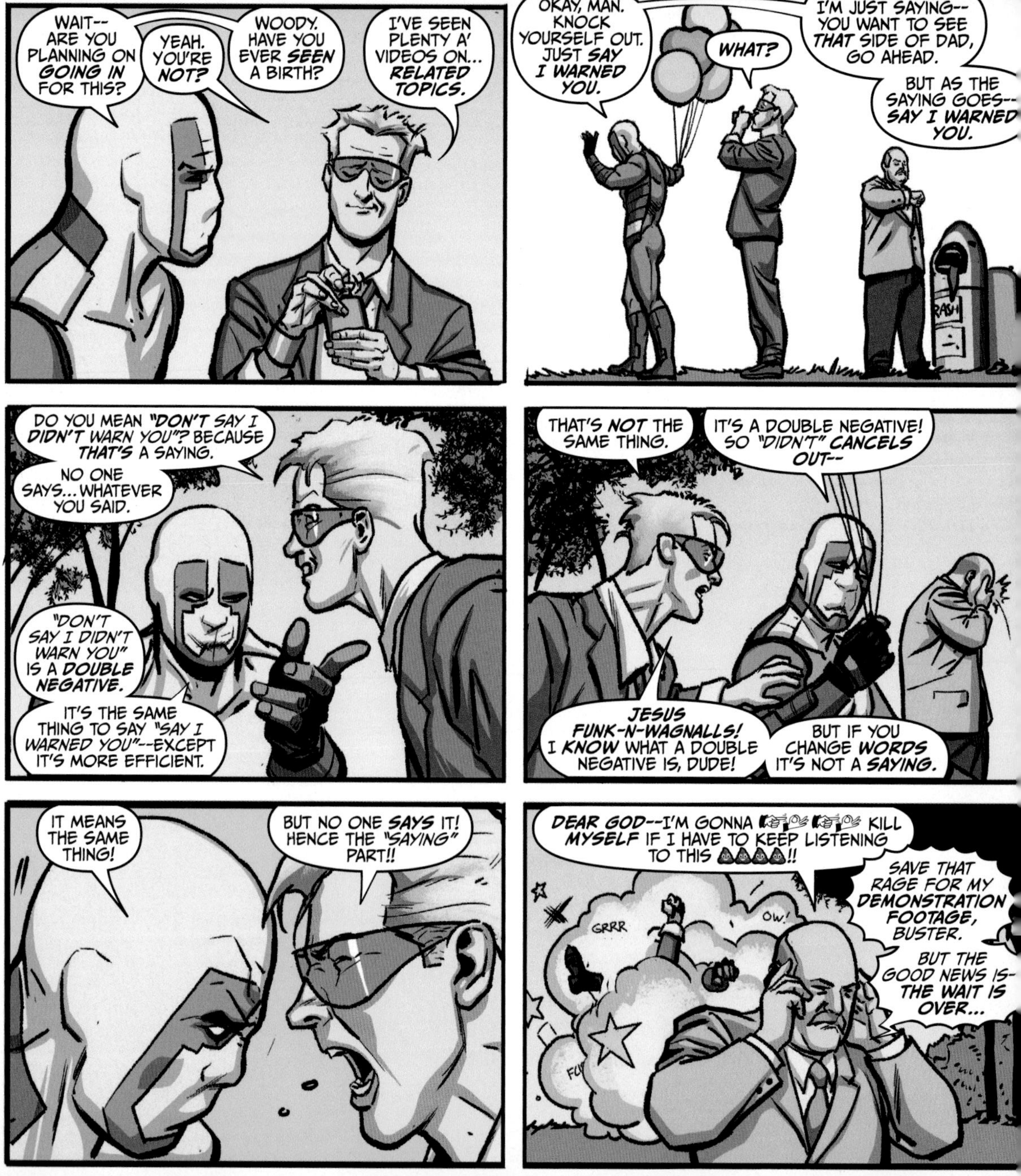
WAIT-- ARE YOU PLANNING ON GOING IN FOR THIS?
YEAH. YOU'RE NOT?
WOODY. HAVE YOU EVER SEEN A BIRTH?
I'VE SEEN PLENTY A' VIDEOS ON... RELATED TOPICS.
OKAY, MAN. KNOCK YOURSELF OUT. JUST SAY I WARNED YOU.
WHAT?
I'M JUST SAYING-- YOU WANT TO SEE THAT SIDE OF DAD, GO AHEAD.
BUT AS THE SAYING GOES-- SAY I WARNED YOU.
DO YOU MEAN "DON'T SAY I DIDN'T WARN YOU"? BECAUSE THAT'S A SAYING.
NO ONE SAYS... WHATEVER YOU SAID.
"DON'T SAY I DIDN'T WARN YOU" IS A DOUBLE NEGATIVE.
IT'S THE SAME THING TO SAY "SAY I WARNED YOU"--EXCEPT IT'S MORE EFFICIENT.
THAT'S NOT THE SAME THING.
IT'S A DOUBLE NEGATIVE! SO "DIDN'T" CANCELS OUT--
JESUS FUNK-N-WAGNALLS! I KNOW WHAT A DOUBLE NEGATIVE IS, DUDE!
BUT IF YOU CHANGE WORDS IT'S NOT A SAYING.
IT MEANS THE SAME THING!
BUT NO ONE SAYS IT! HENCE THE "SAYING" PART!!
DEAR GOD--I'M GONNA KILL MYSELF IF I HAVE TO KEEP LISTENING TO THIS!!
GRRR
OW!
SAVE THAT RAGE FOR MY DEMONSTRATION FOOTAGE, BUSTER.
BUT THE GOOD NEWS IS-- THE WAIT IS OVER...

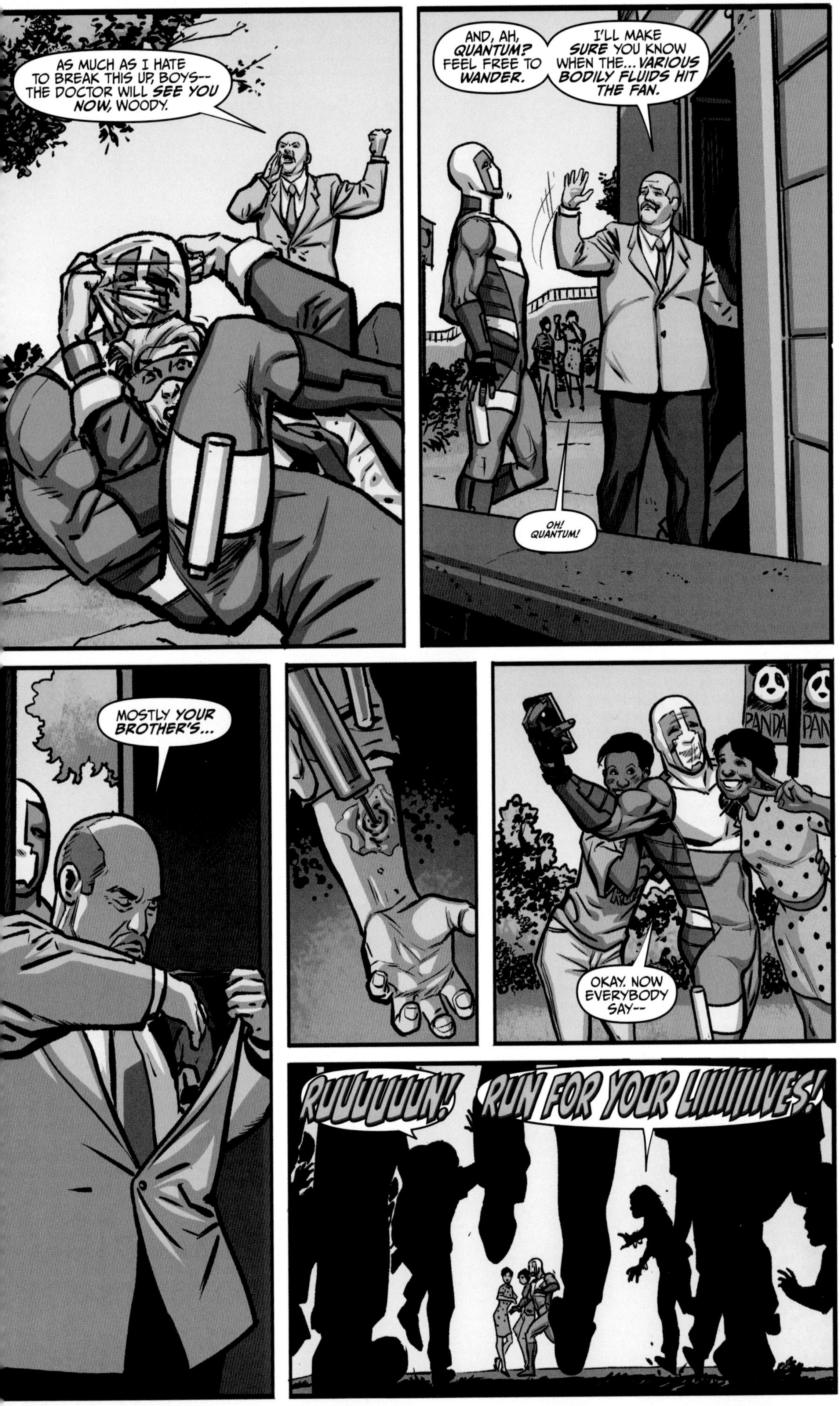
AS MUCH AS I HATE TO BREAK THIS UP, BOYS-- THE DOCTOR WILL SEE YOU NOW, WOODY.
AND, AH, QUANTUM? FEEL FREE TO WANDER.
I'LL MAKE SURE YOU KNOW WHEN THE... VARIOUS BODILY FLUIDS HIT THE FAN.
OH! QUANTUM!
MOSTLY YOUR BROTHER'S...
PANDA
PAN
OKAY. NOW EVERYBODY SAY--
RUUUUUUN! RUN FOR YOUR LIIIIIIVES!

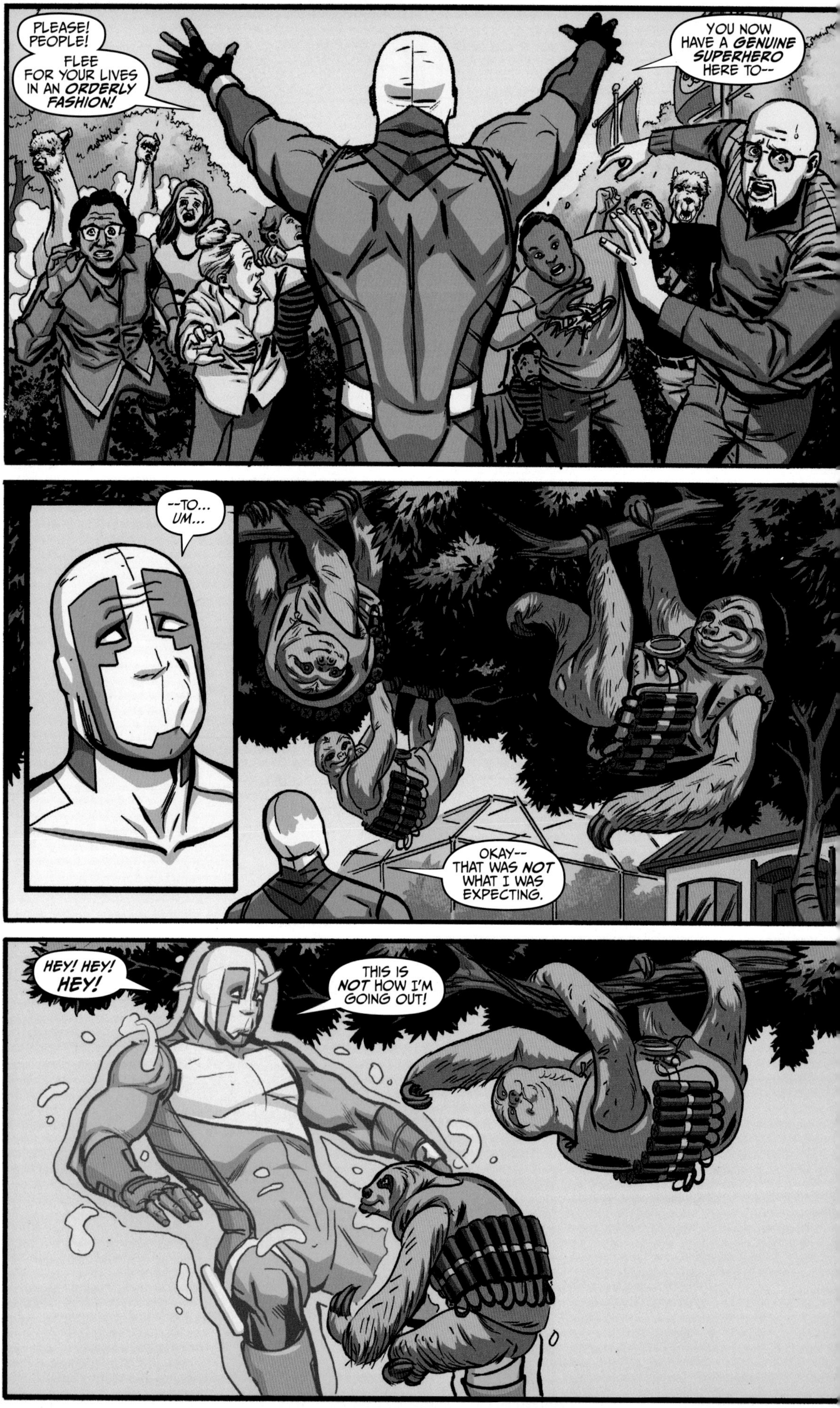
PLEASE! PEOPLE! FLEE FOR YOUR LIVES IN AN *ORDERLY FASHION!*
YOU NOW HAVE A *GENUINE SUPERHERO* HERE TO--
--TO... *UM...*
OKAY-- THAT WAS *NOT* WHAT I WAS EXPECTING.
HEY! HEY! HEY!
THIS IS *NOT* HOW I'M GOING OUT!

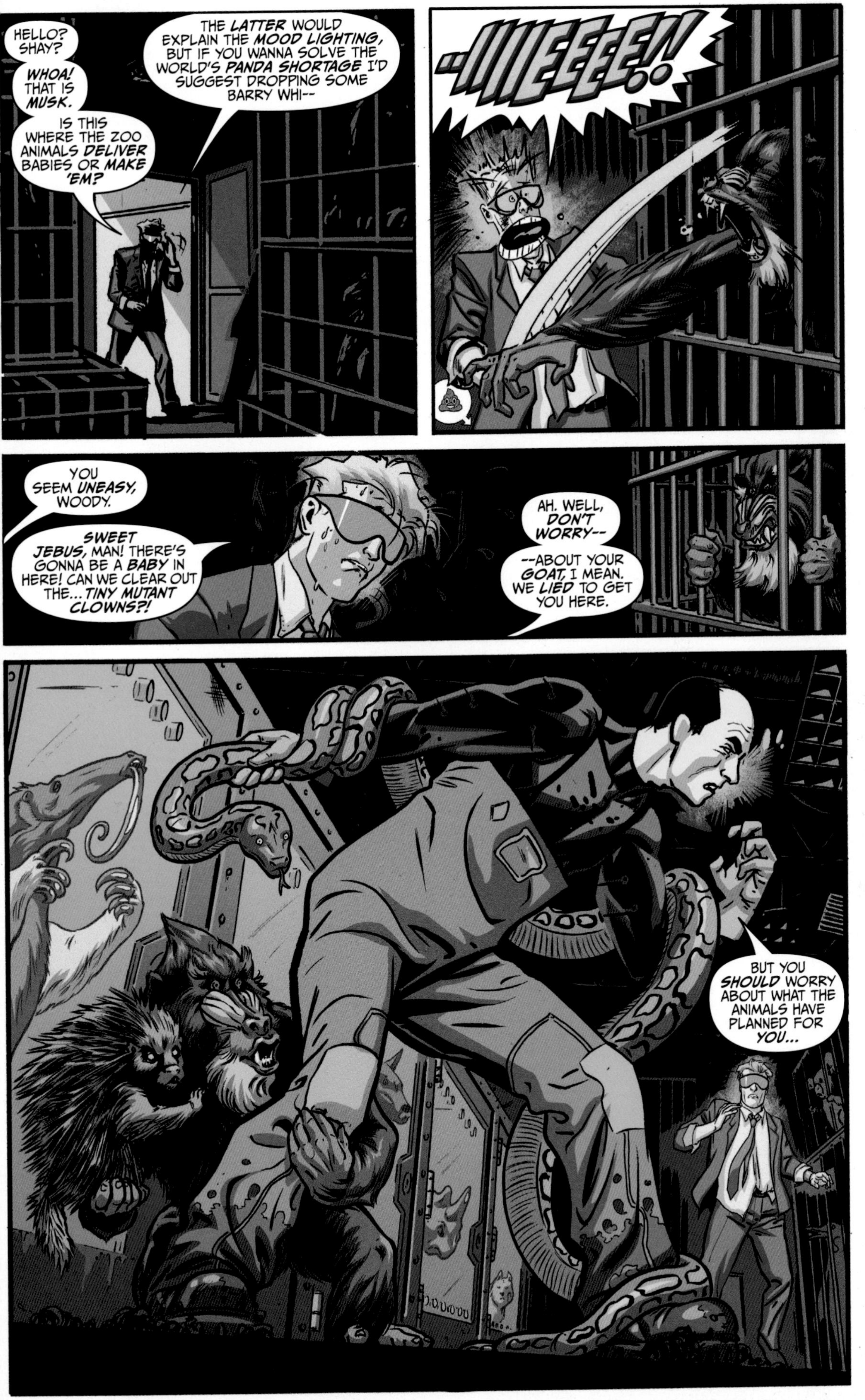

HELLO? SHAY?
WHOA! THAT IS MUSK.
IS THIS WHERE THE ZOO ANIMALS DELIVER BABIES OR MAKE 'EM?
THE LATTER WOULD EXPLAIN THE MOOD LIGHTING, BUT IF YOU WANNA SOLVE THE WORLD'S PANDA SHORTAGE I'D SUGGEST DROPPING SOME BARRY WHI--
-IIIIEEEEE!!
YOU SEEM UNEASY, WOODY.
SWEET JEBUS, MAN! THERE'S GONNA BE A BABY IN HERE! CAN WE CLEAR OUT THE... TINY MUTANT CLOWNS?!
AH. WELL, DON'T WORRY--
--ABOUT YOUR GOAT, I MEAN. WE LIED TO GET YOU HERE.
BUT YOU SHOULD WORRY ABOUT WHAT THE ANIMALS HAVE PLANNED FOR YOU...

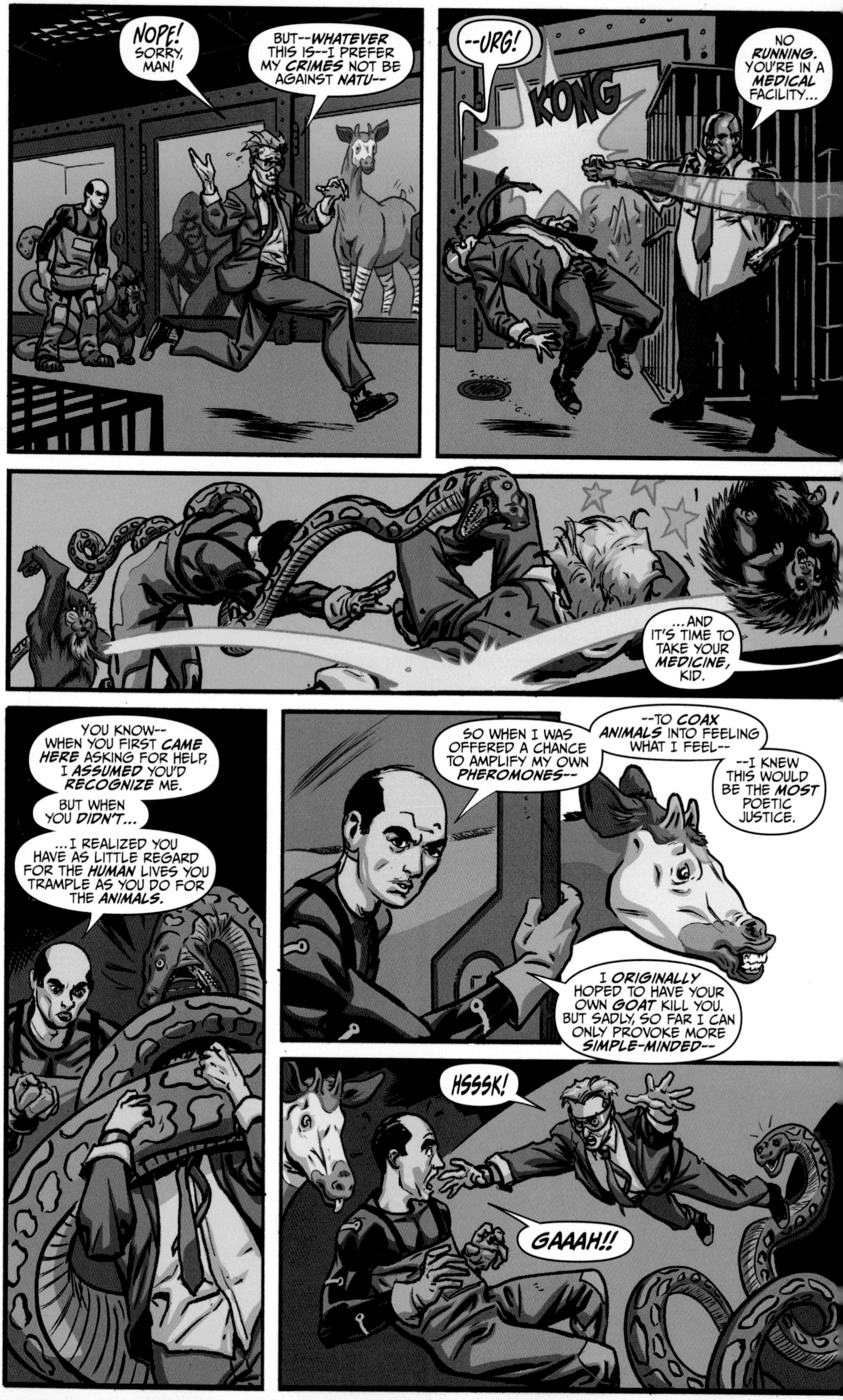
NOPE! SORRY, MAN!
BUT--WHATEVER THIS IS--I PREFER MY CRIMES NOT BE AGAINST NATU--
--URG!
KONG
NO RUNNING. YOU'RE IN A MEDICAL FACILITY...
...AND IT'S TIME TO TAKE YOUR MEDICINE, KID.
YOU KNOW-- WHEN YOU FIRST CAME HERE ASKING FOR HELP, I ASSUMED YOU'D RECOGNIZE ME.
BUT WHEN YOU DIDN'T...
...I REALIZED YOU HAVE AS LITTLE REGARD FOR THE HUMAN LIVES YOU TRAMPLE AS YOU DO FOR THE ANIMALS.
SO WHEN I WAS OFFERED A CHANCE TO AMPLIFY MY OWN PHEROMONES--
--TO COAX ANIMALS INTO FEELING WHAT I FEEL--
--I KNEW THIS WOULD BE THE MOST POETIC JUSTICE.
I ORIGINALLY HOPED TO HAVE YOUR OWN GOAT KILL YOU. BUT SADLY, SO FAR I CAN ONLY PROVOKE MORE SIMPLE-MINDED--
HSSSK!
GAAAH!!

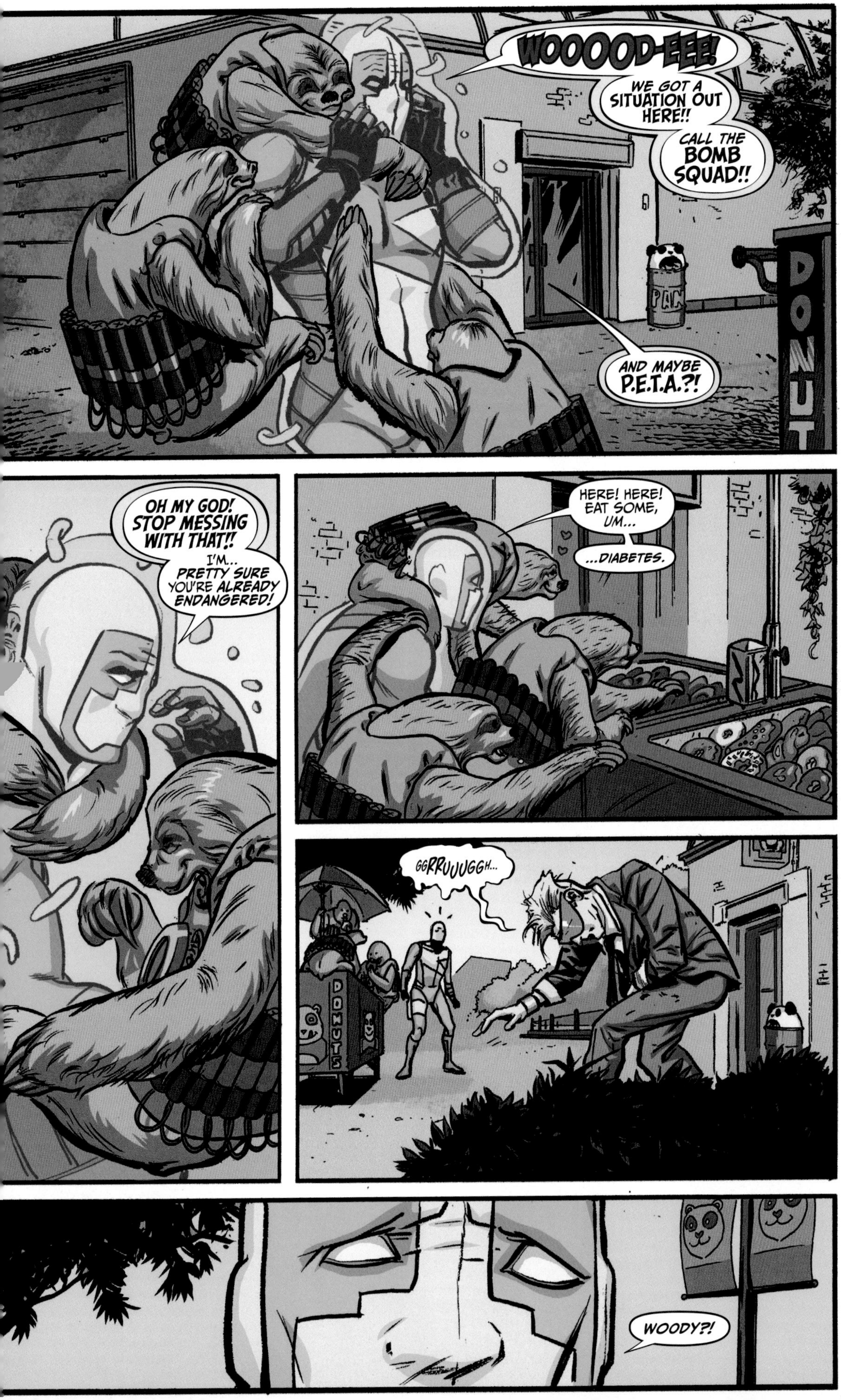
WOOOOD-EEE!
WE GOT A SITUATION OUT HERE!!
CALL THE BOMB SQUAD!!
AND MAYBE P.E.T.A.?!
OH MY GOD! STOP MESSING WITH THAT!!
I'M... PRETTY SURE YOU'RE ALREADY ENDANGERED!
HERE! HERE! EAT SOME, UM...
...DIABETES.
GGRRUUUGGH...
WOODY?!
DONUTS

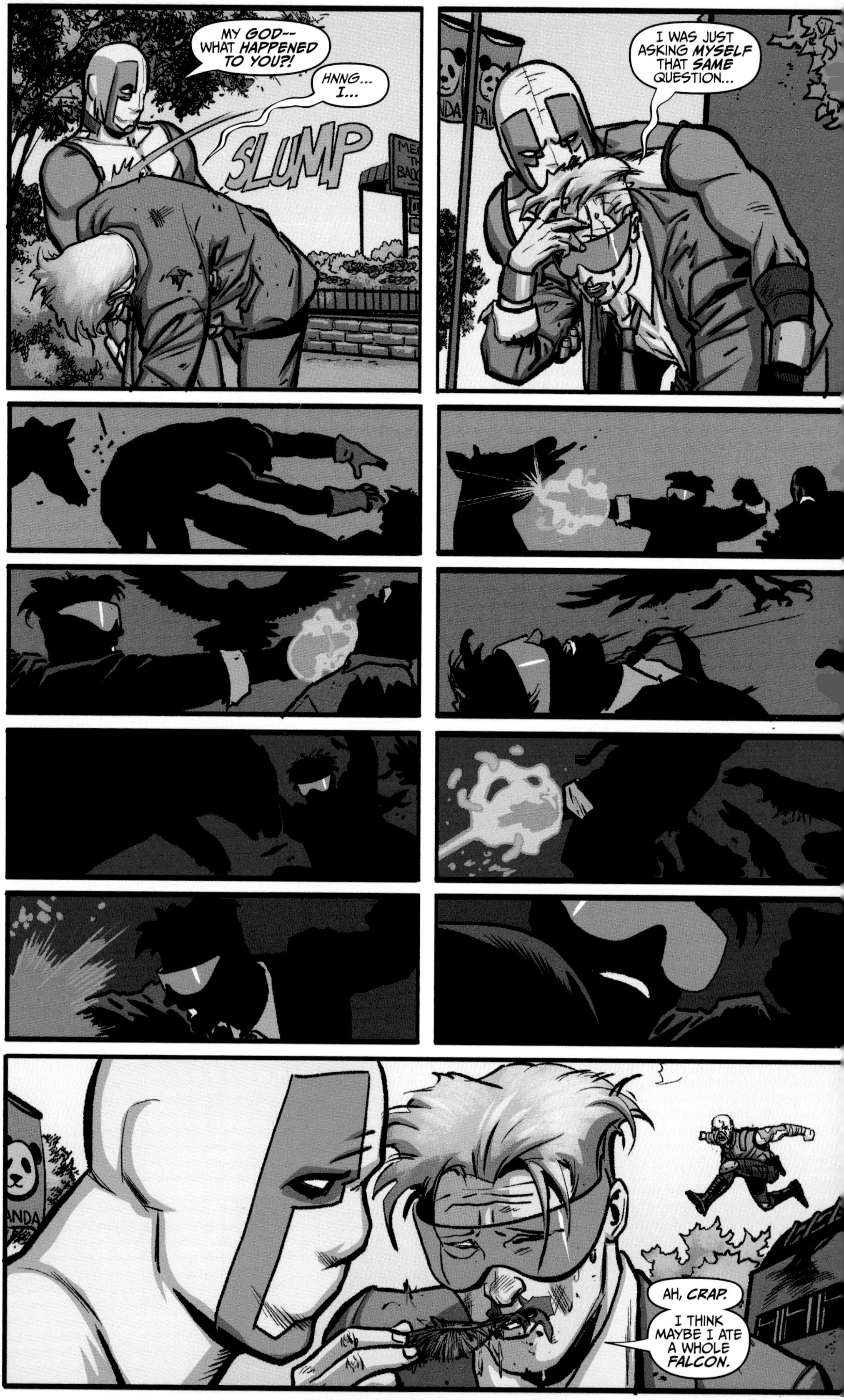
MY GOD-- WHAT HAPPENED TO YOU?!
HNNG... I...
SLUMP
I WAS JUST ASKING MYSELF THAT SAME QUESTION...
AH, CRAP.
I THINK MAYBE I ATE A WHOLE FALCON.

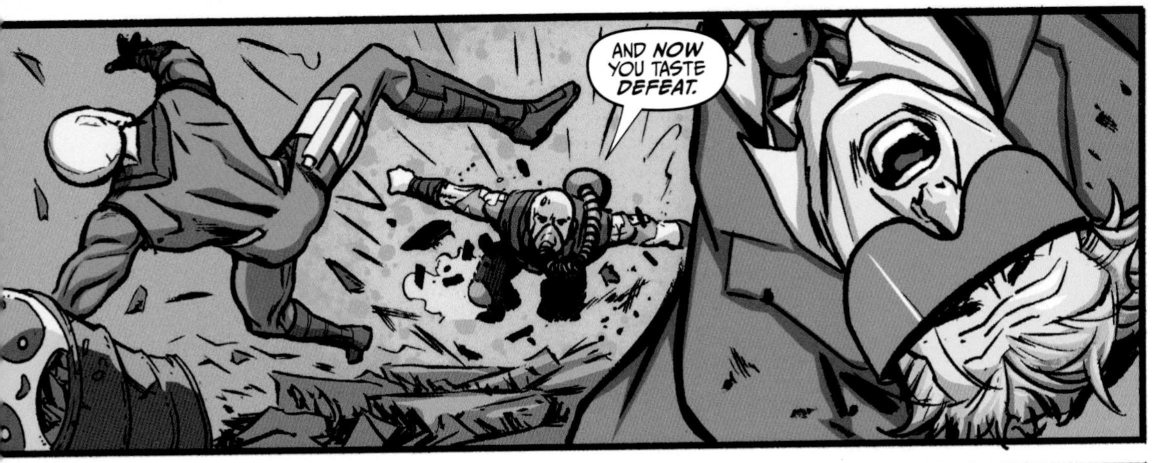
AND NOW YOU TASTE DEFEAT.

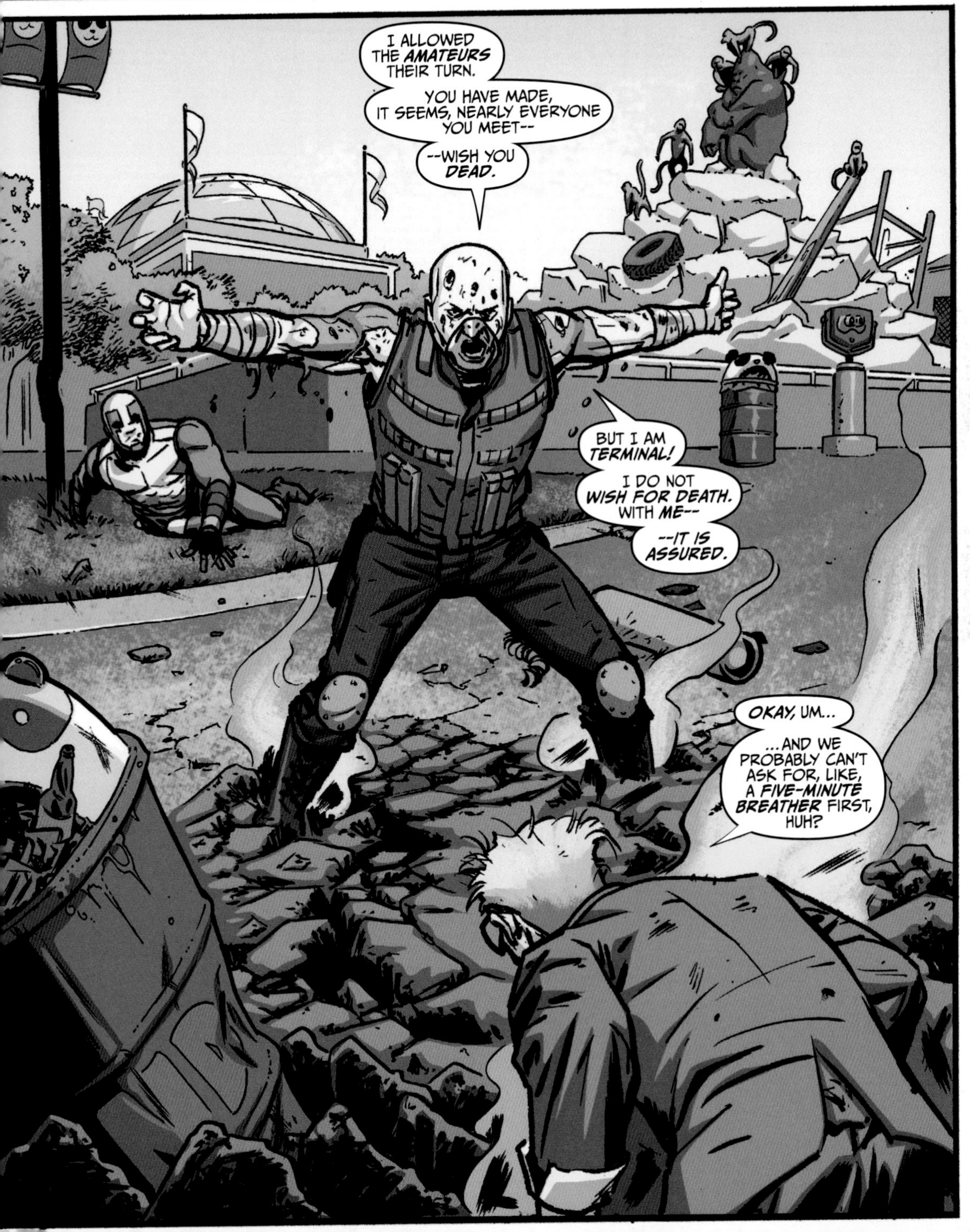
I ALLOWED THE AMATEURS THEIR TURN.
YOU HAVE MADE, IT SEEMS, NEARLY EVERYONE YOU MEET--
--WISH YOU DEAD.
BUT I AM TERMINAL!
I DO NOT WISH FOR DEATH. WITH ME--
--IT IS ASSURED.
OKAY, UM...
...AND WE PROBABLY CAN'T ASK FOR, LIKE, A FIVE-MINUTE BREATHER FIRST, HUH?

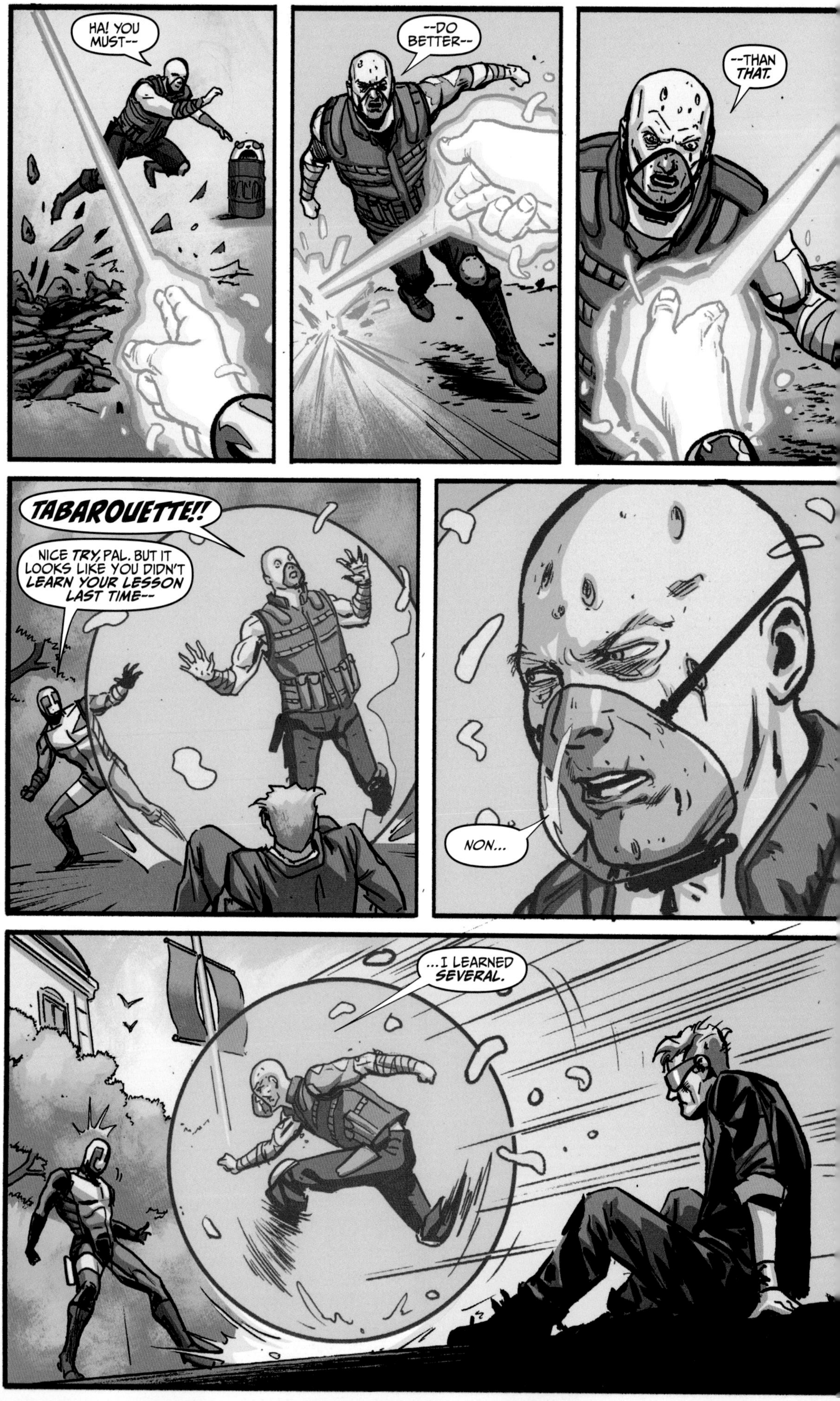

HA! YOU MUST--
--DO BETTER--
--THAN THAT.
TABAROUETTE!!
NICE TRY, PAL. BUT IT LOOKS LIKE YOU DIDN'T LEARN YOUR LESSON LAST TIME--
NON...
...I LEARNED SEVERAL.

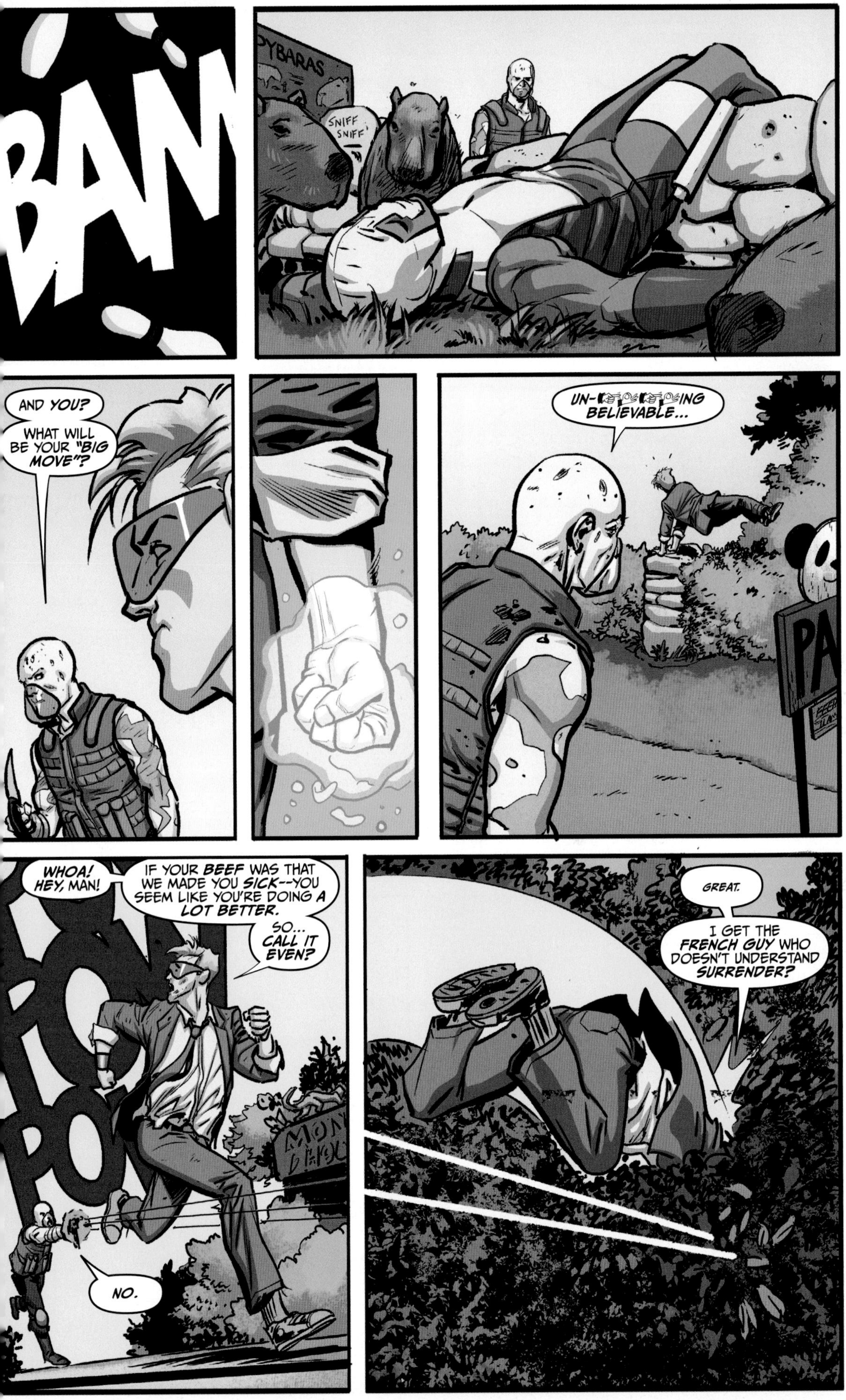
BAM
SNIFF SNIFF
AND YOU?
WHAT WILL BE YOUR "BIG MOVE"?
UN-ING BELIEVABLE...
WHOA! HEY, MAN!
IF YOUR BEEF WAS THAT WE MADE YOU SICK--YOU SEEM LIKE YOU'RE DOING A LOT BETTER.
SO... CALL IT EVEN?
NO.
GREAT.
I GET THE FRENCH GUY WHO DOESN'T UNDERSTAND SURRENDER?

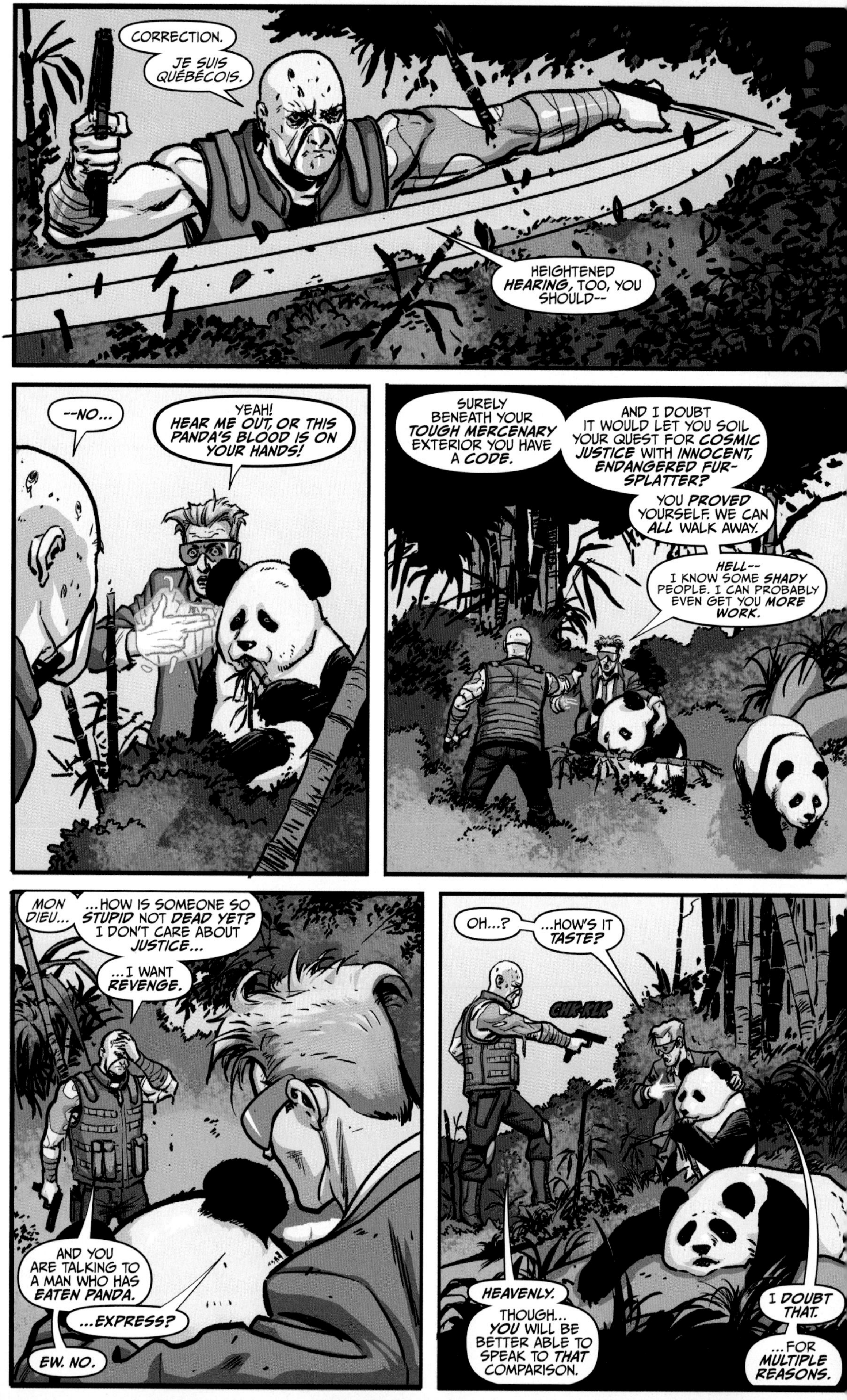
CORRECTION.
JE SUIS QUÉBÉCOIS.
HEIGHTENED HEARING, TOO, YOU SHOULD--
--NO...
YEAH! HEAR ME OUT, OR THIS PANDA'S BLOOD IS ON YOUR HANDS!
SURELY BENEATH YOUR TOUGH MERCENARY EXTERIOR YOU HAVE A CODE.
AND I DOUBT IT WOULD LET YOU SOIL YOUR QUEST FOR COSMIC JUSTICE WITH INNOCENT, ENDANGERED FUR-SPLATTER?
YOU PROVED YOURSELF. WE CAN ALL WALK AWAY.
HELL-- I KNOW SOME SHADY PEOPLE. I CAN PROBABLY EVEN GET YOU MORE WORK.
MON DIEU...
...HOW IS SOMEONE SO STUPID NOT DEAD YET? I DON'T CARE ABOUT JUSTICE...
...I WANT REVENGE.
AND YOU ARE TALKING TO A MAN WHO HAS EATEN PANDA.
...EXPRESS?
EW. NO.
OH...?
...HOW'S IT TASTE?
CHK-KLK
HEAVENLY.
THOUGH... YOU WILL BE BETTER ABLE TO SPEAK TO THAT COMPARISON.
I DOUBT THAT.
...FOR MULTIPLE REASONS.

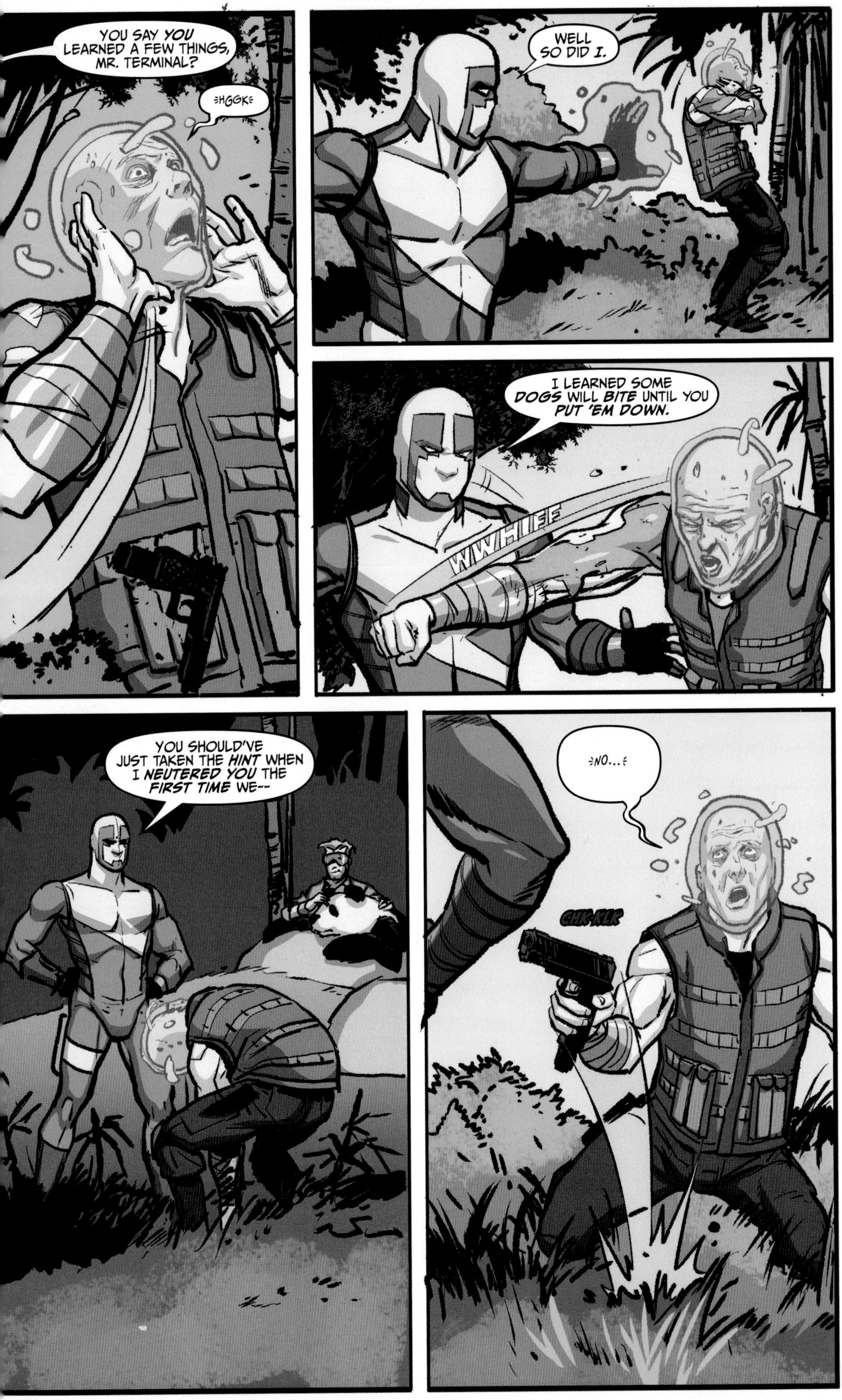
YOU SAY YOU LEARNED A FEW THINGS, MR. TERMINAL?
HGGK
WELL SO DID I.
I LEARNED SOME DOGS WILL BITE UNTIL YOU PUT 'EM DOWN.
WWHIFF
YOU SHOULD'VE JUST TAKEN THE HINT WHEN I NEUTERED YOU THE FIRST TIME WE--
NO...
CHK-KLK

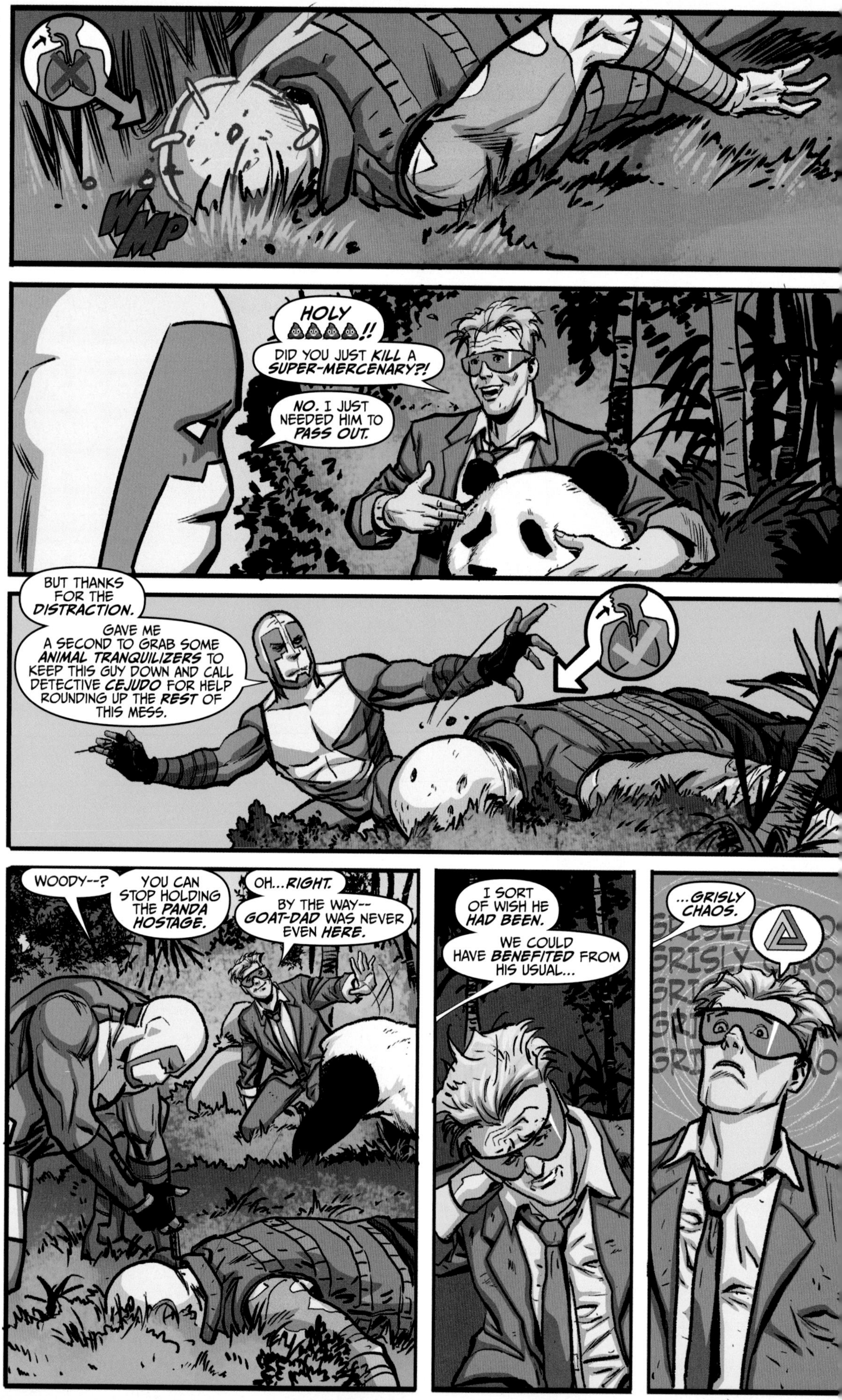
WMP
WMP
HOLY 💩💩💩💩!!
DID YOU JUST KILL A SUPER-MERCENARY?!
NO. I JUST NEEDED HIM TO PASS OUT.
BUT THANKS FOR THE DISTRACTION.
GAVE ME A SECOND TO GRAB SOME ANIMAL TRANQUILIZERS TO KEEP THIS GUY DOWN AND CALL DETECTIVE CEJUDO FOR HELP ROUNDING UP THE REST OF THIS MESS.
WOODY--?
YOU CAN STOP HOLDING THE PANDA HOSTAGE.
OH...RIGHT.
BY THE WAY-- GOAT-DAD WAS NEVER EVEN HERE.
I SORT OF WISH HE HAD BEEN.
WE COULD HAVE BENEFITED FROM HIS USUAL...
...GRISLY CHAOS.

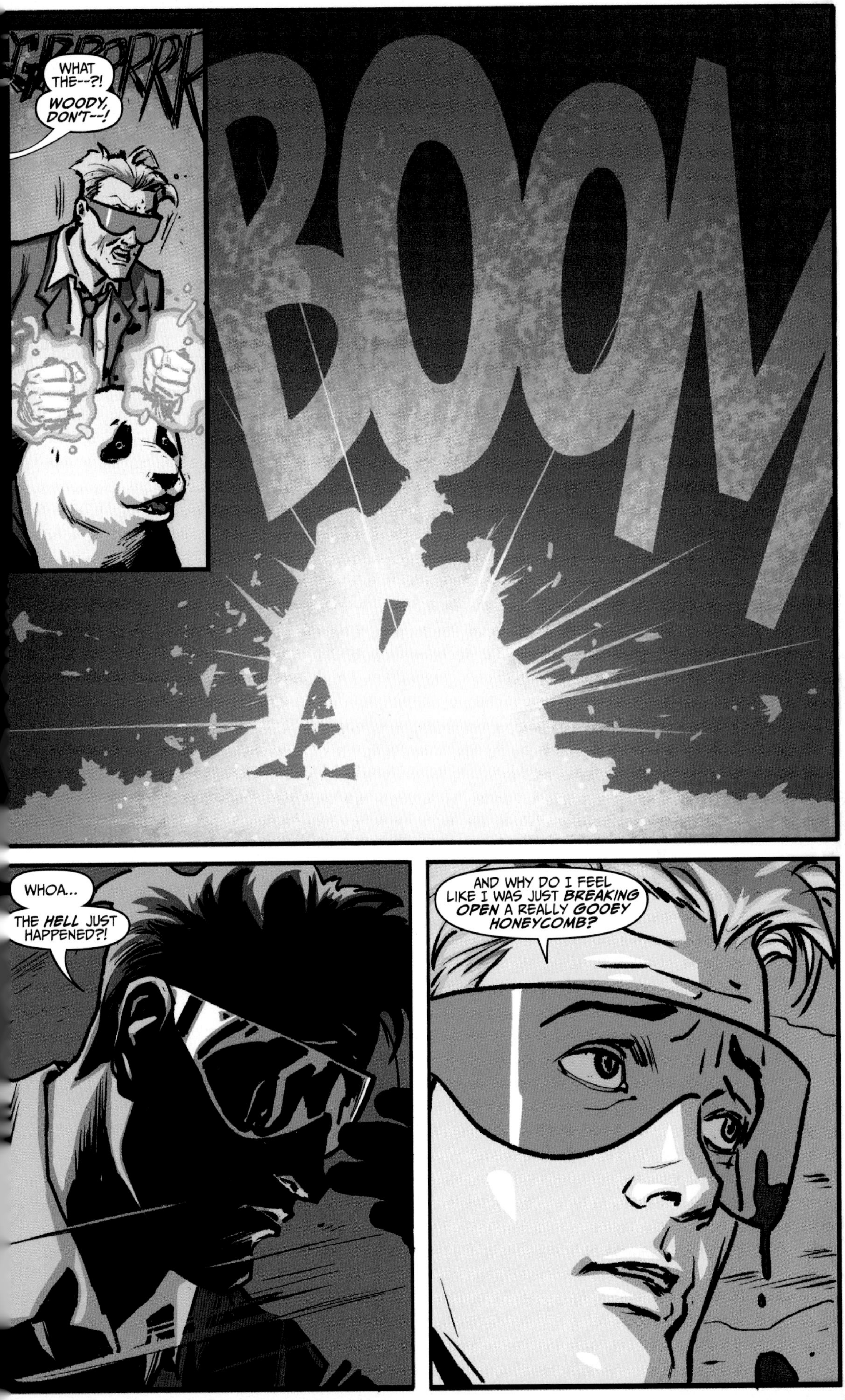
WHAT THE--?!
WOODY, DON'T--!
BOOM
WHOA...
THE HELL JUST HAPPENED?!
AND WHY DO I FEEL LIKE I WAS JUST BREAKING OPEN A REALLY GOOEY HONEYCOMB?

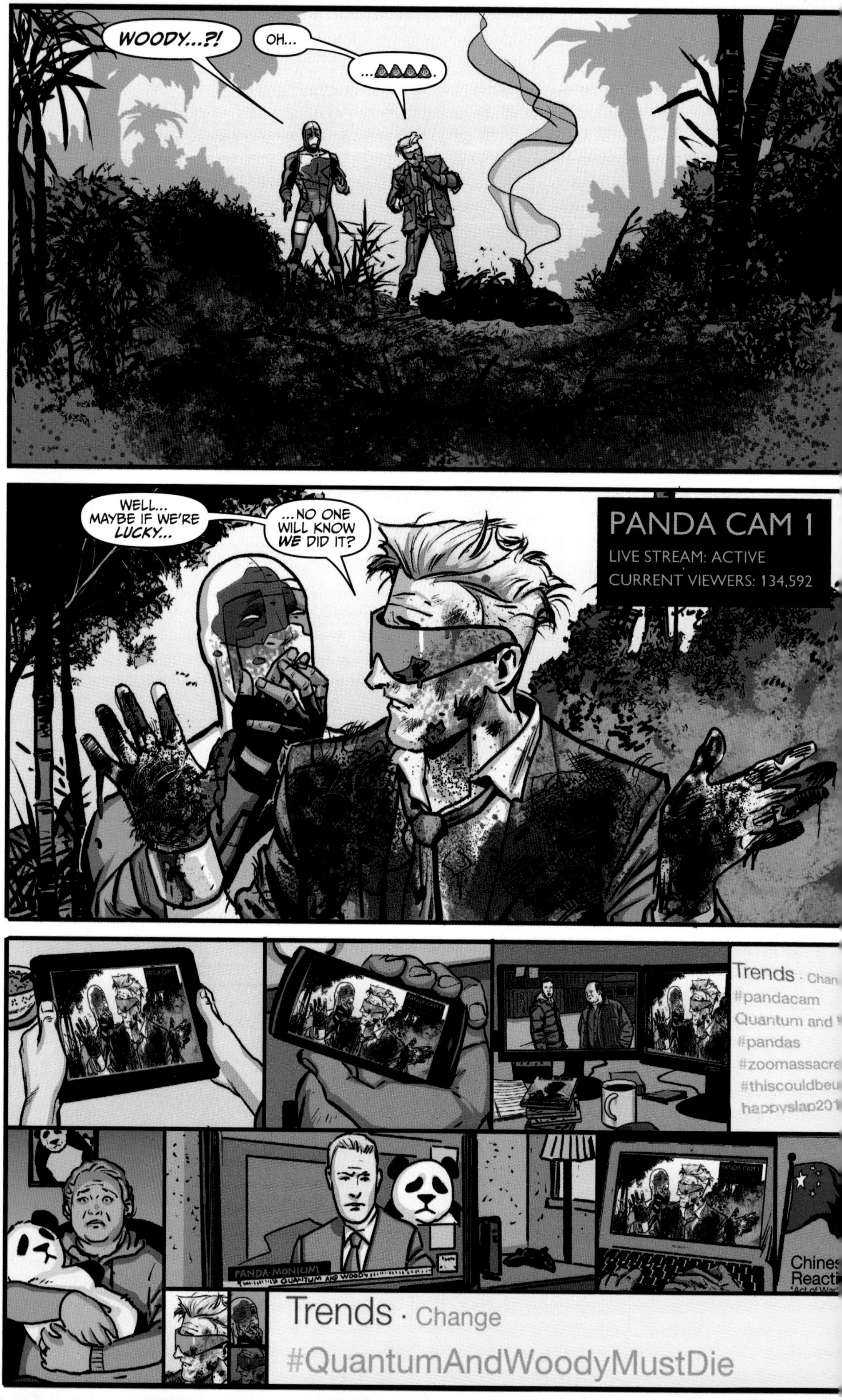
WOODY...?!
OH...
...💩💩💩💩.
WELL... MAYBE IF WE'RE LUCKY...
...NO ONE WILL KNOW WE DID IT?
PANDA CAM 1
LIVE STREAM: ACTIVE
CURRENT VIEWERS: 134,592
Trends · Chan
#pandacam
Quantum and
#pandas
#zoomassacre
#thiscouldbeu
happyslap201
PANDA-MONIUM
QUANTUM AND WOODY
Chines
Reacti
Trends · Change
#QuantumAndWoodyMustDie

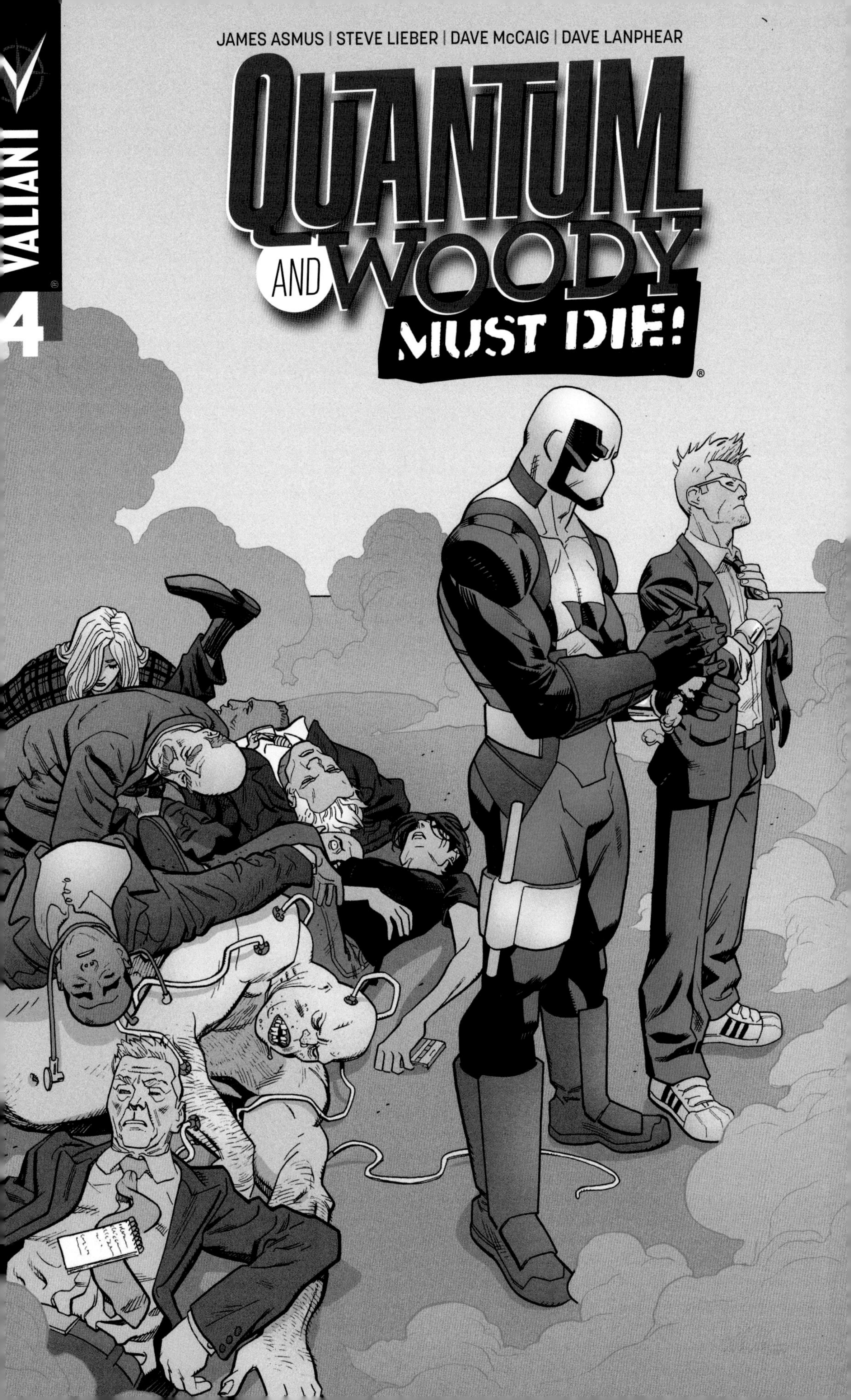
VALIANT
4
JAMES ASMUS | STEVE LIEBER | DAVE McCAIG | DAVE LANPHEAR
QUANTUM AND WOODY
MUST DIE!

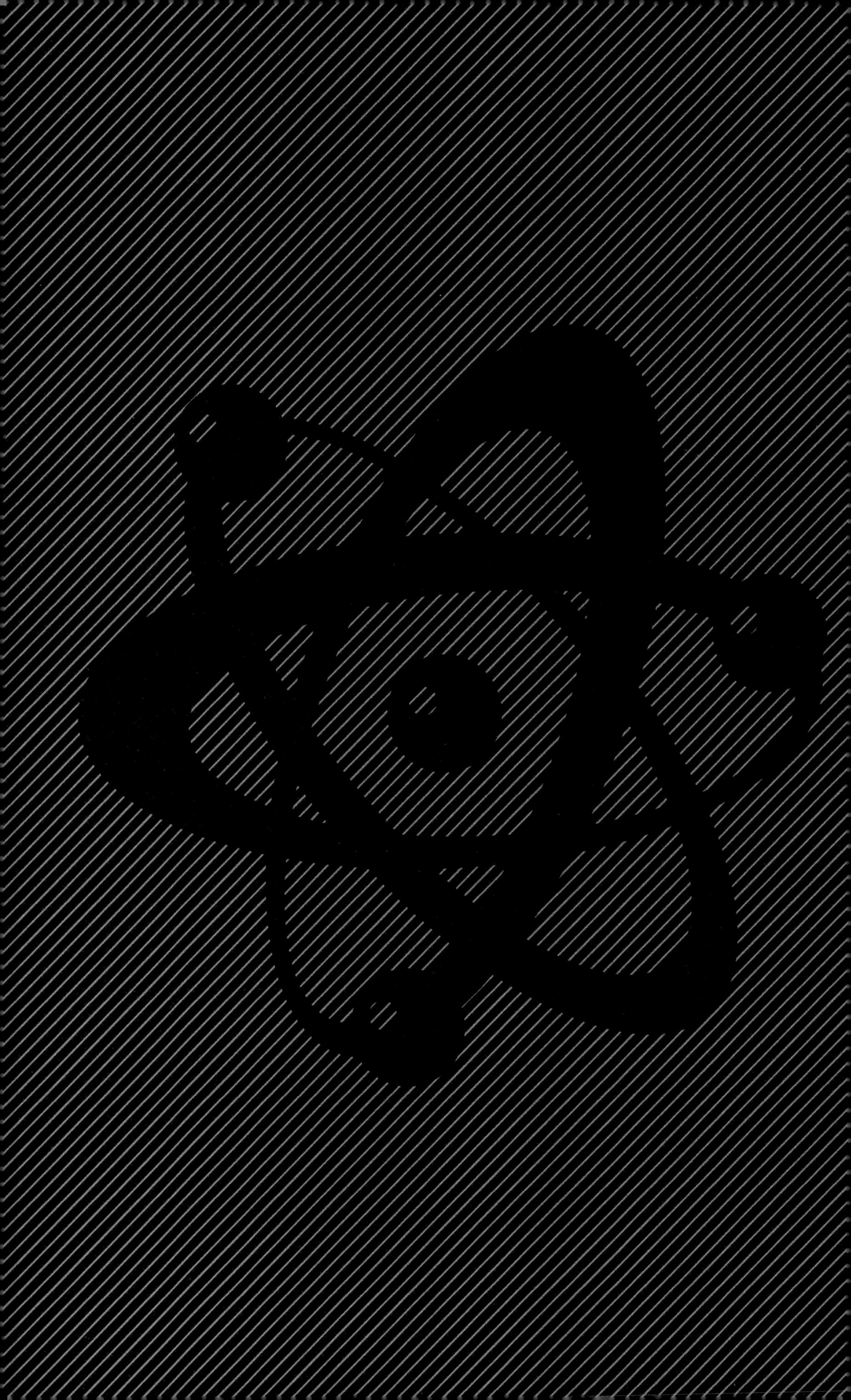

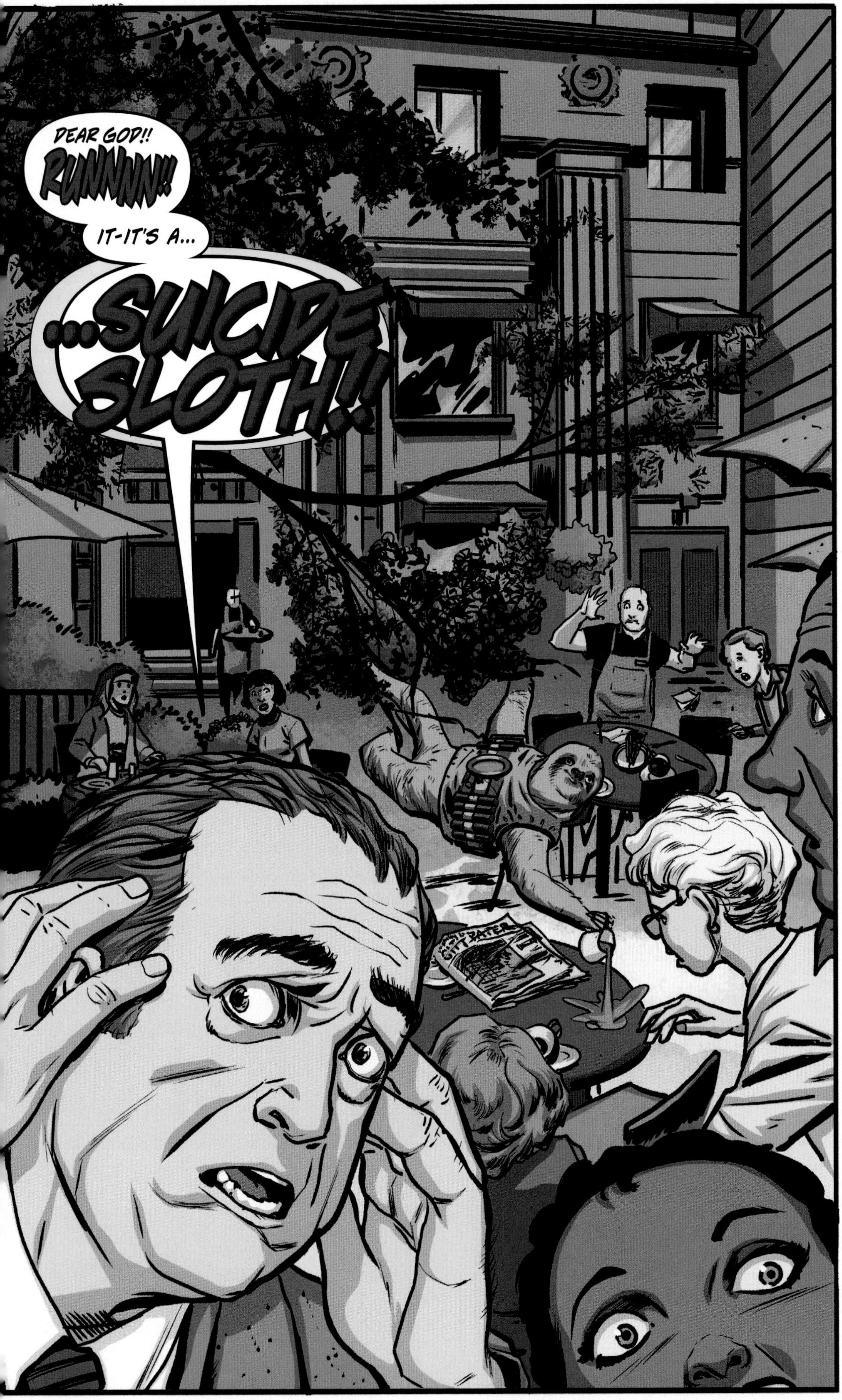
DEAR GOD!! RUNNNN!!
IT-IT'S A...
...SUICIDE SLOTH!!

(Still Probably the Least Deadly Sin.)

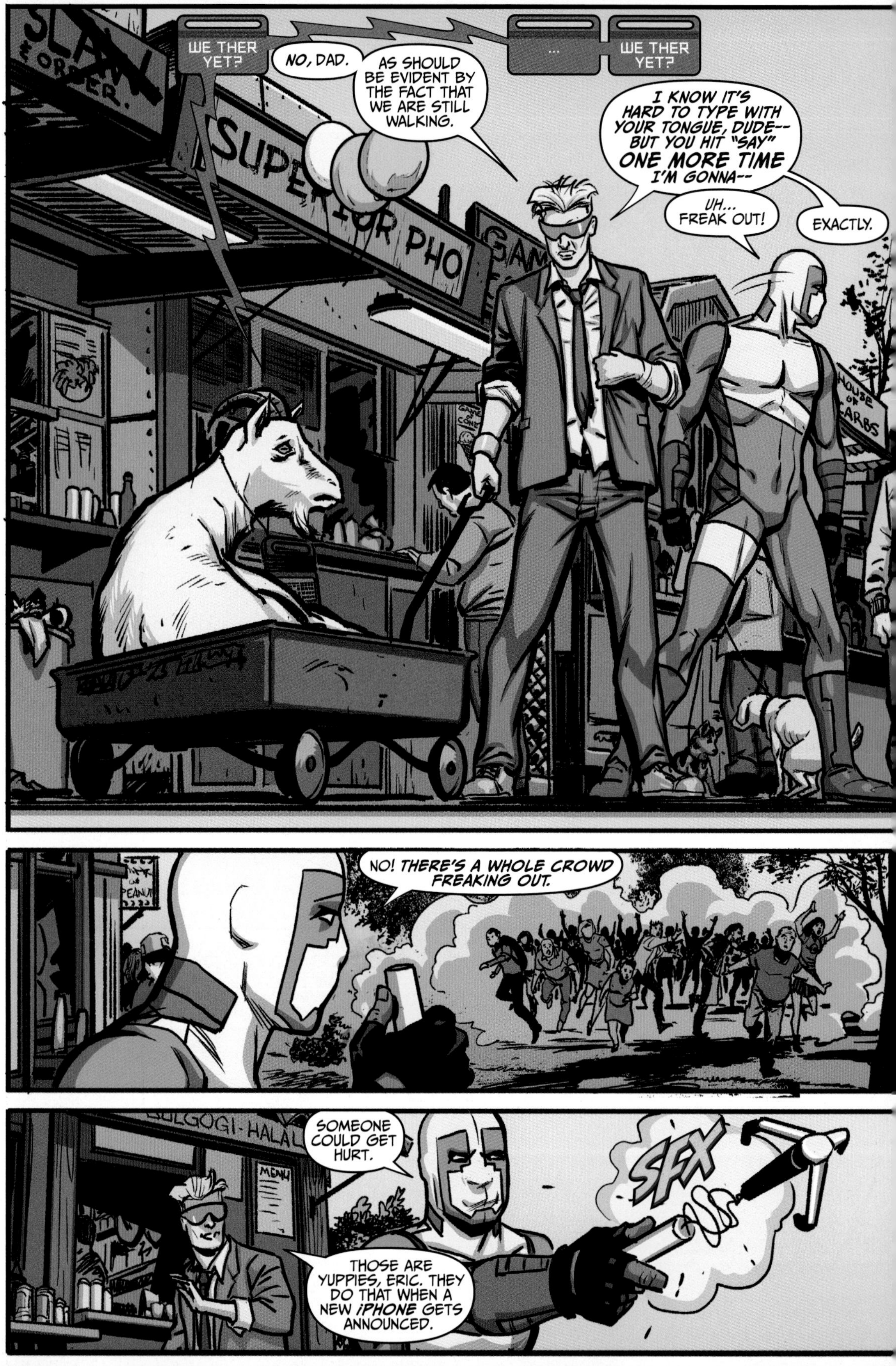
WE THER YET?
NO, DAD.
AS SHOULD BE EVIDENT BY THE FACT THAT WE ARE STILL WALKING.
...
WE THER YET?
I KNOW IT'S HARD TO TYPE WITH YOUR TONGUE, DUDE-- BUT YOU HIT "SAY" ONE MORE TIME I'M GONNA--
UH... FREAK OUT!
EXACTLY.
HOUSE OF CARBS
NO! THERE'S A WHOLE CROWD FREAKING OUT.
SOMEONE COULD GET HURT.
MENU
SFX
THOSE ARE YUPPIES, ERIC. THEY DO THAT WHEN A NEW iPHONE GETS ANNOUNCED.

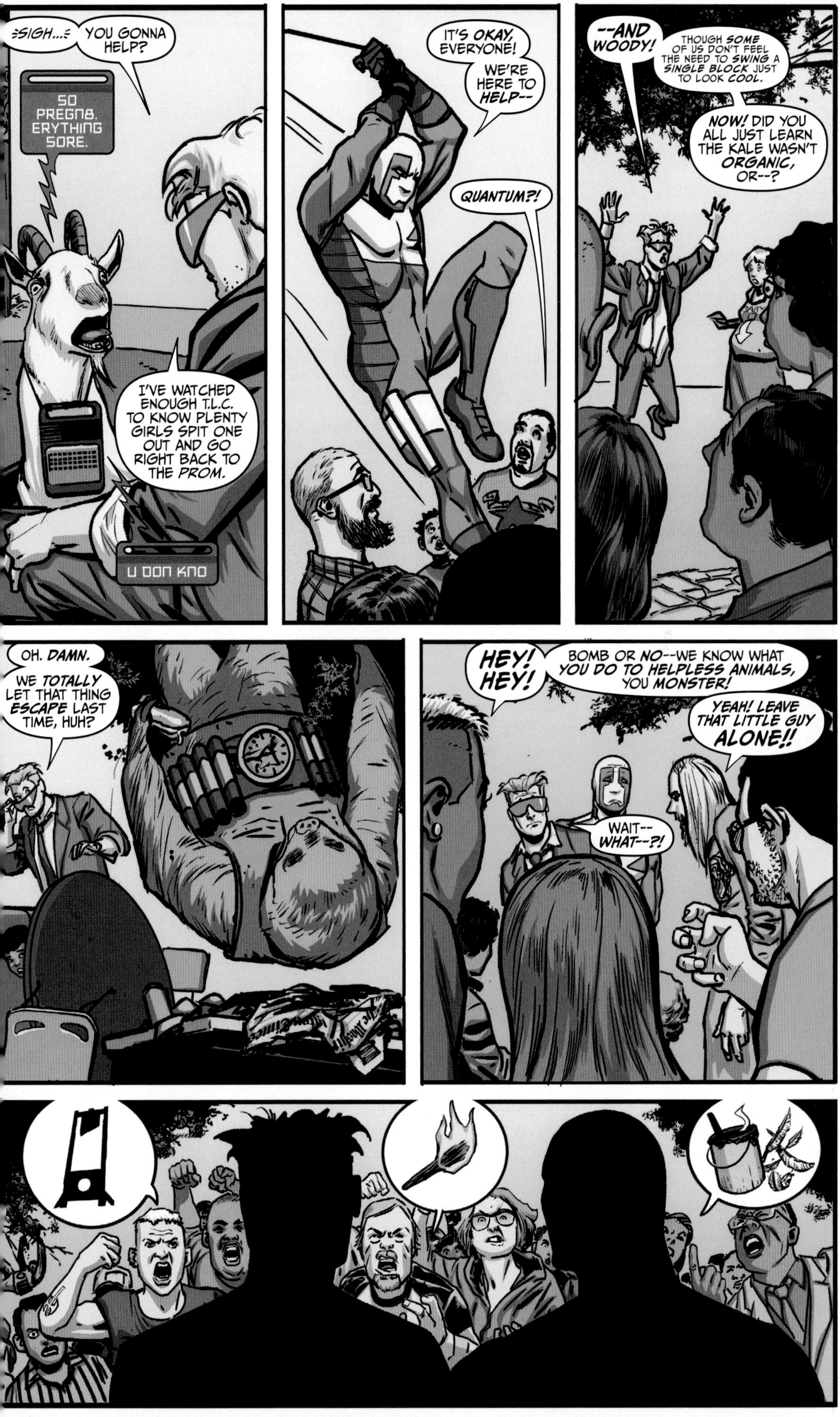

SIGH...
YOU GONNA HELP?
SO PREGN8. ERYTHING SORE.
I'VE WATCHED ENOUGH T.L.C. TO KNOW PLENTY GIRLS SPIT ONE OUT AND GO RIGHT BACK TO THE PROM.
U DON KNO
IT'S OKAY, EVERYONE!
WE'RE HERE TO HELP--
QUANTUM?!
--AND WOODY!
THOUGH SOME OF US DON'T FEEL THE NEED TO SWING A SINGLE BLOCK JUST TO LOOK COOL.
NOW! DID YOU ALL JUST LEARN THE KALE WASN'T ORGANIC, OR--?
OH. DAMN.
WE TOTALLY LET THAT THING ESCAPE LAST TIME, HUH?
HEY! HEY!
BOMB OR NO--WE KNOW WHAT YOU DO TO HELPLESS ANIMALS, YOU MONSTER!
YEAH! LEAVE THAT LITTLE GUY ALONE!!
WAIT-- WHAT--?!

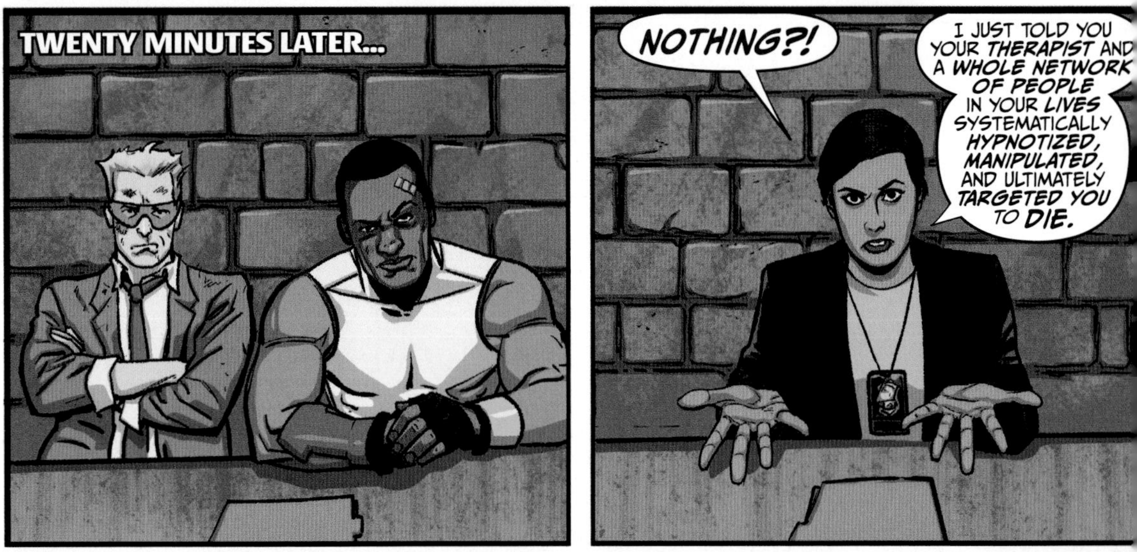
TWENTY MINUTES LATER...
NOTHING?!
I JUST TOLD YOU YOUR THERAPIST AND A WHOLE NETWORK OF PEOPLE IN YOUR LIVES SYSTEMATICALLY HYPNOTIZED, MANIPULATED, AND ULTIMATELY TARGETED YOU TO DIE.

Cop To It.

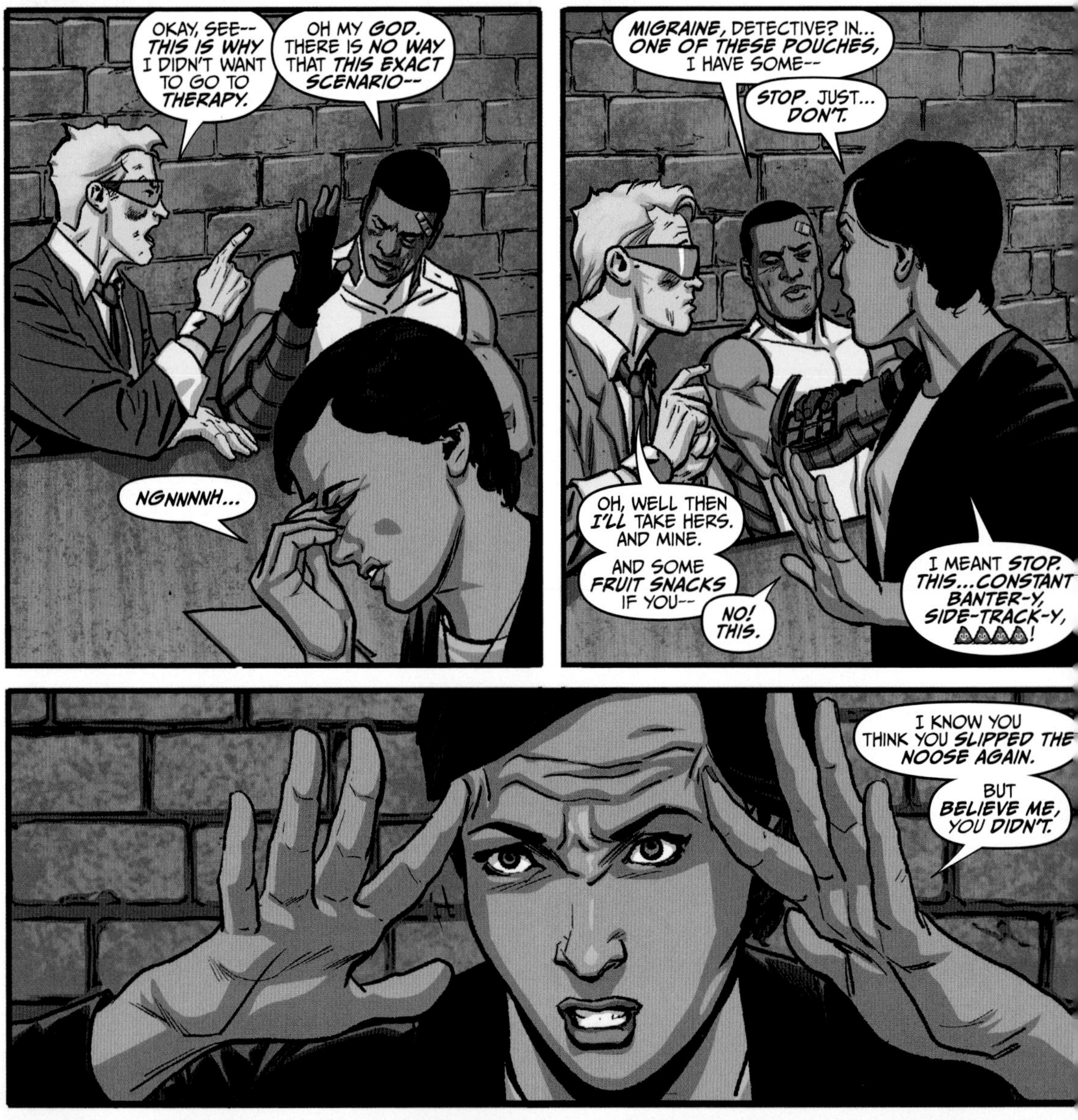
OKAY, SEE-- THIS IS WHY I DIDN'T WANT TO GO TO THERAPY.
OH MY GOD. THERE IS NO WAY THAT THIS EXACT SCENARIO--
NGNNNNH...
MIGRAINE, DETECTIVE? IN... ONE OF THESE POUCHES, I HAVE SOME--
STOP. JUST... DON'T.
OH, WELL THEN I'LL TAKE HERS. AND MINE.
AND SOME FRUIT SNACKS IF YOU--
NO! THIS.
I MEANT STOP. THIS...CONSTANT BANTER-Y, SIDE-TRACK-Y, !
I KNOW YOU THINK YOU SLIPPED THE NOOSE AGAIN.
BUT BELIEVE ME, YOU DIDN'T.

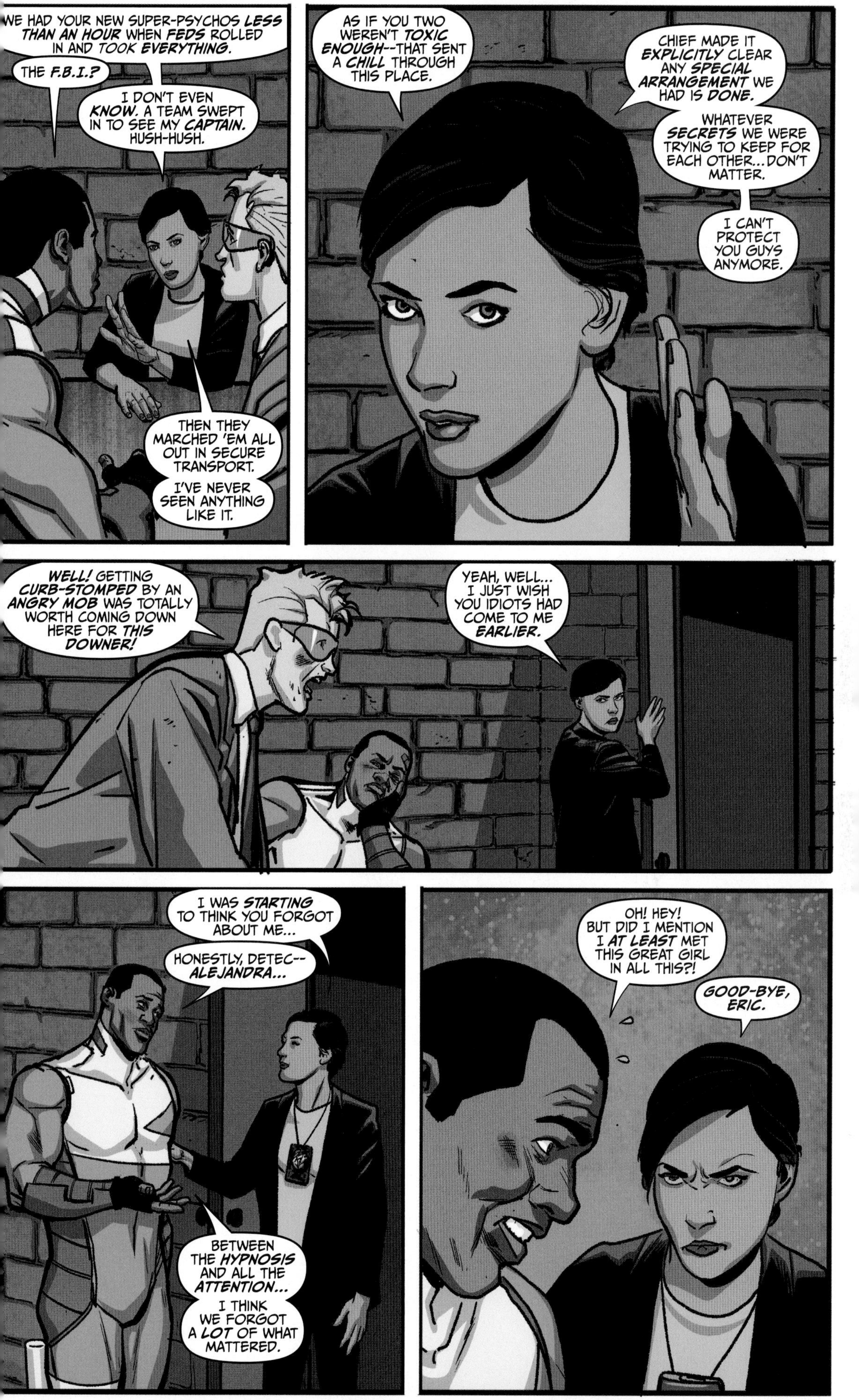
WE HAD YOUR NEW SUPER-PSYCHOS LESS THAN AN HOUR WHEN FEDS ROLLED IN AND TOOK EVERYTHING.
THE F.B.I.?
I DON'T EVEN KNOW. A TEAM SWEPT IN TO SEE MY CAPTAIN. HUSH-HUSH.
THEN THEY MARCHED 'EM ALL OUT IN SECURE TRANSPORT.
I'VE NEVER SEEN ANYTHING LIKE IT.
AS IF YOU TWO WEREN'T TOXIC ENOUGH--THAT SENT A CHILL THROUGH THIS PLACE.
CHIEF MADE IT EXPLICITLY CLEAR ANY SPECIAL ARRANGEMENT WE HAD IS DONE.
WHATEVER SECRETS WE WERE TRYING TO KEEP FOR EACH OTHER... DON'T MATTER.
I CAN'T PROTECT YOU GUYS ANYMORE.
WELL! GETTING CURB-STOMPED BY AN ANGRY MOB WAS TOTALLY WORTH COMING DOWN HERE FOR THIS DOWNER!
YEAH, WELL... I JUST WISH YOU IDIOTS HAD COME TO ME EARLIER.
I WAS STARTING TO THINK YOU FORGOT ABOUT ME...
HONESTLY, DETEC-- ALEJANDRA...
BETWEEN THE HYPNOSIS AND ALL THE ATTENTION...
I THINK WE FORGOT A LOT OF WHAT MATTERED.
OH! HEY! BUT DID I MENTION I AT LEAST MET THIS GREAT GIRL IN ALL THIS?!
GOOD-BYE, ERIC.

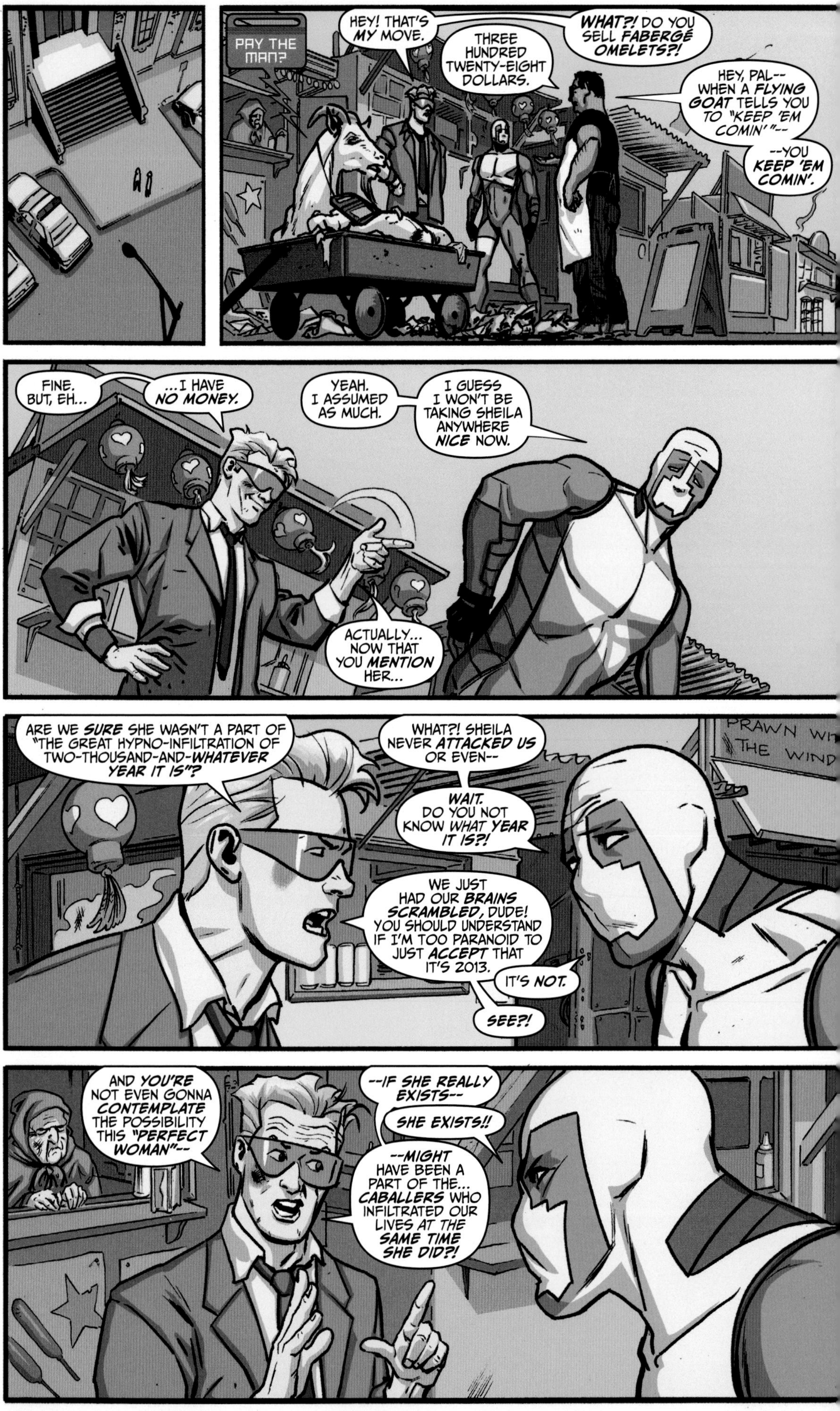
PAY THE MAN?
HEY! THAT'S MY MOVE.
THREE HUNDRED TWENTY-EIGHT DOLLARS.
WHAT?! DO YOU SELL FABERGÉ OMELETS?!
HEY, PAL-- WHEN A FLYING GOAT TELLS YOU TO "KEEP 'EM COMIN'"--
--YOU KEEP 'EM COMIN'.
FINE. BUT, EH...
...I HAVE NO MONEY.
YEAH. I ASSUMED AS MUCH.
I GUESS I WON'T BE TAKING SHEILA ANYWHERE NICE NOW.
ACTUALLY... NOW THAT YOU MENTION HER...
ARE WE SURE SHE WASN'T A PART OF "THE GREAT HYPNO-INFILTRATION OF TWO-THOUSAND-AND-WHATEVER YEAR IT IS"?
WHAT?! SHEILA NEVER ATTACKED US OR EVEN--
WAIT. DO YOU NOT KNOW WHAT YEAR IT IS?!
PRAWN WI THE WIND
WE JUST HAD OUR BRAINS SCRAMBLED, DUDE! YOU SHOULD UNDERSTAND IF I'M TOO PARANOID TO JUST ACCEPT THAT IT'S 2013.
IT'S NOT.
SEE?!
AND YOU'RE NOT EVEN GONNA CONTEMPLATE THE POSSIBILITY THIS "PERFECT WOMAN"--
--IF SHE REALLY EXISTS--
SHE EXISTS!!
--MIGHT HAVE BEEN A PART OF THE... CABALLERS WHO INFILTRATED OUR LIVES AT THE SAME TIME SHE DID?!

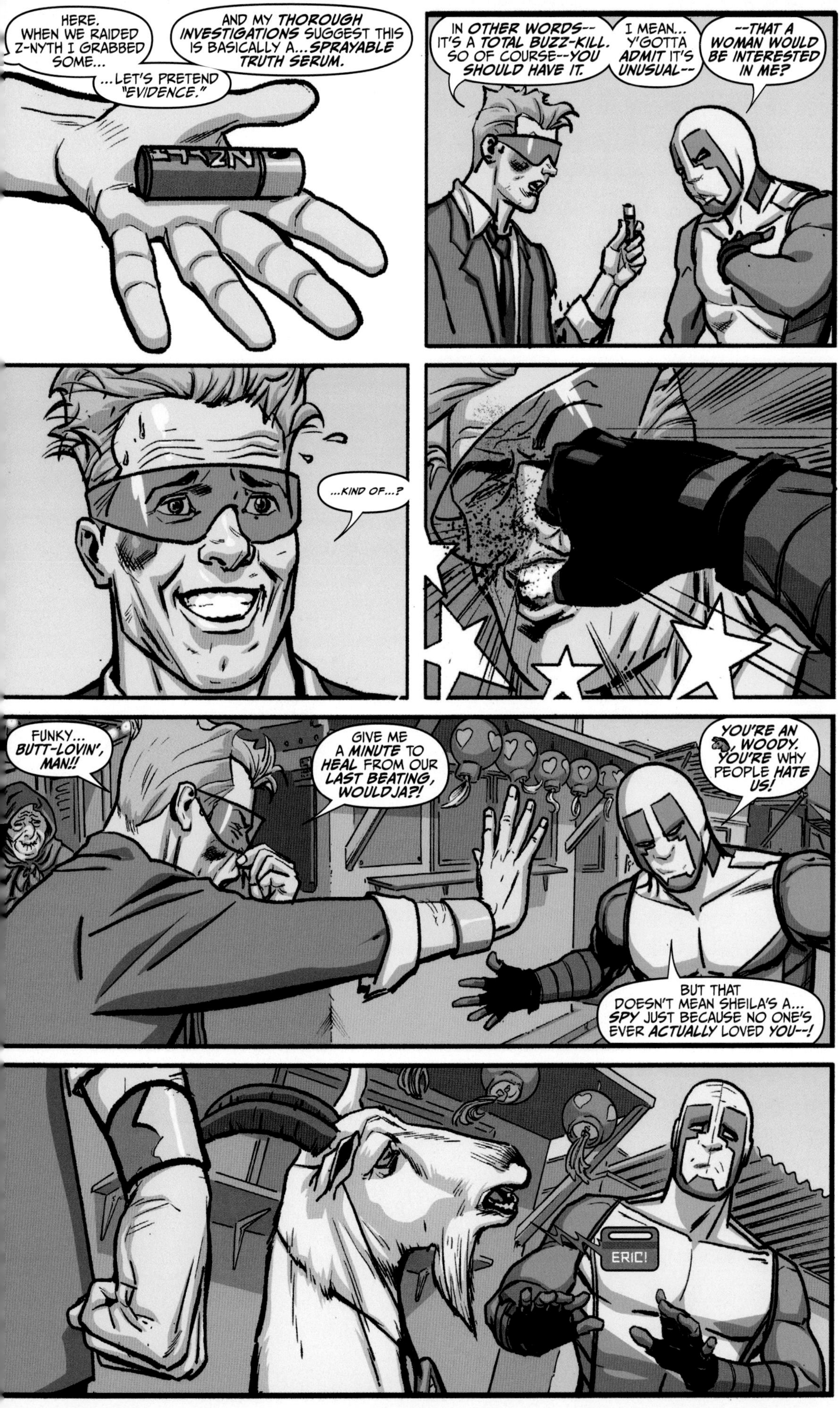
HERE. WHEN WE RAIDED Z-NYTH I GRABBED SOME...
...LET'S PRETEND "EVIDENCE."
AND MY THOROUGH INVESTIGATIONS SUGGEST THIS IS BASICALLY A...SPRAYABLE TRUTH SERUM.
IN OTHER WORDS-- IT'S A TOTAL BUZZ-KILL. SO OF COURSE--YOU SHOULD HAVE IT.
I MEAN... Y'GOTTA ADMIT IT'S UNUSUAL--
--THAT A WOMAN WOULD BE INTERESTED IN ME?
...KIND OF...?
FUNKY... BUTT-LOVIN', MAN!!
GIVE ME A MINUTE TO HEAL FROM OUR LAST BEATING, WOULDJA?!
YOU'RE AN , WOODY. YOU'RE WHY PEOPLE HATE US!
BUT THAT DOESN'T MEAN SHEILA'S A... SPY JUST BECAUSE NO ONE'S EVER ACTUALLY LOVED YOU--!
ERIC!

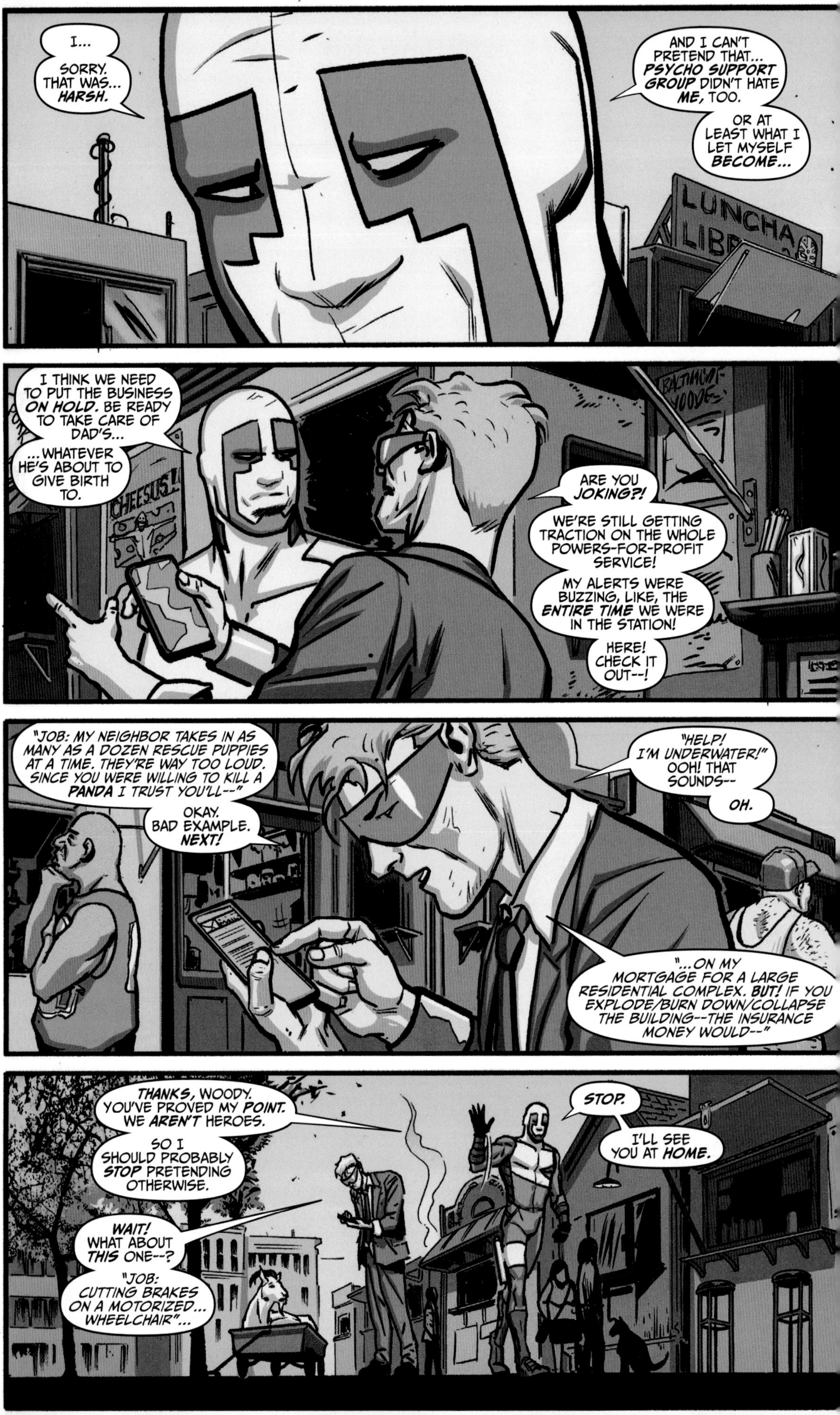
I...
SORRY. THAT WAS... ***HARSH.***
AND I CAN'T PRETEND THAT... ***PSYCHO SUPPORT GROUP*** DIDN'T HATE ***ME,*** TOO.
OR AT LEAST WHAT I LET MYSELF ***BECOME...***
LUNCHA LIBRE
I THINK WE NEED TO PUT THE BUSINESS ***ON HOLD.*** BE READY TO TAKE CARE OF DAD'S...
...WHATEVER HE'S ABOUT TO GIVE BIRTH TO.
CHEESUS!
ARE YOU ***JOKING?!***
WE'RE STILL GETTING TRACTION ON THE WHOLE POWERS-FOR-PROFIT SERVICE!
MY ALERTS WERE BUZZING, LIKE, THE ***ENTIRE TIME*** WE WERE IN THE STATION!
HERE! CHECK IT OUT--!
"JOB: MY NEIGHBOR TAKES IN AS MANY AS A DOZEN RESCUE PUPPIES AT A TIME. THEY'RE WAY TOO LOUD. SINCE YOU WERE WILLING TO KILL A ***PANDA*** *I TRUST YOU'LL--"*
OKAY. BAD EXAMPLE. ***NEXT!***
"HELP! I'M UNDERWATER!" OOH! THAT SOUNDS--
OH.
"...ON MY MORTGAGE FOR A LARGE RESIDENTIAL COMPLEX. ***BUT!*** *IF YOU EXPLODE/BURN DOWN/COLLAPSE THE BUILDING--THE INSURANCE MONEY WOULD--"*
THANKS, WOODY. YOU'VE PROVED MY ***POINT.*** WE ***AREN'T*** HEROES.
SO I SHOULD PROBABLY ***STOP*** PRETENDING OTHERWISE.
STOP.
I'LL SEE YOU AT ***HOME.***
WAIT! WHAT ABOUT ***THIS*** ONE--?
"JOB: CUTTING BRAKES ON A MOTORIZED... WHEELCHAIR"...

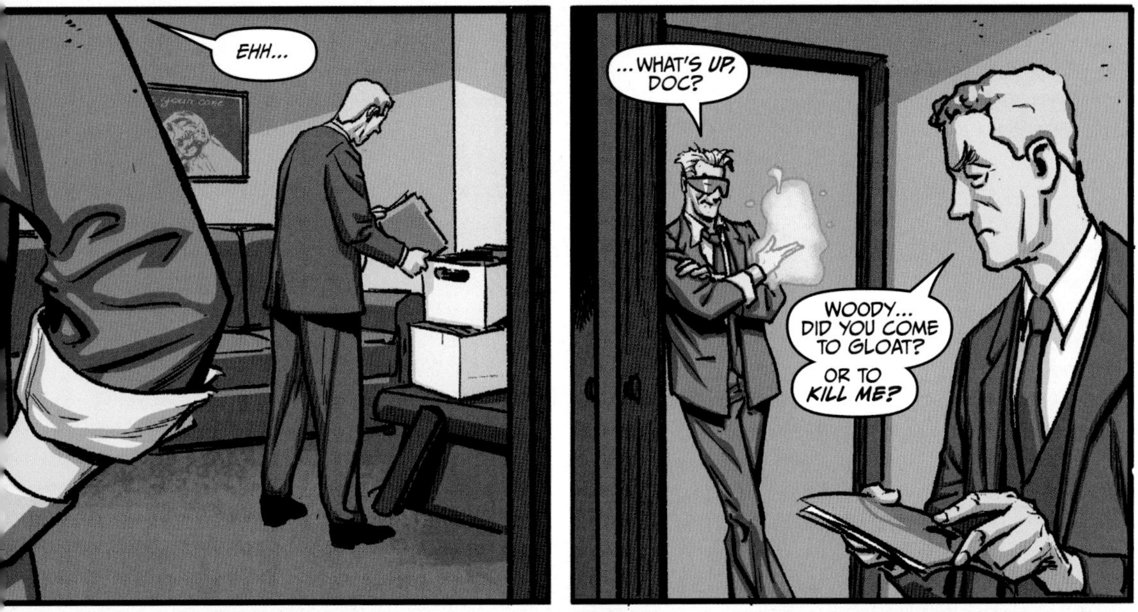
EHH...
...WHAT'S UP, DOC?
WOODY... DID YOU COME TO GLOAT?
OR TO KILL ME?

Breakthrough. (To The Other Side.)

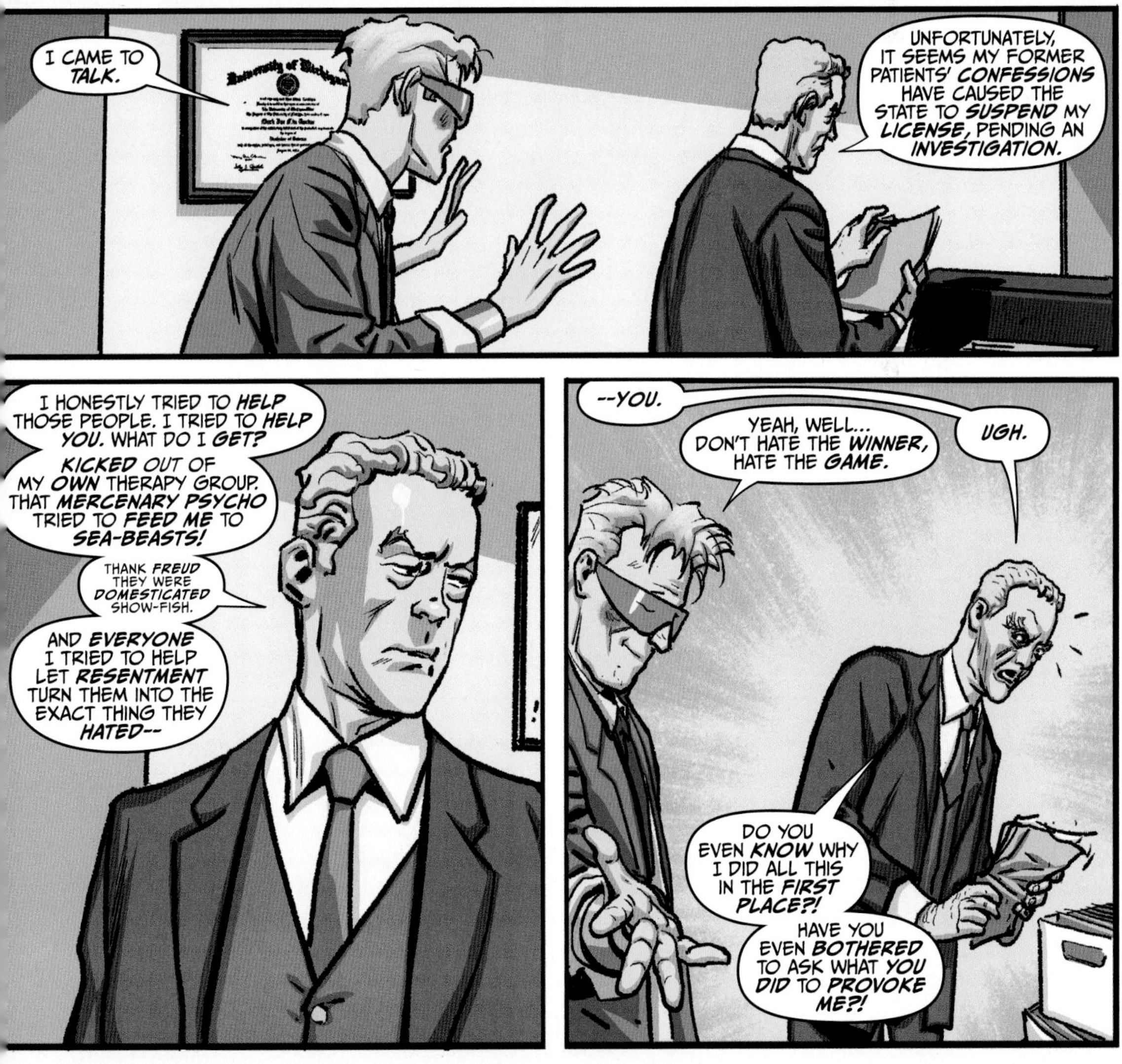
I CAME TO TALK.
UNFORTUNATELY, IT SEEMS MY FORMER PATIENTS' CONFESSIONS HAVE CAUSED THE STATE TO SUSPEND MY LICENSE, PENDING AN INVESTIGATION.
I HONESTLY TRIED TO HELP THOSE PEOPLE. I TRIED TO HELP YOU. WHAT DO I GET?
KICKED OUT OF MY OWN THERAPY GROUP. THAT MERCENARY PSYCHO TRIED TO FEED ME TO SEA-BEASTS!
THANK FREUD THEY WERE DOMESTICATED SHOW-FISH.
AND EVERYONE I TRIED TO HELP LET RESENTMENT TURN THEM INTO THE EXACT THING THEY HATED--
--YOU.
YEAH, WELL... DON'T HATE THE WINNER, HATE THE GAME.
UGH.
DO YOU EVEN KNOW WHY I DID ALL THIS IN THE FIRST PLACE?!
HAVE YOU EVEN BOTHERED TO ASK WHAT YOU DID TO PROVOKE ME?!

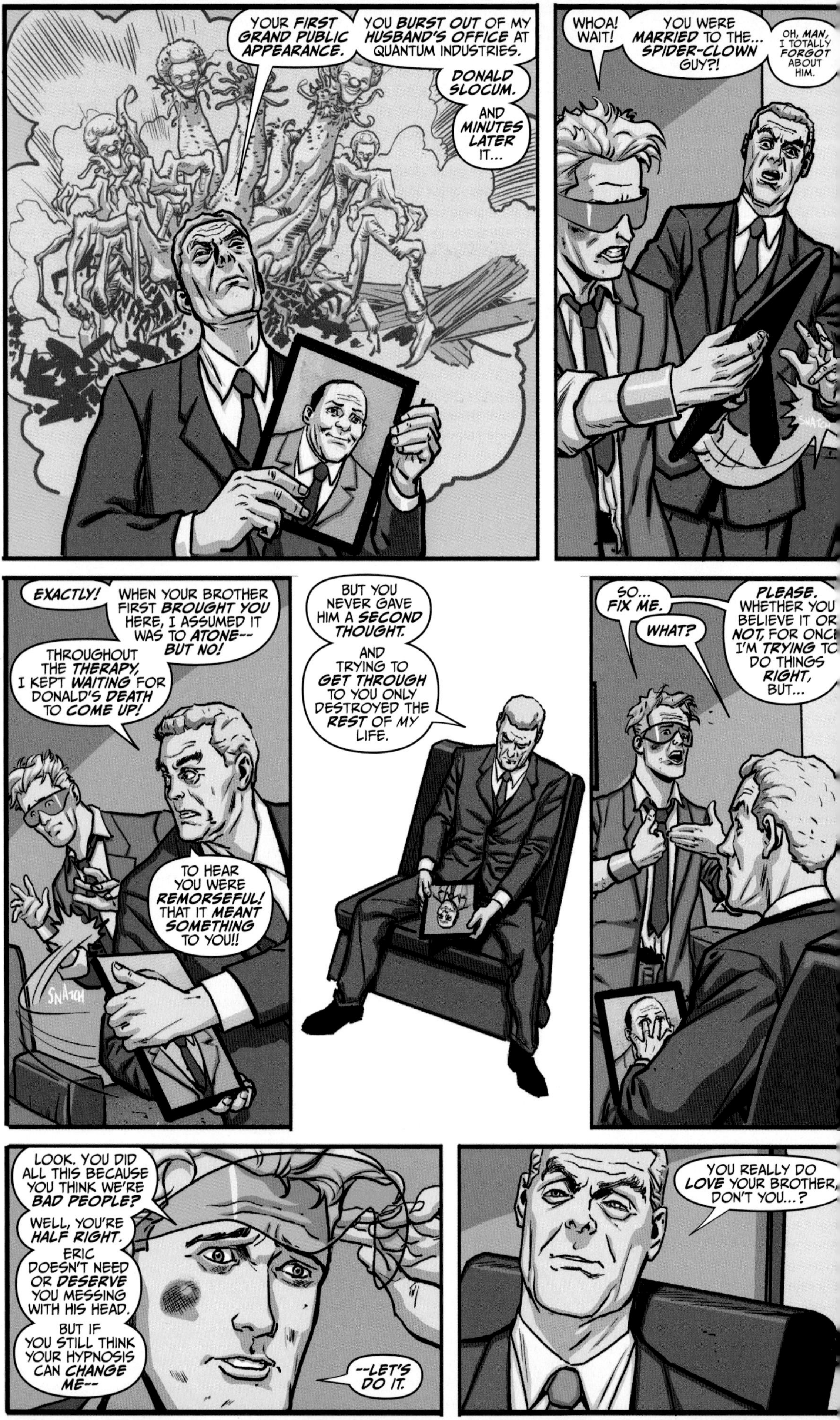

YOUR FIRST GRAND PUBLIC APPEARANCE.
YOU BURST OUT OF MY HUSBAND'S OFFICE AT QUANTUM INDUSTRIES.
DONALD SLOCUM.
AND MINUTES LATER IT...
WHOA! WAIT!
YOU WERE MARRIED TO THE... SPIDER-CLOWN GUY?!
OH, MAN, I TOTALLY FORGOT ABOUT HIM.
SNATCH
EXACTLY!
WHEN YOUR BROTHER FIRST BROUGHT YOU HERE, I ASSUMED IT WAS TO ATONE-- BUT NO!
THROUGHOUT THE THERAPY, I KEPT WAITING FOR DONALD'S DEATH TO COME UP!
TO HEAR YOU WERE REMORSEFUL! THAT IT MEANT SOMETHING TO YOU!!
SNATCH
BUT YOU NEVER GAVE HIM A SECOND THOUGHT.
AND TRYING TO GET THROUGH TO YOU ONLY DESTROYED THE REST OF MY LIFE.
SO... FIX ME.
WHAT?
PLEASE. WHETHER YOU BELIEVE IT OR NOT, FOR ONC I'M TRYING TO DO THINGS RIGHT, BUT...
LOOK. YOU DID ALL THIS BECAUSE YOU THINK WE'RE BAD PEOPLE?
WELL, YOU'RE HALF RIGHT.
ERIC DOESN'T NEED OR DESERVE YOU MESSING WITH HIS HEAD.
BUT IF YOU STILL THINK YOUR HYPNOSIS CAN CHANGE ME--
--LET'S DO IT.
YOU REALLY DO LOVE YOUR BROTHER, DON'T YOU...?

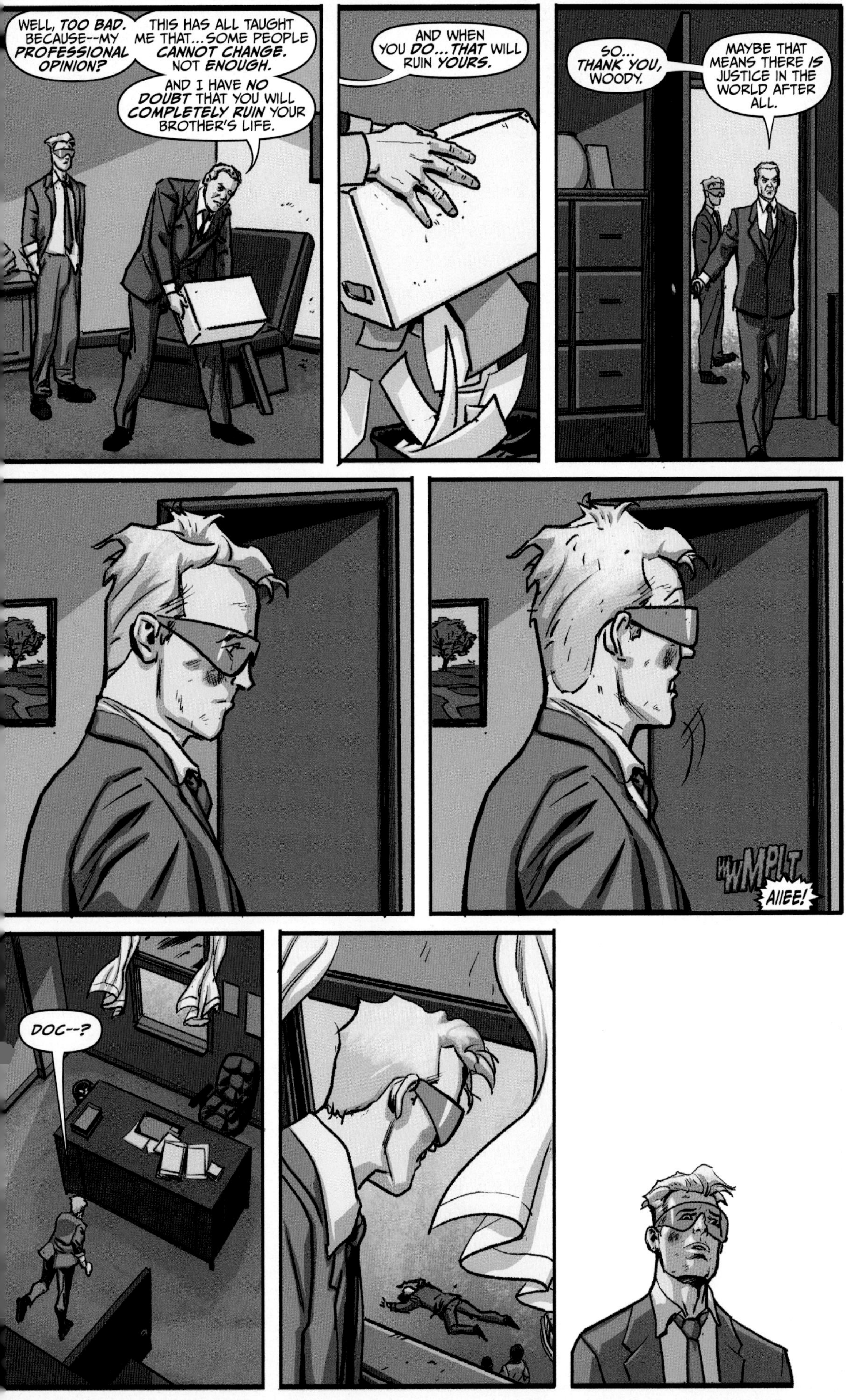
WELL, TOO BAD. BECAUSE--MY PROFESSIONAL OPINION?
THIS HAS ALL TAUGHT ME THAT... SOME PEOPLE CANNOT CHANGE. NOT ENOUGH.
AND I HAVE NO DOUBT THAT YOU WILL COMPLETELY RUIN YOUR BROTHER'S LIFE.
AND WHEN YOU DO... THAT WILL RUIN YOURS.
SO... THANK YOU, WOODY.
MAYBE THAT MEANS THERE IS JUSTICE IN THE WORLD AFTER ALL.
WWMPLT
AIIEE!
DOC--?

Kids (With Brain Damage) Say The Darnedest Things.

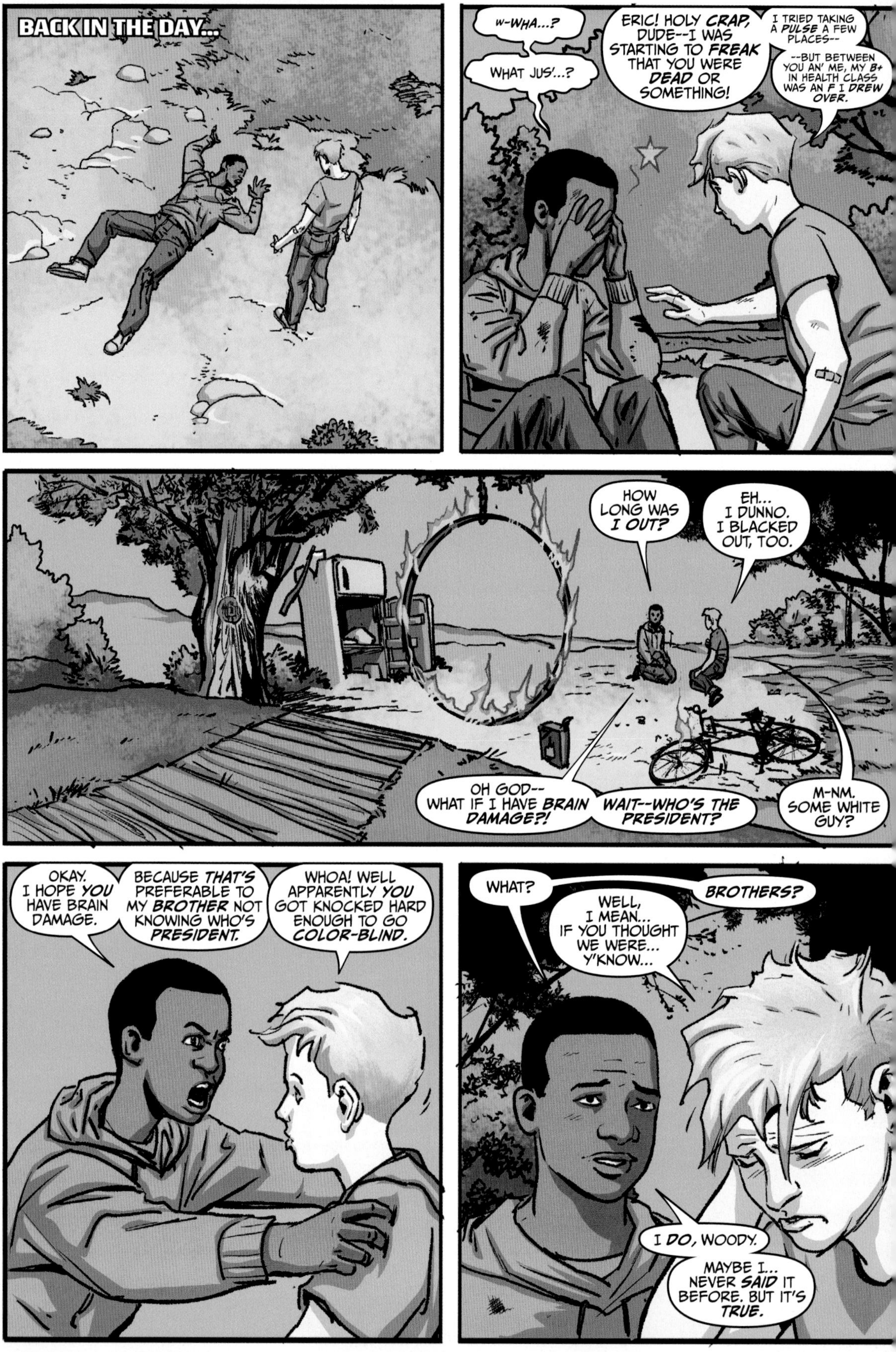

BACK IN THE DAY...
W-WHA...?
WHAT JUS'...?
ERIC! HOLY CRAP, DUDE--I WAS STARTING TO FREAK THAT YOU WERE DEAD OR SOMETHING!
I TRIED TAKING A PULSE A FEW PLACES--
--BUT BETWEEN YOU AN' ME, MY B+ IN HEALTH CLASS WAS AN F I DREW OVER.
HOW LONG WAS I OUT?
EH... I DUNNO. I BLACKED OUT, TOO.
OH GOD-- WHAT IF I HAVE BRAIN DAMAGE?!
WAIT--WHO'S THE PRESIDENT?
M-NM. SOME WHITE GUY?
OKAY. I HOPE YOU HAVE BRAIN DAMAGE.
BECAUSE THAT'S PREFERABLE TO MY BROTHER NOT KNOWING WHO'S PRESIDENT.
WHOA! WELL APPARENTLY YOU GOT KNOCKED HARD ENOUGH TO GO COLOR-BLIND.
WHAT?
BROTHERS?
WELL, I MEAN... IF YOU THOUGHT WE WERE... Y'KNOW...
I DO, WOODY.
MAYBE I... NEVER SAID IT BEFORE. BUT IT'S TRUE.

"AND IT WOULD TAKE A *WORSE BEATING* THAN *THAT* TO MAKE ME *FORGET IT*."

HEY, *UM...* I NEED TO GO CLEAR MY HEAD.

YOU BE OKAY BY YOURSELF?

"DON'T BE AN IDIOT, WOODY."

VOICE LOCK MATCH. WELCOME HOME, GOAT.

OKAY--*SERIOUSLY*-- CAN WE PLEASE MAKE THE *CODE* ANYTHING ELSE?!

OKAY-- THE CHEESE STANDS ALONE.

GO TIME!

GRAND OPENING! FREE DRINKS

FLOOMP!

HUH. I GUESS IT'S TRUE. WHEN GOD CLOSES A DOOR IN YOUR FACE--

--HE OPENS A BAR.

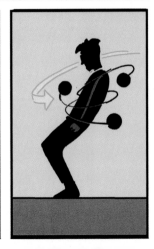

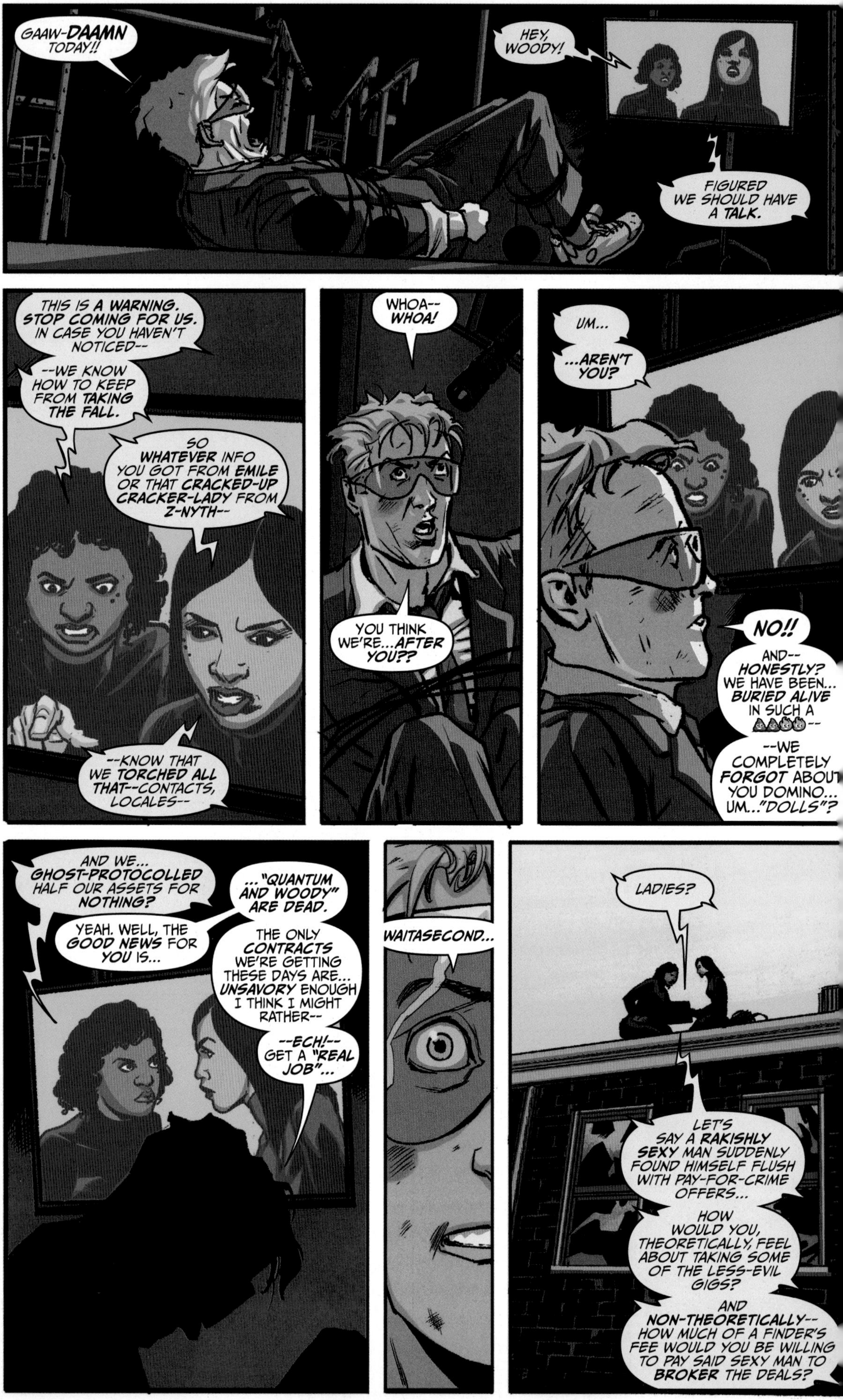
GAAW-DAAMN TODAY!!
HEY, WOODY!
FIGURED WE SHOULD HAVE A TALK.
THIS IS A WARNING. STOP COMING FOR US. IN CASE YOU HAVEN'T NOTICED--
--WE KNOW HOW TO KEEP FROM TAKING THE FALL.
SO WHATEVER INFO YOU GOT FROM EMILE OR THAT CRACKED-UP CRACKER-LADY FROM Z-NYTH--
--KNOW THAT WE TORCHED ALL THAT--CONTACTS, LOCALES--
WHOA-- WHOA!
YOU THINK WE'RE...AFTER YOU??
UM...
...AREN'T YOU?
NO!!
AND-- HONESTLY? WE HAVE BEEN... BURIED ALIVE IN SUCH A --
--WE COMPLETELY FORGOT ABOUT YOU DOMINO... UM..."DOLLS"?
AND WE... GHOST-PROTOCOLLED HALF OUR ASSETS FOR NOTHING?
YEAH. WELL, THE GOOD NEWS FOR YOU IS...
..."QUANTUM AND WOODY" ARE DEAD.
THE ONLY CONTRACTS WE'RE GETTING THESE DAYS ARE... UNSAVORY ENOUGH I THINK I MIGHT RATHER--
--ECH!-- GET A "REAL JOB"...
WAITASECOND...
LADIES?
LET'S SAY A RAKISHLY SEXY MAN SUDDENLY FOUND HIMSELF FLUSH WITH PAY-FOR-CRIME OFFERS...
HOW WOULD YOU, THEORETICALLY, FEEL ABOUT TAKING SOME OF THE LESS-EVIL GIGS?
AND NON-THEORETICALLY-- HOW MUCH OF A FINDER'S FEE WOULD YOU BE WILLING TO PAY SAID SEXY MAN TO BROKER THE DEALS?

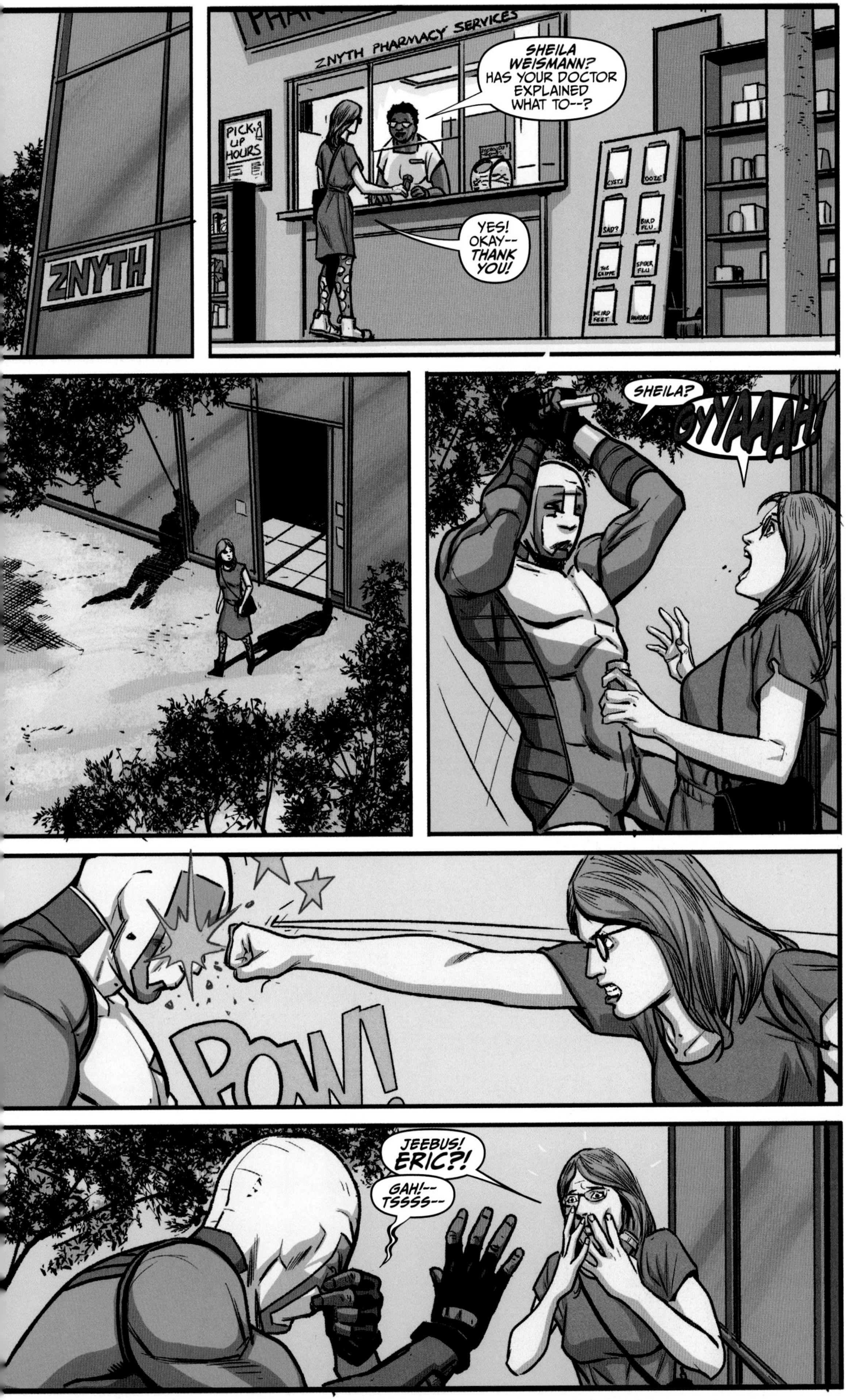
ZNYTH
ZNYTH PHARMACY SERVICES
PICK UP HOURS
SHEILA WEISMANN? HAS YOUR DOCTOR EXPLAINED WHAT TO--?
YES! OKAY-- THANK YOU!
CYSTS
OOZE
SAD?
BIRD FLU.
THE GRIPPE
SPIDER FLU
WEIRD FEET
SHEILA?
GYYAAAAH!
POW!
JEEBUS! ERIC?!
GAH!-- TSSSS--

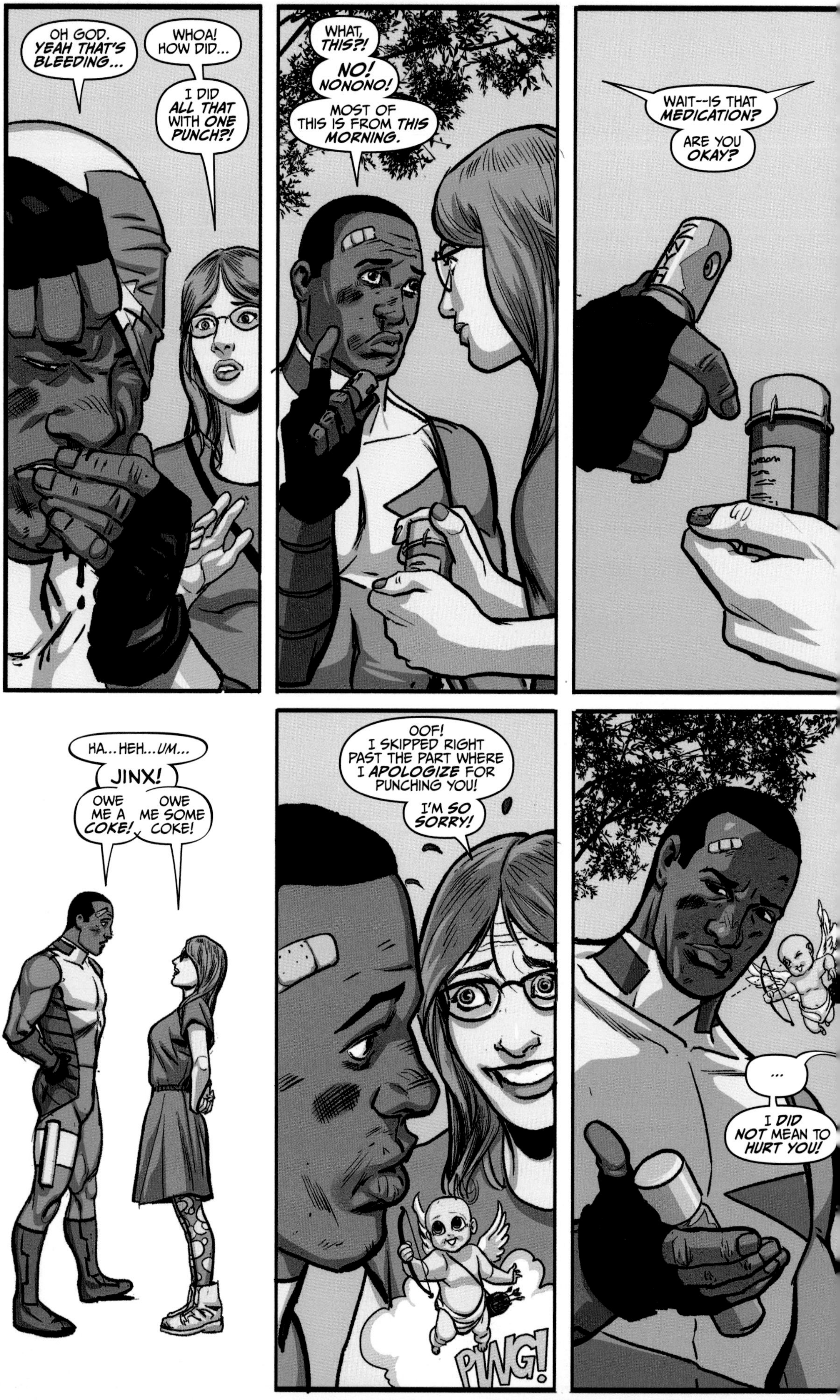
OH GOD. YEAH THAT'S BLEEDING...
WHOA! HOW DID...
I DID ALL THAT WITH ONE PUNCH?!
WHAT, THIS?!
NO! NONONO!
MOST OF THIS IS FROM THIS MORNING.
WAIT--IS THAT MEDICATION?
ARE YOU OKAY?
HA...HEH...UM...
JINX!
OWE ME A COKE!
OWE ME SOME COKE!
OOF! I SKIPPED RIGHT PAST THE PART WHERE I APOLOGIZE FOR PUNCHING YOU!
I'M SO SORRY!
PING!
...
I DID NOT MEAN TO HURT YOU!

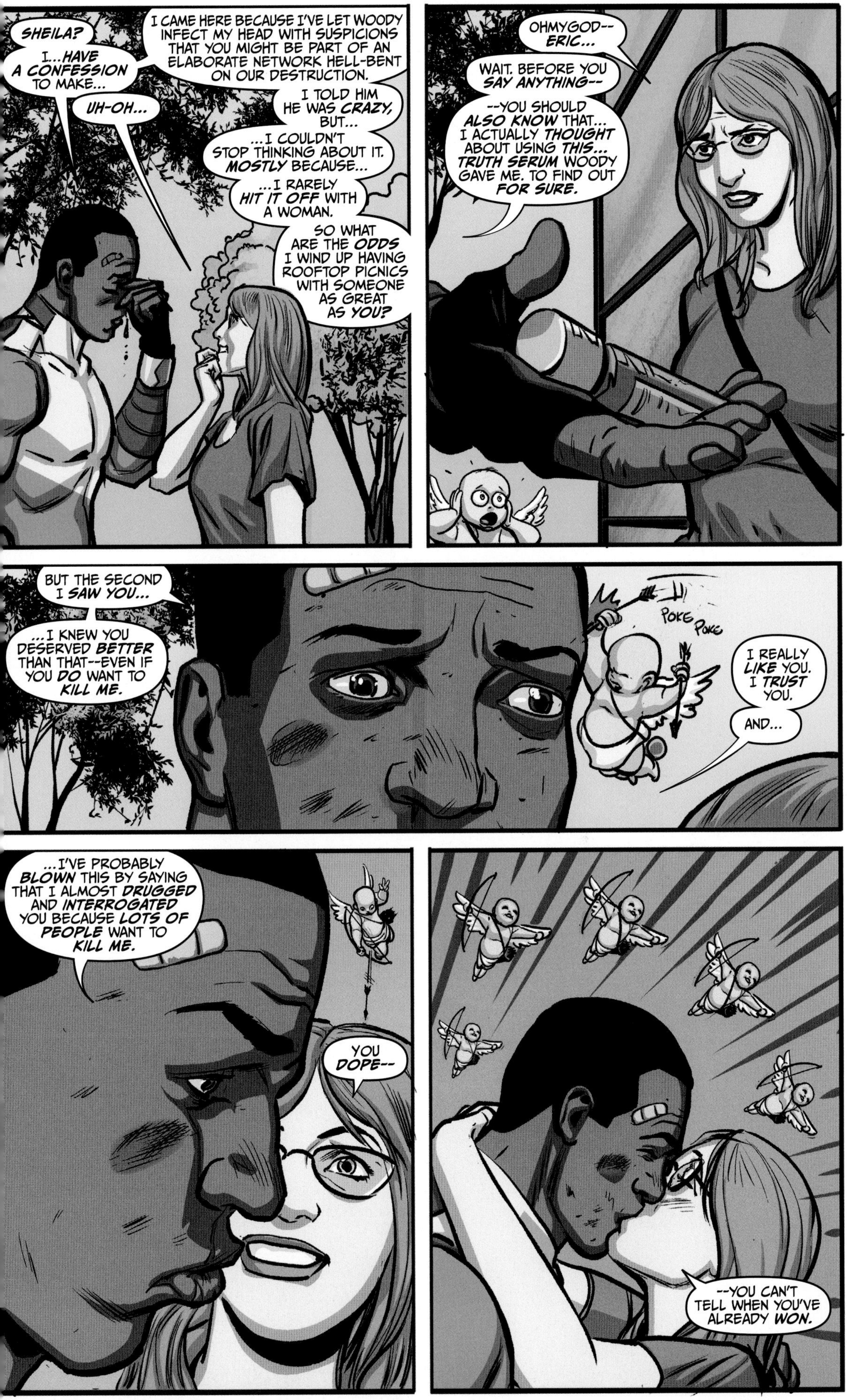
SHEILA?
I...HAVE A CONFESSION TO MAKE...
UH-OH...
I CAME HERE BECAUSE I'VE LET WOODY INFECT MY HEAD WITH SUSPICIONS THAT YOU MIGHT BE PART OF AN ELABORATE NETWORK HELL-BENT ON OUR DESTRUCTION.
I TOLD HIM HE WAS CRAZY, BUT...
...I COULDN'T STOP THINKING ABOUT IT. MOSTLY BECAUSE...
...I RARELY HIT IT OFF WITH A WOMAN.
SO WHAT ARE THE ODDS I WIND UP HAVING ROOFTOP PICNICS WITH SOMEONE AS GREAT AS YOU?
OHMYGOD-- ERIC...
WAIT. BEFORE YOU SAY ANYTHING--
--YOU SHOULD ALSO KNOW THAT... I ACTUALLY THOUGHT ABOUT USING THIS... TRUTH SERUM WOODY GAVE ME. TO FIND OUT FOR SURE.
BUT THE SECOND I SAW YOU...
...I KNEW YOU DESERVED BETTER THAN THAT--EVEN IF YOU DO WANT TO KILL ME.
POKE POKE
I REALLY LIKE YOU. I TRUST YOU.
AND...
...I'VE PROBABLY BLOWN THIS BY SAYING THAT I ALMOST DRUGGED AND INTERROGATED YOU BECAUSE LOTS OF PEOPLE WANT TO KILL ME.
YOU DOPE--
--YOU CAN'T TELL WHEN YOU'VE ALREADY WON.

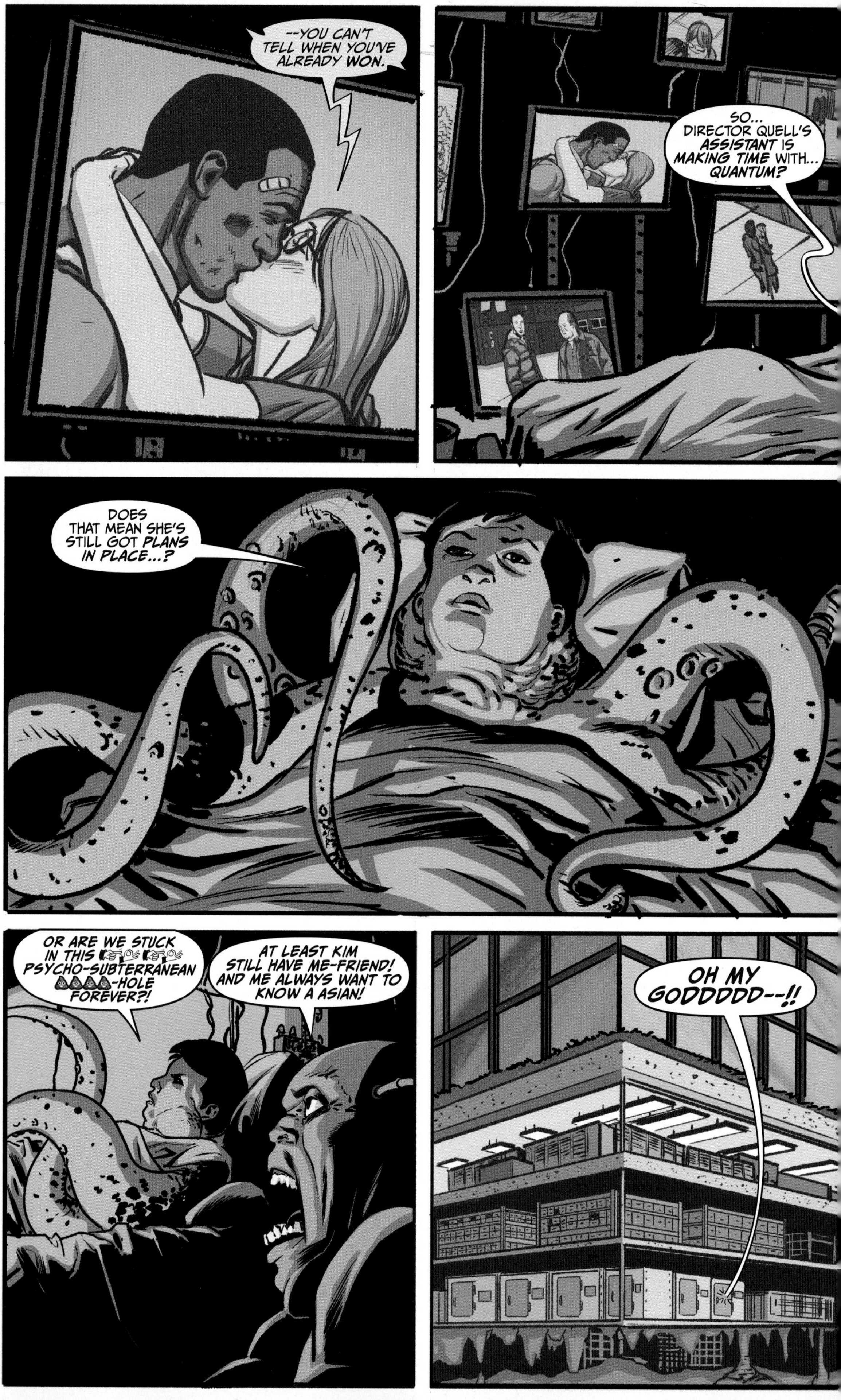
--YOU CAN'T TELL WHEN YOU'VE ALREADY WON.
SO... DIRECTOR QUELL'S ASSISTANT IS MAKING TIME WITH... QUANTUM?
DOES THAT MEAN SHE'S STILL GOT PLANS IN PLACE...?
OR ARE WE STUCK IN THIS PSYCHO-SUBTERRANEAN -HOLE FOREVER?!
AT LEAST KIM STILL HAVE ME-FRIEND! AND ME ALWAYS WANT TO KNOW A ASIAN!
OH MY GODDDDD--!!

--WHERE THE HELL IS EVERYONE?!?!

REAGAN CORRECTIONAL INSTITUTE

UNDER NEW MANAGEMENT

A Peek At Our Private Penal System.

HEY! G-MAN! SOMEBODY HERE BETTER BE ABLE TO TELL ME HOW WE'RE GETTING *SHIPPED TO FEDERAL PRISON* WHEN WE HAVEN'T EVEN HAD *A TRIAL!*

YOU SET LOOSE *EXPLOSIVES* IN A *NATIONAL PARK,* MISTER PRYCE.

AS A *FORMER* LAW MAN, I THINK YOU'D KNOW THAT MAKES YOU BOYS A *TERROR THREAT.*

SO THE *D.O.D.* IS *WELL WITHIN* THEIR RIGHTS TO *DETAIN* YOU *INDEFINITELY* WHILE THE CASE AGAINST YOU IS BEING ASSESSED.

AND A WORD OF *ADVICE?*

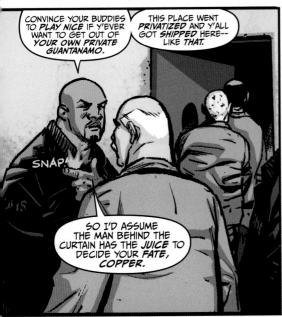

CONVINCE YOUR BUDDIES TO *PLAY NICE* IF Y'EVER WANT TO GET OUT OF *YOUR OWN PRIVATE GUANTANAMO.*

THIS PLACE WENT *PRIVATIZED* AND Y'ALL GOT *SHIPPED HERE*-- LIKE *THAT.*

SNAP!

SO I'D ASSUME THE MAN BEHIND THE *CURTAIN* HAS THE *JUICE* TO DECIDE YOUR *FATE,* COPPER.

GENTLEMEN! WELCOME!

NON...

WHAT?

--THE--?!

I'M NOT *QUITE* YOUR *WARDEN,* BUT I *AM* THE *C.E.O.*--

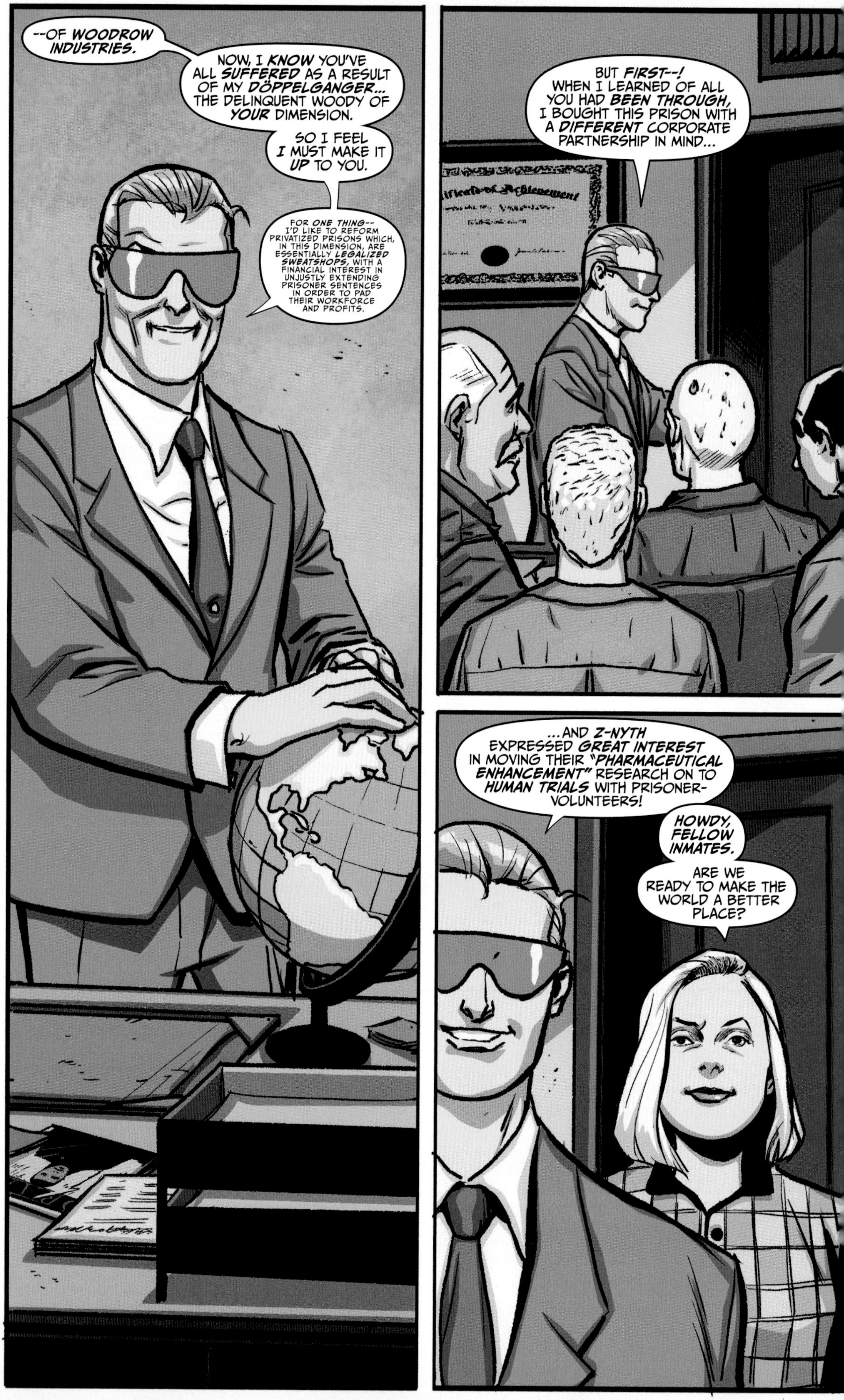
--OF WOODROW INDUSTRIES.
NOW, I KNOW YOU'VE ALL SUFFERED AS A RESULT OF MY DÖPPELGANGER... THE DELINQUENT WOODY OF YOUR DIMENSION.
SO I FEEL I MUST MAKE IT UP TO YOU.
FOR ONE THING-- I'D LIKE TO REFORM PRIVATIZED PRISONS WHICH, IN THIS DIMENSION, ARE ESSENTIALLY LEGALIZED SWEATSHOPS, WITH A FINANCIAL INTEREST IN UNJUSTLY EXTENDING PRISONER SENTENCES IN ORDER TO PAD THEIR WORKFORCE AND PROFITS.
BUT FIRST--! WHEN I LEARNED OF ALL YOU HAD BEEN THROUGH, I BOUGHT THIS PRISON WITH A DIFFERENT CORPORATE PARTNERSHIP IN MIND...
...AND Z-NYTH EXPRESSED GREAT INTEREST IN MOVING THEIR "PHARMACEUTICAL ENHANCEMENT" RESEARCH ON TO HUMAN TRIALS WITH PRISONER-VOLUNTEERS!
HOWDY, FELLOW INMATES.
ARE WE READY TO MAKE THE WORLD A BETTER PLACE?

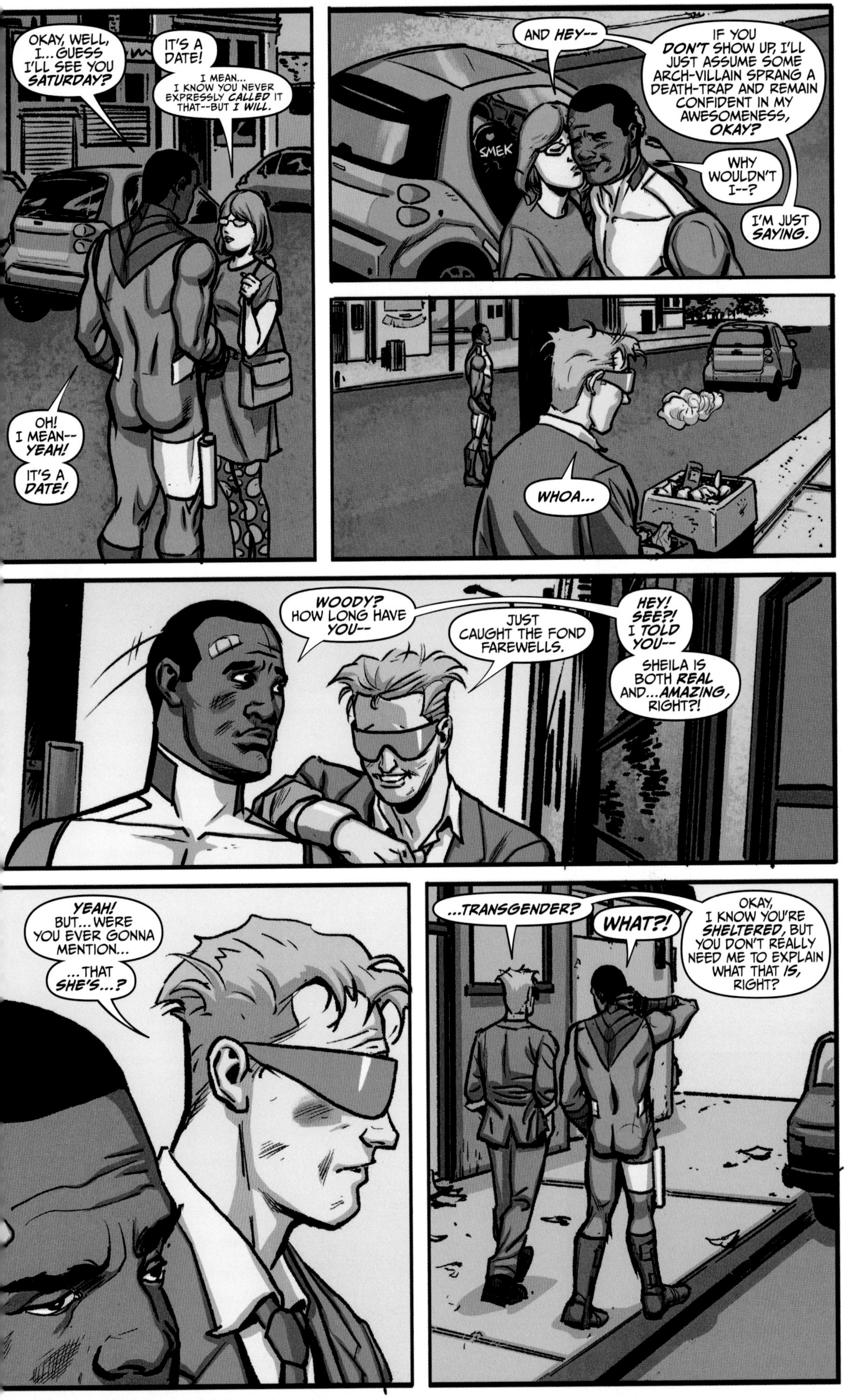
OKAY, WELL, I...GUESS I'LL SEE YOU SATURDAY?
IT'S A DATE!
I MEAN... I KNOW YOU NEVER EXPRESSLY CALLED IT THAT--BUT I WILL.
OH! I MEAN-- YEAH!
IT'S A DATE!
AND HEY--
IF YOU DON'T SHOW UP, I'LL JUST ASSUME SOME ARCH-VILLAIN SPRANG A DEATH-TRAP AND REMAIN CONFIDENT IN MY AWESOMENESS, OKAY?
SMEK
WHY WOULDN'T I--?
I'M JUST SAYING.
WHOA...
WOODY? HOW LONG HAVE YOU--
JUST CAUGHT THE FOND FAREWELLS.
HEY! SEE?! I TOLD YOU--
SHEILA IS BOTH REAL AND...AMAZING, RIGHT?!
YEAH! BUT...WERE YOU EVER GONNA MENTION...
...THAT SHE'S...?
...TRANSGENDER?
WHAT?!
OKAY, I KNOW YOU'RE SHELTERED, BUT YOU DON'T REALLY NEED ME TO EXPLAIN WHAT THAT IS, RIGHT?

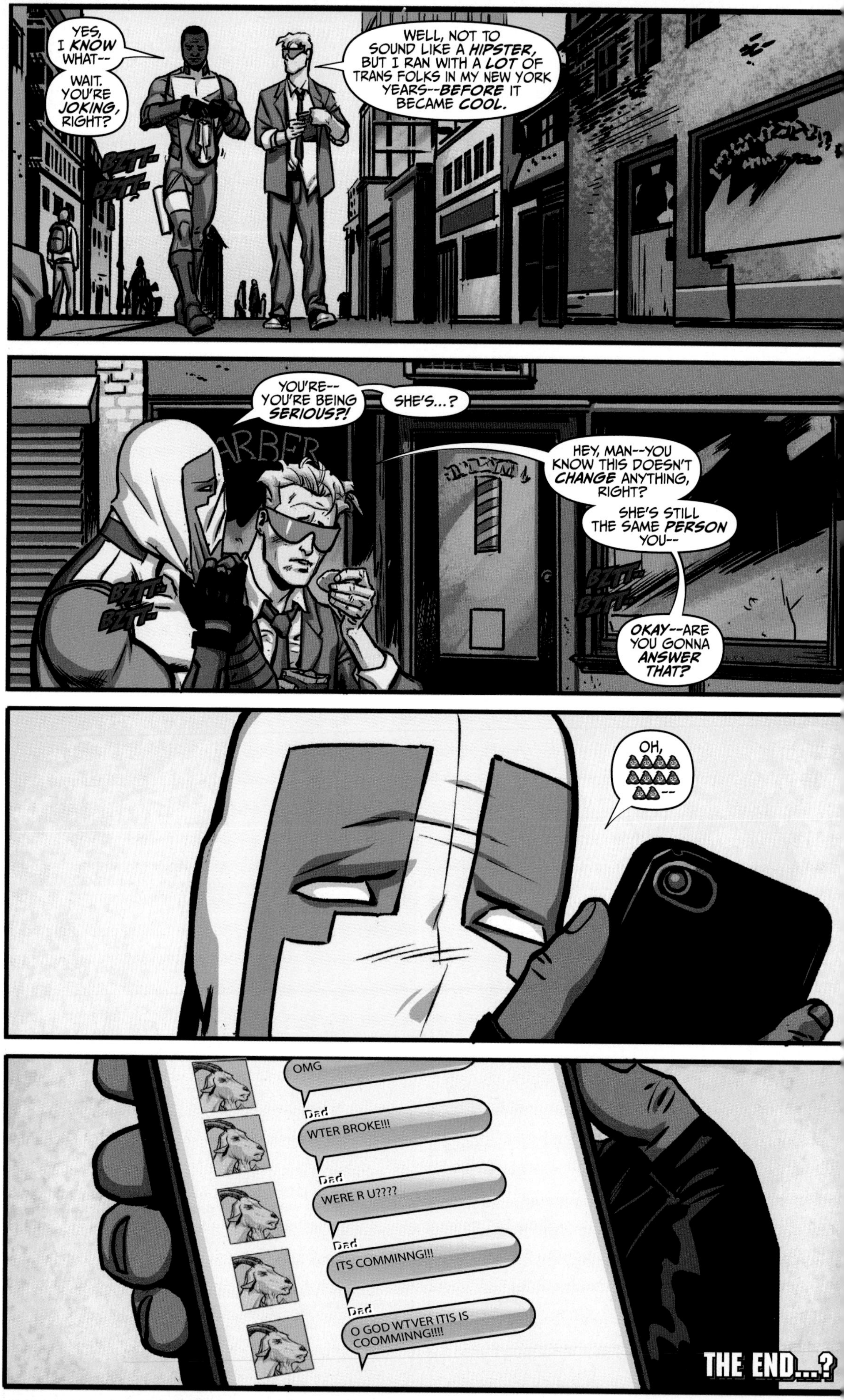
YES, I KNOW WHAT--
WAIT. YOU'RE JOKING, RIGHT?
WELL, NOT TO SOUND LIKE A HIPSTER, BUT I RAN WITH A LOT OF TRANS FOLKS IN MY NEW YORK YEARS--BEFORE IT BECAME COOL.
BZTT- BZTT-
YOU'RE-- YOU'RE BEING SERIOUS?!
SHE'S...?
HEY, MAN--YOU KNOW THIS DOESN'T CHANGE ANYTHING, RIGHT?
SHE'S STILL THE SAME PERSON YOU--
BZTT- BZTT-
OKAY--ARE YOU GONNA ANSWER THAT?
OH, --
OMG
Dad
WTER BROKE!!!
Dad
WERE R U????
Dad
ITS COMMINNG!!!
Dad
O GOD WTVER ITIS IS COOMMINNG!!!!
THE END...?

IT'S WHAT'S
INSIDE
THAT COUNTS.

Dad
WTER BROKE!!!
Dad
WERE R U????
Dad
ITS COMMINNG!!!
Dad

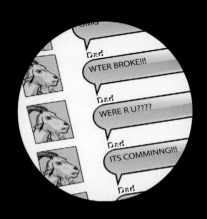

QUANTUM
AND
WOODY
WILL
RETURN!

GALLERY

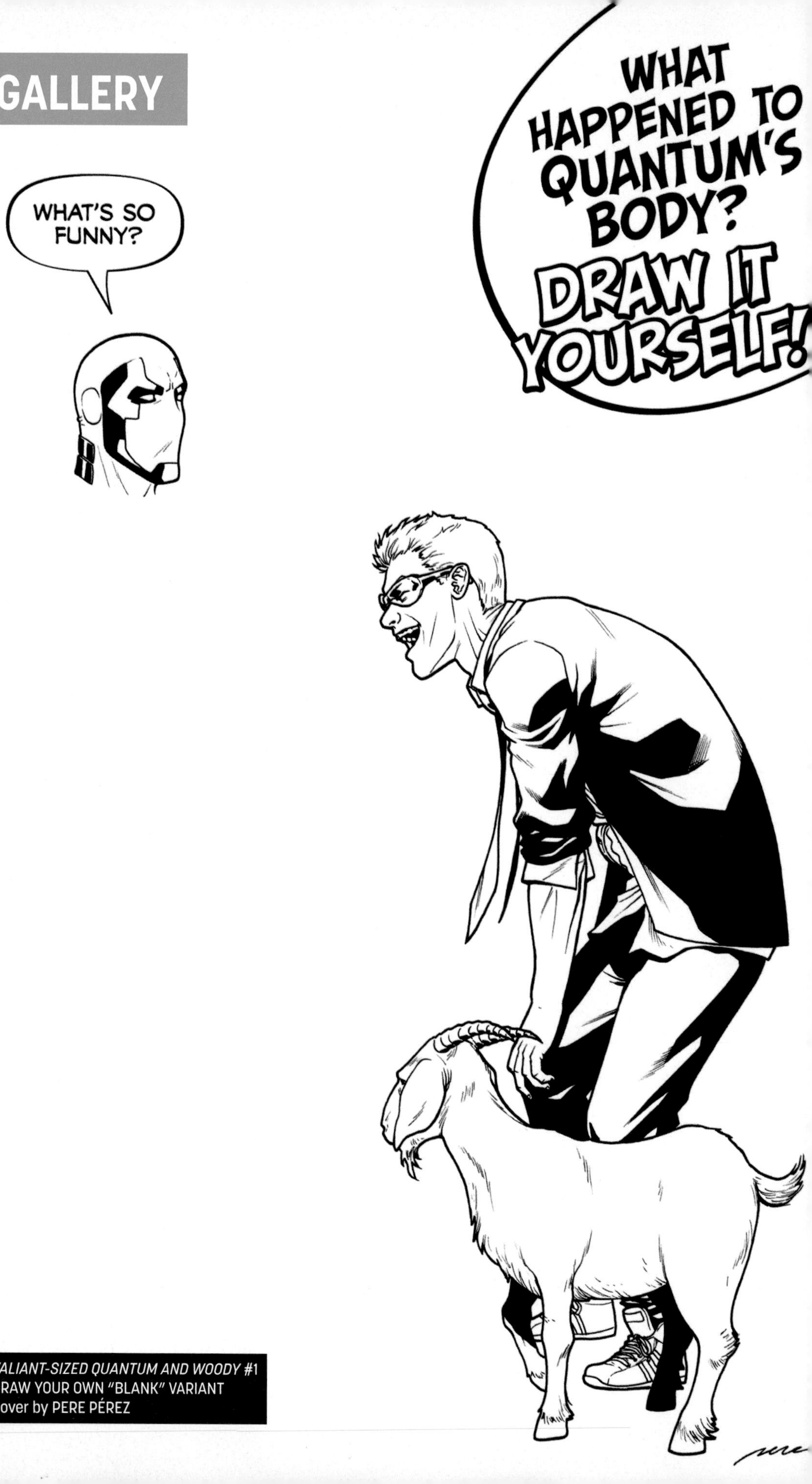
WHAT'S SO FUNNY?
WHAT HAPPENED TO QUANTUM'S BODY? DRAW IT YOURSELF!

VALIANT-SIZED QUANTUM AND WOODY #1
DRAW YOUR OWN "BLANK" VARIANT
Cover by PERE PÉREZ

VALIANT-SIZED QUANTUM AND WOODY #1 VARIANT
Cover by MIKE HAWTHORNE and JORDIE BELLAIRE

QUANTUM AND WOODY MUST DIE! #1 VARIANT
Cover by JOHNNIE CHRISTMAS
and WIL QUINTANA

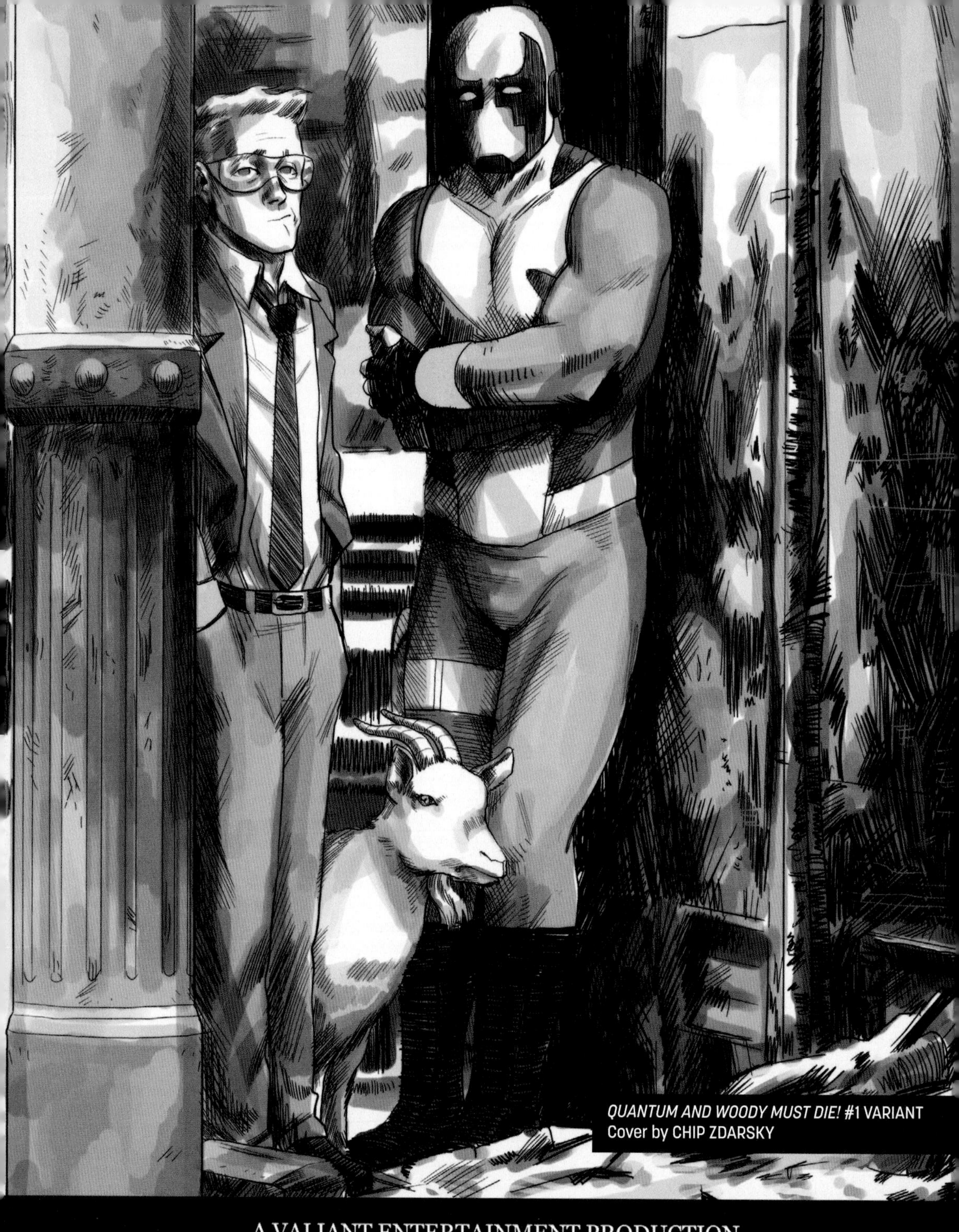

QUANTUM AND WOODY MUST DIE! #1 VARIANT
Cover by CHIP ZDARSKY

A VALIANT ENTERTAINMENT PRODUCTION

“QUANTUM AND WOODY

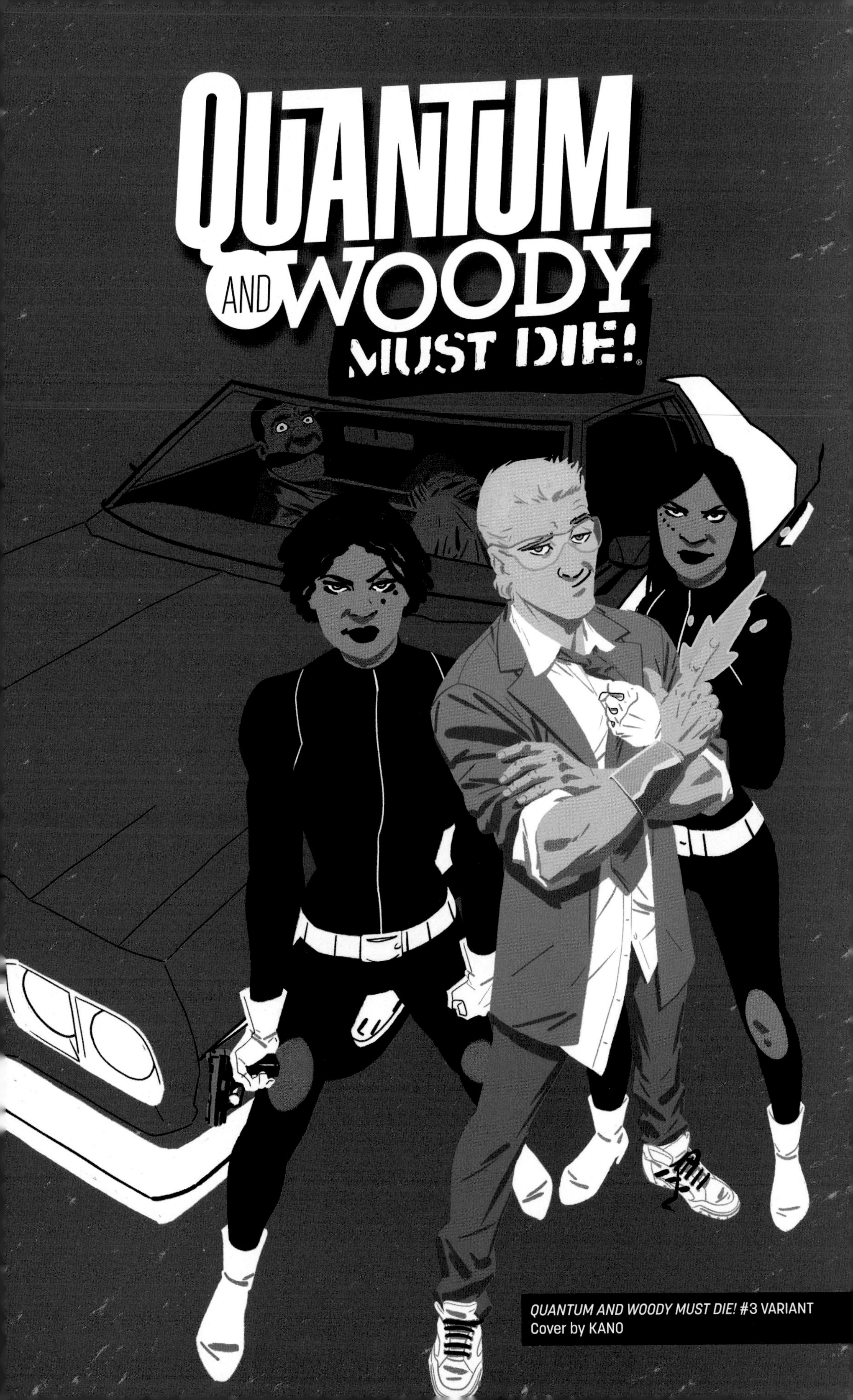
QUANTUM
AND WOODY
MUST DIE!

QUANTUM AND WOODY MUST DIE! #3 VARIANT
Cover by KANO

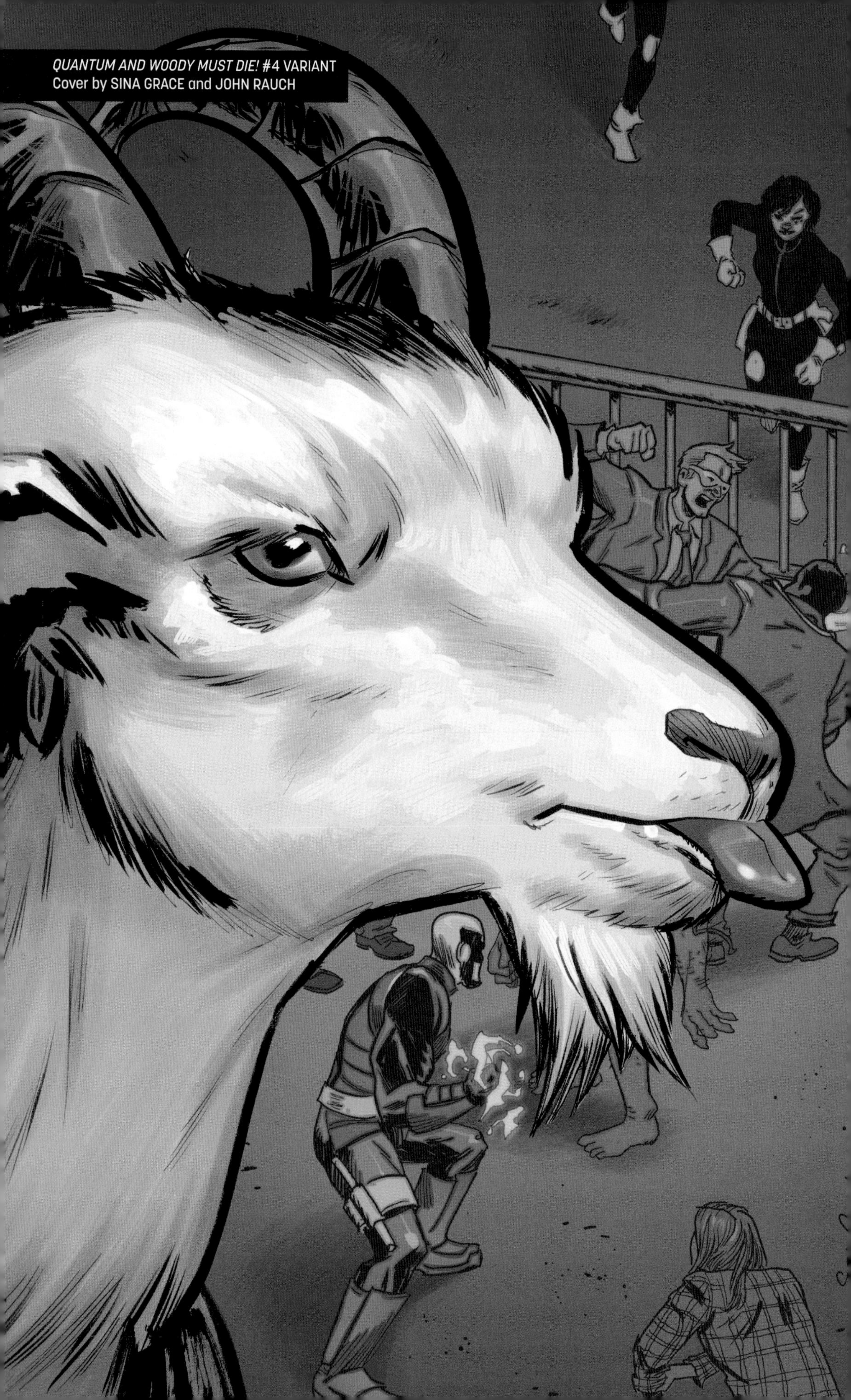

QUANTUM AND WOODY MUST DIE! #4 VARIANT
Cover by SINA GRACE and JOHN RAUCH

VALIANT-SIZED QUANTUM AND WOODY #1,
"UPSIDEDOWNSIDE," p.3
Art by PERE PÉREZ

VALIANT-SIZED QUANTUM AND WOODY #1,
"UPSIDEDOWNSIDE," p.5
Art by PERE PÉREZ

VALIANT-SIZED QUANTUM AND WOODY #1,
"UPSIDEDOWNSIDE," p.12
Art by PERE PÉREZ

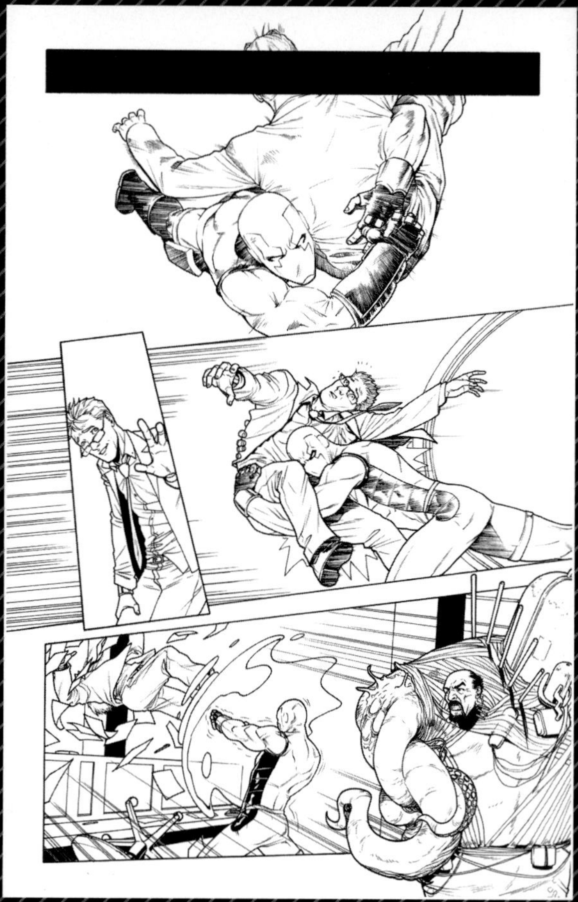

VALIANT-SIZED QUANTUM AND WOODY #1,
"UPSIDEDOWNSIDE," p.18
Art by PERE PÉREZ

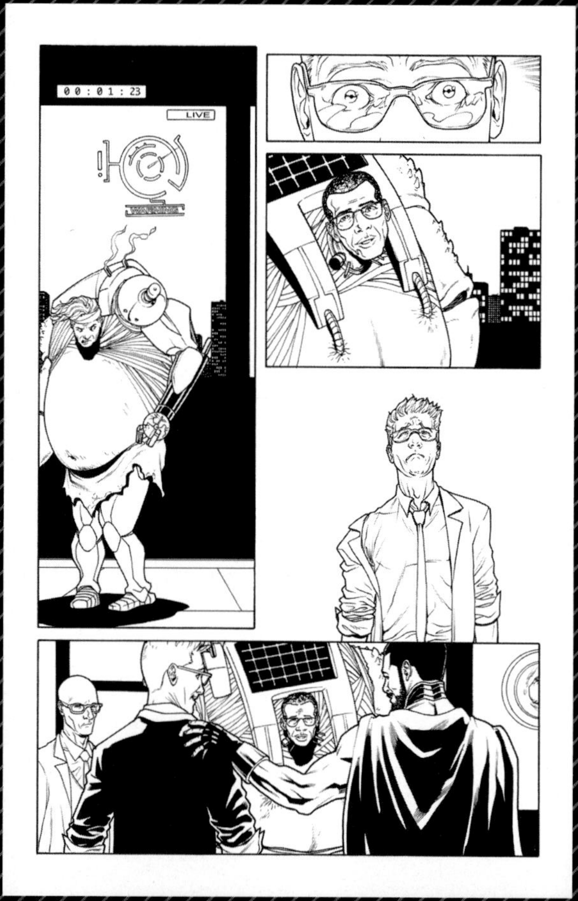
00:01:23
LIVE

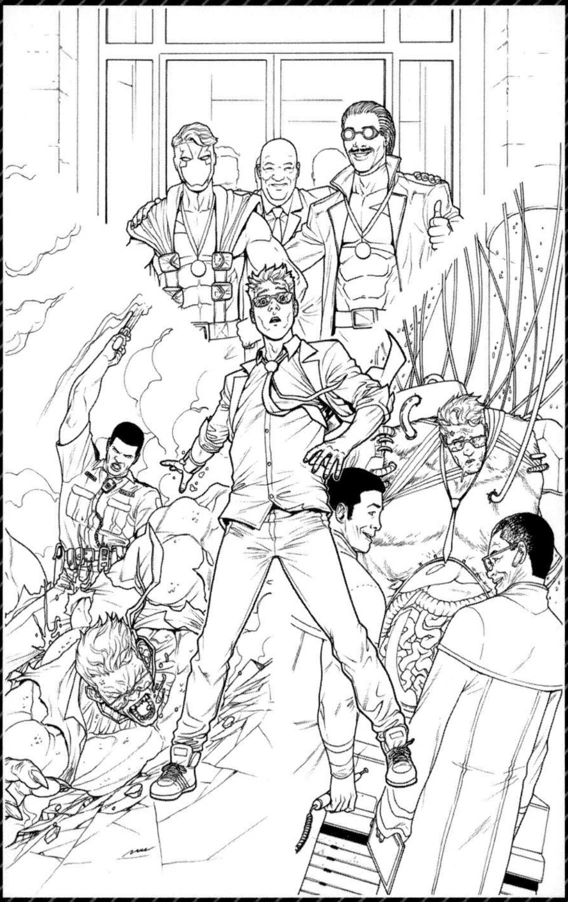

VALIANT-SIZED QUANTUM AND WOODY #1,
"MIRACLE ON 34TH EARTH," p.2
Art by PERE PÉREZ

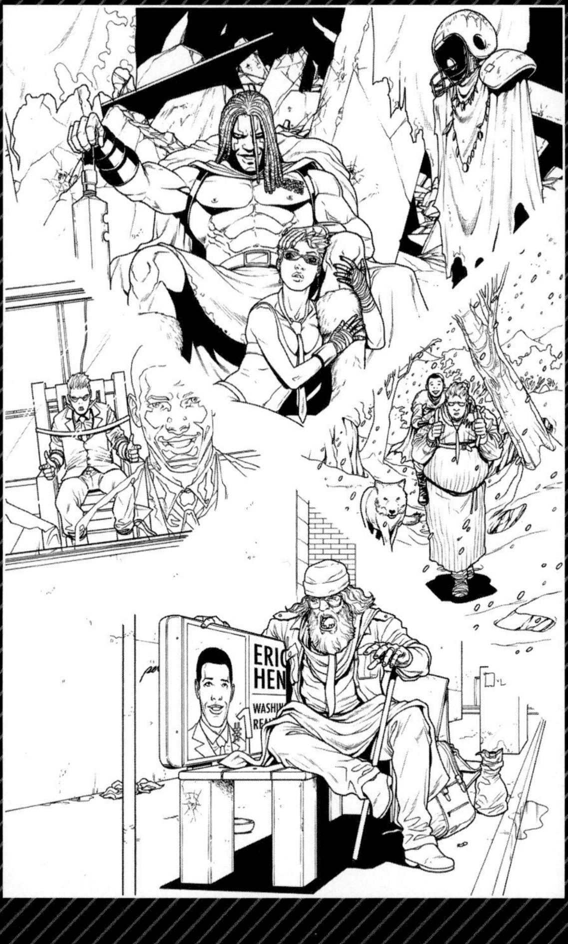
ERIC
HEN
WASHI

VALIANT-SIZED QUANTUM AND WOODY #1,
"MIRACLE ON 34TH EARTH," p.3
Art by PERE PÉREZ

VALIANT-SIZED QUANTUM AND WOODY #1,
"A WOODY RISES," p.4
Art by BRIAN LEVEL

WOODROW
WOODROW
BALLOON TOURS
WOODROW
GLOBAL PARTNERS

VALIANT-SIZED QUANTUM AND WOODY #1,
"A WOODY RISES," p.5
Art by BRIAN LEVEL

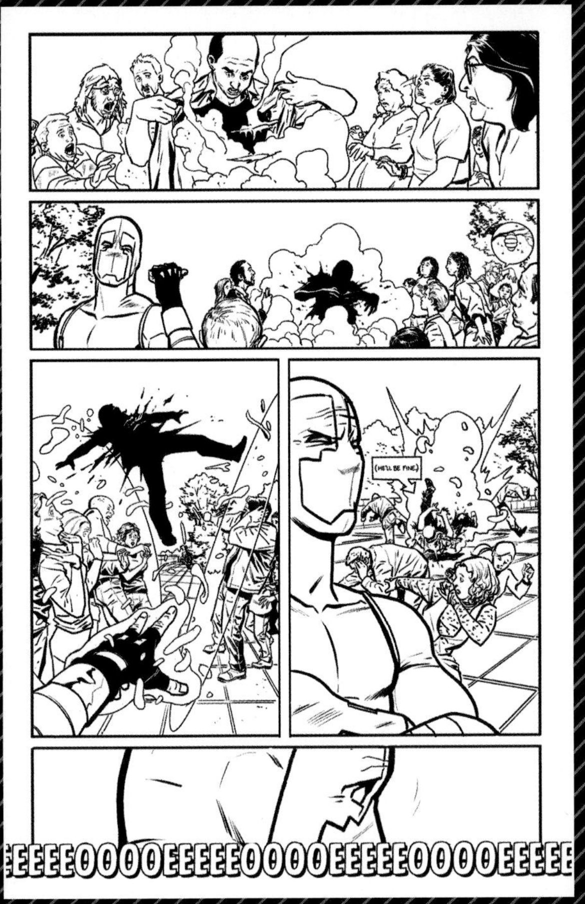
(HE'LL BE FINE)
EEEEEOOOOEEEEEOOOOEEEEEOOOOEEEEE

QUANTUM AND WOODY MUST DIE! #2, p. 17
Art by STEVE LIEBER

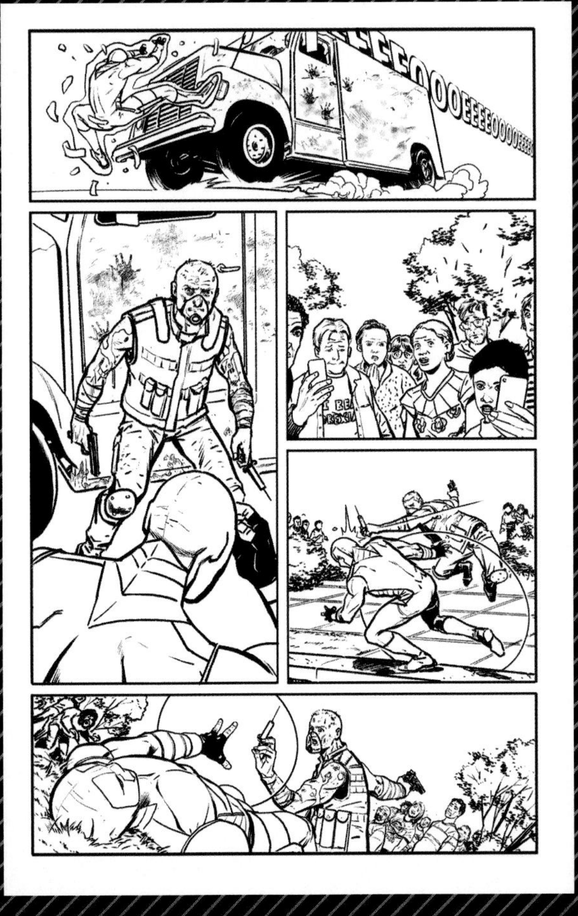

QUANTUM AND WOODY MUST DIE! #2, p. 18
Art by STEVE LIEBER

QUANTUM AND WOODY MUST DIE! #2, p. 20
Art by STEVE LIEBER

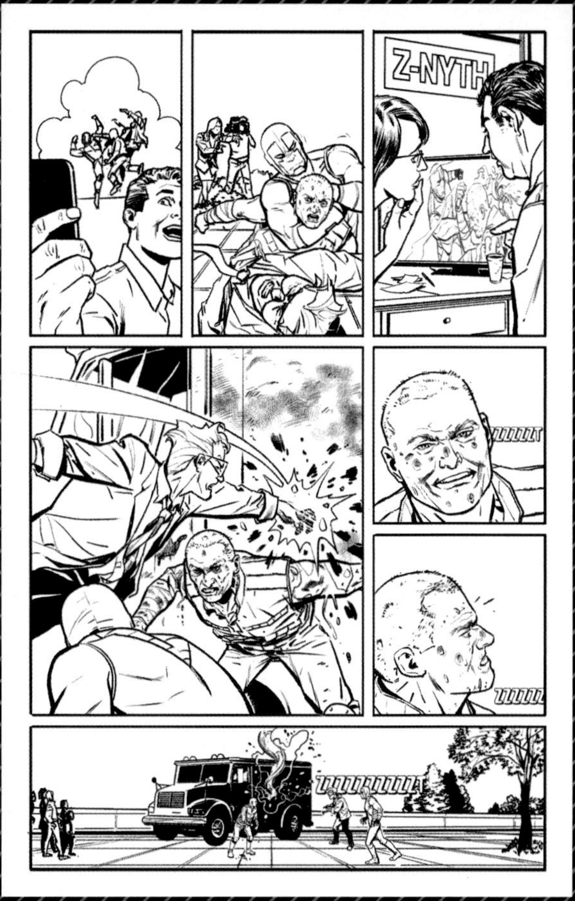
Z-NYTH

QUANTUM AND WOODY MUST DIE! #2, p. 21
Art by STEVE LIEBER

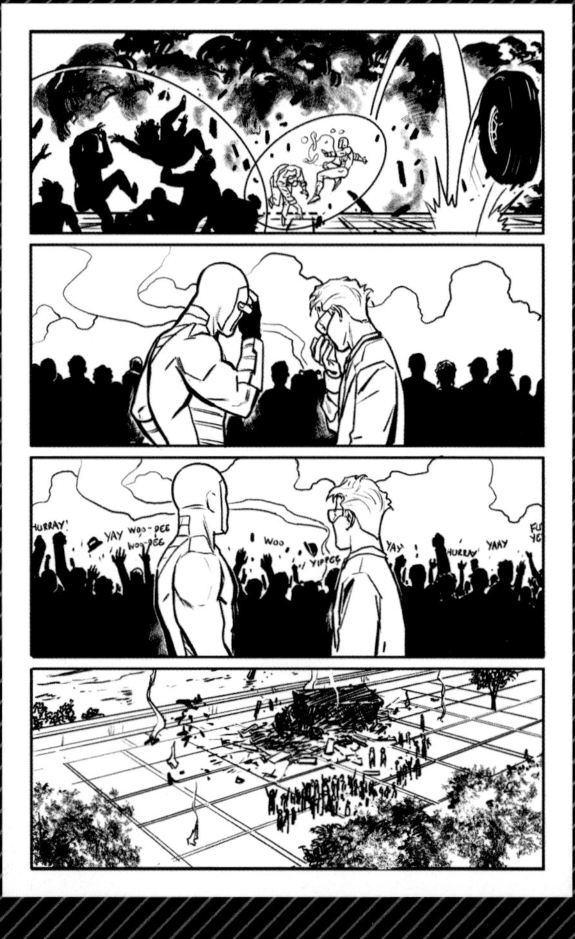
YAY
WOO-PEE
WOO-PEE
WOO
YIPPEE
YAY
YAAY

QUANTUM AND WOODY MUST DIE! #3, p. 1
Art by STEVE LIEBER

QUANTUM AND WOODY MUST DIE! #3, p. 10
Art by STEVE LIEBER

QUANTUM AND WOODY MUST DIE! #3, p. 11
Art by STEVE LIEBER

QUANTUM AND WOODY MUST DIE! #3, p. 21
Art by STEVE LIEBER

BOOM

QUANTUM AND WOODY MUST DIE! #4, p. 14
Art by STEVE LIEBER

QUANTUM AND WOODY MUST DIE! #4, p. 18
Art by STEVE LIEBER

EXPLORE THE VALIANT UNIVERSE

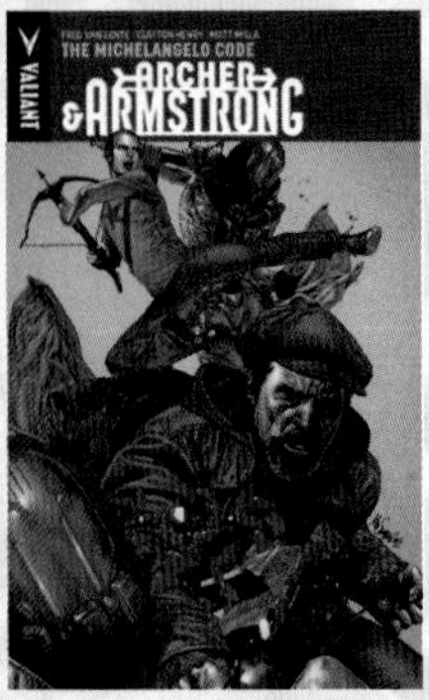
VALIANT
THE MICHELANGELO CODE
ARCHER & ARMSTRONG

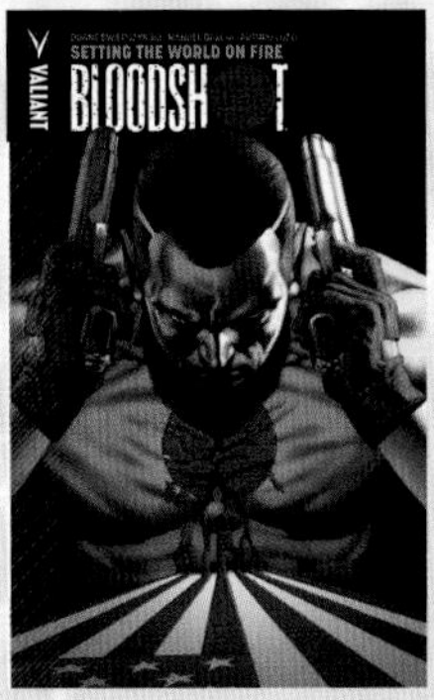
VALIANT
SETTING THE WORLD ON FIRE
BLOODSHOT

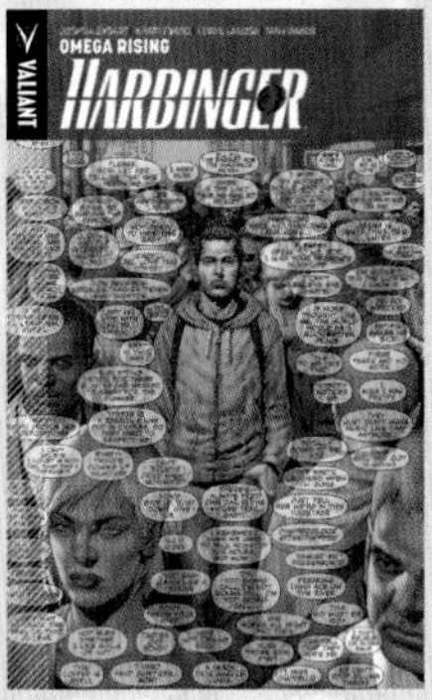
VALIANT
OMEGA RISING
HARBINGER

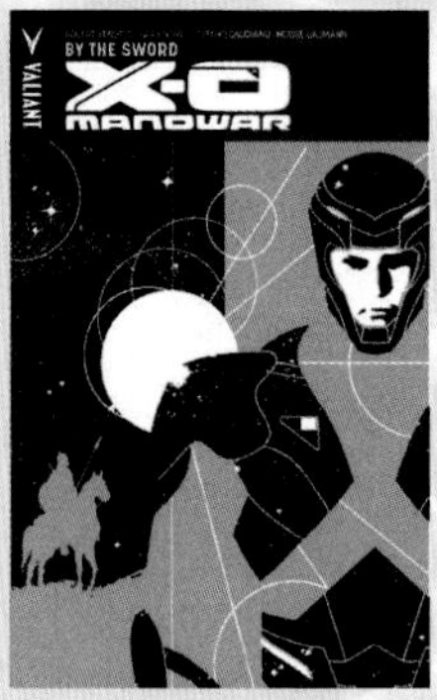
VALIANT
BY THE SWORD
X-O MANOWAR

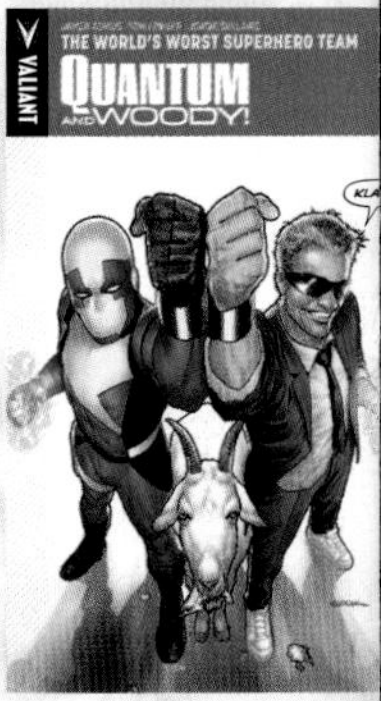
VALIANT
THE WORLD'S WORST SUPERHERO TEAM
QUANTUM AND WOODY!

ARCHER & ARMSTRONG

Volume 1: The Michelangelo Code
ISBN: 9780979640988

Volume 2: Wrath of the Eternal Warrior
ISBN: 9781939346049

Volume 3: Far Faraway
ISBN: 9781939346148

Volume 4: Sect Civil War
ISBN: 9781939346254

Volume 5: Mission: Improbable
ISBN: 9781939346353

Volume 6: American Wasteland
ISBN: 9781939346421

Volume 7: The One Percent and Other Tales
ISBN: 9781939346537

ARMOR HUNTERS

Armor Hunters
ISBN: 9781939346452

Armor Hunters: Bloodshot
ISBN: 9781939346469

Armor Hunters: Harbinger
ISBN: 9781939346506

Unity Vol. 3: Armor Hunters
ISBN: 9781939346445

X-O Manowar Vol. 7: Armor Hunters
ISBN: 9781939346476

BLOODSHOT

Volume 1: Setting the World on Fire
ISBN: 9780979640964

Volume 2: The Rise and the Fall
ISBN: 9781939346032

Volume 3: Harbinger Wars
ISBN: 9781939346124

Volume 4: H.A.R.D. Corps
ISBN: 9781939346193

Volume 5: Get Some!
ISBN: 9781939346315

Volume 6: The Glitch and Other Tales
ISBN: 9781939346711

BLOODSHOT REBORN

Volume 1: Colorado
ISBN: 9781939346674

DEAD DROP

Dead Drop
ISBN: 9781939346858

THE DEATH-DEFYING DOCTOR MIRAGE

The Death-Defying Dr. Mirage
ISBN: 9781939346490

THE DELINQUENTS

The Delinquents
ISBN: 9781939346513

DIVINITY

DIVINITY
ISBN: 9781939346766

ETERNAL WARRIOR

Volume 1: Sword of the Wild
ISBN: 9781939346209

Volume 2: Eternal Emperor
ISBN: 9781939346292

Volume 3: Days of Steel
ISBN: 9781939346742

HARBINGER

Volume 1: Omega Rising
ISBN: 9780979640957

Volume 2: Renegades
ISBN: 9781939346025

Volume 3: Harbinger Wars
ISBN: 9781939346117

Volume 4: Perfect Day
ISBN: 9781939346155

Volume 5: Death of a Renegade
ISBN: 9781939346339

Volume 6: Omegas
ISBN: 9781939346384

HARBINGER WARS

Harbinger Wars
ISBN: 9781939346094

Bloodshot Vol. 3: Harbinger Wars
ISBN: 9781939346124

Harbinger Vol. 3: Harbinger Wars
ISBN: 9781939346117

EXPLORE THE VALIANT UNIVERSE

BY PRIEST & BRIGHT

BATTLE FOR NEW JAPAN
RAI
VALIANT

VALIANT
THE VALIANT

VALIANT
THE DEATH-DEFYING
DOCTOR MIRAGE

VALIANT
DIVINITY

インピリアム MPERIUM

me 1: Collecting Monsters
N: 9781939346759

INJAK

me 1: Weaponeer
N: 9781939346667

UANTUM AND WOODY!

me 1: The World's Worst Superhero Team
N: 9781939346186

me 2: In Security
N: 9781939346230

me 3: Crooked Pasts, Present Tense
N: 9781939346391

me 4: Quantum and Woody Must Die!
N: 9781939346629

UANTUM AND WOODY BY PRIEST & BRIGHT

me 1: Klang
: 9781939346780

me 2: Switch
: 9781939346803

me 3: And So...
: 9781939346865

RAI

Volume 1: Welcome to New Japan
ISBN: 9781939346414

Volume 2: Battle for New Japan
ISBN: 9781939346612

Volume 3: The Orphan
ISBN: 9781939346841

SHADOWMAN

Volume 1: Birth Rites
ISBN: 9781939346001

Volume 2: Darque Reckoning
ISBN: 9781939346056

Volume 3: Deadside Blues
ISBN: 9781939346162

Volume 4: Fear, Blood, And Shadows
ISBN: 9781939346278

Volume 5: End Times
ISBN: 9781939346377

Ivar, Timewalker

Volume 1: Making History
ISBN: 9781939346636

UNITY

Volume 1: To Kill a King
ISBN: 9781939346261

Volume 2: Trapped by Webnet
ISBN: 9781939346346

Volume 3: Armor Hunters
ISBN: 9781939346445

UNITY (Continued)

Volume 4: The United
ISBN: 9781939346544

Volume 5: Homefront
ISBN: 9781939346797

THE VALIANT

The Valiant
ISBN: 9781939346605

VALIANT ZEROES AND ORIGINS

Valiant: Zeroes and Origins
ISBN: 9781939346582

X-O MANOWAR

Volume 1: By the Sword
ISBN: 9780979640940

Volume 2: Enter Ninjak
ISBN: 9780979640995

Volume 3: Planet Death
ISBN: 9781939346087

Volume 4: Homecoming
ISBN: 9781939346179

Volume 5: At War With Unity
ISBN: 9781939346247

Volume 6: Prelude to Armor Hunters
ISBN: 9781939346407

Volume 7: Armor Hunters
ISBN: 9781939346476

Volume 8: Enter: Armorines
ISBN: 9781939346551

Volume 9: Dead Hand
ISBN: 9781939346650

EXPLORE THE VALIANT UNIVERSE

VALIANT
HARBINGER DELUXE EDITION 2

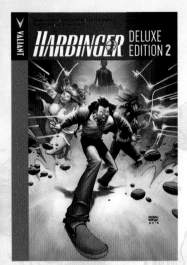

OMNIBUSES

Archer & Armstrong: The Complete Classic Omnibus
ISBN: 9781939346872
Collecting ARCHER & ARMSTRONG (1992) #0-26, ETERNAL WARRIOR (1992) #25 along with ARCHER & ARMSTRONG: THE FORMATION OF THE SECT.

Quantum and Woody: The Complete Classic Omnibus
ISBN: 9781939346360
Collecting QUANTUM AND WOODY (1997) #0, 1-21 and #32, THE GOAT: H.A.E.D.U.S. #1, and X-O MANOWAR (1996) #16

X-O Manowar Classic Omnibus Vol. 1
ISBN: 9781939346308
Collecting X-O MANOWAR (1992) #0-30, ARMORINES #0, X-O DATABASE #1, as well as material from SECRETS OF THE VALIANT UNIVERSE #1

DELUXE EDITIONS

Archer & Armstrong Deluxe Edition Book 1
ISBN: 9781939346223
Collecting ARCHER & ARMSTRONG #0-13

VALIANT
ROBERT VENDITTI MATT KINDT JOSHUA DYSART JOE HARRIS ROBERT GILL DOUG BRAITHWAITE DIEGO BERNARD TREVOR HAIRSINE STEPHEN SEGOVIA
ARMOR HUNTERS DELUXE EDITION

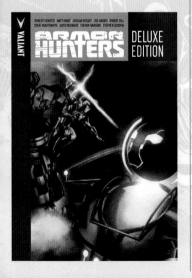

Armor Hunters Deluxe Edition
ISBN: 9781939346728
Collecting ARMOR HUNTERS #1-4, ARMOR HUNTERS: AFTERMATH #1, ARMOR HUNTERS: BLOODSHOT #1-3, ARMOR HUNTERS: HARBINGER #1-3, UNITY #8-11 and X-O MANOWAR #23-29

Bloodshot Deluxe Edition Book 1
ISBN: 9781939346216
Collecting BLOODSHOT #1-13

Harbinger Deluxe Edition Book 1
ISBN: 9781939346131
Collecting HARBINGER #0-14

Harbinger Deluxe Edition Book 2
ISBN: 9781939346773
Collecting HARBINGER #15-25, HARBINGER: OMEGAS #1-3, and HARBINGER: BLEEDING MONK #0

Harbinger Wars Deluxe Edition
ISBN: 9781939346322
Collecting HARBINGER WARS #1-4, HARBINGER #11-14, and BLOODSHOT #10-13

Quantum and Woody Deluxe Edition Book 1
ISBN: 9781939346681
Collecting QUANTUM AND WOODY #1-12 and QUANTUM AND WOODY: THE GOAT #0

Q2: The Return of Quantum and Woody Deluxe Edition
ISBN: 9781939346568
Collecting Q2: THE RETURN OF QUANTUM AND WOODY #1-5

VALIANT
JAMES ASMUS | TOM FOWLER | MING DOYLE
KANO | JORDIE BELLAIRE | DAVE LANPHEAR
QUANTUM AND WOODY! DELUXE EDITION 1
MEH!

Shadowman Deluxe Edition Book 1
ISBN: 9781939346438
Collecting SHADOWMAN #0-10

Unity Deluxe Edition Book 1
ISBN: 9781939346575
Collecting UNITY #0-14

X-O Manowar Deluxe Edition Book 1
ISBN: 9781939346100
Collecting X-O MANOWAR #1-14

X-O Manowar Deluxe Edition Book 2
ISBN: 9781939346520
Collecting X-O MANOWAR #15-22, and UNITY #1-4

VALIANT
JIM SHOOTER | DAVID LAPHAM
CHILDREN OF THE EIGHTH DAY
HARBINGER
VALIANT MASTERS

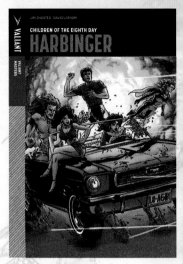

VALIANT MASTERS

Bloodshot Vol. 1 - Blood of the Machine
ISBN: 9780979640933

H.A.R.D. Corps Vol. 1 - Search and Destroy
ISBN: 9781939346285

Harbinger Vol. 1 - Children of the Eighth Day
ISBN: 9781939346483

Ninjak Vol. 1 - Black Water
ISBN: 9780979640971

Rai Vol. 1 - From Honor to Strength
ISBN: 9781939346070

Shadowman Vol. 1 - Spirits Within
ISBN: 9781939346018

VALIANT
KEVIN VANHOOK | DON PERLIN
BLOOD OF THE MACHINE
BLOODSHOT
VALIANT MASTERS

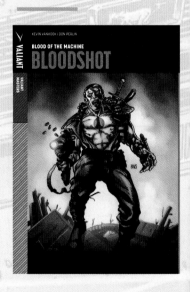

Quantum and Woody Vol. 1:
The World's Worst Superhero Team

Quantum and Woody Vol. 2:
In Security

The Delinquents
(OPTIONAL)

Quantum and Woody Vol. 3:
Crooked Past, Present Tense

Dead Drop
(OPTIONAL)

"Nobody is making superhero books like this... It's simply brilliant." – IGN

"Superbly entertaining... Fun, funny and action packed." – Comic Book Resources

Quantum and Woody Vol. 4:
Quantum and Woody
Must Die!

Read the critically acclaimed (mis)adventures of the world's worst superhero team!

From award-winning writer
JAMES ASMUS
And a celebrated roster of artists including
TOM FOWLER, MING DOYLE, KANO, and STEVE LIEBER

DEAD DROP

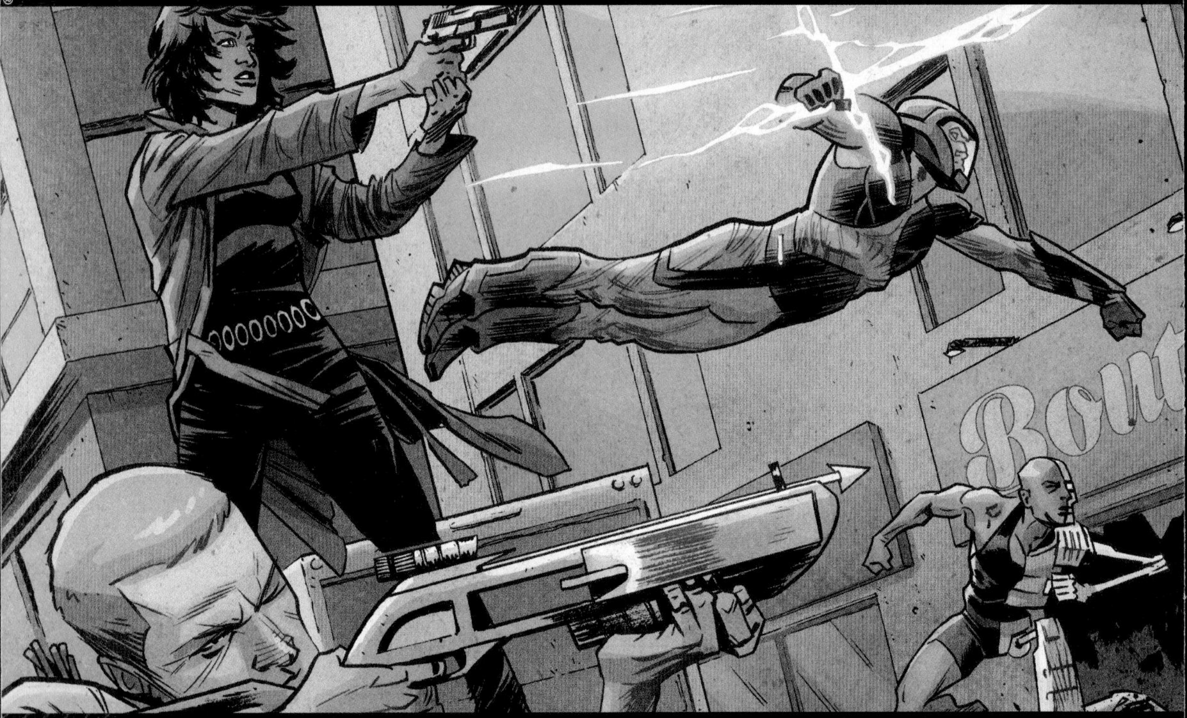

FOUR HEROES. FOUR STORIES. ONE TICKING CLOCK.

There is a secret black market in New York. It is hidden in plain sight - in our streets, trains, restaurants. Those who know how to navigate it exchange secrets of extraordinary nature. But when the secret in circulation is a biological weapon derived from Vine technology, the gloves are off - and the most extraordinary agents are released to stop the disaster before it occurs. Otherwise, in less than thirty minutes, there will be no world to come back to. X-O Manowar, Archer, Neville Alcott, Detective Cejudo, and Betamax are ready to save the world.

Red-hot writer Ales Kot (*Bucky Barnes: The Winter Soldier*) and rising star Adam Gorham (*Zero*) go in deep with an unlikely cast of superhuman operators for an undercover conspiracy action thriller in the darkest corners of the Valiant Universe. Collecting DEAD DROP #1-4.

TRADE PAPERBACK
ISBN: 978-1-939346-85-8

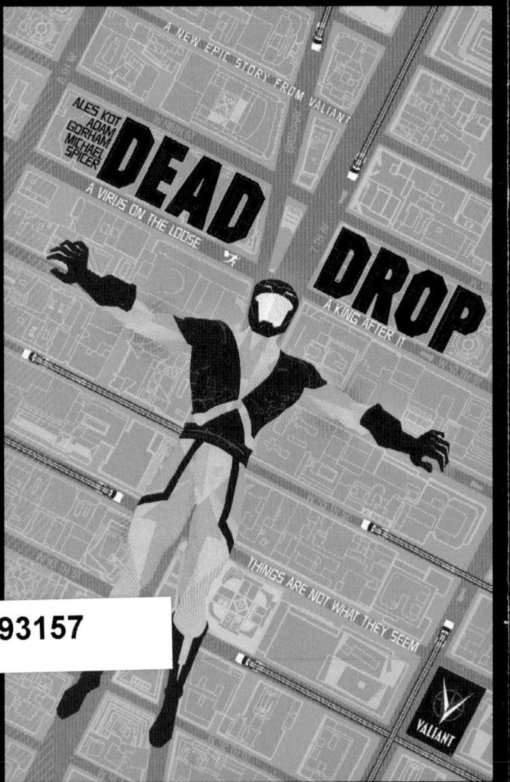
A NEW EPIC STORY FROM VALIANT
ALES KOT
ADAM GORHAM
MICHAEL SPICER
DEAD
A VIRUS ON THE LOOSE
DROP
A KING AFTER IT
THINGS ARE NOT WHAT THEY SEEM
VALIANT